A Place Called Mississippi

A Place Called Mississippi

COLLECTED NARRATIVES

Edited by Marion Barnwell

University Press of Mississippi
JACKSON

This volume is supported in part
by Delta State University
and the Phil Hardin Foundation.

Manufactured in the United States of America
07 06 05 04 03   7 6 5 4 3
The paper in this book meets the guidelines for permanence and
durability of the Committee on Production Guidelines for Book
Longevity of the Council on Library Resources.

Library of Congress Cataloging-in-Publication Data

A Place Called Mississippi: Collected Narratives / Edited by Marion Barnwell.
    p.   cm.
  Includes bibliographical references and index.
    ISBN 0-87805-963-6 (cloth : alk. paper).—ISBN 0-87805-964-4
(paper : alk. paper)
    1. Mississippi—History—Anecdotes.   2. Mississippi—Social life
and customs—Anecdotes.   3. Mississippi—History—Sources.
4. Mississippi—Social life and customs—Sources.   I. Barnwell,
Marion.
F341.M683   1997
977—dc21   96-29607
                                                  CIP

British Library Cataloging-in-Publication data available

For Claiborne, Craig, and Will,
whose stories, like mine, are intertwined
with those of Mississippi

Contents

PART THREE: **Conflict**

PART FOUR: **Social Fabric**

PART FIVE: **Body and Soul**

PART SIX: **Lives and Legends**

Preface

As a child, I had a jigsaw puzzle in the form of a United States map; its pieces taught me to recognize and locate the states according to their shapes. Thus, Mississippi was first a physical shape to me with fixed boundaries, one that could fit easily into the palm of my hand. In seventh grade, I learned that the physical boundaries were not fixed. I made another discovery in 1962 while I was attending a high school in Washington, D. C. and James Meredith was enrolling at the University of Mississippi in Oxford. I learned that the Mississippi I knew with its green fields, big skies, and sleepy towns was not the one described in *The Washington Post* as twenty thousand federal marshals were sent to Oxford to restore order after the riots accompanying Meredith's enrollment. I also learned not to trust easy stereotypes of complex situations.

Still later, when I read the memoirs of my grandmother, Mary Trice Clark, I discovered another Mississippi. She was born on Christmas day in 1879 in Okalona, "the biggest town in northeast Mississippi." She wrote about the advent of trains, telephones, and her first Coke. She described Maréchal Niel roses, a Jersey bull that always broke through the fence, and seeing the steamboat Rosalie when she was five. "Everything was different then," she wrote. "Even the clocks ticked slow and easy. Now they're in such a hurry." As I read, I could see her in the late afternoon, the sun filtering through her white hair, writing on a lapboard she had devised for the purpose, and I could imagine the people and places she described. Compiling this anthology has been, for me, a continuing revision of images, a continuing revelation that the past can, through the written word, come alive again at any moment, and a continuing recognition that Mississippi is not one thing, but multi-layered and complex.

This anthology is a collection of narratives by explorers, travelers, historians, social observers, artists, writers, and musicians all writing about Mississippi—though not necessarily Mississippians—to record the important events and to understand this place and its people. This collection is intended for people of any age and background who want to discover or rediscover the history, diversity, and richness of the state called Mississippi. I have tried to find as many points of view as possible from as many different areas as possible: the Gulf Coast, the Piney Woods, the battlefields of Corinth and Vicksburg, the Delta, and River Country. Providing a perfectly balanced spectrum, however, proved impossible. Natchez, for instance, seems over-represented in the early historical accounts because it was one of the first settlements. Some parts of the state have produced an abundance of writers, while others have not. The anthology covers a wide variety of topics, including an early description of the Chickasaw Indians, a narrative from an ex-slave, "Soggy" Sweat's famous "Whiskey Speech" on Prohibition, and an account of how W. C. Handy discovered the blues in a deserted train station in Tutwiler. Because of the number of fine anthologies of fiction by Mississippi writers (such as the fiction volume of Dorothy Abbott's series, *Mississippi Writers: Reflections of Childhood and Youth*) and because fiction is more readily available than other genres, this collection is limited to non-fictional pieces. However, it does include over a dozen lesser-known nonfiction pieces by some of our best novelists and short story writers.

Beginning with a selection by "A Gentleman from Elvas" written in 1541 and ending with an essay written in 1996 by Ellen Douglas for the Atlanta Olympics, the narratives span a period of over four hundred years. The order of the pieces is chronological within each section, an organization that sheds light on a particular time and place. Chronologically, Belle Kearney follows Nellie Nugent Somerville, a satisfying arrangement since both were elected to the state legislature two years after women won the vote. Eudora Welty, born in 1909, follows Richard Wright, born in 1908, a juxtaposition that caused me to consider how radically different their childhoods were, even though, at one time, both lived in Jackson. It is my hope that readers will find many other such connections and contrasts.

I have made nearly a hundred selections from sources discovered in libraries, attics, and archives. The following pieces will appear in print for the first time: Walter Anderson's journal entry on pelicans, Agnes Anderson's remembrance, Jefferson Davis's account of his capture, James Lucas's ex-slave narrative, Nellie Nugent Somerville's speech, Charlotte Capers's interview with Mrs. Turner, W. B. Allison's "Sacred Harp Sings," and Ruth Bass's "The Singing River." Other works, previously published but out of print or not readily available, include Emy-Lou Biedenharn's memoirs of her father (the first bottler of Coca-Cola), Mary Garrard's preface to the catalog of the Marie Hull exhibit, Dorothy Shawhan's "Mosquito Blues," and Charles East's tribute to the ladies.

Each section of the anthology concerns an aspect of Mississippi's past or present. The first three parts offer narratives about the struggle to get here, settle down, and live together. "Forebears" contains descriptions and records of Native Americans, early explorers, and settlers; "Terrains and Travelers" focuses on the land and how it shaped those who lived on it. The third part undertakes the subject of conflict. The Civil War has indelibly stamped our character, for better and worse. Responding to the oft-asked question as to why the South has produced so many good writers, Walker Percy replied simply, "Because we lost the war." A heritage of racial conflict has spurred thinkers from pre-Civil War days on to take up the pen. Other conflicts such as Reconstruction and women's suffrage have brought forth enormous changes and people who were compelled to write about them.

The fourth and fifth parts explore the topics of pleasure and pastimes. "Social Fabric" looks at the culture as it expresses itself through customs, games, sports, rituals, and religion—the human activities and endeavors that make us what we are and connect us to each other. "Body and Soul" is concerned with food, art, and music, all of which sprang from the hoof of Pegasus, according to Greek myth. On a visit to Mississippi in 1994, the Russian critic Sergai Chekovsky pointed out that sometimes a region's identity must be glimpsed indirectly. He said, "You cannot understand Russia with reason" and speculated that the same is probably true for Mississippi. He added that "Mississippians are like Russians in that they take time out to be human." What we do when we "take time out to be human" reveals much about who we are.

The final section, "Lives and Legends," focuses on people and their stories. It is written by (and about) renegades, imposters, wits, iconoclasts, and raconteurs; by mothers, fathers, firemen, farmers, preachers, doctors, soldiers, and exiles; by blacks, whites, Russians, and Native Americans. These accounts offer the reader a variety of impressions by real people, Mississippians whose colorful lives are part of the ongoing story.

The book ends with Ellen Douglas's essay "Neighborhoods." Evoking a view of Earth as seen from space while contemplating her family home near Natchez, which she says her great-grandmother would still recognize, Douglas enlarges the neighborhood and renders a new vision of sense of place. So too, may the variety of narratives collected here be a reminder that the state we call Mississippi is diverse, multifaceted, and complex. Far from being a fixed piece in a jigsaw puzzle, this place is home to a past kept alive by its treasured stories and to an ever-changing present.

PART ONE

Forebears

The De Soto Chronicles

A GENTLEMAN FROM ELVAS

*In 1541 Hernando de Soto became the first European explorer to reach
the Mississippi River, which he did by capitalizing on the knowledge of
prior explorers Ponce de Leon, Magellan, and Balboa. Ironically, de Soto
died in 1542 and was buried in the river he had "discovered." One of de
Soto's fellow explorers, a Portuguese who called himself "a Gentleman from
Elvas," kept detailed records, published in 1557, of what he observed of
the Native American culture that would soon vanish in the wake of the
explorers. His eyewitness accounts were translated from Portuguese by
James Alexander Robertson in 1933. According to Paul E. Hoffman, who
wrote the introduction to* The De Soto Chronicles, *"The accounts of
the expedition provide a sort of snapshot of populations, political systems,
and seemingly cultural ways that correspond to the late phases of the Mississippian cultural horizon in the Southeast." In chapter 20, "How the
Governor set out from Mavilla for Chicaça, and of What Happened to
Him," selected here from the journal of the Elvas gentleman, de Soto and
his men have just arrived at the Tombigbee River, whereupon de Soto
sends a messenger to the Chicasa (Chickasaw) Indians to herald their
arrival. When the messenger is killed, an uneasy relationship ensues between Governor de Soto and the tribe, with stealing going on from both
sides. Chicasa, which refers to a province, village, and river, was located
in Pontotoc County in the northeastern part of the state.* Cacique *is the
hereditary lord of vassals.*

ALONG THE RIVER were some towns well provided with maize
and beans. From that place to Chicaça, the governor marched for five
days through an unpopulated region. He reached a river where some
Indians on the other side tried to forbid him crossing. In two days another piragua was made. When it was finished, the governor ordered
an Indian to announce to the cacique that he should desire his friendship and should await him peacefully. But the Indians on the other side
of the river killed him in his [the governor's] sight, and immediately
went away uttering loud cries. Having crossed the river next day, December 17, the governor reached Chicaça, a small town of twenty
houses. After they were in Chicaça they suffered great hardships and
cold, for it was already winter, and most of the men were lodged in the

open field in the snow before having any place where they could build houses. This land was very well peopled, the population being spread out as was that of Mavilla. It was fertile and abounding in maize, most of this being still in the fields. The amount necessary for passing the winter was gathered. Certain Indians were captured, among whom was one who was greatly esteemed by the cacique. By means of an Indian the governor sent word to the cacique that he desired to see him and wished his friendship. The cacique came to offer himself to him, together with his person, land, and vassals. He said that he would cause two caciques to come in peace. A few days afterward they came with him accompanied by their Indians, one being named Alimamu and the other Nicalasa. They presented the governor with one hundred and fifty rabbits and some clothing of their land, namely blankets and skins. The cacique of Chicaça came to visit him frequently and sometimes the governor ordered him summoned and sent him a horse to go and come. He [the cacique] made complaint to him [the governor], that one of his vassals had risen against him, withholding his tribute, and asked that he protect him against him, saying that he was about to go to seek him in his land and punish him as he deserved—all pretense, for it was planned that while the governor went with him and the camp was divided into two parts, some would attack the governor and others those who remained in Chicaça. He [the cacique] went to the town where he lived and came with two hundred Indians with their bows and arrows. The governor took thirty horse and eighty foot and went to Saquechuma, as the province of the principal man was called, who he [the cacique] told him [the governor] had rebelled against him. They found an enclosed town which had been abandoned by the Indians, and those who were with the cacique set fire to the houses in order to conceal their treachery. But since the men taken by the governor were very watchful and prudent, as well as those who remained in Chicaça, on that occasion they did not dare attack us. The governor invited the cacique and certain of the principal Indians [to visit him] and gave them some pork to eat. And although they were not accustomed to it, they lusted after it so much that Indians would come nightly to certain houses a crossbow shot away from the camp where the hogs were sleeping and kill and carry off as many as they could. Three Indians were seized in the act, two of whom the governor ordered to be shot with arrows and the hands of the other cut off. In that condition he sent him to the cacique, who expressed regret that they had troubled the governor and was glad that justice had been executed on them.

On the Discovery of
the Mississippi

HENRY DE TONTY

*Thomas Falconer, a writer and explorer, was the first to translate into
English Henry de Tonty's memoir, written in 1693. Contemporary historians argue for Tonty's greatness as an explorer and fur trader and for
his equal standing with his more famous companion, Réne-Robert Cavel-
ier, Sieur de La Salle. Tonty's twenty-five years of exploring the Mississippi made him an uneq___'ed authority on river life, knowledgable about
natives as well as newco___ Here the Italian-born Tonty describes his
first exploration down the ___ssissippi with La Salle. The expedition
began in 1682 and ended with a ceremony claiming for France the entire
Mississippi River and its tributaries. As this passage illustrates, Tonty
wrote vivid descriptions of the land and animals and of encounters with
the Natchez Indians at their various villages along the river. He noted
with equal objectivity the practice of human sacrifice made at the death
of a chief and the civilized system of bartering. Tonty's missing right
hand, referred to in this excerpt, was lost when he fought for France in
the Mediterranean, and his artificial one so fascinated the Native Americans that they called him "Iron Hand" and regarded him as a powerful
chief.*

THE SAVAGES having been informed that we were coming down
the river, came in their canoes to look for us. We made them land, and
sent two Frenchmen as hostages to their village; the chief visited us with
the calumet, and we went to the savages. They regaled us with the best
they had, and after having danced the calumet to M. de la Salle, they
conducted us to their village of Toyengan, eight leagues from Cappa.
They received us there in the same manner, and from thence they went
with us to Toriman, two leagues further on, where we met with the same
reception. It must be here remarked that these villages, the first of
which is Osotonoy, are six leagues to the right descending the river,
and are commonly called Akancas (Arkansas). The three first villages
are situated on the great river (Mississippi). M. de la Salle erected the
arms of the King there; they have cabins made with the bark of cedar;

they have no other worship than the adoration of all sorts of animals. Their country is very beautiful, having abundance of peach, plum and apple trees, and vines flourish there; buffaloes, deer, stags, bears, turkeys, are very numerous. They have even domestic fowls. They have very little snow during the winter, and the ice is not thicker than a dollar. They gave us guides to conduct us to their allies, the Taencas, six leagues distant.

The first day we began to see and to kill alligators, which are numerous and from 15 to 20 feet long. When we arrived opposite to the village of the Taencas, M. de la Salle desired me to go to it and inform the chief of his arrival. I went with our guides, and we had to carry a bark canoe for ten *arpens,* and to launch it on a small lake in which their village was placed. I was surprised to find their cabins made of mud and covered with cane mats. The cabin of the chief was 40 feet square, the wall 10 feet high, a foot thick, and the roof, which was of a dome shaped, about 15 feet high. I was not less surprised when, on entering, I saw the chief seated on a camp bed, with three of his wives at his side, surrounded by more than 60 old men, clothed in large white cloaks, which are made by the women out of the bark of the mulberry tree and are tolerably well worked. The women were clothed in the same manner; and every time the chief spoke to them, before answering him, they howled and cried out several times—"O-o-o-o-o-o!" to show their respect for him, for their chiefs are held in as much consideration as our kings. No one drinks out of the chief's cup, nor eats out of his plate, and no one passes before him; when he walks they clean the path before him. When he dies they sacrifice his youngest wife, his house-steward (*maître d'hotel*), and a hundred men, to accompany him into the other world. They have a form of worship, and adore the sun. There is a temple opposite the house of the chief, and similar to it, except that three eagles are placed on this temple who look towards the rising sun. The temple is surrounded with strong mud walls, in which are fixed spikes on which they place the heads of their enemies whom they sacrifice to the sun. At the door of the temple is a block of wood, on which is a great shell (*vignot*), and plaited round with the hair of their enemies in a plait as thick as an arm and about 20 fathoms (*toises*) long. The inside of the temple is naked; there is an altar in the middle, and at the foot of the altar three logs of wood are placed on end, and a fire is kept up day and night by two old priests (*jongleurs*), who are the directors (*maîtres*) of their worship. These old men showed me a small cabinet within the wall, made of mats of cane. Desiring to see what was inside, the old men prevented me giving me to understand that their God was there. But I have since learnt that it is the place where they keep their treasure, such as fine pearls which they fish up in the neighbourhood, and European merchandise. At the last quarter of the moon all the cabins make an offering of a dish of the best food they have which is placed at the door of the temple. The old men take care to carry it away and to make a good feast of it with their families. Every spring they make a clearing, which they name "the field of the spirit," when all the men work to the sound of the tambour. In the autumn the Indian corn is harvested with much ceremony and stored in magazines until the moon of June in the following year, when all the village assemble, and invite their neighbours to eat it. They do not leave the ground until they have eaten it all, making great rejoicings the whole time. This is all I learnt of this nation. The three villages below have the same customs.

Let us return to the chief. When I was in his cabin he told me with a smiling countenance the pleasure he felt at the arrival of the French. I saw that one of his wives wore a pearl necklace. I presented her with ten yards of blue glass beads in exchange for it. She made some difficulty, but the chief having told her to let me have it, she did so. I carried it to M. de la Salle, giving him an account of all that I had seen and told him that the chief intended to visit him the next day—which he did. He would not have done this for savages but the hope of obtaining some merchandise induced him to act thus. He came the next day with wooden canoes to the sound of the tambour and the music of the women. The savages of the river use no other boats than these. M. de la Salle received him with much politeness, and gave him some presents; they gave us, in return, plenty of provisions and some of their robes. The chiefs returned well satisfied. We stayed during the day, which was the 22nd of March. An observation gave 31° of latitude. We left on the 22nd, and slept in an island ten leagues off. The next day we saw a canoe, and M. de la Salle ordered me to chase it, which I did, and as I was just on the point of taking it, more than 100 men appeared on the banks of the river to defend their people. M. de la Salle shouted out to me to come back, which I did. We went on and encamped opposite them. Afterwards, M. de la Salle expressing a wish to meet them peacefully, I offered to carry to them the calumet, and embarking, went to them. At first they joined their hands, as a sign that they wished to be friends; I, who had but one hand, told our men to do the same thing.

I made the chief men among them cross over to M. de la Salle, who accompanied them to their village, three leagues inland and passed the night there with some of his men. The next day he returned with the chief of the village where he had slept who was a brother of the great chief of the Natches; he conducted us to his brother's village, situated on the hill side, near the river, at six leagues distance. We were very well received there. This nation counts more than 300 warriors. Here the men cultivate the ground, hunt and fish, as well as the Taencas, and their manners are the same. We departed thence on Good Friday, and after a voyage of 20 leagues, encamped at the mouth of a large river, which runs from the west. We continued our journey, and crossed a great canal, which went towards the sea on the right. Thirty leagues further on we saw some fishermen on the bank of the river, and sent to reconnoitre them. It was the village of the Quinipissas, who let fly their arrows upon our men, who retired in consequence. As M. de la Salle would not fight against any nation, he made us embark. Twelve leagues from this village, on the left, is that of the Tangibaos. Scarcely eight days before this village had been totally destroyed. Dead bodies were lying on one another and the cabins were burnt. We proceeded on our course, and after sailing 40 leagues, arrived at the sea on the 7th of April.

Histoire de la Louisiane

LE PAGE DU PRATZ

Le Page Du Pratz's Histoire de la Louisiane *was published in 1758
and translated by the British in 1774 to encourage colonialism. Living
among the Natchez from 1720 to 1728, Du Pratz described firsthand
and in great detail the habits, language, and customs of this tribe at the
height of its power, before the tragic massacre led by Bienville in 1729 to
protect Fort Rosalie. Unlike many of his contemporary observers who saw
the Natchez as savages because of their belief in human sacrifice when a
member of the Sun class died, Du Pratz saw them as fellow human beings
with rules of conduct not unlike his own. In this account, taken from
section 2, "of the language, government, religion, ceremonies, and feasts
of the natives," Du Pratz describes the Natchez belief in the god Coyocop-
chill, or infinite spirit, capable only of good, and of lesser spirits, some of
which were capable of evil. According to Du Pratz's authority, who was
the guardian of the Natchez temple, an emissary from the sun once
brought "excellent precepts" for right living which were similar to the
Judeo-Christian Ten Commandments. He instructed the Natchez to build
a temple and an eternal fire with which to preserve them.*

DURING MY residence among the Natchez I contracted an intimate
friendship, not only with the chiefs or guardians of the temple, but with
the Great Sun, or the sovereign of the nation, and his brother the Stung
Serpent, the chief of the warriors; and by my great intimacy with them,
and the respect I acquired among the people, I easily learned the peculiar language of the nation.

This language is easy in the pronunciation, and expressive in the
terms. The natives, like the Orientals, speak much in a figurative stile,
the Natchez in particular more than any other people of Louisiana.
They have two languages, that of the nobles and that of the people, and
both are very copious. I will give two or three examples to shew the
difference of these two languages. When I call one of the common people, I say to him *aquenan*, that is, hark ye: if, on the other hand, I want
to speak to a Sun, or one of their nobles, I say to him, *magani*, which
signifies, hark ye. If one of the common people call at my house, I say
to him, *tachte-cabanacte, are you there*, or I am glad to see you, which is
equivalent to our good-morrow. I express the same thing to a Sun by

the word *apapegouaiché*. Again, according to their custom, I say to one of the common people, *petchi, sit you down;* but to a Sun, when I desire him to sit down, I say, *caham*. The two languages are nearly the same in all other respects; for the difference of expression seems only to take place in matters relating to the persons of the Suns and nobles, in distinction from those of the people.

Tho' the women speak the same language with the men, yet, in their manner of pronunciation, they soften and smooth the words, whereas the speech of the men is more grave and serious. The French, by chiefly frequenting the women, contracted their manner of speaking, which was ridiculed as an effeminacy by the women, as well as the men, among the natives.

From my conversations with the chief of the guardians of the temple, I discovered that they acknowledged a supreme being, whom they called *Coyococop-Chill*, or *Great Spirit*. The *Spirit infinitely great*, or the *Spirit* by way of excellence. The word *chill*, in their language, signifies the most superlative degree of perfection, and is added by them to the word which signifies *fire*, when they want to mention the Sun; thus *Oua* is *fire*, and *Oua-chill* is the *supreme fire*, or the *Sun;* therefore, by the word *Coyocop-Chill* they mean a spirit that surpasses other spirits as much as the sun does common fire.

"God," according to the definition of the guardian of the temple, "was so great and powerful, that, in comparison with him, all other things were as nothing; he had made all that we see, all that we can see, and all that we cannot see; he was so good, that he could not do ill to any one, even if he had a mind to it. They believe that God had made all things by his will; that nevertheless the little spirits, who are his servants, might, by his orders, have made many excellent works in the universe, which we admire; but that God himself had formed man with his own hands."

The guardian added, that they named those little spirits, *Coyocop-techou*, that is, a *free servant*, but as submissive and as respectful as a slave; that those spirits were always present before God, ready to execute his pleasure with an extreme diligence; that the air was filled with other spirits, some good some wicked; and that the latter had a chief, who was more wicked than them all; that God had found him so wicked, that he had bound him for ever, so that the other spirits of the air no longer did so much harm, especially when they were by prayers entreated not to do it; for it is one of the religious customs of those people to invoke the spirits of the air for rain or fine weather, according as each is needed. I have seen the Great Sun fast for nine days together, eating nothing but maizcorn, without meat or fish, drinking nothing but water, and abstaining from the company of his wives during the whole time. He underwent this rigorous fast out of complaisance to some Frenchmen, who had been complaining that it had not rained for a long time. Those inconsiderate people had not remarked, that notwithstanding the want of rain, the fruits of the earth had not suffered, as the dew is so plentiful in summer as fully to supply that deficiency.

The guardian of the temple having told me that God had made man with his own hands, I asked him if he knew how that was done. He answered, "that God had kneaded some clay, such as that which potters use, and had made it into a little man; and that after examining it, and finding it well formed, he blew up his work, and forthwith that little man had life, grew, acted, walked, and found himself a man perfectly well shaped." As he made no mention of the woman, I asked him how he believed she was made; he told me, "that probably in the same manner as the man; that their *antient speech* made no mention of any difference, only told them that the man was made first, and was the strongest and most courageous, because he was to be the head and support of the woman, who was made to be his companion."

Here I did not omit to rectify his notions on the subjects we had been talking about, and to give him those just ideas which religion teaches us, and the sacred writings have transmitted to us. He hearkened to me with great attention, and promised to repeat all that I had told him to the old men of his nation, who certainly would not forget it; adding, that we were very happy in being able to retain the knowledge of such fine things by means of the speaking cloth, so they name books and manuscripts.

I next proceeded to ask him, who had taught them to build a temple; whence had they their eternal fire, which they preserved with so much care; and who was the person that first instituted their feasts? He replied, "The charge I am entrusted with obliges me to know all these things you ask of me; I will therefore satisfy you: hearken to me. A great number of years ago there appeared among us a man and his wife, who came down from the sun. Not that we believe that the sun had a wife who bore him children, or that these were the descendants of the sun; but when they first appeared among us they were so bright and luminous that we had no difficulty to believe that they came down from the sun. This man told us, that having seen from on high that we did not govern ourselves well; that we had no master; that each of us had presumption enough to think himself capable of governing others, while he could not even conduct himself; he had thought fit to come down among us to teach us to live better.

"He moreover told us, that in order to live in peace among ourselves, and to please the supreme Spirit, we must indispensably observe the following points; we must never kill any one but in defence of our own lives; we must never know any other woman besides our own; we must never take any thing that belongs to another; we must never lye nor get drunk; we must not be avaricious, but must give liberally, and with joy, part of what we have to others who are in want, and generously share our subsistence with those who are in need of it."

"The words of this man deeply affected us, for he spoke them with authority, and he procured the respect even of the old men themselves, tho' he reprehended them as freely as the rest. Next day we offered to acknowledge him as our sovereign. He at first refused, saying that he should not be obeyed, and that the disobedient would infallibly die; but at length he accepted the offer that was made him on the following condition:

"That we would go and inhabit another country, better than that in which we were, which he would shew us; that we would afterwards live conformable to the instructions he had given us; that we would promise never to acknowledge any other sovereigns but him and his descendants; that the nobility should be perpetuated by the women after this manner; if I, said he, have male and female children, they being brothers and sisters cannot marry together; the eldest boy may chuse a wife from among the people, but his sons shall be only nobles; the children of the eldest girl, on the other hand, shall be princes and princesses, and her eldest son be sovereign; but her eldest daughter be the mother of the next sovereign, even tho' she should marry one of the common people; and, in defect of the eldest daughter, the next female relation to the person reigning shall be the mother of the future sovereign, the sons of the sovereign and princes shall lose their rank, but the daughters shall preserve theirs."

"He then told us, that in order to preserve the excellent precepts he had given us, it was necessary to build a temple, into which it should be lawful for none but the princes and princesses to enter, to speak to the Spirit. That in the temple they should eternally preserve a fire, which he would bring down from the sun, from whence he himself had descended, that the wood with which the fire was supplied should be pure wood without bark; that eight wise men of the nation should be chosen for guarding the fire night and day; that those eight men should have a chief, who should see them do their duty, and that if any of them failed in it he should be put to death. He likewise ordered another temple to be built in a distant part of our nation, which was then very populous, and the eternal fire to be kept there also, that in case it should be extinguished in the one it might be brought from the other; in which case, till it was again lighted, the nation would be afflicted with a great mortality."

"Our nation having consented to these conditions, he agreed to be our sovereign; and in presence of all the people he brought down the fire from the sun, upon some wood of the walnut-tree which he had prepared, which fire was deposited in both the temples. He lived a long time, and saw his children's children. To conclude, he instituted our feasts such as you see them."

The Natchez have neither sacrifices, libations, nor offerings: their whole worship consists in preserving the eternal fire, and this the Great Sun watches over with a peculiar attention. The Sun, who reigned when I was in the country, was extremely solicitous about it, and visited the temple every day. His vigilance had been awakened by a terrible hurricane which some years before had happened in the country, and was looked upon as an extraordinary event, the air being generally clear and serene in that climate. If to that calamity should be joined the extinction of the eternal fire, he was apprehensive their whole nation would be destroyed.

One day, when the Great Sun called upon me, he gave me an account of a dreadful calamity that had formerly befallen the nation of the Natchez, in consequence, as he believed, of the extinction of the eternal fire. He introduced his account in the following manner: "Our nation was formerly very numerous and very powerful; it extended more than twelve days journey from east to west, and more than fifteen from south to north. We reckoned then 500 Suns, and you may judge by that what was the number of the nobles, of the people of rank, and the common people. Now in times past it happened, that one of the two guardians, who were upon duty in the temple, left it on some business, and the other fell asleep, and suffered the fire to go out. When he awaked and saw that he had incurred the penalty of death, he went and got some profane fire, as tho' he had been going to light his pipe, and with that he renewed the eternal fire. His transgression was by that means concealed; but a dreadful mortality immediately ensued, and raged for four years, during which many Suns and an infinite number of the people died.

The guardian at length sickened, and found himself dying, upon which he sent for the Great Sun, and confessed the heinous crime he had been guilty of. The old men were immediately assembled, and, by their advice, fire being snatched from the other temple, and brought into this, the mortality quickly ceased." Upon my asking him what he meant by "snatching the fire," he replied, "that it must always be brought away by violence, and that some blood must be shed, unless some tree on the road was set on fire by lightning, and then the fire might be brought from thence; but that the fire of the sun was always preferable.

It is impossible to express his astonishment when I told him, that it was a trifling matter to bring down fire from the sun, and that I had it in my power to do it whenever I pleased. As he was extremely desirous to see me perform that seeming miracle, I took the smallest of two burning glasses which I had brought from France, and placing some dry punk (or agaric) upon a chip of wood, I drew the focus of the glass upon it, and with a tone of authority pronounced the word *Caheuch,* that is, *come,* as tho' I had been commanding the fire to come down. The punk immediately smoking, I blew a little and made it flame to the utter astonishment of the Great Sun and his whole retinue, some of whom stood trembling with amazement and religious awe. The prince himself could not help exclaiming, "Ah, what an extraordinary thing is here!" I confirmed him in his idea, by telling him, that I greatly loved and esteemed that useful instrument, as it was most valuable, and was given to me by my grandfather, who was a very learned man.

Upon his asking me, if another man could do the same thing with that instrument that he had seen me do, I told him that every man might do it, and I encouraged him to make the experiment himself. I accordingly put the glass in his hand, and leading it with mine over another piece of agaric, I desired him to pronounce the word *Caheuch,* which he did, but with a very faint and diffident tone; nevertheless, to his great amazement, he saw the agaric begin to smoke, which so confounded him that he dropt both the chip on which it was laid and the glass out of his hands, crying out, "Ah, what a miracle!"

Their curiosity being now fully raised, they held a consultation in my yard, and resolved to purchase at any rate my wonderful glass, which would prevent any future mortality in their nation, in consequence of the extinction of the eternal fire. I, in the mean time, had gone out to my field, as if about some business; but in reality to have a hearty laugh at the comical scene which I had just occasioned. Upon my return the Great Sun entered my apartment with me, and laying his hand upon mine, told me, that tho' he loved all the French, he was more my friend than of any of the rest, because most of the French carried all their understanding upon their tongue, but that I carried mine in my whole head and my whole body. After this preamble he offered to bargain for my glass, and desired me to set what value I pleased upon it, adding that he would not only cause the price to be paid by all the families of the nation, but would declare to them that they lay under an obligation to me for giving up to them a thing which saved them from a general mortality. I replied, that tho' I bore his whole nation in my heart, yet nothing made me part with my glass, but my affection for him and his brother; that, besides, I asked nothing in return but things necessary for my subsistence, such as corn, fowls, game, and fish, when they brought him any of these. He offered me twenty barrels of maiz, of 150 pounds each, twenty fowls, twenty turkies, and told me that he would send me game and fish every time his warriors brought him any, and his promise was punctually fulfilled. He engaged likewise not to speak any thing about it to the Frenchmen, lest they should be angry with me for parting with an instrument of so great a value. Next day the glass was tried before a general assembly of all the Suns, both men and women, the nobles, and the men of rank, who all met together at the temple; and the same effect being produced as the day before, the bargain was ratified; but it was resolved not to mention the affair to the common people, who, from their curiosity to know the secrets of their court, were assembled in great numbers not far from the temple, but only to tell them, that the whole nation of the Natchez were under great obligations to me.

The Natchez are brought up in a most perfect submission to their sovereign; the authority which their princes exercise over them is absolutely despotic, and can be compared to nothing but that of the first Ottoman emperors. Like these, the Great Sun is absolute master of the lives and estates of his subjects, which he disposes of at his pleasure, his will being the only law; but he has this singular advantage over the Ottoman princes, that he has no occasion to fear any seditious tumults, or any conspiracy against his person. If he orders a man guilty of a capital crime to be put to death, the criminal neither supplicates, nor procures intercession to be made for his life, nor attempts to run away. The order of the sovereign is executed on the spot, and nobody murmurs. But however absolute the authority of the Great Sun may be, and although a number of warriors and others attach themselves to him, to serve him, to follow him wherever he goes, and to hunt for him, yet he raises no stated impositions; and what he receives from those people appears given, not so much as a right due, as a voluntary homage, and a testimony of their love and gratitude.

Life of Apushimataha

GIDEON LINCECUM

*Dr. Gideon Lincecum lived among the Choctaw Indians and kept notes
about their lives. He did not publish these accounts during his lifetime,
although they are now being edited for publication by the Mississippi
Band of Choctaw Indians and scholar Mary Ann Wells. The following
account appeared in the* Publications of the Mississippi Historical
Society *in 1906. On October 18, 1820, in an open field near what is
now Canton, Mississippi, the generals Andrew Jackson and Thomas
Hinds and the Choctaw Indian chiefs Apushimataha (or Pushmataha),
Puckshunubbee, and Mushulatubbee signed the Treaty of Doak's Stand.
Five other treaties had led to this one, whereby 5,500,000 acres in west
and central Mississippi were turned over to the United States government
in exchange for extensive land across the Mississippi between the Arkansas and Red rivers for those Choctaws who chose to remain "wild, wandering hunters." According to Lincecum, the proposed treaty was a
"liberal proposition" for the Choctaws, but the chiefs feared the deal and
knew they had to try to get all they could. Therefore, as shown here,
Apushimataha challenged Jackson on several points before signing the
treaty. Soon after, at the Treaty of Dancing Rabbit, the Choctaws ceded
the rest of their land and headed to Indian territory.*

AT A TREATY held by General Jackson and General Hinds at Doak
Stand, in the Chahta country, during the autumn of 1820, Apushimataha distinguished himself greatly with the two generals by his extraordinary powers; his very correct knowledge of the geography of the far-
off country west of the Mississippi River and his astonishing eloquence.
They had three excellent interpreters, John Pitchlynn, Middleton
Mackey and Edmund Fulsome. All he said was clearly and fairly rendered in good English and General Jackson declared that his speeches
on that occasion would have done honor to any man of the age. He
regretted that he had not prepared himself with a reporter, as his inimi-
table figures so beautifully niched in the immense fabric of his exceedingly fine Chahta oratory were certainly a regretable loss to the literary
world. The object the United States had in holding this treaty was to
exchange, if they could, all that country where the Chahta and Chickasaw nations now reside and claim west of the Mississippi River for a slip

of territory from the lower part of the then Chahta nation, known as the Big Black country, in the State of Mississippi.

General Jackson had conferred the appointment of Brigadier General on Apushimataha, who, with a brigade of Chahta warriors, had served under Jackson during the war of 1818 against the Creeks, Mikisukies and Alocheway Indians. He was at the taking of Fort Baranchas, Pensacola and Mobile, distinguishing himself as a discreet commander and courageous warrior. General Jackson was familiarly acquainted with him, and in his opening speech at the treaty ground seemed to point his discourse mainly to Apushimataha, addressing him in the friendly epithet of "Brother Push." A large portion of the nation was in attendance, and after General Jackson had read the commission and the President's letter to them, in a long speech he opened up the object and purposes for which the people of the great and ever friendly nation of Chahtas had been called together. He declared to that very large assembly in which could be seen the faces of many white people who had attended the treaty, "that to promote the civilization of the Chahta people by the establishment of schools among them and to perpetuate them as a nation was a subject of constant solicitude with the President of the United States. It was an object near to his heart.

To enable the President to effectuate this great national and very desirable object, to accommodate the growing State of Mississippi, and thereby secure greater safety and protection to the Chahtas and their seminaries of learning at home, it was proposed by him to exchange for a small part of their land here a large country beyond the Mississippi River where all, who live by hunting and will not work, and who by the nature of their mode of life are widely scattered, may be collected and settled together in a country of tall trees, many water courses, rich lands and high grass abounding in game of all kinds—buffalo, bear, elk, deer, antelope, beaver, turkeys, honey and fruits of many kinds. In this great hunting ground they might be settled near together for protection and be able to pursue their peculiar vocation without danger.

Another great benefit to be derived from this arrangement would be the removal from among the people at home who are already inclined to progress and civilization of the bad example of those who, in their wild, wandering propensities, do not care for improvement. The project recommended itself to the thinking portion of the industrious community while it would provide ample means for the protection of the careless stragglers of the nation.

The tract of territory which the President proposed to exchange for the Big Black country lay between the Arkansas and Red rivers; it is a large and extensive country. Beginning where the lower boundary line of the Cherokees strikes the Arkansas River, thence up the Canadian to its source, thence due south to the Red River, thence down the Red River to a point three miles below the mouth of Little River, which empties into Red River from the north, thence on a direct line to the beginning.

This extensive rich territory, they were told, was offered in exchange by the President for the little slip of land at the lower part of the present Chahta nation. It is a much larger territory than the whole of the Chahta possessions this side of the Mississippi River and was certainly a very liberal proposition. They were asked, "What say the chiefs and Chahta people to this great offer?"

After the pipe lighters had finished handing the pipes around and order was restored, Apushimataha arose, and addressing himself to his own people first, told them that the man who had just finished his big talk was the great warrior, General Jackson, whom they all had so often heard of, many of them had no doubt seen him and like himself had served under him in many successful battles. His great character as a man and a warrior, in addition to the commission be bore from the President of the United States, demanded from the Chahta people respectful replies to his propositions, and for that purpose he moved that the council adjourn until the middle of the day to-morrow, which motion was carried and the council adjourned accordingly.

The chiefs and headmen went into a secret council that night where they very deliberately discussed the merits of the proposition that had been made by the United States commissioners. They considered it a wise and benevolent proposition, and notwithstanding the land they offered to exchange the large tract of western territory for was worth more to them at this time than two such countries as the one they were offering, with the Chahtas the thing stood very different, particularly in relation to the fixing of a home for the wandering hunters in the midst of a game country. However good as the proposition was they decided that they must in this case adopt the white man's rules in the transaction and get all they could from them. They recognized the fact that General Jackson was a great man, but in his talk in making the proposition to exchange countries they said he had been guilty of misrepresentations which he knew were such, and others which he was not perhaps apprised of. Their plan was to meet him in the treaty with his own policy and let the hardest reap the profits. If they could do no better they would accept the offer already made. This much and the appointment of Apushimataha to do the talking next day was the result of the secret council.

When at twelve o'clock the next day the council assembled the commissioners enquired of the chiefs if they had come to any conclusions on the subject of the proposition made to them yesterday in relation to the exchange of countries. Apushimataha arose and said that the chiefs and leaders of his country had appointed him to reply to the commissioners on that subject. He remarked that he fully appreciated the magnitude of the proposition and his incompetency to do it justice, especially while in contact with two such master minds as he would have to deal with. He further remarked that when any business was intended to be fairly and honestly transacted it made no difference as to the capacity of the contracting parties. One party might be as great a man as General Jackson, the other a fool, but the result would be the same. The wise man, in such cases would protect the rights of the fool, holding him firm on the safe ground. From what he had already heard he had discovered that this great transaction, now about to take place between friendly nations, who dwell almost in mixed society together, was not to be conducted on those equitable principles and that it would not be safe for him, fool as he was, to rely upon such expectation. He was to come to the contest with such powers as he possesses, do the best he could, and his people must be satisfied and abide the results. The object and benefits to be derived by the United States were great and very desirable or they would not have sent two of their greatest warrior generals to conduct the treaty in their behalf. He was friendly towards the United States, and particularly so to their two distinguished agents, for he had served under and side by side with them in the hour of peril and deathly strife, and had aided them in the acquisition of Florida and a considerable portion of the Muskogee country with his manhood, as had as many of his countrymen as he could persuade to take part in the dangers of the enterprise. Under all these considerations he intended to strike the bargain in the exchange of countries with them if he could. He thought it was one of those kind of swaps if it could be fairly made that it would accommodate both parties. He should do his best and he hoped to succeed in presenting the thing in such form as to convince the commissioners that further misrepresentation would be entirely unnecessary. He then took his seat calmly, without even a glance from his eyes either towards the red or the white audiences, when General Jackson rose and gravely remarked:

"Brother Push, you have uttered some hard words. You have openly accused me of misrepresentation and indirectly of the desire to defraud the red people in behalf of my government. These are heavy charges, charges of a very serious character. You must explain yourself in a manner that will clear them up or I shall quit you."

Apushimataha arose, took the speakers' stand very deliberately and casting his eyes, which were now beaming with the light that fired his great soul, upon his audience, said:

"As men grow older, especially great men, enthralling themselves with much business on the field of growing fame, they become impatient and irritable. They dare not stop on the path of their rushing and varying necessities to parley with the ignorant. They must make short work with all such obstructions. There is no honor in permitting the feeble or the foolish he may meet in his precipitate course to pass. No allowance is to be made or forgiveness offered for him. He must yield to the mere say so of the warily moving seeker of fame or be crushed. I have been making observation on that cast of character a long time, and find but little difference in their public action. In their private intercourse the whole thing is changed.

"My great friend, General Jackson, who familiarly calls me brother, whom my inner soul loveth, and in whose presence I always felt myself a mere boy, has become excited at some of my remarks, and has hastily called on me to explain them, and that explanation must be satisfactory or he will 'quit us,' the meaning of which, as I suppose, is that should I fail to make the *amende honorable* he returns to his government and informs them that the insulting obstinacy of the Chahta people is such that an honorable treaty cannot be negotiated with them. Then comes the horrors of war against us. All I have to say about it is that I hope they will have the good sense and the justice to put it upon those only who have raised the fuss to do the fighting. It would indeed be a great error in the justice of any government to involve the innocent inhabitants of two nations in the ruinous consequences of war on account of a misunderstanding betwixt two of their ministers.

"You gentlemen, General Jackson and General Hinds, are filling, as I understand from the letter you read before the council yesterday, the place of commissioners from the government of the United States to hold a treaty for certain purposes with the people of the Chahta country. Am I right?" and both the generals nodding assent, Apushimataha resumed and said: "I informed you in the outset, which I here repeat, that I occupy the same position. I, too, have been appointed by my government as commissioner to hold a treaty through you gentlemen with your people. I am therefore your equal, as far as appointment can make us so. I have already recognized your appointment and authority as being in all respects on an equal basis with my own. You, gentlemen, must reciprocate." And he seated himself on the bench with the commissioners, looking remarkably sedate.

General Jackson, in a remarkably good humor, rose and said: "General Apushimataha, in all respects in this treaty we acknowledge you to be vested with powers equal to ourselves and precisely on the same footing in relation to your country that we are to ours. You shall have no complaint to make against us in that respect. And now, as we are all equals, not of our own creation, but by the appointment of our respective nations, you are in a condition to go on and explain wherein I have misrepresented any fact in the propositions I have made in the name of my government. The nature of our position demands it, and we expect it from you."

Apushimataha said: "I shall take much pleasure in my explanation to render a plain and irrefutable interpretation of what I have said, and I will present in a very clear light the misrepresentations in relation to the quality of the country west of the Mississippi and the size of the country outside of the great river by my highly esteemed friend.

"In the first place he speaks of the country he wishes to obtain in the swap as 'a little slip of land at the lower part of the present Chahta nation,' whereas it is a very considerable tract of country. He has designated the boundaries of it himself, and I am very familiar with the entire tract of land it will cut off from us. In the second place, he represented the country he wishes to exchange for the 'little slip' as being a very extensive country 'of tall trees, many water courses, rich lands and high grass, abounding in game of all kinds—buffalo, bear, elk, deer, antelope, beaver, turkeys, honey and fruits of many kinds.' I am also well acquainted with that country. I have hunted there often, have chased the Commanchee and the Ovashsashi over those endless plains, and they have sometimes chased me there. I know the country well. It is indeed a very extensive land, but a vast amount of it is exceedingly poor and sterile, trackless, sandy deserts, nude of vegetation of any kind. As to tall trees, there is no timber anywhere except on the bottom lands, and it is low and boukey even there. The grass is everywhere very short, and for the game it is not plenty, except buffalo and deer. The buffalo in the western portion of the tract described and on the great plains into which it reaches are very numerous and easily taken; antelope, too, are there and deer almost everywhere except in the dry, grassless, sandy deserts. There are but few elk, and the bear are plenty only on Red River bottom lands. Turkeys are plentiful on all the water courses. There are, however, but few beavers, and the honey and fruit are rare things. The bottoms on the rivers are generally good soil, but liable to inundation during the spring season, and in summers the rivers and creeks dry up or become so salt that the water is awful for use. It is not at these times always salt, but often bitter, and will purge a man like medicine. This account differs widely from the description given by my friend yesterday and constitutes what in my reply to him I styled a misrepresentation. He has proven to me by that misrepresentation and one egregious error that he is entirely ignorant of the geography of the country he is offering to swap, and therefore I shall acquit him of an intention at fraud. The testimony that he bears against himself in regard to his deficiency of a knowledge of the geography of that far off country manifests itself in the fact that he has offered to swap to me an undefined portion of Mexican territory. He offers to run the line up the Canadian River to its source and thence due south to Red River. Now I know that a line running due south from the source of the Canadian would never touch any portion of Red River, but would go into the Mexican possessions beyond the limits even of my geographical knowledge."

General Jackson, interrupting him, said: "See here, Brother Push, you must be mistaken. Look at this map; it will prove to you at once that you are laboring under a great geographical error yourself;" and he spread out the map.

Apushimataha examined it very minutely while General Jackson traced out and read the names of the rivers for him. Apushimataha said, "the paper is not true." He then proceeded to mark out on the ground with the handle of the pipe hatchet which he held in his hand while speaking, the Canadian and the upper branches of Red River and said, holding the end of the hatchet handle on the ground:

"Here is the south, and you see the line between the two points do not touch any portion of Red River, and I declare to you that that is the natural position of the country and its water course."

"You must be mistaken," said General Jackson; "at any rate I am willing to make good the proposition I have named."

"Very well," replied Apushimataha, "and you must not be surprised nor think hard of me if I point your attention to another subject within the limits of the country you have designated west of the Mississippi which you do not seem to be apprised of. The lower portion of the land you propose to swap is a pretty good country. It is true that as high up the Arkansas River as Fort Smith the lands are good and timber and water plenty; but there is an objectionable difficulty lying in the way. It was never known before in any treaty made by the United States with the red people that their commissioners were permitted to offer to swap off or sell any portion of their citizens. What I ask to know in the stipulations of the present treaty is whether the American settlers you propose to turn over to us in this exchange of countries are, when we get them in possession, to be considered Indians or white people?"

General Jackson rejoined and told the speaking chief that "As for the white people on the land it was a mere matter of moonshine. There were perhaps a few hunters scattered over the country, and he would have them ordered off."

"I beg your pardon," replied Apushimataha. "There are a great many of them, many of them substantial, well to do settlers, with good houses and productive farms, and they will not be ordered off."

"But," replied General Jackson, "I will send my warriors, and by the eternal I'll drive them into the Mississippi or make them leave it."

"Very well," replied the chief; "and now the matter is settled as far as the land west of the great river is concerned. We will next consider the boundary and country the Chahtas are to give you for it, and if we can agree upon that the trade will be completed. You have defined its boundaries, and they include a very valuable tract of country, of considerable extent, capable of producing corn, cotton, wheat and all the crops the white man cultivates. Now, if we do agree on terms and run this line, it must, as a part of this contract, be very clearly understood, and put on paper in a form that will not die nor wear out, that no other alteration shall be made in the boundaries of that portion of our territory that will remain until the Chahta people are sufficiently progressed in the arts of civilization to become citizens of the State, owning land and homes of their own, on an equal footing with the white people. Then it may be surveyed and the surplus sold for the benefit of the Chahta people."

"That," said General Jackson, "is a magnificent arrangement, and we consent to it readily."

The day being well spent he proposed to the chiefs an adjournment until eleven o'clock the next day. It would give the chiefs and warriors time to discuss and arrange the details of the treaty and opportunity to his secretary for preparing his big paper upon which the articles and stipulations of the great contract between two friendly nations should be placed.

The chiefs assenting, an adjournment took place immediately.

The chiefs and people were highly pleased with the proceedings of the day and they went into secret council where they agreed and arranged what they intended to demand in detail to finish the swap, and put it on Apushimataha to do the talking again the coming day. They were all of opinion that the treaty would be finished in one more day and that it would result favorably to the red people they did not seem to doubt.

FROM

Life and Confession of the Noted Outlaw James Copeland

J. R. S. PITTS

Copeland's infamous career as an outlaw began when he was twelve and stole a neighbor's knife in Perry County, in the Piney Woods of Mississippi. Soon after, he became a member of Gale Wages's clan of outlaws, who were known for lawlessness and even murder. Before he was hanged in 1857, Copeland gave the following controversial confession to a sheriff named Pitts, who, upon publishing the work, was convicted of libel. The narrative describes the illegal activities of the outlaws Copeland, Wages, and a man named Charles McGrath, who masqueraded as an itinerant minister. In his prefatory pages, Pitts contextualizes Copeland's activities as part of the flush times of the 1830s and 1840s, when travelers invited lawlessness by carrying thousands of dollars. The scholar John D. W. Guice points out in the introduction to the facsimile edition of the confession that, apart from its sensational aspects, the story provides us with knowledge of the thriving livestock and timber industries on the Mississippi Gulf Coast at the time. In the following excerpt, "They Plan a Distribution of Their Booty—Honor Among Thieves," Copeland describes typical challenges for the outlaws, foraging for food and dividing their booty. The thirty thousand dollars referred to here was later buried in three oak barrels in the Catahoula Swamp in Hancock County. Then, in an unbelievably ironic twist of fate, Copeland lost the map of the hidden treasure in what he called "the famous Harvey battle."

OUR UNDERSTANDING with Harden was that he was to return to the vicinity of Mobile in the fall or early in the winter. The next morning early Harden, Wages and I paid our landlord and left; Harden, up the river to Tennessee, and Wages and I went to the New Basin, took passage on a wood freighting schooner to the Bay of St. Louis, and up Wolf river to a landing in the piney woods. We had provided ourselves with some biscuit, cheese and meat. We landed and walked to Allen Brown's again, where we landed the second night, very tired. McGrath, when we returned, was over on Black creek at Daniel Smith's hard up courting his daughter, Mary Smith, whom he married the next June following. He soon got the word that Wages and I had returned, and came over to Brown's.

Now we were all easy, with plenty of time to feast and frolic. We soon sent off to Pass Christian for flour, sugar, coffee, and whiskey, too, tobacco, cigars, and other little nicknacks. We first tried our hand at hunting deer and fishing in Red Creek, and did kill a few deer and caught some fish, but we found that too fatiguing in that hot season, and we resorted to other means to procure our fresh meat. And the way he slung old Bill Griffin's fine, fat heifers and yearlings was a caution. Their meat was very fat and remarkably fine flavored.

We remained at Brown's and in the vicinity until after the middle of August, and I don't believe that old Brown and his family had ever lived so well in his or their lives before. It was then that Wages commenced courting old Brown's daughter, whom he afterward married; and it was then that Brown made the proposition to Wages to go into the "counterfeiting business;" and I am here compelled to say that the association of Allen Brown with us was the main cause of our exposure, the death of Wages and McGrath, and the annihilation of our clan, and the prime cause of my fate.

Well, we rusticated at Brown's our time out, and all of us were fully satiated to our heart's content, and now the time had arrived for us to leave for our places near Mobile. A small consultation as to the way of our departure was necessary, and as McGrath was a member of the church, and had made frequent visits to Brother Smith's and Brother Bounds, he could go publickly any way, and was to go by way of the back Bay of Biloxi to visit the brethren about Evans', while Wages and I prepared ourselves with three days provisions, and started one moonlight night—Brown with us, and two of his horses. He went with us about thirty miles that night, and left us in the morning and returned home. We lay-by that day near the road, and started a little before sunset and crossed Pascagoula at Fairley's ferry before daylight next morning. We were then on our own native hills. We again laid by. The next night we crossed Dog river at Ward's bridge, and reached home early in the morning. McGrath arrived about ten days after us. Our first business was, after resting a while, to gather all our money and have a correct settlement and distribution of our funds.

Now it was honor among thieves! I disgorged all into the hands of Wages; he said to McGrath that he knew I had given up all. "Now, McGrath," said Wages, "shell out." So McGrath did turn out the seventeen hundred and twenty-five dollars. Wages said to him "where is that gospel money?" to which McGrath replied that the amount was small, and that he thought he ought to retain that for pocket and spending money. Wages then came out upon him in plain terms, and said: "McGrath, you came in with us upon equal terms, and if you wish to bulk or fly back, take your seventeen hundred dollars and leave, but look out for the consequences!" McGrath soon forked over about thirteen hundred dollars more. We had, when properly estimated, thirty-one thousand eight hundred and seventy-five dollars. This money was in joint stock between us three, and a proper appropriation and distribution of that sum was what we had next to look to.

"Now," said Wages, "boys, we have this amount of money, part in possession, and the balance at command. Let us devise some plan to save it; this, however, you may reflect upon. Our next business is to get the whole in possession; when we have done that, our next business is to make the proper disposition of it. So now we have buried at one place four thousand five hundred dollars, and our deposits in bank in New Orleans six thousand six hundred and seventy-five dollars, and what we now have makes our account tally; our next business is to get it altogether. When we have done that we must reflect well; and," said Wages to me, "James. I would rather that you and McGrath would lie down and sleep until I have all that matter accomplished, for I am fearful of your youthful imprudence, and McGrath's imprudent Irish brogue to go in blind right or wrong, and always come out at the little end of the horn, as they did at Vinegar Hill, or as Mitchell, Meagher and others did in their recent effort in Ireland to obtain their liberty." I then proposed to McGrath to give Wages the whole and sole control, to which he finally consented, though, I discovered, with some reluctance. . . .

Now to our affairs. Wages had returned to New Orleans, with all our money, and had purchased five barrels of whiskey, in one of which he had placed all the money. He had procured the whole of it in gold, and made a long, slim canvass bag, which he could pass through the bung-hole of the barrel, and in this bag he had placed his gold, mostly sovereigns, and five and ten-dollar pieces of American coin. After placing the money in the barrel he put in the bung tight, and nailed on the tin; shipped it as an ordinary barrel of whiskey, and hauled it out to one of our camps, where we opened it, and took out the gold. We had on hand a considerable amount of bank notes of New Orleans and Mobile Banks. We then agreed that Wages should take it all, and exchange it for gold, under pretense of entering land for some company in Mississippi. Wages took his little two-horse wagon, loaded with pickets, and went to Mobile. The first trip he brought home near eight thousand dollars in gold, which was deposited with the rest. I then proposed to Wages and McGrath to make the amount in gold, thirty thousand dollars even, and bury it in some safe place, secure, so that we might have it for any emergency; and in case of the death of one of us, the other two were to share it; and if two died, one had all. So the next trip Wages made to Mobile, he brought the balance to make up the amount. We had three strong kegs made in Mobile, well iron-hooped, and we placed in each ten thousand dollars; filled all the crevices with clean, white sand, headed the kegs up, gave them three coats of paint, and after they were thoroughly dry, we buried them in a thick swamp on Hamilton's creek. The balance of our money we then divided between us equally, which gave each share about six hundred and twenty-five dollars.

To accomplish our settlement of affairs, brought about the middle of November, 1843. McGrath left for the back Bay of Biloxi, and I saw nothing more of him until after his marriage.

About two weeks after, Harden arrived at Wages' riding a very fine horse, and had with him a likely mulatto fellow, riding on a very fine horse also, both of which he told me he sold to a man by the name of Jenkins. The first object to be effected was to kill and rob old man Sumrall. Mr. Newton was to turn preacher and go to Mr. Sumrall's house, and by some means effect the object; but by some misstep his intention was discovered through one of the house servants, the alarm was given, and brother Newton was ordered to leave brother Sumrall's premises. Wages and I lay in ambush, and had our appointed places to meet. We soon learned the result of Harden's adventure at Sumrall's. I returned to Mobile, Harden went to Louisiana, and Wages, by Jasper county, to Mobile. We were all to meet again about the last of February, on Black Creek, at the Pearlington road. We did meet, and a very few days after old Robert Lott was killed and all his money taken. This was sometime early in March, 1844. Wages was with Harden that night, and helped; I did not happen there. I met Wages next morning, at our camp, and he told me what was done and turned me back. Harden and Wages had divided a little over two thousand dollars. Harden left a few nights after for the Mississippi swamp in Louisiana, and Wages and I for Mobile, and traveled altogether in the night, to avoid discovery.

Natchez: The Antebellum Diary of a Free Negro

WILLIAM JOHNSON

William Johnson was in the unique position of being a freed mulatto slave who worked as a barber in pre–Civil War days. His mother had been freed by her master in 1814, and Johnson was freed in 1820. His business prospered, and by the 1830s he owned three barbershops. Prosperity brought about the ironic situation of his becoming a slaveowner himself. He was murdered in 1851 over a property dispute. Between 1835 and 1851, he kept a diary of over two thousand pages filled with accounts of betting on horse races, hunting and fishing, and attending political rallies. The following daily entries from 1837 indicate his immersion in the social life of Natchez, where he was held in high regard (from chapter 10, "The Negro: The Negro Speaks").

NOTHING HAS TRANSPIRED that is worth a Comment. I gave French $2.25 to day and the Boys $3 both for Bath Buisness

—Mr William H. Chambers Died Last night about 9 Oclock—Mrs Rebecka Bingham Died this evening Mr Chambers was buried out at the Family Burial Ground

—I bought of young Mr Harris to day $10 Rail Road Scrip for Seven & 1/2 of our paper Currency

—A fight took place this morning between Mr George Lancaster and Big Frank Little in the Market House, Frank Little it appears whiped Mary Lattimore[1] as she terms herself, for being at the Bench Drinking Coffee She was Left in Charge of Mr Lancaster and as soon as he herd that F Little had whiped her he went into market and commenced On F. Little as hard as he could with his fists They had a pretty sharp fight but was at Last Separated by the bystanders, I herd Mr P. Gemmell walk past my Shop Door Cursing N. L. Williams He was about to Flake him and did attempt to Jump the counter after him and was prevented by Mr Neibut. He cursed him for a d—d scoundrell and a greate many more things.[2]

—Nothing new worth recording—Mr Walker Gets the Girl that ran away from him some time ago

—Mr. Woodville P. Ward, the Post Master at Vicksburg, Died to day with Small pox—Extracted from N. Paper . . .

—The carpenters Commenced To repair the gallery the next Door at Capt Dossens, and very Glad I am to have thet place Stoped up. I Received a Letter from Captain Miller to day from Vicksburgh

—Mr A. Spielman owes me to this date the sum of three hundred Dollars

—To day Mr N. L. Williams Came To me To know if I had made any arrangement with Mr Gemmell. I told him that I had not but was waiting for a tittle for the wall from Mr Gemmell, and he Said Mr Gemmell Cannot give you a title for the wall, for he has treated me very shabbyly Lately, and I will not do anything To oblige him in any way. He would Sooner put his head in the River and hold it there a half hour than ask me to Sign a deed for it You had better Seys he, waight untill I get back from the North, and then we will have the buisness fixed for He Cannot give you a tittle and I have not passed my deed to Captain Dossen yet but will do it when I return from the North. He gave me to understand that he would sell me the wall for the Same Sum that I was to pay Mr Gemmel for it.

—To Days paper Announces the Ellction of Mr Izod to the Office of Sherriff—He had a majority of three hundred and fifty two over Col Woods—To Day Mr McGetrick paid me One months rent that was due on the 15th ins—the Amount of Rent was $79.00 I took 59 Dollars in Branch paper and $20 in Rail Road Scrip—He Left One hundred Dollars in Scrip—After taking Out the $20 it Leaves a Ballance of Eighty Dollars in Scrip in his favor of which I am to take Out Every month twenty Dollars as Long as it will Last To Day I herd Mr Paterson Driving Mr Abonette from his Store, saying go off! Go off—and I herd that they had takin him by the Collar and Led him to the door—Mr Bell had him put in Jail this Evening for debt . . .

—To day I paid Mr Mark Breden & Spielman & Co. the Sum of One Hundred and fifty three Dollars for Building a Bake Oven—very high price Mother paid me twelve Dollars on the above Amount, This will Leave a Ballance of One hundred and forty One Dollars—I Loaned Mr McFadden $50 to be paid On Tuesday next, 27th instant

—Business unusually dull, I wrode out and took Bill Winston with me To get Black Berrys. We got a greate many in a short time, Capt Pomp, or Mr Strickland is appointed Deputy Sherriff—Aunt F. McCary Stayd all night at our house

—I Read a prety tight burlesque to day in the Jackson paper of the

Duel that was to have Taken place between Mr Armatt & Besancon It apeared to be a Burlesque on Mr Armatt alone

—Judge Rawlins called To Know Something Respecting my whishing to have a petition for a reduction of taxes on my Property—To Day we had a first rate fight between Bill Rushelow & Bill Winston—They made a Stand of[f]—Neither whiped

—I herd this morning of the Dreadfull attack of Mr Rogers of Manchester on a Dr Reigna of the Same place, what the fight Grew Out of I Have not herd, but appears that Mr Rogers Saw Dr Reigna on his gallery and was in company with his family, ie, his wife and Children Mr Rogers drew a pistol and fired on him then Jumped To him, Knocked him down and stabed him clear through the body and screwed it around in his Dead Boddy—Latest accounts that he was put in Irons—to stand his tryal, Mr. R. Parker came in this Evening to Know how many Slaves I had about my yard as my property I told him that I had five and that I had Several Boys and they were not mine and they were not Bound to me yet.

—I Caught old Mary to night with a Basket with 7 or 8 unbaked Buiscuit—I have reason to believe that she got them at the City Hotell, and the way I cursed her was the wright way and if Ever I can hear of her doing the Like again I will whip her untill I make her faint

—This morning M[other] Commenced as usual to quarrell with Everything and Every body, I, Knowing perfectly well what it Grew Out of, I thought I would take the quickest way to stop it, and I accordingly took a whip and gave her a few Cuts; As soon as that was done M. Commenced to quarrell and abuse me Saying that I done it to oblige Sarah and advancing on me at the same time Dareing me to strike, which I would not do for anything in the world. I shoved her back from me three times

N·O T E S

[1] Mary Lattimore was a slave, the property of Dr. David Lattimore. On September 8, 1838, he swapped "a Mulatto woman named Mary," aged about twenty-one, to "Nancy [Lattimore] a free person of color" in exchange for another female slave, aged about eighteen, and $1.00. Adams County Deed Records, DD. 46.

[2] On May 6, 1836, Nathaniel L. Williams had purchased the three-story brick store building, occupied by the firm of Neibert & Gemmell and owned by Peter Gemmell and John G. Taylor. William Johnson's barbershop was immediately adjacent. Adams County Deed Records, X, 164–65. In 1837, Williams opened a new "Book and Drug Store," probably in the building he owned. Natchez *Courier*, November 27, 1837.

Southern Belle

MARY CRAIG SINCLAIR

Born in 1882, Mary Craig Kimbrough Sinclair describes in this excerpt from "When the World Was Young," the first chapter of Southern Belle, *published in 1957, her years of growing up in Greenwood, Mississippi, and at Ashton Hall, on the Mississippi Gulf Coast, where the Kimbroughs became close friends with their neighbors, the Jefferson Davises. Her father, Judge Allan Kimbrough, managed the Davis estate. Here she evokes with joy the privileged life she led when she had all the time in the world to watch black servants seine the ocean in Mississippi City on the Gulf Coast, fell firewood from the Piney Woods, or gather nuts and persimmons in the Delta. The chapter concludes with young Craig Kimbrough, attending the Gardner School for Young Ladies, visiting Mrs. Davis in New York in 1898. At the time of these visits, she was gathering material for a novel based on the life of Winnie Davis, "the daughter of the Confederacy," a biography that was never finished. Not long after these visits with Mrs. Davis, Kimbrough married the novelist and socialist Upton Sinclair. Her novel* Sylvia, *about a southern girl much like herself, was published under Sinclair's name.*

I WAS BORN in the midst of vast cotton plantations. It was from them that my father's wealth came, and in our winter home in Greenwood, Mississippi, I spent more than half of each year of my childhood.

The owners of the plantations had inherited them. After the Civil War devastated the land, and set free their slaves, they had gone down the Mississippi to New Orleans, or up to St. Louis, and borrowed money from the banks to restock and re-equip their places and recoup their fortunes. The ex-slaves had been put back to work in the cottonfields, and so by the time I was born, things were about as they had been during the days of slavery.

These proud white people thought they were the lords of creation, and no "damyankees" could make them change their minds or their ways. Pleasure was the chief concern of their lives, and they sought it and had it, just as their parents had done in the old days. The Negroes also were a pleasure-loving people, not far in their minds from the jungles of Africa where their ancestors had lived.

My father, a hard-working judge, banker, and plantation owner, used to look at them and deplore the "natural defect in the blood of the Negro" which made him shiftless and averse to responsibility. There were people who thought that God had ordained this, and it was fortunate for the cotton planter, who could not have labored to raise his own crops in a sun that was as hot as Africa's. And it was fortunate for Mama too, for how could she have lived with so many babies, and so many parties to give, if there had not been Negro mammies and housegirls and cooks?

Aunt Catherine was a fixture in our kitchen long before I arrived on earth. She had been a slave, and though slavery had been abolished many years earlier, it had made no difference in Catherine's status as she knew it; she still "belonged," and nothing on earth could have separated her from the family whose social prestige she shared. "Us colored peoples wuz happier then," I heard her say many times. "Us colored peoples had no 'sponsibility. De white folks had dat. An' dat's what I doan like about freedom, I doan want no 'sponsibility."

Among their former masters these black people had enough to eat, enough to wear, and roofs over their heads. The white planter furnished these because he could not afford not to; and the blacks had that thing precious to them, security.

Once one of the shopkeepers' wives in the town made an effort to seduce Catherine away from the family, and she came home and told Mama about it. "You know what dat white ooman done—she 'vited me in an' tole me to set down in her parlor! I wouldn't work for *no* white ooman what told me to set down in her parlor."

There were at least half a dozen ex-slaves of the family, both men and women, who lived in the cabins of our lane, and did a little work only when they felt like it. All of them had food from our house or from the plantation, and if they became sick, a doctor was called by the white folks. We were taught to treat these elderly blacks with the respect due to their age; without exception they were called "aunts" and "uncles." Catherine would say to one of my brothers, "Doan you give me no sass, boy. If you give me sass, I'll tell yo' mammy." And she never had to.

From infancy on I was used to black arms holding white children, and to black caresses. I never had anything from the black people but love. I heard their stories of slavery days, and learned much about the Civil War from them. Today in memory I plainly hear the voice of white-haired "Uncle" Henry telling a child how he was "the bodyguard" of my real Uncle William Morgan all through "de War"—there was only one war in the mind and speech of any Southerner, white or black, in those days. "I done carry him off de battlefiel' when he got shot," Uncle Henry would say; "wid dese yere arms I carried him, an' he tell you I save his life."

One night a fight broke out among our black people who were attending a dance in a cabin beside our woods. My father seized the empty shotgun which was always in the hall closet; he rushed off into the darkness, and my mother seized his loaded rifle and followed, ordering me to stay in the house. She was going to protect my six-foot-two father!

Unnecessary, because on the plantation, Papa's will was the law. These were "his" Negroes, and he would not shoot them because he knew they would obey him, and he needed their labor in the cotton fields. He waded among them, wielding the shotgun as a club and shouting to them to "get out." He was a powerful man, and they ran in a drove, scattering as they reached their homes. And then there was the task of binding up the wounds, which were made by razors, folded back, so that cuts were not deep but were long and bloody. Trusted house servants were sent to do this work. There was no doctor for ten or twenty miles, and if the foreman and the plantation manager happened not to be at hand, the plantation owner had to go with the servants to look after "his own."

This was in the Delta district of Mississippi, where we had our winter home, on the banks of the deep and dangerous Yazoo River—the Indian name means "river of death." My father became a judge, and after that he had to deal with other men's Negroes as well as his own.

Every year, at the approach of hot weather, Mama would move us from Greenwood to Ashton Hall, our summer home on the Mississippi Sound between Gulfport and Biloxi. The old house was set well back from the beach road in the midst of wide-spreading liveoak trees. It was spacious, and hospitable-looking, with wide galleries, roofed, and with banisters on all sides. It was built by slaves before the Civil War, out of hand-sawn lumber brought from Florida by schooners, and Papa was proud of the fact that it was still as "sound as a dollar" because nothing but well-cured lumber had gone into it.

Back of it was another ancient structure, a two-story building in which were the large kitchen and upstairs the servants' rooms. The kitchen was separate from the "big house" so that no odors from the enormous meals of sea foods prepared in it could reach the noses of the white folks.

The "big house" was always packed with guests, and the servants were busy during the daylight hours preparing elaborate meals, mainly of sea food, for this company. The menservants sat on wooden benches under the great oak trees, cracking the crab claws, peeling the shrimp, opening the oyster shells, and cutting up the okra, onions and bell peppers which went into the famed crab-gumbo of the Gulf Coast.

Back of the kitchen was an enormous arbor of scuppernong grapes, the vines so old that no one knew whether they were antebellum like the houses. We did know that these grapes made delicious wine, and that in some bygone day they had been used for this purpose. Mama was not the kind of homemaker who bothered with supervising canning or bottling—she was too busy with her children and guests. There was every kind of excellent wine to be bought in nearby New Orleans.

The world was young because we were young. The freshness of the dawn lasted through all hours of the day, for we were seeing and feeling only the joy of being alive on an earth which had no diseases, no perils, no sorrows; at least we did not know there were such things. When the west wind became too strong, it brought to us swarms of mosquitoes from the Louisiana marshes. We were uncomfortable when these insects bit us, and we slapped at them and anointed ourselves with oil of citronella and ran to shelter behind gauze wire and mosquito netting. But we did not dream that these pests, which came only occasionally, brought in their stings the germs of malaria, and sometimes of the deadly yellow fever.

We felt that we were immortal, that all things were immortal, and that Papa and Mama were all-powerful. These two would always know how to heal our sicknesses and disperse our sorrows. We were entirely safe and secure from all harm forever. This is the glory of childhood.

Papa never came to the coast until September, except for weekends. He had to stay in the hot and dangerous Delta until after the late sessions of court. When he came to play for a happy month with his precious family, he went to the beach every morning to see the seine pulled by the Negro menservants. This was a daily event of great excitement, and everyone except Mama gathered on the beach to see the contents of the net when it was dragged up on the clean, dry sands. My tall, dignified father never left his room in the morning until he was fully dressed in one of his clean blue-and-white-striped seersucker suits. And Mama never returned to the beach after the morning swim; she did not want to spoil her peaches-and-cream complexion with sunburn. But the rest of us still wore our bathing suits and were barefooted when the seine was pulled.

This net was perhaps 50 feet long, with weights at the bottom; two Negroes would wade out for some distance, one following in the other's footsteps, and then the front man would turn and wade to right or left, and when the net was parallel to the beach each would haul his end to the shore. The treasures which came out of that subtropical water outshone those which Aladdin found in his magical cave. Jewels are dead things, but here for the delight of a brood of healthy children was life abounding—leaping, wriggling, quivering, kicking. There were shrimp, crabs and a dozen kinds of fish, striped or banded or spotted, black or white or red or brown; fishes flat, or long and thin, or puffed up like balloons; fishes that croaked, fishes that flopped about madly and had to be grabbed before they got back into the water.

Now and then there would be a thrilling novelty, mysterious, perhaps dangerous: a horseshoe crab, for example, fairly round and flat, with a long tail and spikes on it—and could it sting you? We were never sure. We knew that the salt-water catfish, with their black needles sticking out, could give poisonous stabs.

Dink, our lively fox terrier, would rush in barking to challenge an energetic crab, and rush away again yelping. Some of the crabs were formidable, with powerful claws eight inches long, always upraised for battle; they would scuttle this way and that, trying to get back into the water. They had a disconcerting way of darting to one side or the other, and Dink could never learn this trick.

Out of two or three haulings of the seine would come buckets full of shrimp, and of crabs and fish—more than the family could consume at its largest, when there were several children, and the servants, and many guests. The surplus was dumped into a big pot in the back yard and boiled for the caretaker's chickens, and we ate the chickens he raised for us.

We had a wharf, extending far out into the water, and also we had what was called the "oyster pier" about a mile from the shore; almost every winter the storms damaged these wooden structures, and sometimes swept them away entirely. Mr. Bebb, the caretaker, wrote us when this happened and Papa had them replaced before we came to the coast. There were big lumber schooners out on the Sound, heavily loaded, and now and then they were caught in severe storms and had to dump part of their cargo; whatever was washed onto our beach went into rebuilding wharf and pier. The beach was ours, and also the water, or so we thought, and no one ever disputed the claim. Ours also was the oyster bed, a mile out; Papa had "planted" it, and he would order a schoonerload of oysters to replenish it now and then. All summer long we would row or sail to the "pier" and a colored boy would "tong up" oysters and open them for us to eat on the spot.

A good part of the day we children wore bathing suits. A boy's suit came to his knees, but girls wore bloomers which came to their ankles, not for beauty but for modesty. At low tide we splashed about and had water "fights"; at high tide we swam and floated, and so learned to take care of ourselves. One scene is forever impressed on my mind: several of the little ones were in the water when there was a warning shout—the black fin of a shark was cutting the water nearby. We splashed wildly to the beach, and one of my little brothers, Hunter, clambered up a slimy post which had been left in the water from a previous year's pier. There he clung until a rescue boat took him off; he was cut by barnacles, but not by sharks.

The wharf had a bathhouse with a covered porch around it, from which we children could fish and catch crabs. Farther out on the wharf was a sort of summerhouse, and if the mosquitoes were bad we would have pallets carried out to this place and sleep there. These swarms of mosquitoes came only when there was a high west wind, but when they did come, no gauze wire, no sort of netting could keep them out of the house.

My brothers had a sailboat as soon as they were old enough to sail it, and I had a rowboat. Mama didn't like me to row, because she said it would make my hands large, and that was not aristocratic; but somehow I managed to wheedle this privilege, and at dawn would row out toward the pier and watch the sunrise. I could never tire of that silent glory; the sun half out of the water, the clouds painted with a dozen shades I could not name, and these reflected on the water below. I would greet Papa being rowed out by a Negro boy to the oyster pier to fish. This boy always came with him, and carried his basket of shrimp for bait; he would bait Papa's hook and take off the fish as Papa caught them. Large ones could be caught from this pier, and here my harassed father got his rest from the cares and problems of plantation life and the court-room.

Oh, how kind and patient he was—and how I loved him! That I should ever do anything to displease him was wholly beyond the possibility of my thinking. I was taught to believe in God, and this was easy for me, for I knew He must be like Papa. . . .

Memorials of a Southern Planter

SUSAN DABNEY SMEDES

First published in 1887, the memoirs of Susan Dabney Smedes describe the life of her father, Thomas Smith Dabney, prominent owner of Burleigh Plantation near Raymond, Mississippi, in Hinds County. The book provides a detailed description of daily life on a plantation before, during, and after the Civil War, the circumstances of which Mrs. Smedes knew well. After the death of her mother and her husband, Lyell Smedes, a minister from Vicksburg, Mrs. Smedes became the mistress of Burleigh. Familiar with Harriet Beecher Stowe's Uncle Tom's Cabin, *Mrs. Smedes wanted to illustrate the positive side of slave-holding. Thomas Dabney made Burleigh into four thousand acres of cultivated farmland where he grew cotton, tobacco, corn, and other vegetables. He had a labor force of five hundred slaves, and, in the family's most prosperous years, over twenty-seven house servants. Burleigh was considered a model plantation, where, as we learn from the following excerpt from chapter 6, "Plantation Management," many slaves were taught to read and write. During the Civil War, Federal troops camped only a half mile away, sending the family and its slaves into exile in Mobile, Alabama, and Macon, Georgia. After the war, Dabney and his children were able to hold the plantation together, until 1882, partly because many of the freed slaves chose to stay on in the benign environment. In the following excerpt, the reader will note that Mrs. Smedes refers to her mother and father as Sophia and Thomas. Mammy Harriet was a slave who migrated to Mississippi with Dabney from Virginia.*

THOMAS OWNED more Negroes than could work with advantage on one place. He was advised to put a part on a second plantation, but he refused to let a consideration of profit induce him to place his servants where he could not personally attend to their welfare. All the Negroes were encouraged to come freely to the house to see the master and mistress, and they were very fond of making visits there. . . .

The master and mistress taught the Negroes truthfulness and honesty, as they taught their own children, by not tempting them, and by trusting them. It was a maxim with the master that it made a child honest and truthful to believe its word. He was by nature so unsuspicious that it required no effort to carry this out in his daily life.

On one occasion one of his daughters was at a reception in New York given to the House of Bishops. The honored guest of the evening was that great missionary Bishop Selwyn, of Lichfield, who had come over from England to our General Convention. Among other subjects the dishonesty of the Negro race was discussed, and someone asked if all Negroes were thieves. Thomas Dabney's daughter felt diffident about speaking, but she regretted afterwards that she had not said that a very large portion of her father's Negroes could be trusted to any extent. The interrogator had probably confounded Negroes who were trusted with those who were not. The confidence shown in them by the heads of her Southern home had taught the Negroes so much self-respect that a thoroughly thievish Negro was put under the ban in his own little world. Thomas had the control of about five hundred of them. About two hundred were his own, and on the Burleigh plantation. The others belonged to his wards, and were nearly all family Negroes, closely related to his, and living on neighboring plantations. He had the management of four estates belonging to minors. It was a saying in the family that the estates of his wards were better managed than his own, and their property increased faster than his, "Of course, I put the best overseers on their plantations," he said. "You see, I am here to look after my own." The Negroes of these came to him as to their master, and he treated them as his own.

He bought a cook, one of his mother's Negroes, after he went to Mississippi, at the same time making the arrangement to buy her husband. For some reason both did not go out together. A cook was always a belle on a plantation, and this young Alcey soon had all the unmarried men at her feet, among others a young fellow named Bob. One Sunday evening, as the rival suitors were sitting with her, Bob, who was thought to be a favored one, got his jawbone caught back in an unfortunate yawn, and spent several hours speechless, with his mouth wide open, while a messenger was despatched for the doctor. But this did not seem to disillusionize the object of his address, for she wrote a letter to her husband in Virginia that quite decided him not to join her. He also, it was said, had been casting his eyes around for a more congenial mate. When Mrs. Chamberlayne spoke to him of going out to Mississippi, he answered that Alcey had given him an account in a letter of the terrible ocean that had to be gone over on the way. Mrs. Chamberlayne said that if a woman could stand the journey a strong man certainly could. "Yes, Miss Marthy, but Alcey know more 'bout dem mysteries dan I does."

When Alcey was spoken to on the subject, she said, "Tell marster not to bother 'bout sendin' for him. He lazy an' puny an' no 'count." Bob's charms had triumphed.

On wedding occasions, in addition to the materials for a cake, the bride always expected a good many gifts, and some of the master's family to be present. The mistress's big prayer-book was taken over, and the marriage service read by one of the young masters. They would not be satisfied unless the bride and the cake were duly complimented. The children of the house-servants were married in the dining-room at Burleigh, and it was a saying in the family that these turned out to be happy marriages. . . .

The nurse who took care of the women when their babies were born received a fee each time. The mothers themselves looked on these seasons as gala times. They were provided with flour, sugar, dried fruit, and often meals from the table, and a woman to do all their cooking, washing, and house-work for a month. During the rest of the year they did little more than take care of the babies. Their cabins were clean and orderly, their beds gay with bright quilts, and often the pillows were snowy enough to tempt any head.

When we children were allowed to go to see some of the servants, they delighted in setting out a little feast. If they had nothing else, we were not allowed to go without a new-laid egg or two. Once at Christmas Mammy Harriet gave a "high tea" to us children. I was at that time about fourteen years of age, the oldest of the invited. A friend of my own age, Arabella Foote, the youngest daughter of Henry S. Foote (Governor and United States Senator), was spending her Christmas holidays with me. Mammy felt some modesty about inviting the young lady into her house, but I took Arabella, and she enjoyed it as much as any of us. Mammy had made a nice cake and hot biscuits and tea for the occasion, set out in her choicest cups, some of rare old china, and with sugar in the sugar-bowl that she had inherited from her mother. She gave us, besides, sweetmeats, nuts, raisins, fruits of several kinds—indeed, a delightful tea. And she stood behind us waiting on the table, her bright bandanna kerchief towering aloft on her head, and she looking so pleased.

The children delighted in teaching the house-servants. One night the whole family were formally invited, the master, mistress, governess, and guests, by a twelve-year-old school-mistress to hear her pupils recite poetry. She had about a dozen of the maids, old and young, Mammy

Maria among them. One of the guests was quite astonished to see his own servant, whom he had with him spending several months at Burleigh, get up and recite a piece of poetry that had been learned with pains for this occasion.

Some of the sons taught those of the plantation Negroes who cared to learn, but very few were willing to take the trouble to study. Virginius was successful with his scholars. Five of them learned to read so well that they became preachers. For this service he got one dozen eggs a month; or occasionally in lieu of this he received a pullet at the end of two months. He taught in the kitchen by the light of pine torches. His method of enforcing discipline on these middle-aged men was truly ludicrous. As his tutor, being one of the old-fashioned sort, did not spare the rod in the morning, so at night Virginius belabored the backs of his sturdy fellows. His beatings were received with shouts of laughter, the whole school would be in an uproar, the scholars dodging about to escape the young pedagogue's stick, and the cook and other on-lookers roaring with laughter. One of his graduates asked his advice as to a course of reading, suggesting history as the branch that he wished to pursue. The youthful teacher promptly advised *Robinson Crusoe,* and lent his own handsome copy to this promising pupil. After reading one hundred pages Joe came to him and said, "Mars Virginius, did you say dat book was history?" Virginius explained as well as he could what fiction was, on which Joe said, "I bin mistrustin' all 'long dat some o' de things what Robinson Crusoe say warn't true."

With Negro slaves it seemed impossible for one of them to do a thing, it mattered not how insignificant, without the assistance of one or two others. It was often said with a laugh by their owners that it took two to help one to do nothing. It required a whole afternoon for Joe, the aspirant for historical knowledge, and another able-bodied man like himself, to butcher a sheep. On a plantation the work of the women and children, and of some of the men also, amounted to so little that but small effort was made to utilize it. Of course, some kind of occupation had to be devised to keep them employed a part of the time. But it was very laborious to find easy work for a large body of inefficient and lazy people, and at Burleigh the struggle was given up in many cases. The different departments would have been more easily and better managed if there had been fewer to work. Sometimes a friend would say to the master that he made smaller crops than his Negroes ought to make. His reply was that he did not desire them to do all that they could.

The cook at Burleigh had always a scullion or two to help her, besides a man to cut her wood and put it on the huge andirons.* The scullions brought the water and prepared the vegetables, and made themselves generally useful. The vegetables were gathered and brought from the garden by the gardener, or by one of the half-dozen women whom he frequently had to help him. A second cook made the desserts, sweetmeats, etc. As children, we thought that the main business of the head cook was to scold the scullion and ourselves, and to pin a dish-rag to us if we ventured into her kitchen. Four women and a boy were in charge of the dairy. As the cows sometimes wandered to pastures several miles away, this number did not seem excessive. The boy brought the cows up, sometimes with one of the women to help him. Two of the women milked; the third held the semi-sinecure office, taking charge of the milk; and the fourth churned.

There were no blooded cattle on the plantation for many years, but thirty cows in the cowpen gave all the milk and butter that was needed for the house and plantation, and a good deal of butter was sold. The pastures were so good that the cattle increased rapidly and were sold, a hundred at a time. Southdown sheep were imported from Kentucky and pigs from England. Everything looked well and fat at Burleigh. The master was amused on being asked by a neighboring farmer if he would let him have some of his curly-tailed breed of pigs. The man innocently added that he noticed they were always fat, not knowing, as Thomas used to say, in repeating this, that corn would make the straightest tail curl. His beeves were fattened two years, after they had worked two years as oxen to make the flesh firm. One year they ran in the cornfield before the corn was gathered, and the next they were stalled. As all the oxen were fattened for beeves after two years of work, no old ox was on the place. He killed every winter eight or ten of these stalled oxen. The stalled sheep were so fat that they sometimes died of suffocation. . . .

One day, on the occasion of a large dinner, the master was hastily summoned to the kitchen, to see there a huge saddle of Southdown mutton that had by its own weight torn itself from the big kitchen spit, and was lying in the basting-pan.

During the spring and summer lambs were butchered twice a week, or oftener if required. That did not keep down the flock sufficiently, and a great many were sold. The hides from the beeves almost supplied

---

* The cook's husband, who for years had looked on himself as nearly blind, and therefore unable to do more than work about her, and put her wood on the fire sometimes cutting a stick or two, made no less than eighteen good crops for himself when the war was over. He was one of the best farmers in the country.

the plantation with shoes. Two of the Negro men were tanners and shoemakers. A Southern plantation, well managed, had nearly everything necessary to life done within its bounds. At Burleigh there were two carpenters in the carpenter-shop, two blacksmiths in the blacksmith-shop, two millers in the mill, and usually five seamstresses in the house. In the laundry there were two of the strongest and most capable women on the plantation, and they were perhaps the busiest of the corps of house-servants. Boys were kept about, ready to ride for the mail or to take notes around the neighborhood. There was no lack of numbers to fill every place; the trouble was rather to find work for supernumeraries, as already intimated.

One of the overseers, who was ambitious to put in a large crop, begged to have some of these hangers-on sent to the field. There were twenty-seven servants in the service of the house, he said.

The land in cultivation looked like a lady's garden, scarcely a blade of grass to be seen in hundreds of acres. The rows and hills and furrows were laid off so carefully as to be a pleasure to the eye. The fences and bridges, gates and roads, were in good order. His wagons never broke down. All these details may seem quite out of place and superfluous. But they show the character of the man in a country where many such things were neglected for the one important consideration—the cotton crop.

He never kept a slow mule; all must be fast and strong. They were sold as soon as they failed to come up to these requirements. Thomas raised all his own mules and nearly all his own horses—his thoroughbred riding-horses always—and frequently he had more than he needed of both. The great droves of mules and horses brought annually from Tennessee and Kentucky to less thrifty planters found no sale at Burleigh unless the master happened to need a pair of carriage-horses. Two teams of six mules each carried off his cotton crop, going to the station every working day for months. It was only ten miles off, but the eight bales of cotton, that weighed nearly five hundred pounds apiece, and the heavy, deeply cut-up roads, made it a day's journey. As the returning wagon-drivers came up in the evenings they were met by other men, who took the mules out and cared for them, and loaded up the wagons for the next day. It was not considered right by the master that those who occupied the responsible position of drivers should have these labors to perform. They had nothing to do but to go to the house to deliver the cotton receipts, get a drink of whiskey, and some tobacco too, if the regular allowance issued had run short, and then home to supper and to rest, ready for a fresh start in the morning.

Hog-killing time was a high carnival on the plantation. There were usually about a hundred and fifty or a hundred and seventy-five hogs, sometimes more. They supplied the house all the year round, and the Negroes for six months. He had taken out to Mississippi the Virginia art of cutting bacon. His hams were famous among his friends and guests, as were the chops and saddles of Southdown mutton, the legs of venison, wild or from his park, the great rounds and sirloins of beef, and the steaks cut with the grain.

It was no waste or useless lavishness that these great roasts of beef or mutton were seldom put on the table a second time, or that the number of chickens in the fattening coops were in the season not allowed to fall below sixty, or that during the winter and spring turkeys were on the table twice a week. Not only the house-servants, but usually several sick and favorite ones, were fed from the table. In addition to these, there were almost always the servants of guests and neighbors in the house.

It was customary on many plantations for boys to drive the mules in the cotton-gin. Under them the mules did not thrive, and had frequently to be changed. On the Burleigh place the most experienced and trustworthy of the drivers had charge of the ginmules. Under them the same team ginned out the entire crop, working at it every day for months. At the end of the season they were as fat and well as at the beginning.

Fodder-pulling was looked on with dread by most planters, as the hot work among the corn-stalks gave the Negroes chills and fevers. The master of Burleigh guarded his Negroes against sickness by providing two barrels of whiskey for this season. Every man and woman came for a cup of it when the day's work was over. The wag of the plantation, Uncle Beverly, was always given two cups, because he had a very funny way of opening his enormous mouth and throwing the contents of the cup into it as if he were throwing it into a bucket. Everybody laughed when he did it, the master enjoying it as much as as any of them.

The heart-warming laugh with his master seemed to be the best part.

Indulgent as he was when he thought his servants needed liquor, he was equally strict in forbidding them to touch it at other times. It was his boast that he was always obeyed in this, and also that under his system he had never had a drunkard on his plantation. Our friends and neighbors were not sure at Christmas and other festive seasons that the dining-room servants would not be intoxicated. At Burliegh the servants knew that the eggnog-bowl and the other things would be handed to them at the proper time, and they felt a pride in not displeasing the family by bad conduct. Likewise, his wagon-drivers were put on their good behavior as long as they had the wagons and teams under their care. The servants who went with the carriage to dinner-parties and at night about in the neighborhood had the lives of wife and children in their keeping, he used to say, and he chose them for their steadiness, and was never deceived or disappointed. In connection with this, his children and a number of young people, guests at Burleigh, were near meeting with an accident one cold winter's night. The roads were heavy, having been cut up by the cotton-wagons, and it was thought unsafe to go over five miles of a bad road on a dark night in anything less substantial than a six-mule plantation wagon. There was great glee and fun in the getting off. It was at the Christmas season, and everybody felt in spirit for enjoying the Christmas-parties at the country-houses. There had been a series of them. As the wagon was loaded up with its gay, living freight, there was some talk of firing off some of the children's fire-crackers in order to put mettle into the mules. In the lightness of his heart the master called out to the steady Lewis, his trusted driver, "Lewis, don't bring them back till you have upset them twice." And with that parting speech, which was received with cheers, he went back into the house. He did not dream that Lewis, who had never disobeyed him in his life, did not mean to disobey him this time. We thought that Lewis was surely intoxicated, from the manner in which he brought us back home. But we had not had time to tell papa of our grave suspicions before Lewis's honest face appeared at the door with his apology to the amazed master. "I do my ve'y bes', marster, to tu'n dat waggin ober, sir. I run it in all de gullies I could fin', but I couldn't tu'n it ober, sir."

Southern children were taught to call the colored people "aunt" and "uncle" as titles of respect. They resented being called by their names without the title, and considered that it spoke ill for the manners of a child who would do so rude a thing. They called each other "brer" and "sis." This referred, not to the natural relationship, but to their relationship in the church. On formal occasions they were "Mr." and"Mrs." Ignorance of this led me into sad disgrace one night with my usually indulgent Mammy Maria. She had taken me to see her brother married. I heard her address him as Mr. Ferguson, and at once asked, "Mammy, what makes you call Henry Mr. Ferguson?" "Do you think 'cause we are black that we cyarn't have no names?" was Mammy's indignant reply. She could not be angry more than a minute with "her white chillun." She never went to wedding or party or quilting without bringing to us an apple or a cake or a bouquet—whatever was given to her there. I do not think that her own children fared as well. The mistress had wet-nurses for her babies, chosen from among her Negro servants. The devotion of the nurses to these foster-children was greater than their love for their own. One of them, with a baby at home very sick, left it to stay with the white child. This one she insisted on walking the night through, because he was roaring with the colic, though the mistress entirely disapproved, and urged her to go home to her own child, whose illness was more serious, if less noisy, than the white nursling with its colic.

FROM

Trials of the Earth

MARY HAMILTON

*Mary Hamilton may have been the first white woman to cross the Sun-
flower River in the Mississippi Delta. A pioneer with great strength and
courage, she lived from 1866 to 1966. At the urging of her friend (and
later editor) Helen Dick Davis, she wrote down in great detail the adventures and hardships of her life as the wife of Frank Hamilton, a timber-
man and farmer, describing her role as cook, laborer and mother to nine
children, four of whom died young. Her sister and brother-in-law, Jane
and Jim Thompson, and another sister, Lucy, lived and worked with
them at the time. In this selection, from the chapter entitled "Concordia
Island," Hamilton and her family have moved to Mississippi from Arkansas in the year 1896 because they hope the climate will improve Frank
Hamilton's health, not knowing at the time that he had Bright's disease.
In her forward to this book, Ellen Douglas writes:*

> *We have journals written by upperclass educated white southerners, male
> and female, and by visitors to the South. We have volumes of letters. But I
> know of no account of life in the timber camps and on small isolated farms
> before and after the turn of the century written by a white woman who lived
> and worked and raised her family in the camps and on the farms during
> the period when the huge tracts of virgin forest in the American South were
> being clear cut and the clear-cut land was just beginning to be farmed.*

I T   W A S   A   C O L D   gloomy morning in January 1896 when I started
with my two little girls, my sister Lucy, and my brother Johnny, to what
was to us a new world, the Mississippi Delta. Frank sent us directions
how to go to Memphis, but no further, as he was to meet us there, and
we were to go on by boat, the *Kate Adams,* to our new home on the
Concordia Island, five miles from Gunnison, Mississippi. Through a
mistake, we missed Frank and had to take a train to Gunnison. Frank
got to Memphis and came tearing across town just in time to see our
train pulling out. He knew we wouldn't get to Gunnison until the next
day, as we had to lay over night in Delta, Mississippi. So he came right
back by boat and met us the next day at Gunnison.

Oh, I was so glad to see him again. He was tanned, the white chalky
color all gone, and was fifteen pounds heavier than when he left Missouri. Nina knew him, but baby Leslie wouldn't have a thing to do with

him. He hadn't seen her since she was a few weeks old, and now she was running everywhere and talking some.

Frank and Jim Thompson were working together. Jim was there to meet us, with Frank.

"Wait till you see your beautiful new homes," Jim said, and I could see my good jolly brother as of old was a little uneasy for fear I would be disappointed, as this was going to be my first experience of camp life.

We went from Gunnison in a two-horse buggy, Frank and Jim on horseback. We drove down the Mississippi River levee about a mile, then turned off the levee down into the thickest timber I had ever seen. Oak, gum, ash, hackberry, and poplar stood so thick, with no underbrush, only big blue cane growing rank and tall, almost to the limbs of the trees. It looked so odd, but what looked odder still to me was the black mud, "gumbo," Frank said it was. When we came out on the Mississippi River, the ground was sandy, but it was black sand, and the woods were thinner; there were fewer trees but larger—big old cottonwoods and sycamores that seemed to me when I looked up like their tops were lost in the sky. It was a pretty sight, except the road. The soft black sand was almost hub deep, but at last we came in sight of our future home, and what a sight!

Jim's office and commissary and bedrooms were built of clapboards, his cook shanty the same, with a small dining room for the white men, who were never more than four, as he worked Negroes altogether. Then there were the Negroes' cooking shanties and a few cabins; it was altogether like a little town. Jim rode alongside the buggy and asked me what I thought of "Clapboard City." I choked back a sob, I don't know whether of relief or disappointment. I didn't know then. But I managed to say, "Fine. I have always wanted to try camp life."

Frank had stopped at the roadway to see about some teams, and Jim went on with us. He explained to us that at Gunnison the river began a forty-mile bend, coming back almost to Gunnison again, and that was why the land lying between the river and the levee was called Concordia Island, although it was really a long neck of land surrounded by water— all but a little strip at Gunnison. Beyond Jim's place we saw a big white tent, the largest I ever saw. Nina pointed to it and said, "Pretty white house." Nothing would satisfy her but to drive right on down there. It was a big tent thirty by twenty feet, floored and boxed in four feet high; there was a nice big cookstove in the front end and a big Kind heater in the middle. The back was curtained off into bedrooms, small but large enough. This was to be our home, as Frank had to live and sleep out of doors. I had left Lucy at the hotel in Gunnison until our things came, and I was glad I had known better than to let her come out in camp before we got fixed up.

We stayed that first night with Jim. Nina took up with him, and he said it was like finding his own little girl. Nina, like me, had never got over her brother's death, but the change to this new country, and being with her father, was helping us both already. She had always seemed to love Frank so much, and he worshipped her.

The next day our things came, and I sent after Lucy. She was, as I knew she would be, disgusted with everything, but I kept her so busy she couldn't say much. We put down carpet in the back of our tent house. It reached from the back of the tent to the heater, and I had rugs for the other side of it. We put up our beds, two bedsteads and a child's bed. I had four big feather beds besides the child's feather bed and eight big feather pillows. That sounds silly now, but those days the more feather beds you had the better off you were supposed to be. And I had plenty of nice bedclothes. So when we got all our things in, our dining table, little cook table, cupboard for dishes, cupboard for clothes, trunks, and small, splintbottom homemade chairs, we were all fixed up nice. We had plenty to cook, and, oh, how you can eat in camp. Jim took his meals with us. He had a big commissary and wouldn't let Frank charge hardly anything to himself. He never went to town without bringing us all kinds of choice cuts of meat, and fruit, and he never forgot the children. Would bring them toys, clothes, anything he could see that he thought they would like.

One time when he was in Greenville he got Nina a beautiful white silk dress and six yards of white ribbon with pale blue and yellow violets "to trim it in," he said. I told him I would lay it away until she got older or until we got in a house. He said, "Make it now. She looks just like a fairy or an angel. I can't understand how a child as handsome as Nina could be the child of you and Frank. I guess you want to save it for her wedding dress."

Nina spoke up so serious. "Uncle Jim, I don't want a wedding dress. Mamma is going to make it now and I am going to wear it and wear it for you, and I am going to wear it when I go to heaven."

Then she ran out to play, and Jim said, "Why does she talk so much of going to heaven? It isn't right to put such stuff in a child's head, Mary."

I told him I had not, and I couldn't understand it either, unless it was her brother Oswald. Ozzie had always talked that way, and they were so devoted to each other. When he died, and they told her he had gone to heaven, she ran to him and clung to him, crying, "Wait, Ozzie, wait. I go with you. I want to go. I want to go." They couldn't console her. Lucy tried to get her to notice the baby, Leslie, but she would only say, "It is sweet, but I want to go to heaven with Ozzie." She was in bed several days with fever after he died.

When I got hold of myself a little, I told them they must ignore her talk of going to heaven, but it did little good. In time she talked less of Oswald and heaven, but when something like this would come up and she would talk so natural about going to heaven, I sometimes thought it was never out of her mind. How little we can know what is in the mind of a child.

Jim said, "I have heard her mention heaven several times. She is so happy and contented, full of fun and mischief, yet she has the saddest look at times. You make that dress, Mary, and I will see she wears it out, and I will never get her another white dress." He kept his word and got her every other kind, but never white.

Once settled, I had time to look around me, see more of the strange country and people, and adopt them as my own, for why shouldn't I love a country that gave Frank back his health, his very life? It was a mild winter, and almost every day I took my children and Lucy and went to the river bank to watch the men build their raft. It was fine to go up there well-wrapped and build us a fire; the children and I never tired watching the stream of boats and the waves rolling behind them. But Lucy, not her! She didn't like anything about camp life.

Either Frank or Jim was at the raft all the time, the other one in the woods. They had from six to eight log wagons going all the time; eight-wheeled wagons, the wheels boxed in to keep them from bogging up in the mud, and from eight to ten oxen to a wagon. Many of the logs were so large they couldn't get but one on a wagon. I have seen Frank stand on the ground beside the butt cut of a tree, and he could just lay his hand on top of it. They hauled the logs to the river bank and rolled them off in the river; then the men would float them up against the raft and fasten them together with poles. Gum and oak they called "sinkers"; these they would pin between cottonwoods, ash, and cypress, "floaters," to keep them from sinking. A large rope was tied every fifty feet with wire cables to trees along the bank or to posts driven in the ground. When they got enough logs rafted together to send to Greenville, they would send for tugboats, bunch the rafts together, and float them there to be sold.

I was happy and contented and so were the children. Every day brought a new adventure. Soon winter was over, and spring came with warm rains. Violets were everywhere, and green grass, and the trees putting out new leaves. Spring was in the air, in our blood, in the frogs, too, for they held a concert every night. Bees were flying around gathering honey from the holly blooms, and the holly trees were shedding their old leaves and putting on new. Every day in falling timber they would find a bee tree, and Frank would bring in three or four gallons of fine white honey.

We were all happy but Lucy. She was gloomy, blue, discontented. Said she couldn't stand this godforsaken place any longer. The lady that ran the hotel in Gunnison had visited us several times, and she and Lucy took a liking to each other. Lucy's romantic dreams weren't coming true, camping and living like Indians as we did, and I wasn't surprised when she came to me one day and said, "I'm going to Gunnison to stay at the hotel with Mrs. Huse. I will help her enough to pay my board, until you get out of this hole."

I was sorry, but she was twenty-four years old and knew her own business. She had taken her life in her own hands ten years before. So Johnny took her out to Gunnison, and she left the island to return only on short visits. I am afraid we all felt relieved when she left, for she was so dissatisfied she took lots of the brightness out of our lives. But she was so good to my children I missed her lots.

FROM

Wild Bill Sullivan

ANN R. HAMMONS

Ann Hammons was the great-granddaughter of the man called Wild Bill Sullivan, who lived from 1851 to 1932. Much of her account is taken from an unpublished manuscript of Sullivan's story as told to her father, Virgil M. Howell. The story of the Mississippi Sullivans, of Scotch-Irish descent, begins with Thomas, who was born around 1775 and came to Mississippi by way of South Carolina and Alabama. Thomas Sullivan had two wives, who lived across the road from each other and who each bore him eleven children. Because the children named their children after their brothers and sisters (and because there was some intermarriage among the descendants), prefixes such as "Wild Bill," "Big Bud," or "Red Jack" were soon necessary. The Sullivan clan settled deep in the Piney Woods in an area known as Sullivan's Hollow, which encompassed the southwest corner of Smith County and parts of Covington and Simpson counties in south Mississippi. Ruggedly independent and sometimes violent, the clan made their living primarily in the timber industry, but also raised cattle and hunted deer. In 1903, along with his son Andrew Jack, Bill Sullivan was accused of murdering his own brother, Wilson Sullivan. Andrew Jack went into hiding and accidentally killed himself before he could be brought to trial. "Wild Bill" was found guilty by a lower court, a decision that was reversed in 1904 by the Mississippi Supreme Court. The true nature of the man Bill Sullivan, known as "the king of the Hollow," has been the subject of much conversation and of many articles in magazines such as Life *and* Colliers, *all of which have found him to be paradoxical, since he was known to be violent but also steadfastly loyal to his friends and family. As the following chapter, "The Humorist," reveals, one thing that can be agreed upon about him is that he was a colorful prankster.*

WILD BILL SULLIVAN is often characterized as a man with a dry sense of humor. The essence of this type of humor cannot be captured with the written word. The nature of the individual himself, the inflection of the words which he said, the vast storehouse of past experiences—all of these must be understood and perceived in their correct relationship in order to see why certain anecdotes about Wild Bill can produce reactions, varying from chuckles to hilarious laughter, even among the Sullivans today. Some episodes, when viewed from the distance of the hundred years that have passed since their occurence, seem to be crude comedy almost bordering on slapstick nonsense. For example, once Bill caught a salesman in the Hollow, proceeded to paint his horse black, and then proclaimed emphatically that the horse belonged to him. . . .

Dovie Sullivan tells the story of how Wild Bill went fishing one day, and upon his return home, his wife Juriah exclaimed: "Why, Bill, are you wet?" Whereupon he replied, deadpan without a trace of a smile, "Well, Juriah, I guess I am. There is no reason for me not to be. I fell into a creek." No scribe, however brilliant, can recount that story and get a laugh. Yet those who know Wild Bill can conjure up the scene vividly. Such is the power of the memory of Wild Bill. . . .

Randall Howell, a grandnephew of Bill's, remembers him as a great fisherman but also as a man to be avoided if possible. Bill was a good friend of Randall's father, Judge W. M. Howell. Randall said that although Bill was easily agitated, he was "easy to forget grievances." He told of many times when Bill would come to Judge Howell, wanting the judge to fill out papers so that he could bring a suit against someone who had crossed him. On these occasions Judge Howell would ask Bill to sit on the porch, and they would talk about the prospects of good or bad crops. Then, at the judge's invitation Bill would eat supper and spend the night there. After breakfast the next morning, Judge Howell might say, "Now, Bill, what kind of papers were you wanting me to draw up?" and Bill might stroke his big mustache and say with a droll wit, "Judge, just forget them papers. Just say I came after me something to eat." Then these two grey-haired fellows would shake hands, each with a twinkle in his eyes, and off Bill would go until the next time he decided to fix up some papers on someone.

Shep Sullivan said his grandfather was one of the gentlest men he ever knew and loved to pull innocent pranks, yet he could laugh at himself. After Shep's mother died in 1914, when he was twelve, Shep lived with his Grandpa Bill and Grandma Juriah for awhile. Shep slept in the same bed with his grandfather, who complained about Shep's tendency to kick during the night. Shep, in an effort to please his grandfather, decided to cure himself of his kicking habit. "I got me a string, tied one end to my big toe and one end to the bed rail, and just waited the next morning until Grandpa started in on his usual complaints about the bad kicking during the night. He didn't do it in a mean way, just picking at me. I was fumbling trying to find that there string when he said, 'Boy, what in the world are you doing?' I showed him my big toe tied to the rail, and he laughed so hard he couldn't get out of bed."

. . . Another incident recalls the day Bill and Neece went fishing in Cohay swamp around some stumps that stood out in the water. Bill saw a big catfish down in the hollow of a stump and was unable to reach it with his hand. He called Neece over to help him. His plan was for Neece to hold his feet while he went headfirst into the stump and groped for the catfish. Neece would then pull both him and the fish out. However, when Bill had gone all the way down into the stump, Neece let go of his feet and wouldn't pull him out. Bill's arms, head, shoulders, and chest were under water, and he almost drowned before he could let go of the catfish. After then, the very mention of going catfishing would evoke uncontrollable mirth from the brothers.

In 1963 in the governor's race in Mississippi, legends about the Hollow were used to make a telling political point. Among the candidates was Charles Sullivan, a Clarksdale attorney whose forebears came out of the Hollow. He assured his listeners that a few days in Sullivan's Hollow would do a world of good for Bobby Kennedy and Chief Justice Earl Warren. Old-timers throughout the state laughed at the remark. They knew exactly what Mr. Sullivan implied.

Violence itself was often the basis for the humor. Regular battles were fought at Shiloh Church in Covington County, but the fight best remembered was one in which two men were killed, and Bill's brother Neece was stabbed a dozen times and virtually disemboweled by Tom Chain. Someone pulled Chain off just in time, and Neece, "holdin' his innards with his hands, drug hisself over to his mule and got away." Some twenty years later, Neece's boys came in one night with their clothes in tatters and their bodies bruised and cut from head to foot. They explained, "We been fightin' Tom Chain's boys over to Shiloh Church." Old Neece looked up and said, "Well, if Ah'd known yuh was gonna do that, Ah'd hev told yuh to wear yuh old clothes."

. . . As early as 1947, *Collier's* published a feature entitled "The Sullivans of Sullivan's Hollow" which pointed out that Wild Bill and his brother Neece loved a good joke; in fact, all the Sullivans did, and even today, the real test in Sullivan's Hollow is whether a person can play a better joke than the other fellow can. The *Collier's* reporter ran into the Sullivan trait of impish delight when he met Fred Sullivan, who, in an interview, squinted, frowned, and said, "Us Sullivans are jest about the meanest people there is. Hain't no crime we ain't committed. We're guilty of 'em all, 'n' we're just so mean we doan' care." When the reporter said he didn't believe it, Fred just sighed with disappointment: "Shucks, ev'y now 'n' then yuh git aholt of a fella who's skitterish, 'n' boy, when we git one like thet, we sure like to lay hit on."

. . . Many fights occurred with resultant loss of lives, and their fights were the beginning of many long, drawn-out family quarrels and feuds.

One of these occurred at a time when Bill and Neece were invited to have dinner with the owner of the sawmill in Bunker Hill. Some of Bill and Neece's enemies were also invited. Not being pleased with the guests present at this dinner, Neece rushed for a knife, and asked Bill to help him clear the house. Bill replied, "Do it yourself and let me eat," at which Neece jerked out Bill's shirttail and cut it off. Bill slashed Neece on the shoulders and arms with his knife. The guests, seeing the floor becoming spotted with Neece's blood, cleared out quickly without further controversy.

Another incident typifies their mischief and violence. One day when the family preacher was to visit their father's home for dinner, Bill and Neece, with their two sisters, were to prepare dinner and entertain him. For some reason the rest of the family were not at home. The boys decided that a good joke would be to prevent the sisters from preparing the dinner. They placed a long ladder beside the house and climbed to the housetop to look over the farm and surrounding country. After a few minutes, they came down hurriedly and told the girls they had just seen a pack of wolves on the farm. The girls, very much alarmed, were allowed to climb up to the housetop and see the wolves. While they were on the roof, Bill and Neece removed the ladder and then hid it. Thus when the preacher came for dinner, he found only the two girls at home, both perched upon the roof of the house, and no dinner prepared. . . .

Sullivan's Hollow, after its name became famous, was rarely pestered with peddlers, although one happened through once in a while. A Bible salesman once reached the Hollow and paid a visit to the Henderson Sullivan home. Before the salesman had time to introduce his wares, he was suspected to be a peddler, and Bill and Neece raised a panel of rail fence, poked the salesman's head through the crack, and let the fence down on him. There was barely room in the fence crack for his neck. They then placed a beehive near him, leaving the bees to become fearfully familiar with the peddler. After a few minutes, they released the peddler who thought he might find a better sale for Bibles elsewhere.

Bill's father was once having trouble with something stealing his chickens at night. He suspected 'coons and 'possums as the thieves. He was watching his flock very closely one night when Bill and Neece sneaked to the chicken house, quietly took an old hen from the roost, tied a coonskin over her and set her loose. Of course, she made a great outcry and ran about the premises struggling with the coonskin. At last the hen had shaken the skin loose except for a string tied to one of her feet. The skin dragged after her. Meanwhile the boys' father had gotten out of bed and was trying to shoot whatever was after the hen. Of course, he saw the coon after the hen and shot several times at it, but some of his shot killed the hen. Not until he had examined the hen did he know that he had been the butt of this joke. . . .

In 1880, Bill and Neece ran afoul of the law in the Bryant Craft murder case, which will be told later. They took to the woods for about four years. Even then, their love of pranks continued to play an important part in their lives. Wild Bill tells it best in his own words.

Me and Neece shore had lots o' fun when we was lyin' out. I recollect one night when we was a fixin' to camp out and sleep in the woods we had a little fire built and Neece had stretched out by the side uv it and went to sleep. I wanted to pull some kind o' prank on 'im 'cause 'twenrn't but a few days fo' that he had pushed me off'n a foot log, into the creek. I happened to think about a big chicken snake we had killed that day and was not but about a quarter of a mile back from the fire. I slipped back and got it and when I got back Neece was sleeping like a log. I tied the snake to his foot and got over on the other side of the fire from him and shot my gun twice and hollered "snake." Neece jumped up and when he drawed his foot up to get up the snake follered along arter it. Neece tried his best to jump out 'o the way o' the snake but it looked to him lack it was jumpin arter him. Neece throwed his hat off and started to run out across a little ol' fiel' but soon foun' the snake was tied to him. He eased back to the fire and said, "I'll just be damned if I don't keep you awake all night, just for that."

Another time me and Neece was a'settin' on a log by the road and I told Neece I was goin't have some fun. I said the first one comes down this road is a' goin' to dance for us. I hadn't hardly more'n said it when I seed a' old man a' comin' down the road a' ridin' a horse and when he got close to us I ast him where he was goin' he said, "to Mize." I said, "Did you ever dance any?" "Not much" he said. "Well, we want to see you get down off that horse and try it." He looked at me for a minit and didn't move. I said "You must not know who I am. If you don't know, I'll tell you. I am Wild Bill Sullivan, an' I mean fur you to git down and shake your feet." He didn't hesitate this time. He danced 'till the sweat was a' pouring off his face, and then I said, "That will do." The old man said, "Before you told me who you was, I had a' min' not to dance, but now, if you won't tell anybody about this prank in Mize, I'll give you a good drink o' whiskey." I said, "I shore won't tell it." I put my gun down and he reached in his saddle pocket to get what I thought was the whiskey. The first thing I seed a' comin' out was the handle of a big navy pistol. He said, "Did you ever dance any?" I said, "No, but by golly I am goin' at it right now." (Here there was a loud laugh by all) "When I had danced 'till my knees began to wobble, he said, "That will do." We shook han's an' he went on down the road and me and Neece went back to the woods. . . .

The truth about Wild Bill has become so entwined with legend that it is difficult to separate the two. In writing of Sullivan's Hollow, John K. Bettersworth of Mississippi State University did not try to do so. He referred to the way Mississippians speak "with genuine delight of the numerous feuding Sullivans of Sullivan's Hollow, whose capital was Mize, where the best watermelons and some of the liveliest tall tales in Mississippi were produced."

Autobiography of an Ex-Slave

JAMES LUCAS

A collection of narratives of ex-slaves was sponsored by the Works Progress Administration, a relief program created to stimulate the economy after the depression. This autobiography of ex-slave James Lucas was recorded by Edith Wyatt Moore, one of the many, mostly middle-class workers recruited for the program. The interviewers tried to preserve as closely as possible the dialect of the ex-slaves. Lucas was living in Natchez when he gave this live account. His interviewer described him as small, wrinkled, slightly stooped, and neatly dressed, with wooly white hair, grizzled mustache, and bright eyes. Here he tells of growing up on a plantation in Wilkinson County in the southwest corner of the state and of being owned by several masters in Adams County, one of whom was Jefferson Davis. When the Civil War broke out, he was put in a Yankee uniform, serving the army first on a gunboat, then digging a canal at Vicksburg. He claims to have witnessed the moment when General Lee turned over his sword to General Grant. At the time of the interview, he was living on a federal pension and longing for the days before the Civil War.

''MISS YOU CAN count up for yo'se'f. I was born on October 11, 1833. My young Marster give me my age when he heired de prope'ty of his uncle, Marse W. B. Withers. He was a-goin' through de papers an' a-burnin' some of 'em when he foun' de one 'bout me. Den he says, 'Jim, dissen's 'bout you. It gives yo' birthday.'

"I recollec' a heap 'bout slav'ry-times, but I's all by myse'f now. All o' my frien's has lef' me. Even Marse Fleming has passed on. He was a little boy when I was a grown man.

"I was born in a cotton fiel' in cotton pickin' time, an' de wimmins fixed my mammy up so she didn' hardly lose no time atall. My mammy sho' was healthy. Her name was Silvey an' her mammy come over to dis country in a big ship. Somebody give her de name o' Betty, but twant her right name. Folks couldn' un'erstan' a word she say. It was some sort o' gibberish dey called gulluh-talk, an' it soun' *dat* funny. My pappy was Bill Lucas.

"When I was a little chap I used to wear coarse lowell-cloth shirts on de week-a-days. Dey was long an' had big collars. When de seams ripped de hide would show through. When I got big enough to wait 'roun' at de Big House an' go to town, I wore clean rough clo'es. De pants was white linsey-woolsey an' de shirts was rough white cotton what was wove at de plantation. In de winter de sewin' wimmins made us heavy clothes an' knit wool socks for us. De wimmins wore linsey-woolsey dresses an' long leggin's lak de sojers wear. Dis was a long narrow wool cloth an' it wropt 'roun' an' 'roun' dey legs an' fas'n at de top wid a string.

"I never went to no church, but on Sund'ys a white man would preach an' pray wid us an' when he'd git through us went on 'bout us own business.

"At Chris'mus de Marster give de slaves a heap o' fresh meat an' whiskey for treats. But you better not git drunk. No-sir-ree! Den on Chris'mus Eve dey was a big dance an' de white folks would come an' see de one what dance de bes'. Marster an' Mistis laugh fit to kill at de capers us cut. Den sometimes dey had big weddin's an' de young white ladies dressed de brides up lak dey was white. Sometimes dey sont to N'awleans for a big cake. De preacher married 'em wid de same testimony dey use now. Den ever'body'd have a little drink an' some cake. It sho' was larrupin'. Den ever'body'd git right. Us could dance near 'bout all night. De old-time fiddlers played fas' music an' us all clapped han's an' tromped an' sway'd in time to de music. Us sho' made de rafters ring.

"Us slaves didn' pay no 'tention to who owned us, leastways de young ones didn'. I was raised by a marster what owned a heap o' lan's. Lemme see, dey is called Artonish, Lookdale, an' Lockleaven. Dey is plantations 'long de river in Wilkinson County, where I was raised. Dey is all 'long together.

"I's sho' my firs' marster was Marse Jim Stamps an' his wife was Miss Lucindy. She was nice an' sof'-goin'. Us was glad when she stayed on de plantation.

"Nex' thing I knowed us all b'longed to Marse Withers. He was from de nawth an' he didn' have no wife. (Marsters wid-out wives was de debbil. I knows a-plenty what I oughtn' tell to ladies. Twant de marsters whut was so mean. Twas dem po' white trash overseers an' agents. Dey was mean; dey was meaner dan bulldogs. Yes'm, wives made a big diffe'nce. Dey was kin' an' went 'bout mongst de slaves a-lookin' after 'em. Dey give out food an' clo'es an' shoes. Dey doctored de little babies.) When things went wrong de wimmins was all de time puttin' me up to tellin' de Mistis. Marse D. D. Withers was my young marster. He was a little man, but ever'body stepped when he come 'roun'.

"Don' rightly know how it come 'bout. Lemme see! De bes' I 'member my nex' Marster was Pres'dent Jefferson Davis hisse'f. Only he warnt no pres'dent den. He was jus' a tall quiet gent'man wid a pretty young wife what he married in Natchez. Her name was Miss Varina Howell, an' he sho' let her have her way. I spec I's de only one livin' whose eyes ever seed 'em bofe. I talked wid her when dey come in de big steamboat. 'Fore us got to de big house, I tol' her all 'bout de goins'-on on de plantations. She was a fine lady. When I was a boy 'bout thirteen years old dey took me up de country toward Vicksburg to see a place call Briarsfield. It mus'-a been named for her old home in Natchez what was called 'de Briars.' I didn' b'long to Marse Jeff no great while, but I aint never fo'git de look of 'im. He was always calm lak an' savin' on his words. His wife was jus' de other way. She talked more dan a-plenty.

"I b'lieves a bank sol' us nex' to Marse L. Q. Chambers. I 'members him well. I was a house-servant an' de overseer dassent hit me a lick. Marster done lay de law down. Mos' planters lived on day plantations jus' a part o' de year. Dey would go off to Saratogy an' places up nawth. Sometimes Marse L. Q. would come down to de place wid a big wagon filled wid a thousan' pair o' shoes at one time. He had a nice wife. One day whilst I was a-waitin' on de table I see old Marse lay his knife down jus' lak he tired. Den he lean back in his chair, kinda still lak. Den I say, 'What de matter wid Marse L. Q.?' Den dey all jump an' scream an', bless de Lawd, if he warnt plumb dead.

"Slaves didn' know what to 'spec from freedom, but a lot of 'em hoped dey would be fed an' kep' by de gov'ment. Dey all had diffe'nt ways o' thinkin' 'bout it. Mos'ly though dey was jus' lak me, dey didn' know jus' zackly what it meant. It was jus' somp'n dat de white folks an' slaves all de time talk 'bout. Dat's all. Folks dat ain' never been free don' rightly know de *feel* of bein' free. Dey don' know de meanin' of it. Slaves like us, what was owned by quality-folks, was sati'fied an' didn' sing none of dem freedom songs. I recollec' one song dat us could sing. It went lak dis:

> 'Drinkin' o' de wine, drinkin' o' de wine,
> Ought-a been in heaven three-thousan' yeahs
> A-drinking' o' dat wine, a-drinkin' o' dat wine.'

Us could shout dat one.

"I was a grown-up man wid a wife an' two chillun when de War broke out. You see, I stayed wid de folks 'til 'long cum de Yanks. Dey took me off an' put me in de War. Firs', dey shipped me on a gunboat an', nex', dey made me he'p dig a canal at Vicksburg. I was on de gunboat when it shelled de town. It was turrible, seein' folks a-tryin' to blow each other up. Whilst us was bull-doggin' Vicksburg in front, a Yankee army slipped

in behin' de Rebels an' penned 'em up. I fit at Fort Pillow an' Harrisburg an' Pleasant Hill an' 'fore I was ha'f through wid it I was in Ba'ti-
more an' Virginny.

"I was on han' when Gin'l Lee handed his sword to Gin'l Grant. You
see, Miss, dey had him all hemmed in an' he jus' natchally had to give
up. I seen him stick his sword up in de groun'.

"Law! It sho' was turrible times. Dese old eyes o' mine seen more
people crippled an' dead. I'se even seen 'em saw off legs wid hacksaws.
I tell you it aint right, Miss, what I seen. It aint right atall.

"Den I was put to buryin' Yankee sojers. When nobody was lookin' I
stript de dead of dey money. Sometimes dey had it in a belt a-roun' dey
bodies. Soon I got a big roll o' foldin' money. Den I come a-trampin'
back home. My folks didn' have no money but dat wuthless kin'. It was
all dey knowed 'bout. When I grabbed some if it an' throwed it in de
blazin' fiah, dey thought I was crazy, 'til I tol' 'em, 'dat aint money; it's
no 'count!' Den I give my daddy a greenback an' tol' him what it was.

"Aftah de War was over de slaves was worse off dan when dey had
marsters. Some of 'em was put in stockades at Angola, Loosanna, an'
some in de turrible corral at Natchez. Dey warnt used to de stuff de
Yankees fed 'em. Dey fed 'em wasp-nes' bread, 'stead o' corn-pone an'
hoe cake, an' all such lak. Dey caught diseases an' died by de hund'eds,
jus' lak flies. Dey had been fooled into thinkin' it would be good times,
but it was de wors' times dey ever seen. Twant no place for 'em to go;
no bed to sleep on; an' no roof over dey heads. Dem what could git
back home set out wid dey min's made up to stay on de lan'. Most of
dey mistis' took 'em back so dey wuked de lan' ag'in. I means dem what
lived to git back to dey folks was more'n glad to wuk! Dey done had a
sad lesson. Some of 'em was worse'n slaves after de War.

"Dem Ku Kluxes was de debbil. De Niggers sho' was scared of 'em,
but dey was more after dem carpet-baggers dan de Niggers. I lived right
in 'mongst 'em, but I wouldn't tell. No Ma'am! I knowed 'em, but I
dasn' talk. Sometimes dey would go right in de fiel's an' take folks out
an' kill 'em. Aint some of 'em lef' now. Day is all dead an' gone, but
dey sho' was rabid den. I never got in no trouble wid 'em, 'cause I
tended my business an' kep' out o' dey way. I'd-a been kilt if I'd-a run
'roun' an' done any big talkin'.

"I never knowed Marse Linc'um, but I heard he was a pow'ful good
man. I 'members plain as yesterd'y when he got kilt an' how all de flags
hung at ha'f mas'. De Nawth nearly went wil' wid worryin' an' blamed
ever'body else. Some of 'em even tried to blame de killin' on Marse

Davis. I fit wid de Yankees, but I thought a might heap o' Marse Davis. He was quality.

"I guess slav'ry was wrong, but I 'members us had some mighty good times. Some marsters was mean an' hard but I was treated good all time. One thing I does know is dat a heap of slaves was worse off after de War. Dey suffered 'cause dey was too triflin' to work widout a boss. Now dey is got to work or die. In dem days you worked an' rested an' knowed you'd be fed. In de middle of de day us rested an' waited for de horn to blow to go back to de fiel'. Slaves didn' have nothin' turrible to worry 'bout if dey acted right. Dey was mean slaves de same as dey was mean marsters.

"Now-a-days folks don' live right. In slav'ry times when you got sick a white doctor was paid to git you well. Now all you gits is some no-count paten' medicine. You is 'fraid to go to de horspital, 'cause de docters might cut on yo' stummick. I think slav'ry was a lot easier dan de War. Dat was de debbil's own business. Folks what hankers for war don' know what dey is askin' for. Dey ain' never seen no bloodshed. In war-times a man was no more dan a varmint.

"When my white folks tol' us us was free, I waited. When de sojers come dey turnt us loose lak animals wid nothin'. Dey had no business to set us free lak dat. Dey gimme 160 acres of lan', but twant no 'count. It was in Mt. Bayou, Arkansas, an' was low an' swampy. Twant yo' lan' to keep lessen you lived on it. You had to clear it, dreen it, an' put a house on it.

"How I gwine-a dreen an' clear a lot o' lan' wid nothin' to do it wid? Reckon somebody livin' on my lan' now.

"One of de rights of bein' free was dat us could move 'roun' and change bosses. But I never cared nothin' 'bout dat.

"I hear somebody say us gwine-a vote. What I wanta vote for? I don' know nothin' 'bout who is runnin'.

'I draws a Federal pension now. If I lives 'til nex' year I'll git $125 a mont'. It sho' comes in handy. I paid $800 for my house an', if I'd-a thought, I'd-a got one wid no' lan'. I don' wan' to plant nothin'. I do want to put a iron fence a-roun' it an' gild it wid silver paint. Den when I's gone, dar it will be.

"Yes'm. I'se raised a big fambly. Den what ain't dead, some of 'em looks as old as I does. I got one gran-chil' I loves jus' lak my own chillun. I don' rightly 'member dis minute how many chillun I had, but I aint had but two wives. De firs' one died long 'bout seventeen years ago, an' I done what de Good Book say. It say, 'when you goes to de graveyard to bury yo' firs' wife, look over de crowd an' pick out de nex' one.'

"Dat's jus' what I done. I picked Janie McCoy, 'cause she aint never been married b'fore. She's a good cook, even if she does smoke a pipe, an' don' know much 'bout nothin'.

"I sho' don' live by no rules. I jus' takes a little dram when ever I wants it, an' I smokes a pipe 'ceptin when de Mistis give me a seegar. I can't chew tobacco on 'count my teeth is gone. I ain't been sick in bed but once in seventy years.

"I is five feet, five inches tall. I used to weigh 150 pounds, but dis old carcass o' mine done los' fifty pounds of meat.

"Now-a-days I has a heap of misery in my knee, so I can't ride 'roun' no mo'. Durin' de War I got a muskit ball in my hip an' now dat my meat's all gone, it jolts a-roun' an' hurts me worse. I's still right sprightly though. I can jump dat drainage ditch in front of de house, an' I sho' can walk. Mos' every day I walks to de little sto' on Union Street. Dar I rests long enough to pass de time-o-day wid my neighbors. My eyes is still good, but I wears glasses for show an' for seein' close.

"De longer I lives de plainer I see dat it ain' right to want mo' den you can use. De Lawd put a-plenty here for ever'body, but shucks! Us don' pay no min' to his teachin'. Sometimes I gits lonesome for de frien's I used to know, 'cause aint nobody lef' but me. I's sho' been lef' a fur piece b'hin'. De white folks say, 'Old Jim is de las' leaf on de tree,' an' I 'spec day's 'bout right."

PART TWO

Terrains and Travelers

Audubon's America

JOHN J. AUDUBON

John J. Audubon, famous for his Birds of America, *was not always
well known or successful. He was born Fougere Rabin in 1785, the ille-
gitimate son of a wealthy Frenchman and his Haitian paramour. A year
later, when his mother died, his father adopted him, took him home to
France and changed his name to John James Audubon. (Despite rumors
to the contrary, he was not the Lost Dauphin of France.) As a young boy,
Audubon drew birds, hunted, and learned the art of taxidermy. Later,
his father sent him to America to escape conscription into Napoleon's
army. In Kentucky, he set up a frontier store and married Lucy Bakewell,
daughter of his hunting companion, the Englishman William Bakewell.
Because Aububon spent his days hunting and drawing life-sized pictures
of animals instead of tending the store, he soon fell into bankruptcy. He
escaped poverty by drawing portraits for a time on Jackson Square in
New Orleans. His keen observations made Audubon an excellent diarist.
In this chapter, called "The Cougar," he describes a hunt in the backwoods of the Mississippi Valley in the northwestern section of the state
when it was a raw wilderness, a time when killing bear, deer, coon, and
the dreaded cougar was deemed necessary.*

THERE IS AN extensive swamp in the section of the State of Mississippi which lies partly in the Choctaw territory. It commences at the
borders of the Mississippi, at no great distance from a Chickasaw village
situated near the mouth of a creek known by the name of Vanconnah,
and partly inundated by the swellings of several large bayous, the principal of which, crossing the swamp in its whole extent, discharges its waters not far from the mouth of the Yazoo River. This famous bayou is
called False River. The swamp of which I am speaking follows the wind-
ings of the Yazoo, until the latter branches off to the northeast, and at
this point forms the stream named Cold Water River, below which the
Yazoo receives the draining of another bayou inclining towards the
northwest and intersecting that known by the name of False River at a
short distance from the place where the latter receives the waters of the
Mississippi. This tedious account of the situation of the swamp is given
with the view of pointing it out to all students of nature who may happen to go that way, and whom I would earnestly urge to visit its interior,

as it abounds in rare and interesting productions—birds, quadrupeds, and reptiles, as well as molluscous animals, many of which, I am persuaded, have never been described.

In the course of one of my rambles, I chanced to meet with a squatter's cabin on the banks of the Cold Water River. [The Coldwater River runs through the northwest counties of Coahoma, Tunica, and De-Soto.] In the owner of this hut, like most of those adventurous settlers in the uncultivated tracts of our frontier districts, I found a person well versed in the chase, and acquainted with the habits of some of the larger species of quadrupeds and birds. As he who is desirous of instruction ought not to disdain listening to any one who has knowledge to communicate, however humble may be his lot, or however limited his talents, I entered the squatter's cabin, and immediately opened a conversation with him respecting the situation of the swamp, and its natural productions. He told me he thought it the very place I ought to visit, spoke of the game which it contained, and pointed to some Bear and Deer skins, adding that the individuals to which they had belonged formed but a small portion of the number of those animals which he had shot within it. My heart swelled with delight, and on asking if he would accompany me through the great morass, and allow me to become an inmate of his humble but hospitable mansion, I was gratified to find that he cordially assented to all my proposals. So I immediately unstrapped my drawing materials, laid up my guns, and sat down to partake of the homely but wholesome fare intended for the supper of the squatter, his wife, and his two sons.

The quietness of the evening seemed in perfect accordance with the gentle demeanor of the family. The wife and children, I more than once thought, seemed to look upon me as a strange sort of person, going about, as I told them I was, in search of birds and plants; and were I here to relate the many questions which they put to me in return for those I addressed to them, the catalogue would occupy several pages. The husband, a native of Connecticut, had heard of the existence of such men as myself, both in our own country and abroad, and seemed greatly pleased to have me under his roof. Supper over, I asked my kind host what had induced him to remove to this wild and solitary spot. 'The people are growing too numerous now to thrive in New England,' was his answer. I thought of the state of some parts of Europe, and calculating the denseness of their population compared with that of New England, exclaimed to myself, 'How much more difficult it must be for men to thrive in those populous countries!' The conversation then changed, and the squatter, his sons and myself, spoke of hunting and fishing until at length, tired, we laid ourselves down on pallets of Bear skins, and reposed in peace on the floor of the only apartment of which the hut consisted.

Day dawned, and the squatter's call to his hogs, which, being almost in a wild state, were suffered to seek the greater portion of their food in the woods, awakened me. Being ready dressed I was not long in joining him. The hogs and their young came grunting at the well-known call of their owner, who threw them a few ears of corn, and counted them, but told me that for some weeks their number had been greatly diminished by the ravages committed upon them by a large *Panther,* by which name the Cougar is designated in America, and that the ravenous animal did not content himself with the flesh of his pigs, but now and then carried off one of his calves, notwithstanding the many attempts he had made to shoot it. The *Painter,* as he sometimes called it, had on several occasions robbed him of a dead Deer; and to these exploits the squatter added several remarkable feats of audacity which it had performed, to give me an idea of the formidable character of the beast. Delighted by his description, I offered to assist him in destroying the enemy, at which he was highly pleased, but assured me that unless some of his neighbors should join us with their dogs and his own, the attempt would prove fruitless. Soon after, mounting a horse, he went off to his neighbors several of whom lived at a distance of some miles, and appointed a day of meeting.

The hunters, accordingly, made their appearance, one fine morning, at the door of the cabin, just as the sun was emerging from beneath the horizon. They were five in number, and fully equipped for the chase, being mounted on horses which in some parts of Europe might appear sorry nags, but which in strength, speed, and bottom, are better fitted for pursuing a Cougar or a Bear through woods and morasses than any in that country. A pack of large, ugly curs were already engaged in making acquaintance with those of the squatter. He and myself mounted his two best horses, whilst his sons were bestriding others of inferior quality.

Few words were uttered by the party until we had reached the edge of the swamp, where it was agreed that all should disperse and seek for the fresh track of the Painter, it being previously settled that the discoverer should blow his horn, and remain on the spot, until the rest should join him. In less than an hour, the sound of the horn was clearly heard, and, sticking close to the squatter, off we went through the thick woods, guided only by the now and then repeated call of the distant huntsmen. We soon reached the spot, and in a short time the rest of the party came up. The best dog was sent forward to track the Cougar, and in a few moments the whole pack were observed diligently trailing, and bearing in their course for the interior of the Swamp. The rifles were immediately put in trim, and the party followed the dogs, at separate distances, but in sight of each other, determined to shoot at no other game than the Panther.

The dogs soon began to mouth, and suddenly quickened their pace. My companion concluded that the beast was on the ground, and putting our horses to a gentle gallop, we followed the curs, guided by their voices. The noise of the dogs increased, when, all of a sudden their mode of barking became altered, and the squatter, urging me to push on, told me that the beast was *treed*, by which he meant that it had got upon some low branch of a large tree to rest for a few minutes, and that should we not succeed in shooting him when thus situated, we might expect a long chase of it. As we approached the spot, we all by degrees united into a body, but on seeing the dogs at the foot of a large tree, separated again, and galloped off to surround it.

Each hunter now moved with caution, holding his gun ready, and allowing the bridle to dangle on the neck of his horse, as it advanced slowly towards the dogs. A shot from one of the party was heard, on which the Cougar was seen to leap to the ground, and bound off with such velocity as to show that he was very unwilling to stand our fire longer. The dogs set off in pursuit with great eagerness and a deafening cry. The hunter who had fired came up and said that his ball had hit the monster, and had probably broken one of his fore-legs near the shoulder, the only place at which he could aim. A slight trail of blood was discovered on the ground, but the curs proceeded at such a rate that we merely noticed this, and put spurs to our horses, which galloped on towards the centre of the Swamp. One bayou was crossed, then another still larger and more muddy; but the dogs were brushing forward, and as the horses began to pant at a furious rate, we judged it expedient to leave them and advance on foot. These determined hunters knew that the Cougar being wounded, would shortly ascend another tree, where in all probability he would remain for a considerable time, and that it would be easy to follow the track of the dogs. We dismounted, took off the saddles and bridles, set the bells attached to the horses' necks at liberty to jingle, hoppled the animals, and left them to shift for themselves.

Now, kind reader, follow the group marching through the swamp, crossing muddy pools, and making the best of their way over fallen trees and amongst the tangled rushes that now and then covered acres of ground. If you are a hunter yourself, all this will appear nothing to you; but if crowded assemblies of 'beauty and fashion,' or the quiet enjoyments of your 'pleasure grounds' alone delight you, I must mend my pen before I attempt to give you an idea of the pleasure felt on such an expedition.

After marching for a couple of hours, we again heard the dogs. Each of us pressed forward, elated at the thought of terminating the career of the Cougar. Some of the dogs were heard whining, although the greater number barked vehemently. We felt assured that the Cougar was treed, and that he would rest for some time to recover from his fatigue. As we came up to the dogs, we discovered the ferocious animal lying across a large branch, close to the trunk of a cottonwood tree. His broad breast lay towards us; his eyes were at one time bent on us and again on the dogs beneath and around him; one of his fore-legs hung loosely by his side, and he lay crouched, with his ears lowered close to his head, as if he thought he might remain undiscovered. Three balls were fired at him, at a given signal, on which he sprang a few feet from the branch, and tumbled headlong to the ground. Attacked on all sides by the enraged curs, the infuriated Cougar fought with desperate valor; but the squatter, advancing in front of the party, and almost in the midst of the dogs, shot him immediately behind and beneath the left shoulder. The Cougar writhed for a moment in agony, and in another lay dead.

The sun was now sinking in the west. Two of the hunters separated from the rest to procure venison, whilst the squatter's sons were ordered to make the best of their way home, to be ready to feed the hogs in the morning. The rest of the party agreed to camp on the spot. The Cougar was despoiled of its skin, and its carcass left to the hungry dogs. Whilst engaged in preparing our camp, we heard the report of a gun, and soon after one of our hunters returned with a small Deer. A fire was lighted, and each hunter displayed his *pone* of bread, along with a flask of whiskey. The deer was skinned in a trice, and slices placed on sticks before the fire. These materials afforded us an excellent meal, and as the night grew darker, stories and songs went round, until my companions, fatigued, laid themselves down, close under the smoke of the fire, and soon fell asleep.

I walked for some minutes round the camp, to contemplate the beauties of that nature from which I have certainly derived my greatest pleasures. I thought of the occurrences of the day, and glancing my eye around, remarked the singular effects produced by the phosphorescent qualities of the large decayed trunks which lay in all directions around me. How easy, I thought, would it be for the confused and agitated mind of a person bewildered in a swamp like this, to imagine in each of these luminous masses some wondrous and fearful being, the very sight of which might make the hair stand erect on his head. The thought of being myself placed in such a predicament burst over my mind, and I hastened to join my companions, beside whom I laid me down and slept, assured that no enemy could approach us without first rousing the dogs, which were growling in fierce dispute over the remains of the Cougar.

At daybreak we left our camp, the squatter bearing on his shoulder the skin of the late destroyer of his stock, and retraced our steps until we found our horses, which had not strayed far from the place where we had left them. These we soon saddled, and jogging along, in a direct course, guided by the sun, congratulating each other in the destruction of so formidable a neighbor as the Panther had been, we soon arrived at my host's cabin. The five neighbors partook of such refreshment as the house could afford, and dispersing, returned to their homes, leaving me to follow my favorite pursuits.

Mississippi Scenes

JOSEPH B. COBB

*Joseph Beckham Cobb, planter, editor, author, and Whig, moved to Nox-
ubee County from Georgia in 1838. His sketches in* Mississippi Scenes
*show the influence of the southwestern humor of Augustus Baldwin
Longstreet, to whom the book is dedicated, and also of eighteenth-century
English writers such as Addison, Steele, and Johnson. Cobb's urbane
narrator comments on abhorrent excesses of the age. This excerpt depicts
the narrator, called Rambler, as a newcomer to Columbus, a reflection of
Cobb himself, who moved to Longwood Plantation near Columbus in
1844. Here the narrator's geniality finally overrides his scepticism about
a man who was more newly arrived than he, the shoeblack J. H. B.
Bigbug (from chapter 3, "On Humbugs: The Allegory of the Shoeblacks").*

I HAD PAUSED listlessly, one summer morning, at the corner of
Main and Market, opposite the drug establishment of A. N. Jones & Co.,
and was admiring the peculiar beauties of Columbus at such a moment
when, in the absence of all active trade, nothing is to be seen on the
streets but a dashing equipage containing some lovely votary of fashion
engaged in her diurnal round of shopping, or the contented countenance of a *nonchalant* loafer as he perambulates from one corner to the
other in that delectable occupation of *killing time*. It is only at such season, my fair friend, that we are enabled to appreciate *les modes* (in every
sense of the term) of this little interior city. But, small as Columbus is,
we have yet here a sufficiency of all necessary materials to paint a miniature of the world. The residence of only a twelvemonth will serve to
convince the veriest skeptic who presumes to doubt the fact.

I shall here (and, maybe, hereafter) adduce evidences to sustain
what I have asserted; and, by way of beginning, let me say that, on the
morning in question, I was amused with a very striking and forcible
illustration. On every side, and for some distance up and down this
main thoroughfare of the city, my eye caught sight of blazing and gorgeous advertisements, some in large gilt or wooden frames, others simply nailed to doors and facings—all, however, garnished with varied
colors, and setting forth the unheard-of and never-to-be-equaled qualities of some newly-discovered or long-established medical preparation,

with a farewell hint about what places and what persons have been fixed upon as agencies through which to help mankind to their healthful benefits. Upon entering one or two shops on Main Street, I found, besides the usual display of a fancy establishment, that a great part of the room was decorated with ornaments of this description. There were elixirs, and tinctures, and crack plasters, and sanative salves, and pills, and electuaries, and, in short, more special curatives than I believe there are diseases. You might naturally have supposed that *Death,* on beholding such a fearful preparation of armor to ward off his attacks, would have quit his business in utter despair, and presented the counterpart of "Patience on a monument smiling at Grief."

. . . Leaving the shops, I continued my walk leisurely up the street, and whilst still meditating on the medicinal wonders I had just seen, I was attracted by several notices, full pompous notes of exclamation which loomed forth from the trees and posts along the edge of the pavement. I had the curiosity to stop and read one of these, when the following annunciation met my eye, strangely illustrating more potently the thoughts which had occurred to me when looking over the all-healing nostrums and invaluable medical discoveries.

☞ S T O P   A N D   R E A D ! ! ! ! ☜

J.H.B. Bigbug, Shoeblack, having determined to settle in Columbus, respectfully offers his professional services to all such as will favor him with their patronage. He belongs to the new school of shoeblacks, having taken his degrees at Goodenbrush College, Ireland, and hopes, should occasion offer, to prove that those who style themselves the *regulars* are the true quacks. The citizens of Columbus may not be aware that new and important discoveries have been made recently in the science of shoeblacking. Under the benign influence of these valuable discoveries, many boots and shoes which are now fast wearing out and dropping to untimely decay under the pernicious system used at present to keep them bright, will be beautifully restored. The whole substance and constitution of the leather will be resuscitated miraculously quick, without leaving any injurious poisons to undermine and weaken the strength. This may be done, too, at one quarter of the usual expense, and by the use of one hundredth less of blacking than is employed under the old system. His materials being prepared either by himself or experienced agents at the north, he will avouch their being genuine and efficacious. He may always be found (when not professionally engaged) at No. 23 Market St.

You can well imagine, my dear S——, that surprise was my first emotion on reading this unique card, and I found myself involuntarily laughing at the singular assurance, as I then thought it to be, which characterized its author. But, on mixing in with some few friends and acquaintances, I soon found that I must use some caution in speaking out my impressions, and that this Mr. Bigbug was already beginning to take the town by storm. Most every person was his advocate, and many ardently testified to his superior and unheard-of dexterity. I saw that imagination had taken wing, and the numerous instances of his skill which were momentarily recited in my presence almost convinced me that Mr. Bigbug was going to prove the eighth and greatest wonder of the world.

The Cotton Kingdom

FREDERICK LAW OLMSTEAD

Frederick Olmstead, the architect who designed New York's Central Park and the grounds of the Biltmore mansion in Asheville, North Carolina, traveled through the South during the relatively calm time after the Compromise of 1850 and the election of Lincoln and wrote about what he saw for the New York Daily Times. *His expenses were about two dollars a day. His moderate view on abolition became a source of hot debate with his friend Charles Brace, a rabid abolitionist. Although, like Brace, he saw the system as morally degrading to the slaves and even more so to their owners, he also recognized the severe economic blow that would be dealt to the slaveholders if emancipation came. Although his primary concern was to report the conditions of the slaves throughout the region, he also vividly described the music, religion, drinking habits, and class distinctions of the people. Dependent on strangers to take him in, Olmstead often slept in bug-infested beds and struggled to obtain water and feed for his horse, Belshazzar. In this passage, from the chapter entitled "The Exceptional Large Planters," he has just traveled through eastern Texas and Louisiana and has arrived in Woodville, Mississippi, in Wilkinson County near the Louisiana-Mississippi state line. Through the conversations he recorded, the extreme wealth as well as the extreme poverty of the region are made clear.*

I ARRIVED SHORTLY after dusk at Woodville, a well-built and pleasant court-town, with a small but pretentious hotel. Court was in session, I fancy, for the house was filled with guests of somewhat remarkable character. The landlord was inattentive, and, when followed up, inclined to be uncivil. At the ordinary—supper and breakfast alike—there were twelve men besides myself, all of them wearing black cloth coats, black cravats, and satin or embroidered waistcoats; all, too, sleek as if just from a hairdresser's, and redolent of perfumes, which really had the best of it with the exhalations of the kitchen. Perhaps it was because I was not in the regulation dress that I found no one ready to converse with me, and could obtain not the slightest information about my road, even from the landlord.

I might have left Woodville with more respect for this decorum if I had not, when shown by a servant to my room, found two beds in it, each of which proved to be furnished with soiled sheets and greasy pillows, nor was it without reiterated demands and liberal cash in hand to the servant, that I succeeded in getting them changed on the one I selected. A gentleman of embroidered waistcoat took the other bed as it was, with no apparent reluctance, soon after I had effected my own arrangements. One wash-bowl, and a towel which had already been used, was expected to answer for both of us, and would have done so but that I carried a private towel in my saddle-bags. Another requirement of a civilized household was wanting, and its only substitute unavailable with decency.

The bill was excessive, and the black hostler, who had left the mud of yesterday hanging all along the inside of Belshazzar's legs, and who had put the saddle on so awkwardly that I resaddled him myself after he had brought him to the door, grumbled, in presence of the landlord, at the smallness of the gratuity which I saw fit to give him.

The country, for some distance north of Woodville, is the most uneven, for a non-mountainous region, I ever saw. The road seems well engineered, yet you are nearly all the time mounting or descending the sides of protuberances or basins, ribs or dykes. In one place it follows along the top of a crooked ridge, as steep-sided and regular for nearly a quarter of a mile, as a high railroad embankment. A man might jump off anywhere and land thirty feet below. The ground being too rough here for cultivation, the dense native forest remains intact.

This ridge, a man told me, had been a famous place for robberies. It is not far from the Mississippi bottoms.

"Thar couldn't be," said he, "a better location for a feller that wanted to foller that business. There was one chap there a spell ago, who built himself a cabin t'other side the river. He used to come over in a dug-out. He could paddle his dug-out up the swamp, you see, to within two mile of the ridge; then, when he stopped a man, he'd run through the woods to his dug-out, and before the man could get help, he'd be t'other side the Mississippi, a sittin' in his housen as honest as you be."

. . . Not far north of the ridge, plantations are found again, though the character of the surface changes but little. The hill-sides are carefully ploughed so that each furrow forms a contour line. After the first ploughing the same lines are followed in subsequent cultivation, year in and year out, as long as enough soil remains to grow cotton upon with profit. On the hills recently brought into cultivation, broad, serpentine ditches, having a fall of from two to four inches in a rod, have been frequently constructed: these are intended to prevent the formation of gullies leading more directly down the hill during heavy rains. But all these precautions are not fully successful, the cultivated hills, in spite of them, losing soil every year in a melancholy manner.

I passed during the day four or five large plantations, the hillsides worn, cleft, and channelled like icebergs; stables and negro quarters all abandoned, and everything given up to nature and decay.

In its natural state the virgin soil appears the richest I have ever seen, the growth upon it from weeds to trees being invariably rank and rich in colour. At first it is expected to bear a bale and a half of cotton to the acre, making eight or ten bales for each able fieldhand. But from the cause described its productiveness rapidly decreases.

Originally, much of this country was covered by a natural growth of cane, and by various nutritious grasses. A good Northern farmer would deem it a crying shame and sin to attempt to grow any crops upon such steep slopes, except grasses or shrubs which do not require tillage. The waste of soil which attends the practice is much greater than it would be at the North, and, notwithstanding the unappeasable demand of the world for cotton, its bad economy, considering the subject nationally, cannot be doubted.

If these slopes were thrown into permanent terraces, with turfed or stone-faced escarpments, the fertility of the soil might be preserved, even with constant tillage. In this way the hills would continue for ages to produce annual crops of greater value than those which are at present obtained from them at such destructive expense—from ten to twenty crops of cotton rendering them absolute deserts. But with negroes at fourteen hundred dollars a head, and fresh land in Texas a half a dollar an acre, nothing of this sort can be thought of. The time will probably come when the soil now washing into the adjoining swamps will be brought back by our descendants, perhaps on their heads, in pots and baskets, in the manner Huc describes in China,—and which may be seen also in the Rhenish vineyards,—to be relaid on these sunny slopes, to grow the luxurious cotton in.

The plantations are all large, but, except in their size and rather unusually good tillage, display few signs of wealthy proprietorship. The greater number have but small and mean residences upon them. No poor white people live upon the road, nor in all this country of rich soils are they seen, except *en voyage*. In a distance of seventy-five miles I saw no houses without negro-cabins attached, and I calculated that there were fifty slaves, on an average, to every white family resident in the country under my view. (There is a small sandy region about Woodville, which I passed through after nightfall, and which, of course, my note does not include.)

I called in the afternoon, at a house, almost the only one I had seen during the day which did not appear to be the residence of a planter or overseer, to obtain lodging. No one was at home but a negro woman and children. The woman said that her master never took in strangers; there was a man a few miles further on who did; it was the only place she knew at which I was likely to "get in."

I found the place: probably the proprietor was the poorest white man whose house I had passed during the day, but he had several slaves; one of them, at least, a very superior man, worth fully $2,000.

Just before me, another traveller, a Mr. S., from beyond Natchez, had arrived. Learning that I was from Texas, he immediately addressed me with volubility.

"Ah! then you can tell us something about it, and I would be obliged to you if you would. Been out west about Antonio? Ranching's a good business, eh, out west there? Isn't it? Make thirty per cent. by it, eh? I hear so. Should think that would be a good business. How much capital ought a man to have to go into ranchering, good, eh? So as to make it a good business?"

He was a middle-aged, well-dressed man, devouring tobacco prodigiously; nervous and wavering in his manner; asking questions, a dozen at a breath, and paying no heed to the answers. He owned a plantation in the bottoms, and another on the upland; the latter was getting worn out, it was too unhealthy for him to live in the bottoms, and so, as he said, he had had "a good notion to go into ranchering. Just for ease and pleasure."

"Fact is, though, I've got a family, and this is no country for children to be raised in. All the children get such foolish notions. I don't want my children to be brought up here. Ruins everybody. Does, sir, sure. Spoils 'em. Too bad. 'Tis so. Too bad. Can't make anything of children here, sir. Can't, sir. Fact."

He had been nearly persuaded to purchase a large tract of land at a point upon a certain creek where, he had been told, was a large courthouse, an excellent school, etc. The waters of the creek he named are brackish, the neighbouring country is a desert, and the only inhabitants, savages. Some knavish speculator had nearly got a customer, but could not quite prevail on him to purchase until he examined the country personally, which it was his intention soon to do. He gave me no time to tell him how false was the account he had had, but went on, after describing its beauties and advantages—

"But negro property isn't very secure there, I'm told. How is't? Know?"

"Not at all secure, sir; if it is disposed to go, it will go: the only way you could keep it would be to make it always contented to remain. The road would always be open to Mexico; it would go when it liked."

"So I hear. Only way is, to have young ones there and keep their mothers here, eh? Negros have such attachments, you know. Don't you think that would fix 'em, eh? No? No, I suppose not. If they got mad at anything, they'd forget their mothers, eh? Yes, I suppose they would. Can't depend on niggers. But I reckon they'd come back. Only be worse off in Mexico—eh?"

"Nothing but—"

"Being free, eh? Get tired of that, I should think. Nobody to take care of them. No, I suppose not. Learn to take care of themselves."

Then he turned to our host and began to ask him about his neighbours, many of whom he had known when he was a boy, and been at school with. A sorry account he got of most. Generally they had run through their property; their lands had passed into new hands; their negroes had been disposed of; two were now, he thought, "strikers" for gamblers in Natchez.

"What is a striker?" I asked the landlord at the first opportunity.

"Oh! to rope in fat fellows for the gamblers; they don't do that themselves, but get somebody else. I don't know as it is so; all I know is, they don't have no business, not till late at night; they never stir out till late at night, and nobody knows how they live, and that's what I expect they do. Fellows that come into town flush, you know—sold out their cotton and are flush—they always think they must see everything, and try their hands at everything—they get hold of 'em and bring 'em in to the gamblers, and get 'em tight for 'em, you know."

"How's —— got along since his father died?" asked Mr. S.

"Well, ——'s been unfortunate. Got mad with his overseer; thought he was lazy and packed him off; then he undertook to oversee for himself, and he was unfortunate. Had two bad crops. Finally the sheriff took about half his niggers. He tried to work the plantation with the rest, but they was old, used-up hands, and he got mad that they would not work more, and tired o' seein' 'em, and 'fore the end of the year he sold 'em all."

Another young man, whom he inquired about, had had his property managed for him by a relative till he came of age, and had been sent North to college. When he returned and got it into his own hands, the first year he ran in debt $16,000. The income from it being greatly reduced under his management, he had put it back in the care of his relative, but continued to live upon it. "I see," continued our host, "every time any of their teams pass from town they fetch a barrel or a demijohn. There is a parcel of fellows, who, when they can't liquor anywhere else, always go to him."

"But how did he manage to spend so much," I inquired, "the first year after his return, as you said,—in gambling?"

"Well, he gambled some, and run horses. He don't know anything about a horse, and, of course, he thinks he knows everything. Those fellows up at Natchez would sell him any kind of a tacky for four or five hundred dollars, and then after he'd had him a month, they'd ride out another and make a bet of five or six hundred dollars they'd beat him. Then he'd run with 'em, and of course he'd lose it."

"But sixteen thousand dollars is a large sum of money to be worked off even in that way in a year," I observed.

"Oh, he had plenty of other ways. He'd go into a bar-room, and get tight and commence to break things. They'd let him go on, and the next morning hand him a bill for a hundred dollars. He thinks that's a smart thing, and just laughs and pays it, and then treats all around again."

. . . At supper, Mr. S., looking at the daughter of our host, said—

"What a pretty girl that is. My dear, do you find any schools to go to out here—eh? I reckon not. This isn't the country for schools. There'll not be a school in Mississippi 'fore long, I reckon. Nothing but Institutes, eh? Ha! ha! ha! Institutes, humph! Don't believe there's a school between this and Natchez, is there?"

"No, sir."

"Of course there isn't."

"What sort of a country is it, then, between here and Natchez?" I asked. "I should suppose it would be well settled."

"Big plantations, sir. Nothing else. Aristocrats, Swell-heads, I call them, sir. Nothing but swell-heads, and you can't get a night's lodging, sir. Beyond the ferry, I'll be bound, a man might die on the road 'fore he'd get a lodging with one of them. Eh, Mr. N.? So, isn't it? 'Take a stranger in, and I'll clear you out!' That's the rule. That's what they tell their overseers, eh? Yes, sir; just so inhospitable as that. Swell-heads! Swell-heads, sir. Every plantation. Can't get a meal of victuals or a night's lodging from one of them, I don't suppose, not if your life depended on it. Can you, Mr. N.?"

"Well, I believe Mr. ——, his place is right on the road, and it's half way to the ferry, and I believe he tells his overseer if a man comes and wants something to eat, he must give it to him, but he must not take any pay for it, because strangers must have something to eat. They start out of Natchez, thinking it's as 'tis in other countries; that there's houses along, where they can get a meal, and so they don't provide for themselves, and when they get along about there, they are sometimes desperate hungry. Had to be something done."

"Do the planters not live themselves on their plantations?"

"Why, a good many of them has two or three plantations, but they don't often live on any of them."

"Must have ice for their wine, you see," said Mr. S., "or they'd die. So they have to live in Natchez or New Orleans. A heap of them live in New Orleans."

"And in summer they go up into Kentucky, do they not? I've seen country houses there which were said to belong to cotton-planters from Mississippi."

"No, sir. They go North. To New York, and Newport, and Saratoga, and Cape May, and Seneca Lake. Somewhere that they can display themselves more than they do here. Kentucky is no place for that. That's the sort of people, sir, all the way from here to Natchez. And all round Natchez, too. And in all this section of country where there's good land. Good God! I wouldn't have my children educated, sir, among them, not to have them as rich as Dr. ———, every one of them. You can know their children as far off as you can see them. Young swell-heads! You'll take note of 'em in Natchez. You can tell them by their walk. I noticed it yesterday at the Mansion House. They sort o' throw out their legs as if they hadn't got strength enough to lift 'em and put them down in any particular place. They do want so bad to look as if they weren't made of the same clay as the rest of God's creation."

Some allowance is of course to be made for the splenetic temperament of this gentleman, but facts evidently afford some justification of his sarcasms. This is easily accounted for. The farce of the vulgar-rich has its foundation in Mississippi, as in New York and in Manchester, in the rapidity with which certain values have advanced, especially that of cotton, and, simultaneously, that of cotton lands and negroes.[1] Of course, there are men of refinement and cultivation among the rich planters of Mississippi, and many highly estimable and intelligent persons outside of the wealthy class, but the number of such is smaller in proportion to that of the immoral, vulgar, and ignorant newly-rich, than in any other part of the United States. And herein is a radical difference between the social condition of this region and that of the sea-board Slave States, where there are fewer wealthy families, but where among the few people of wealth, refinement and education are more general.

I asked how rich the sort of men were of whom he spoke.

"Why, sir, from a hundred thousand to ten million."

"Do you mean that between here and Natchez there are none worth less than a hundred thousand dollars?"

"No, sir, not beyond the ferry. Why, any sort of a plantation is worth a hundred thousand dollars. The niggers would sell for that."

"How many negroes are there on these plantations?"

"From fifty to a hundred."

"Never over one hundred?"

"No; when they've increased to a hundred they always divide them; stock another plantation. There are sometimes three or four plantations adjoining one another, with an overseer for each, belonging to the same man. But that isn't general. In general, they have to strike off for new land."

"How many acres will a hand tend here?"

"About fifteen—ten of cotton, and five of corn; some pretend to make them tend twenty."

"And what is the usual crop?"

"A bale and a half to the acre on fresh land and in the bottom. From four to eight bales to a hand they generally get: sometimes ten and better, when they are lucky."

"A bale and a half on fresh land? How much on old?"

"Well, you can't tell. Depends on how much it's worn and what the season is so much. Old land, after a while, isn't worth bothering with."

"Do most of these large planters who live so freely, anticipate their crops as the sugar planters are said to—spend the money, I mean, before the crop is sold?"

"Yes, sir, and three and four crops ahead generally."

"Are most of them the sons of rich men? are they old estates?"

"No, sir; lots of them were overseers once."

"Have you noticed whether it is a fact that these large properties seldom continue long in the same family? Do the grandsons of wealthy planters often become poor men?"

"Generally the sons do. Almost always their sons are fools, and soon go through with it."

"If they don't kill themselves before their fathers die," said the other.

"Yes. They drink hard and gamble, and of course that brings them into fights."

This was while they were smoking on the gallery after supper. I walked to the stable to see how my horse was provided for, and took my notes of the conversation. When I returned they were talking of negroes who had died of yellow fever while confined in the jail at Natchez. Two of them were spoken of as having been thus "happily released," being under sentence of death, and unjustly so, in their opinion.

A man living in this vicinity having taken a runaway while the fever was raging in the jail at Natchez, a physician advised him not to send him there. He did not, and the negro escaped; was some time afterward recaptured, and the owner having learned from him that he had been once before taken and not detained according to law, he made a journey to inquire into the matter, and was very angry. He said, "Whenever you catch a nigger again, you send him to jail, no matter what's to be feared. If he dies in the jail, you are not responsible. You've done your duty, and you can leave the rest to Providence."

"That was right, too," said Mr. P. "Yes, he ought to a' minded the law. Then if he'd died in jail, he'd know 'twasn't his fault."

Next morning, near the ferry house, I noticed a set of stocks, having holes for the head as well as the ankles; they stood unsheltered and unshaded in the open road.

I asked an old negro what it was.

"Dat ting, massa?" grinning; "well, sah, we calls dat a ting to put black people, niggers, in, when dey misbehaves bad, and to put runaways in, sah. Heaps o' runaways, dis country, sah. Yes, sah, heaps on 'em round here."

Mr. S. and I slept in the same room. I went to bed some time before him; he sat up late, to smoke, he said. He woke me when he came in, by his efforts to barricade the door with our rather limited furniture. The room being small, and without a window, I expostulated. He acknowledged it would probably make us rather too warm, but he shouldn't feel safe if the door were left open. "You don't know," said he; "there may be runaways around."

He then drew two small revolvers, hitherto concealed under his clothing, and began to examine the caps. He was certainly a nervous man, perhaps a madman. I suppose he saw some expression of this thought in my face, for he said, placing them so they could be easily taken up as he lay in bed, "Sometimes a man has a use for them when he least expects it. There was a gentleman on this road a few days ago. He was going to Natchez. He overtook a runaway, and he says to him, 'Bad company's better'n none, boy, and I reckon I'll keep you along with me into Natchez.' The nigger appeared to be pleased to have company, and went along, talking with him, very well, till they came to a thicket place, about six miles from Natchez. Then he told him he reckoned he would not go any further with him. 'What! you black rascal,' says he; 'you mean you won't go in with me? You step out and go straight ahead, and if you turn your face till you get into Natchez, I'll shoot you.' 'Aha! massa,' says the nigger, mighty good-natured, 'I reckon you ain't got no shootin' irons'; and he bolted off into the thicket, and got away from him."

At breakfast, Mr. S. came late. He bowed his head as he took his seat, and closed his eyes for a second or two; then, withdrawing his quid of tobacco and throwing it in the fire-place, he looked round with a smile, and said:—

"I always think it a good plan to thank the Lord for His mercies. I'm afraid some people'll think I'm a member of the church. I aint, and never was. Wish I was. I am a Son, though [of Temperance?]. Give me some water, girl. Coffee first. Never too soon for coffee. And never too late, I say. Wait for anything but coffee. These swell-heads drink their coffee after they've eaten all their dinner. I want it with dinner, eh? Don't nothing taste good without coffee, I reckon."

Before he left, he invited me to visit his plantations, giving me careful directions to find them, and saying that if he should not have returned before I reached them, his wife and his overseer would give me every attention if I would tell them he told me to visit them. He said again, and in this connection, that he believed this was the most inhospitable country in the world, and asked, as I had been a good deal of a traveller, didn't I think so myself? I answered that my experience was much too small to permit me to form an opinion so contrary to that generally held.

If they had a reputation for hospitality, he said, it could only be among their own sort. They made great swell-head parties; and when they were on their plantation places, they made it a point to have a great deal of company; they would not have anything to do if they didn't. But they were all swell-heads, I might be sure; they'd never ask anybody but a regular swell-head to see them.

His own family, however, seemed not to be excluded from the swell-head society.

Among numerous anecdotes illustrative of the folly of his neighbours, or his own prejudices and jealousy, I remember none which it would be proper to publish but the following:—

"Do you remember a place you passed?" (describing the locality).

"Yes," said I; "a pretty cottage with a large garden, with some statues or vases in it."

"I think it likely. Got a foreign gardener, I expect. That's all the fashion with them. A nigger isn't good enough for them. Well, that belongs to Mr. A. J. Clayborn[?]. He's got to be a very rich man. I suppose he's got as many as five hundred people on all his places. He went out to Europe a few years ago, and sometime after he came back, he came up to Natchez. I was there with my wife at the same time, and as she and Mrs. Clayborn came from the same section of country, and used to know each other when they were girls, she thought she must go and see her. Mrs. Clayborn could not talk about anything but the great people they had seen in Europe. She was telling of some great nobleman's castle they went to, and the splendid park there was to it, and how grandly they lived. For her part, she admired it so much, and they made so many friends among the people of quality, she said, she didn't care if they always stayed there. In fact, she really wanted Mr. Clayborn to buy one of the castles, and be a nobleman himself. 'But he wouldn't,' says she; 'he's such a strong Democrat, you know.' Ha! ha! ha! I wonder what old Tom Jeff. would have said to these swell-head Democrats."

I asked him if there were no poor people in this country. I could see no houses which seemed to belong to poor people.

"Of course not, sir. Every inch of the land bought up by the swell-heads on purpose to keep them away. But you go back on to the pine ridge. Good Lord! I've heard a heap about the poor folks at the North; but if you ever say any poorer people than them, I should like to know what they live on. Must be a miracle if they live at all. I don't see how these people live, and I've wondered how they do a great many times. Don't raise corn enough, great many of them, to keep a shoat alive through the winter. There's no way they can live, 'less they steal."

At the ferry of the Homochitto I fell in with a German, originally from Düsseldorf, whence he came seventeen years ago, first to New York; afterward he had resided successively in Baltimore, Cincinnati, New Orleans, Pensacola, Mobile, and Natchez. By the time he reached the last place he had lost all his money. Going to work as a labourer in the town, he soon earned enough again to set him up as a trinket peddler; and a few months afterward he was able to buy "a leetle coachdray." Then, he said, he made money fast; for he would go back into the country, among the poor people, and sell them trinkets, and calico, and handkerchiefs, and patent medicines. They never had any money. "All poor folks," he said; "dam poor; got no money; oh no; but I say, 'dat too bad, I don't like to balk you, my frind; may be so, you got some egg, some fedder, some cheeken, some rag, some sass, or some skin vot you kill.' I takes dem dings vot they's got, and ven I gets my load I cums to Natchez back and sells dem, alvays dwo or dree times so much as dey coss me; and den I buys some more goots. Not bad beesnes—no. Oh, dese poor people dey deenk me is von fool ven I buy some dime deir rag vat dey bin vear; dey calls me de ole Dutch cuss. But dey don't know nottin' vot it is vorth. I deenk dey neever see no money; may be so dey geev all de cheeken vot they been got for a leetle breaspin vot cost me not so much as von beet. Sometime dey be dam crazy fool; dey know not how do make de count at all. Yees, I makes some money, a heap."

NOTES

[1] As "A SOUTHERN LAWYER," writing for *Harper's Weekly* (February, 1859), observes: "The sudden acquisition of wealth in the cotton-growing region of the United States, in many instances by planters commencing with very limited means, is almost miraculous. Patient, industrious, frugal, and self-denying, nearly the entire amount of their cotton-crops is devoted to the increase of their capital. The result is, in a few years large estates, as if by magic, are accumulated. The fortunate proprietors then build fine houses, and surround themselves with comforts and luxuries to which they were strangers in their earlier years of care and toil."

FROM

Rough Riding Down South

J. F. H. CLAIBORNE

*This essay about the Piney Woods of Mississippi was originally published
in* Harper's New Monthly Magazine *in 1862. Son of General F. L.
Claiborne and nephew of Gov. W. C. C. Claiborne, J. F. H. Claiborne
was born in Natchez in 1807 into a highly political family. He was at
various times a lawyer, newspaperman, legislator, and historian. Called
the "Grand Old Man" of Mississippi history, he published the first volume of* Mississippi As a Province, Territory, and State *in 1881. The
manuscript of the second volume was never published because it was
destroyed by fire, and Claiborne died two months later, grief-stricken over
his loss. In this account, Claiborne describes the land and inhabitants of
the Piney Woods, as well as some of the political goings-on that he observed.*

A L O N G   T H E   Gulf of Mexico, or what the United States Coast Survey
styles the Mississippi Sound, extending across the State of Mississippi,
with a depth in the interior of about one hundred miles, there lies a
region of country usually denominated the Pine Woods. The soil is
sandy and thin, producing small crops of rice, potatoes, and corn, a
little cotton, indigo, and sugar-cane, for home consumption. But it sus-
tains a magnificent pine forest, capable of supplying for centuries to
come the navies of the world. The people are of primitive habits, and
are chiefly lumbermen or herdsmen. Exempt from swamps and inundation, from the vegetable decomposition incidental to large agricultural
districts, fanned by the sea-breeze and perfumed by the balsamic exhalations of the pine, it is one of the healthiest regions in the world. If the
miraculous fountain, in search of which the brave old Ponce de Leon
met his death in the lagoons of Florida in 1512, may be found any
where, it will be in the district I am now wandering over. I have never
seen so happy a people. Not afflicted with sickness or harassed by litiga-
tion; not demoralized by vice or tormented with the California fever;
living in a state of equality, where none are rich and none in want;
where the soil is too thin to accumulate wealth, and yet sufficiently productive to reward industry; manufacturing all that they wear; producing
all they consume; and preserving, with primitive simplicity of manners,
the domestic virtues of their sires. Early marriages are universal. Fathers

yet infants in law, and happy grandams yet in the vigor of womanhood, may be found in every settlement; and numerous are the firesides around which cluster ten or a dozen children, with mothers still lovely and buoyant as in the days of their maiden bloom.

Leaving the Gulf shore at Pascagoula for the interior, in a couple of hours the traveler finds himself on the banks of a broad, deep, beautiful river, the Escatawba, curving gently down to mingle with the ocean. It flows through a forest of colossal growth. Many of these hoary Titans were overthrown by the great hurricane of '52, which began at 10 A.M., August 24, and blew with increasing fury until 12 M. next day, raging with undiminished violence until 12 at night, when it began to abate. It tore away whole masses of bluff on the sea-shore, dug up the earth from the roots of trees, blew down the potato hills as it swooped along the surface, and prostrated forests in its mad career.

Here, at what is now called Elder's Ferry, once stood the lodge of the last chieftain of the Pascagoulas. His warriors had all perished in the fatal wars with the Muscogees of Alabama. Sole survivor of the last conflict, the enemy still upon his trail, he led the women and children from the Escatawba to the sea, preferring death in its much loved waters to captivity and slavery. You have heard of the mysterious music which at midnight chimes along these shores; a low, lute-like strain, sometimes a vesper hymn, sometimes like a harp-string breaking. When the winds and surges sleep, in the still hours of night, I have often heard this plaintive anthem; and tradition says it is the death-chant of the Pascagoulas that wails along the sea.

The Indian village stood on a picturesque bluff, the gentle river, flowing through prairies of verdure, margined by aged oaks that lift their heads among the clouds and bathe their mossy beards in the silver spray beneath. The country spreads out into a continuous meadow of boundless extent, on every side dotted with little islets of palm-like trees. At intervals a serpentine line of ravine comes sweeping along, fringed with dwarf laurel, myrtle, jasmine, and other parasites, and the whole plain around is embroidered with flowers of every hue. Ah! it is pleasant to bivouac in these solitary plains, the quiet stars smiling upon you, and the fragrant winds singing in the trees around. There is a charm in these grand old woods—in these laughing waters—in these remote retreats, where only an echo of the storms of life is heard. No wonder the imaginative ancients peopled them with divinities: for here, at every step, one can but feel the presence of a God; and the feeling chastens and refines the heart. It is not in your gorgeous temples, with coquettish eyes and Shylock countenances around, and vanity peeping out even from the pulpit, that one truly feels the sentiment of religion in its humanizing and exalting influences. . . .

I was now approaching the ancient village of Augusta, once the stamping-ground of the famous Coon Morris. Being advised to take a near cut when within three miles, I turned to the right and drove ahead through leafy by-paths and across deserted fields grown over with stunted pines. For three hours I drove about, describing three segments of a circle, and finally got back to the point I started from. [*Nota bene:* Let all travelers stick to the beaten road, for in this country one may travel twenty miles without meeting a traveler or a finger-board.] The country through which I passed was poor, the population sparse, and no indications of the proximity of a town that I had heard of for twenty-five years. I drove on, however, expectation on tip-toe, the sun pouring down vertically, and my flagging steed sinking above his fetlocks in the sand, when, lo! the ancient village stood before me—an extensive parallelogram, garnished round with twelve or fifteen crumbling tenements, the wrecks of by-gone years! Not a tree stood in the gaping square for the eye to rest upon; the grass was all withered up; the burning sun fell on the white and barren sand as on a huge mirror, and was reflected back until your cheeks scorched and your eyes filled with tears. Even of these dilapidated houses several were unoccupied, and we drove round two-thirds of the square before we could find a human being to direct us to the tavern. It was a log-cabin, with one room, a deal table, some benches and cots, and a back shed for kitchen. Stable there was none, nor bar, nor servant, nor landlord visible. I turned my horse on the public square and took peaceable possession of the establishment. Nobody was to be seen. I was hungry and fatigued. The idea of a town once famous, and its hundred-and-one little comforts for the traveler, had buoyed me up during the morning drive, and fancy had diagramed something very different from what I was then realizing. In a few hours, however, the bachelor landlord came in. Not expecting company he had gone out on a foraging expedition. He feasted us on delicious venison, and, being a Virginian, soon concocted an ample julep. The mint grew near the grave of a jolly lawyer, a son of the "Old Dominion," who died there a few years before. No man can live in such a place without losing his energies. The mind stagnates, and in six months one would go completely asleep. I never saw such a picture of desolation. All was silence and solitude. In reply to my inquiry, my old friend, Colonel Mixon, said that times were dull; there was a little activity in one line only; and hobbling off he soon returned with a pair of babies in his arms—twin gems, plump, blue-eyed, rosy-cheeked, hanging around his neck like flowers on the stump of a storm-battered oak. Counselor Barrett, who seemed thoroughly posted in this branch of statistics, informed me that, during the last twelve months, thirteen matrons of that vicinity had produced doublets! The Colonel said that any disconsolate pair who would board with him six months, and drink from a peculiar spring on the premises, without having their expectations realized, should have a free ticket at his table for sixty days to try it again.

These infant phenomena, however, are by no means confined to Perry County. East Mississippi every where is equally prolific. In the *Paulding Clarion* I read the following, from the Rev. Marmaduke Gardiner, of Clarke County:

> *Falling Spring,* Feb. 2.
>
> "More than one hundred persons have visited my house since Saturday last, for the purpose of seeing three beautiful boy babies which my wife gave birth to on the 28th ult. One weighs 7^1/$_2$, the others 6^1/$_2$ *each,* and are perfectly formed. We have named them Abraham, Isaac, and Jacob. I married my wife twenty years ago, and she has given me nine sons and nine daughters, but no triplets until the last."

Married couples in search of heirs often cross the Atlantic, or drug themselves with nostrums and stinking mineral waters, when a single summer in these pine-woods would accomplish what they desire without extraordinary efforts, and at one-twentieth of the expense.

The old town next day presented a more lively scene. That certain premonitory of a piny-woods' gathering, the beer and ginger-bread cart, came rumbling into the square.—Rickety vehicles, of odd shapes, laden with melons, trundled along behind. A corner shanty displayed several suspicious-looking jugs and kegs. Buck negroes, dressed in their holiday suits, strode in, looking about for the candidates as one would for the giraffe. No candidate except the Hon. Robert J. Walker had visited the defunct town for years. It was quite an event. Finally, the stout sovereigns from the country came in, and the comedy commenced. The largest portion of the crowd was in the court-house to hear the orators, but a pretty considerable group was posted about the doggery. A number were playing "old sledge" on the heads of empty whisky barrels, and others were discussing the preliminaries of a quarter race.

Three of the candidates had spoken, when the late Judge Mitchell (formerly a well-known Member of Congress from Tennessee) rose. After an elaborate reply to the arguments of two of them, he turned to the third, and laying his hand on his head, said, "I have only one word to say in answer to my young friend. He has a leetle soft spot right here, *and it is mushy all round it.*"

When R. J. Walker was canvassing against George Poindexter for the Senate, he was accompanied, said Colonel Mixon, by a queer fish, one Isaac M'Farren, a fellow of infinite jest, and whose countenance was a comedy of itself. On a certain occasion they put up with a new settler, and had to sleep on the floor, while the man and his wife occupied a bunk in the same room. A very buxom damsel slept in a small kitchen near by. Mac had cast sheep's-eyes at her, and being uncomfortable on the floor, concluded to go and whisper a few soft nothings in her ear. He slipped out very quietly; but it being a crispy and frosty night, the door of the kitchen creaked upon its hinges, and the woman exclaimed, "Husband! husband! one of them men's arter Sally!" He sprang up, seized his rifle, and was rushing out, when Mr. Walker seized his arm. M'Farren hearing the noise, appeared at the other door rather *en désha-billé.* "Je-men-y!" cried the man, and cocked his rifle. Mr. Walker threw it up, and Mac, running forward, seized him by the hand, exclaiming, "Sir, it is only a frolic and an indiscretion; I am a man of honor, incapable of injuring sleeping innocence. Sir, I throw myself on your generosity. I see that you belong to the honorable fraternity of free and accepted masons. Brother, I give you *the right hand of fellowship!*" The man was overwhelmed with this volubility, and flattered at the notion of being mistaken for a mason. He accompanied the party over the county, but finally voted the Poindexter ticket, because Walker would persist in running when M'Farren was the proper man for the place!

"I was in ——," said Counselor Barrett, "when Governor ——, who was a candidate for re-election, came there. The county had been recently organized, and few of the people had been there long enough to vote under the Constitutional provision which requires six months' residence in the county and twelve in the State. They were anxious to vote, and got up a petition to the Board of Police (which has the supervision of elections) *to dispense with the requisitions of the Constitution.*"

"Did the Board comply with the petition?"

"I can't exactly say," said the Counselor; "*but as they all voted,* I presume the order was duly made. The best of the joke was, *the Governor signed the petition!*"

Next day the Counselor accompanied me a few miles on my way. Showing me a road running down toward the swamp, he inquired if I knew how that road came to be made. On replying that I did not, he said: "Some years ago I was down in that swamp with some fellows after wild hogs. I was standing on the edge of it hallooing on the hounds, my gun resting against a tree, when out rushed an enormous boar and charged right at me. I could only straddle my legs to escape his furious onset; but as he passed under, being rather low in the crotch, I found myself astride of him. Almost unconscious from terror, I involuntarily seized his tail, and stuck my heels under his shoulders. At every stride he took my spurs goaded him on. Thus he ran some three miles through the brush-wood, making a clean sweep as he went, but finally fell exhausted, when I dispatched the monster with my bowie-knife. The road is now used for hauling timber from Leaf River swamp, and is called Barrett's trail."

The country through which I am journeying is sparsely settled, and is only adapted to grazing. Its surface undulates like the roll of the ocean, and hill and valley are covered with luxuriant grass and with flowers of every hue. Herds of cattle stand in the plashy brooks. Red deer troop along the glades; wild turkeys run before you along your road, and the partridge rises from every thicket. But for these the solitude would be painful. Settlements are often twenty miles apart; the cheering mile-post and gossiping wayfarer are rarely met with. The gaunt pines have a spectral aspect, and their long shadows fall sadly upon the path. At nightfall, when the flowers have faded away, no fire-flies gem the road; one hears no tinkling bell; the robber owl skims lazily by; fantastic shades chase each other into deeper gloom; and instead of "the watch-dog's cheerful cry," the "wolf's long howl" comes from the reed-brakes, and is echoed by its prowling mate on the neighboring hills.

The day was dark and lowering. For weeks nor rain nor gentle dews had refreshed the calcined earth. A heavy cloud hung overhead, and its pent-up fury burst upon the forest. The few birds that tenant these silent woods flew screaming to their eyries; some cattle dashed across the hills for shelter. The whole wilderness was in motion. The pines swayed their lofty heads, and the winds shrieked and moaned among the gnarled and aged limbs. A few old ones fell thundering down, casting their broken fragments around; and then the hurricane rushed madly on, tearing up the largest trees, and hurling them like javelins through the air. The sky was covered as with a pall; and lurid flashes, like sepulchral lights, streamed and blazed athwart it. The earthquake voice of nature trembled along the ground, and, ere its running echoes died away, came again, crash after crash thundering forth. But at length, as though weary of the agony, it paused, and the phantom clouds scudded away. The scene around was appalling! Hundreds of trees lay prostrate, while, here and there, others stood shivered by the bolt of heaven and smoking with its fires. God preserve me from another ride through these giant pines in such a tempest!

Travels on the Lower Mississippi 1879–80

ERNST VON HESSE-WARTEGG

Ernst von Hesse-Wartegg, who lived from 1854 to 1918, was an Austro-German aristocrat with a gargantuan lust for travel. In Travels *he wrote three detailed chapters about Mississippi at the end of Reconstruction. A feature story in the* New York Times, *January 30, 1882, praised him as a "traveler of the stamp of Dickens and Mrs. Trollope." Named a baron in Germany and a chevalier in France, he observed classes of people he wrote about through aristocratic eyes: anti-Semitic, he also viewed blacks as inferior and thought that they would be better off as slaves. He traveled by train through Meridian, Jackson, and Vicksburg, and in chapter 9, "Through the State of Mississippi," he comments on the Civil War, the crops, and the inefficiency of trains. Hesse-Wartegg circled the globe four times and published over forty travel books, from which, it is said, Mark Twain borrowed heavily. When he married the American prima donna Minnie Hawk, an opera luminary and also a traveler, he became an American citizen at her request.*

EITHER MISSISSIPPI or Alabama dwarfs many a European power. Together they compose a domain of colossal proportions. Both, in spite of their miseries, stand on a threshold of magnificence greater than the old slavocratic splendor.

To the foreigner, Mississippi with a million inhabitants seems practically uninhabited and in something of the pristine condition still found in Dakota or West Texas. Giant primeval forests cover it. Tall oaks, cottonwoods, and elms—magnolias among them here and there—still prevail in hundreds of thousands of acres of virgin land where nobody has set foot. Thick vines twist upward and around giant trunks. Heaps of gray-green Spanish moss overload the limbs and branches, droop in long beards, and make the trees look like huge weeping willows. The Mississippi and Yazoo's vast bayous flood the area in spring and summer, rendering them inaccessible.

Mississippi's railroads traverse hundreds of miles that are untouched by the plow. Slaveholders, of course, put their plantations in the best and most accessible places. They prospered. The *"freedman"* lives there now. He struggles with self-government. A problem the white has not solved, it remains a mystery to the black, he being newly emancipated.

Plantations realized worth through slaves bound to them. Slaves were as necessary as sun and rain. Plantations therefore lost their worth the moment they lost their slaves. Perhaps it has been reserved to the present generation to restore by rational agriculture the former glory of this land. A modicum of money and the financial independence that accompanies it would lift the people beyond measure. But the money cannot be found now.

Mississippi, though without important minerals, enjoys splendid soil, expanses ideal for cotton, corn, tobacco, hemp, flax, and in the north, every sort of grain. Fruits of the moderate climates flourish there; in the south, oranges and figs. Since the war, however, as I have said, land values and the state's wealth have disappeared. The worth of real and personal property, over $500 million in 1860, fell to $150 million in 1870. The cotton output, 1.25 million bales in 1860, shriveled to a half million in 1870. It has returned only to 1.25 million.

Perhaps the least developed and most backward of the states, it is scantily populated, having not one city of 10,000 except Vicksburg. It lacks enough railroads and therefore suffers from too little transportation and thus faulty communication. For, in the South (especially the Mississippi valley), navigable rivers and the railroad do not supplement and extend the footpath and the highway; transportation and communication originate on the river and with the railroad. Farmers and planters reach one another and get to town by traveling cross-country or, under the best of circumstances, by following their own *"trails."* Highways and thoroughfares, drained, marked out, and in any other way improved, do not exist in these states. Nor is there familiarity between Mississippi's people and the world outside. Travelers to and from New Orleans, going north or south, speed through at night in sleeping cars. Nobody so much as dreams of pausing in one of the notorious little railroad towns, ill-reputed because precarious; and Mississippi, especially the southern part, barely smacks of civilization.

Fifty to a hundred miles often separate one city or town from another. Nothing passes between them. You can imagine what hardships planters suffer in these remote regions, getting food and other necessities and bringing harvests to market. Yet they persevere, planter and town. Every planter rests assured that the railroad will pass his plantation someday; every town, that it will be selected as terminus for some transcontinental railroad. As not a breath of such success has stirred, patience must equal optimism.

The inclemency, the harshness of this countryside surprised me when I traveled by train through the middle of the state. Sluggish, muddy streams toil through sandy, yellow soil. A stagnant pool or a green pond fills the forest's every depression. No more than a little rain has turned the fields to muck. In the northern part more people occupy a better-cultivated countryside. In the southern an Indian primitiveness still reigns supreme. The railroads themselves are an example. Make a connection? Arrive on time? Not a chance. Trains often stop at will on the open tracks or at plantations and regularly arrive one or more hours late at appointed destinations. Mine stopped frequently because the short-winded locomotive labored on hills. We often stalled two or three times an hour while the locomotive spun its wheels but advanced not an inch. Passengers dismounted. Many helped by pushing or pulling. But the old jade would not go. Repeated retreats and roaring assaults, sand on the rails, other measures: only after all had been taken did the enterprise succeed. Such railway exercises at night in the wilderness do not rank (as you can well imagine) among the joys of travel. Even the otherwise phlegmatic Yankees lost their composure.

I could quote the volcano of curses. It would make interesting reading but expand the book by several chapters. Mississippi is prodigal of curses. So I must limit myself to a short and general discussion. Now, an occasional, brief, pithy curse ought usually to serve the purpose and, like the counterpart in my country, be forgiven in tense moments that provoke them. But such a trifle satisfies neither *"Yankee"* nor *"Southerner."* The high and nasal voice spins a thread of curses instead, but so long and flimsy that the effect crumbles. (A cursing Yankee resembles a miaowing cat.) The curser shoves his hands into his pockets, pulls his soft hat low on this brow, and betrays no agitation. The objective European sees an utterly silly person. Curses among us [on this Mississippi excursion] continued longest when the train would stop in solitary stations where nobody got on or off and our engine struggled its best in vain to move the cars and resume the journey. Meanwhile the villages reminded me of southern Hungary and the Banat: squat shacks and log cabins with pigsties; an expansive square at the station; here and there a few primeval trees, spared the axe; and at the station, bales upon countless bales of cotton everywhere. I got off in Meridian, in the interior [east-central part], at a junction with the train to Vicksburg. I intended to see city and environs in a few days.

The clerk looked at the register, thunderstruck. A flesh-and-blood European, off the train, alive and breathing at *his* desk?

"*You are a fool,* sir, daring to come here!"

I asked the reason. He replied with candor.

"Life and property aren't safe, really, in this part of Mississippi, outside of town. There's no industry at all. Everything depends on cotton and hogs. Farmers haven't got a cent. The niggers are in the hands of bloodsucking Jewish '*storekeepers*' and purveyors. Things are in sad shape around here."

I toured the environs anyway. The land is excellent everywhere. Water, forest, prairie: they lack only settlers, railways, roads. Toughs roam these parts, however, scoundrels not likely to inspire trust. When I had to stop for a night in one of the many taverns in Marion, I spent the evening conversing with a young planter. How charming was his shout to me, *"Stranger, I bet you a hundred-dollar bill you won't see your folks alive again!"* But he had ruined his chances. Not about to let him win so much money, I took the next night train to Jackson, the capital.

The Mississippi, the artery of commerce, passes nearby; and the capital of the South [New Orleans] lies but twelve hours away by train. The dual influence manifests itself here. The people you meet, white or black, are well dressed and impress you as prosperous. Pleasant houses and nicely kept gardens confirm the impression. In the valley's prettiest city between Cairo and New Orleans, part of the old planter aristocracy retains its residences. Avenues everywhere; lovely gardens with palms and palmettoes, cacti and orange groves; government buildings open to the public; and on a slight elevation, the elegant and distinguished state capitol, seat of the government. Being the majority in Mississippi, blacks enjoy a big share of government, and hold many important offices, as we have observed: lieutenant-governor, secretary of state, commissioner of education, among others. At the capitol I also noted interesting details about finance and education. The state supports numerous schools. Its two universities are at Oxford, for whites, and on the banks of the Mississippi near Rodney, for blacks (named after a former governor, Alcorn).

By contrast the state's political affairs leave much to be desired. In the rural areas nobody looks after the safety of property or life. The situation, always bad, worsens during elections, when *"rowdies"* often impose a political persuasion on planters and Negroes. Consequently, in the last few years, black landowners have wanted to leave and resettle in Texas or the prairie states.

I stayed overnight in the hotel beside the station. During the night the train brought passengers who, like me, got off here. In the morning after breakfast, they crowded up to the desk, pulled rolls of banknotes out of their pockets, and paid their bills, $3.00 each. They received neither invoice nor receipt. When I saw others pay $2.00, I plunked down $2.00. The clerk looked at me. After a moment he asked with some surprise, *"Are you a drummer, sir?* Another dollar!" I added the third and continued on my journey, richer for the knowledge that the common traveler must pay more than drummers pay for lodging. What are drummers? Traveling salesmen: America's *"commercials."*

. . . Next I intended some side trips from Vicksburg into the famous *"Mississippi bottom."* So I returned from Jackson to the Mississippi by train.

Planters are always calling this *"bottomland"* the richest, the most fertile agricultural land in the valley; yet it remains primitive and uninhabitable. It extends some 300 miles, running along the Mississippi's left bank from Memphis to Vicksburg. Thirty to forty miles wide, it amounts to an area that dwarfs the kingdom of Würtemburg. A considerable system of ample rivers, mostly navigable, flows through this wilderness, tributary chiefly to the Yazoo, or River of the Dead, as the Indians call it. At many points the rivers communicate with other tributaries of the Mississippi. But the Yazoo is *the* bottomland river. It joins the Mississippi at Vicksburg. The Mississippi's annual floods inundate most of the bottom to depths of three to six feet. The water recedes in summer, leaving a thick crust of mud that resists cultivation. The bottom nonetheless produces one bumper crop—insects. Oxen and horses, stung by poisonous flies, often die an agonized death in a few hours. In the mostly oak, sassafras, cypress, and silver-poplar forests you will find many deer. Panthers and small black bears dwell in low-lying reed thickets. On numerous crescent-shaped lakes (obviously parts of the old riverbed), pelicans, swans, and countless other birds, and even alligators, disport themselves. In a word, this is a wilderness of a kind described in prior chapters, with the unique features and the advantages and disadvantages of such a wild place. Yet its days are numbered. In time, with the growing incursion of northerners, the land will be cleared and expanses brought under the plow.

No place but Vicksburg, in all the United States, evokes so many sad memories of the terrible anti-slavery war of the last decade. Every hill, every cliff thrusting a sheer face from the river, knows legendary acts of martial heroism. Every square foot of the environs has drunk soldiers' blood. In the river itself, evidence endures of modern history's biggest and bloodiest siege. Indeed, bent by the siege to a different course, the river has kept it.

The city, Mississippi's largest, rises imposingly on steep upthrusts, the *"bluffs"* of the river, which ascend to the plateau at the top. The more distinguished homes of planters join the beautiful courthouse there. And on the heights above them, even now you can see traces of the old fort. From its walls, "Whistling Dick," the Confederates' infamous cannon, hurled hideous death into enemy ranks. Grass flourishes on the ruins but the elevation still commands the river. A long panorama sweeps the Mississippi's twists and bends, the twin cities of De-Soto and Delta on the opposite shore, and the throb of all that riverfront life in the port. Nearer our vantage point, large and handsome hotels and stores line Washington Street, Vicksburg's thoroughfare. The many short, narrow streets seem to plunge from there to the river, to the many massive warehouses and magazines along its banks. People pant and wheeze to the top of the steep streets. Wheeled vehicles cannot use them. To walk is to sink into a foot of debris; the streets are not paved. In every one, fifty Negroes and white vagabonds loaf. Indeed, nothing looks hospitable, nor does the city evoke trust or inspire confidence.

True, nineteen steamboat lines maintain wharves and anchorages, and an impressive traffic bustles on the river and the rails below us. Vicksburg is still one of the cotton country's important commercial centers. True, many of the South's first and oldest planter families live here. But Vicksburg has meant *infamy* since the war. Multifarious riff-raff, found in every port city, assert themselves with exceptional energy here. People carry revolvers as a matter of habit, as they might pencils or toothpicks. Lynching, murder, gunplay occurred almost weekly for years. If things have improved in latter days, have the rowdies become as meek as lambs? Not at all!

I see, this time from a boat, a tall flagpole and the Stars and Stripes, marking the national cemetery about two miles off. Many of its occupants died in the siege. The graves extend across fourteen acres of well-cared-for terraces: 180,000 graves, not one empty!

In the regions below Vicksburg and even in Natchez (the state's second-largest river port), Negroes constitute the majority and thus hold the most-important county and municipal offices. Much political and social friction has harassed the state since the war. The status of Negroes has been one of the chief causes. In Natchez the races live in peace. But schools, churches, and communities divide along racial lines: all white or all black, no exceptions. Cotton reigns supreme, as everywhere in this part of the country.

Olden Times Revisited

W. L. CLAYTON

*Washington Lafayette Clayton, who lived from 1836 to 1904, published
his memories of Itawamba County, Mississippi, in the* Tupelo Journal
*during the year 1905. He called these reminiscences "Pen Pictures," and
his intention was to draw them with such detail that the reader could
"see" them, too. Clayton, whose family settled outside of Tupelo in Fulton
when he was four, was a circuit-riding lawyer who knew the countryside
and its people. He served in the Civil War as a captain and later had
the honorary title of colonel bestowed upon him. In these selections, from
the chapter " 'Scorpions' and Stagecoaches," Clayton describes the countryside, the custom of corn shucking, and the stagecoaches he knew as a
young boy. His writings were popular because of his simple narrative
style and his direct addresses to the reader.*

May 26, 1905

HOW LONG THE Indians roamed over these magnificent forests,
and looked upon these great uplifting and overtopping poplar, walnut,
chestnut, hickory, oak and gum trees, and chased the deer and shot the
wild turkey with his bow and arrow, speared the fish in the wild-wooded
streams and cultivated his little patch of maize by the side of the wig-
wam, no man will ever know. They wrote no history, however much they
may have made. But when they left this country in 1836, they left to the
white man the same virgin forest they had enjoyed so long, save the
little maize clumps beside their lodges, the deer roaming over the hills
and valleys as of yore, the trout in the lake, the birds amid the trees,
and the furrow unturned. What a lovely picture to look upon had we in
those olden days! What a view for a landscape painter to set his cultivated eye upon! About the time we came here and soon thereafter,
great herds of cattle could have been seen grazing upon the wide
stretch of native grassplains and small prairies, with a deer occasionally
slipping away from them, and which could be seen sometimes for almost or quite a mile, the country being open, and nothing to obstruct
the view, save the great trunks of the forest trees. But year by year and
month by month the pioneer pushed in, and began filling in the space,
and the forest fires became less and less frequent and the present
growth that now so thickly covers the woodlands began springing up

and filling in the vacant places, and the axe of the settler felled the great trees, making them into boards and rails, and occasionally into plank by means of the whip saw.

Many of my readers doubtless have never seen a whip saw at work, and so I will describe it. The whip saw is a straight saw having a handle at each end, not like the common cross-cut saw, but entering through the saw laterally and extending an equal distance on each side of the blade. In order to saw, the log is elevated upon a scaffolding so high that a man can stand straight under it; then two men do the sawing, one on top the log and the other underneath, the man on the ground having his face covered with a veil to protect his eyes from the saw dust. By this means did our fathers procure what plank they then used. I have often seen my father and my oldest brother thus sawing lumber and longed for the time when I should be large enough to handle the saw myself, but I never did. It passed out of use before I arrived to manhood. In the early days we always broke out lands for corn with the bulltongue plow and crossed it off and dropped the corn the same way we first ran with the plow in running it off, and covered with the hoe. The cotton was drilled,[1] but covered with two furrows with the bulltongue and knocked off with a board or home-made wooden harrow. The corn was worked till silking and tasseling. One of the good old customs, I have often thought, might have been kept up, but which disappeared many years ago, was "corn shucking." It was then customary for each neighbor to make a "corn shucking," invite his friends, and they would come in crowds, and shuck out all his corn, the good women at the same time having a quilting, and by these means the men and women of the neighborhood would often get together and spend many pleasant hours. The husking often extended into the night and was generally crowned by placing a darkey on the corn pile to lead the song while the other negroes present would join in the chorus. Their happy, joyous countenances, their weird expressions and their deep bass voices, mingled with an occasional scream from the screech owl, was a thing not to be forgotten and especially when the negro minstrel, at the hooting of the owl, would often stop his leadership, and break out, "Nigger, you hear dat bird? Time we gittin' 'way from dis place. Shore gwine ter be somethin' done. Le' me down from here." So, with the corn shucking and the quilting gatherings and the log rollings and the young peoples' parties, there was much social intercourse between the different neighborhoods, and life passed in a pleasant and joyous manner. As the years rolled on and the country became more thickly settled, church facilities increased and were fairly good, the preacher, however, ordinarily working in the field, or giving his attention to merchandise during the week, and dispensing the Word from the sacred desk on the Sabbath; but there were no Sabbath schools. I was a grown young man before I ever had an opportunity of attending a Sabbath school.

Up to some time in the fifties, there were but few renters in the country. Almost all owned their farms and if anyone did not own a home, he ordinarily worked for wages or "overseered" for someone having slaves.

Very few white women then worked in the fields. They kept the house, spun the thread, wove the cloth and made clothes for the family and bed clothing for the beds, including as beautiful counter-pieces as my eyes ever beheld. They also dyed wool with walnut bark and made lovely homespun winter wear for the men and boys and with different colors made a kind of woolen linsey for their own underwear.

The farmer raised everything he needed for home consumption, except sugar, coffee and molasses, and a supply of that was laid in once a year when the crop was sold. Wheat was raised in abundance for home use and I never saw a barrel of flower[2] till in the fifties. But no sorghum was raised till about 1854, but some molasses were made in parts of the country from maple water, however only in a few places.

Fire hunting was common. May be you don't know what that is and how conducted. Well, the vessel carrying the fire and light was made by crossing iron strips, bending and fastening them to another strip at the top, thus making an oblong open pan, say twelve by eighteen inches and about a foot deep. This pan was attached to a long handle by which to carry it. The light was made by burning rich pine in the pan, which was carried on the shoulder of the fire hunter, the pan in his rear and having someone along as an assistant to carry the gun and the supply of lightwood for the trip and look after the dog, if one was carried. The game thus hunted was deer, and they were discovered by the shining of their eyes, which look like two great stars. The deer seem to be entranced by the light and will permit the hunter to get so close to him that his body may be readily seen. The usual course is for the assistant to carry the gun and extra wood for the fire, walking at the heels of the hunter until he sights the deer's eyes; and he then simply reaches back his hand for the gun saying nothing, and the assistant hands him the gun, takes hold of the dog and never moves again until the gun fires. . . . I remember to have gone with my brother, John, on Saturday night and again on Monday following, and we never went over half a mile from the house, and yet we carried in a fine doe Saturday night and a nice buck on Monday night. The shot just creased the buck, and but for the faithful old dog, we would have lost him, but the dog held the deer down till another shot was fired into his head. This fire hunting was pretty dangerous to horses and cows, as it took a practiced hand to distinguish the eye of a horse or cow from that of a deer, and many an unlucky wight has been very much crestfallen over his mistake and that to his neighbor's sorrow. But fire hunting, like the deer of the forest, is a thing of the past.

June 2, 1905

. . . A little incident occurred while I was attending school at old Richmond[3] in 1856 which convinced me that people will enjoy word picturing if done in a natural way and in plain English free from Latin, French, or other foreign language, which they do not understand. We had a public examination and Composition reading at the close of the spring session and I wrote a composition on an imaginary country, called "Buncom," describing its hills and valleys, mountains and rocks, rooks and rills, its fields of waving grain, the flowers of its spring and the beauty of its scenery in the hazy months of October and November, all tinted with purple and gold and carnation with the farm houses dotting the hill sides and climbing up the foot hills of the mountains, and the smoke rising from the dwellings, the lowing cattle browsing on the meadows, and the fowls cackling round the barnyard. I read it to brother James, who was attending the same school. "Well," said he, "I'll people that country for you in my Composition." And so he wrote a composition in which he described the inhabitants of "Buncom," their dwellings, their dress and manners, the kind of occupations they followed, how they cultivated their fields, their social gatherings, and the kind of food they ate. We indicated to the teacher that our compositions were connected and which one should be read first. We captivated the house and yet there were many compositions read that day which, for thought and expression, were equal, and probably superior to them, but it was that simple narrative style which pleased. Now, if after all these years, I can confine my word painting to the same simple style, and remain true to nature, I shall not lack for readers. . . .

As the people moved in and settled up the country, and the forests were felled, the corn and wheat and cotton planted, the stores opened and the blacksmith shop established, the doctors and lawyers settled in their practice, there also came along with them the liquor traffic. In all the towns of any size there was from one to three "groceries," as they were then called, where liquor was sold by the drink, and in addition to this, at every place where anything else was sold, the beverage could be bought by the gallon, and at many cross roads nothing was sold but liquor. The whiskey could be bought for forty cents a gallon, and I suppose as good quality as you can now buy for two dollars and a half. A dime each would furnish four men a gallon, and then such drinking as they had, for you must know they did not buy it to divide and carry home for medicine,[4] but to drink somewhere on the ground. In my raising it was a general thing for the men to visit saloons and drink whiskey. Few men would refuse a drink. Do you ask, "how was drunkenness then compared with now?" You would then see a dozen drunk men where you will not see one now. At old Mooreville and Richmond, on Saturdays and public days, you would frequently see men lying on the corners down, and many more still going but staggering and swearing as they went. It was very seldom men refused a drink when offered, but I must say my father always refused to drink "with the boys," and I never saw him take a drink nor did I ever hear of his doing so.

One of the old time institutions I must not forget, and that is the stage coach. It was one of the last of the olden time institutions to give way before advancing improvements. When the stage coach arrived in the towns and hamlets, it was like the coming in of a railroad train now, so far as the excitement of the curious is concerned. The driver who was at once conductor and engineer, brakeman and fireman, often felt his power and importance. As he came into the towns and villages where he was to change his team, he sounded his bugle blast clear and keen, dashed in at better speed, and cracked his whip, turned his team over to the hostler whose business it was to take and replace them with fresh horses, and himself strode away for a drink and his meal. The old stage coach was never supposed to be full, but to hold one more, either inside or on top, and the movements of the great old things were like that of a ship at sea, and many had "stage sickness" from riding in or on it. It was one of the last relics of the olden time, only giving way to this country just before the civil war. But, until the railroads came, it was the only means of public travel unless the trip could be made by water. In those olden times all our cotton was flat boated on the river to Mobile, New Orleans or Memphis, after being hauled to the river side. It was very inconvenient, and often the river did not rise till in the spring and sometimes not at all. I have known my father to sell cotton in New Orleans after waiting months for returns at four cents per pound.

NOTES

[1] Sown by being dropped along a shallow furrow.

[2] Flour.

[3] A small settlement, 1830–60, 5 miles south of Mooreville.

[4] Drug stores also sold whiskey, but were not supposed to sell it unless it was prescribed by a physician as medicine.

Mississippi

WILLIAM FAULKNER

In 1954, William Faulkner gave a "tour" of his home state of Missis-sippi in a rare nonfiction article for Holiday *magazine. Born in 1897 in New Albany, Mississippi, Faulkner soon moved his family to nearby Oxford, where he would live and write for most of his life. In this essay, Faulkner sets up the semiautobiographical point of view of "the boy" and blends real names and places with fictional ones to describe the land-scapes, the people, and their rich history. Malcolm Cowley notes in his introduction to this piece that Faulkner "loves the Mississippi earth, the vegetation, the rivers—especially the Old Man of them all—the animals up or down to Mississippi mules. He loves—not likes—most of the people, while he hates a few of them with an intensity of emotion that he would never waste on Northerners." Faulkner attended high school until his senior year, trained in the Royal Air Force in Canada during World War I, and took courses at the University of Mississippi. His body of work includes nineteen novels, more than eighty short stories, and many poems, sketches, and film scripts. His experiments with point of view and perceptions of time and his depiction of generational families in the myth-ical kingdom of Yoknapatawpha have brought recognition from critics and readers around the world, and many have regarded him as the most important writer of the twentieth century. In 1950 Faulkner was awarded the Nobel Prize for literature. He died in 1962 and was buried in St. Peter's cemetery in Oxford.*

MISSISSIPPI BEGINS in the lobby of a Memphis, Tennessee hotel and extends south to the Gulf of Mexico. It is dotted with little towns concentric about the ghosts of the horses and mules once teth-ered to the hitch-rail enclosing the county courthouse and it might almost be said to have only those two directions, north and south, since until a few years ago it was impossible to travel east or west in it unless you walked or rode one of the horses or mules; even in the boy's early manhood, to reach by rail either of the adjacent county towns thirty miles away to the east or west, you had to travel ninety miles in three different directions on three different railroads.

In the beginning it was virgin—to the west, along the Big River, the alluvial swamps threaded by black almost motionless bayous and impen-

etrable with cane and buckvine and cypress and ash and oak and gum;
to the east, the hardwood ridges and the prairies where the Appalachian mountains died and buffalo grazed; to the south, the pine barrens and the moss-hung liveoaks and the greater swamps less of earth
than water and lurking with alligators and water moccasins, where Louisiana in its time would begin.

And where in the beginning the predecessors crept with their simple
artifacts, and built the mounds and vanished, bequeathing only the
mounds in which the succeeding recordable Algonquian stock would
leave the skulls of their warriors and chiefs and babies and slain bears,
and the shards of pots, and hammer- and arrow-heads and now and
then a heavy silver Spanish spur. There were deer to drift in herds
alarmless as smoke then, and bear and panther and wolves in the brakes
and bottoms, and all the lesser beasts—coon and possum and beaver
and mink and mushrat (not muskrat: mushrat); they were still there
and some of the land was still virgin in the early nineteen hundreds
when the boy himself began to hunt. But except for looking occasionally out from behind the face of a white or a Negro, the Chickasaws and
Choctaws and Natchez and Yazoos were as gone as the predecessors,
and the people the boy crept with were the descendants of the Sartorises and De Spains and Compsons who had commanded the Manassas
and Sharpsburg and Shiloh and Chickamauga regiments, and the Mc-
Caslins and Ewells and Holstons and Hogganbecks whose fathers and
grandfathers had manned them, and now and then a Snopes too because by the beginning of the twentieth century Snopeses were everywhere: not only behind the counters of grubby little side street stores
patronised mostly by Negroes, but behind the presidents' desks of
banks and the directors' tables of wholesale grocery corporations and
in the deaconries of Baptist churches, buying up the decayed Georgian
houses and chopping them into apartments and on their death-beds
decreeing annexes and baptismal fonts to the churches as mementos
to themselves or maybe out of simple terror.

They hunted too. They too were in the camps where the De Spains
and Compsons and McCaslins and Ewells were masters in their hierarchial turn, shooting the does not only when law but the Master too said
not, shooting them not even because the meat was needed but leaving
the meat itself to be eaten by scavengers in the woods, shooting it simply
because it was big and moving and alien, of an older time than the little
grubby stores and the accumulating and compounding money; the boy
a man now and in his hierarchial turn Master of the camp and coping,
having to cope, not with the diminishing wilderness where there was

less and less game, but with the Snopeses who were destroying that little which did remain.

These elected the Bilboes and voted indefatigably for the Vardamans, naming their sons after both; their origin was in bitter hatred and fear and economic rivalry of the Negroes who farmed little farms no larger than and adjacent to their own, because the Negro, remembering when he had not been free at all, was therefore capable of valuing what he had of it enough to struggle to retain even that little and had taught himself how to do more with less: to raise more cotton with less money to spend and food to eat and fewer or inferior tools to work with: this, until he, the Snopes, could escape from the land into the little grubby side street stores where he could live not beside the Negro but on him by marking up on the inferior meat and meal and molasses the price which he, the Negro, could not even always read.

In the beginning, the obsolescent, dispossessed tomorrow by the already obsolete: the wild Algonquian—the Chickasaw and the Choctaw and Natchez and Pascagoula—looking down from the tall Mississippi bluffs at a Chippeway canoe containing three Frenchmen—and had barely time to whirl and look behind him at a thousand Spaniards come overland from the Atlantic Ocean, and for a little while longer had the privilege of watching an ebb-flux-ebb-flux of alien nationalities as rapid as the magician's spill and evanishment of inconstant cards: the Frenchman for a second, then the Spaniard for perhaps two, then the Frenchman for another two and then the Spaniard again and then the Frenchman again for that last half-breath before the Anglo-Saxon, who would come to stay, to endure: the tall man roaring with Protestant scripture and boiled whiskey, Bible and jug in one hand and like as not an Indian tomahawk in the other, brawling, turbulent, uxorious and polygamous: a married invincible bachelor without destination but only motion, advancement, dragging his gravid wife and most of his mother-in-law's kin behind him into the trackless wilderness, to spawn that child behind a log-crotched rifle and then get her with another one before they moved again, and at the same time scattering his inexhaustible other seed in three hundred miles of dusky bellies: without avarice or compassion or forethought either: felling a tree which took two hundred years to grow, to extract from it a bear or a capful of wild honey.

He endured, even after he too was obsolete, the younger sons of Virginia and Carolina planters coming to replace him in wagons laden with slaves and indigo seedlings over the very roads he had hacked out with little else but the tomahawk. Then someone gave a Natchez doctor a Mexican cotton seed (maybe with the boll weevil already in it since, like the Snopes, he too has taken over the southern earth) and changed the whole face of Mississippi, slaves clearing rapidly now the virgin land lurking still (1850) with the ghosts of Murrell and Mason and Hare and the two Harpes, into plantation fields for profit where he, the displaced and obsolete, had wanted only the bear and the deer and the sweetening for his tooth. But he remained, hung on still; he is still there even in the boy's middle-age, living in a log or plank or tin hut on the edge of what remains of the fading wilderness, by and on the tolerance and sometimes even the bounty of the plantation owner to whom, in his intractable way and even with a certain dignity and independence, he is a sycophant, trapping coons and muskrats, now that the bear and the panther are almost gone too, improvident still, felling still the two-hundred-year-old tree even though it has only a coon or a squirrel in it now.

Manning, when that time came, not the Manassas and Shiloh regiments but confederating into irregular bands and gangs owning not much allegiance to anyone or anything, unified instead into the one rite and aim of stealing horses from Federal picket-lines; this in the intervals of raiding (or trying to) the plantation house of the very man to whom he had been the independent sycophant and intended to be again, once the war was over and presuming that the man came back from his Sharpsburg or Chickamauga majority or colonelcy or whatever it had been; trying to, that is, until the major's or colonel's wife or aunt or mother-in-law, who had buried the silver in the orchard and still held together a few of the older slaves, fended him off and dispersed him, and when necessary even shot him, with the absent husband's or nephew's or son-in-law's hunting gun or dueling pistols,—the women, the indomitable, the undefeated, who never surrendered, refusing to allow the Yankee *minie* balls to be dug out of portico column or mantelpiece or lintel, who seventy years later would get up and walk out of *Gone with the Wind* as soon as Sherman's name was mentioned; irreconcilable and enraged and still talking about it long after the weary exhausted men who had fought and lost it gave up trying to make them hush: even in the boy's time the boy himself knowing about Vicksburg and Corinth and exactly where his grandfather's regiment had been at First Manassas before he remembered hearing very much about Santa Claus.

In those days (1901 and -2 and -3 and -4) Santa Claus occurred only at Christmas, not like now, and for the rest of the year children played with what they could find or contrive or make, though just as now, in '51 and -2 and -3 and -4, they still played, aped in miniature, what they had been exposed to, heard or seen or been moved by most. Which was true in the child's time and case too: the indomitable unsurrendered old women holding together still, thirty-five and forty years later, a few of the old house slaves: women too who, like the white ones, declined, refused to give up the old ways and forget the old anguishes. The child himself remembered one of them: Caroline: free these many years but who had declined to leave. Nor would she ever accept in full her weekly Saturday wages, the family never knew why unless the true reason was the one which appeared: for the simple pleasure of keeping the entire family reminded constantly that they were in arrears to her, compelling the boy's grandfather then his father and finally himself in his turn to be not only her banker but her bookkeeper too, having got the figure of eighty-nine dollars into her head somehow or for some reason, and though the sum itself altered, sometimes more and sometimes less and sometimes it would be she herself who would be several weeks in arrears, it never changed: one of the children, white or Negro, liable to appear at any time, usually when most of the family would be gathered at a meal, with the message: 'Mammy says to tell you not to forget you owe her eighty-nine dollars.'

To the child, even at that time, she seemed already older than God, calling his grandsire 'colonel' but never the child's father nor the father's brother and sister by anything but their christian names even when they themselves had become grandparents: a matriarch with a score of descendants (and probably half that many more whom she had forgotten or outlived), one of them a boy too, whether a great grandson or merely a grandson even she did not remember, born in the same week with the white child and both bearing the same (the white child's grandsire's) name, suckled at the same black breast and sleeping and eating together and playing together the game which was the most important thing the white child knew at that time since at four and five and six his world was still a female world and he had heard nothing else that he could remember: with empty spools and chips and sticks and a scraped trench filled with well-water for the River, playing over again in miniature the War, the old irremediable battles—Shiloh and Vicksburg, and Brice's Crossroads which was not far from where the child (both of them) had been born, the boy because he was white arrogating to himself the right to be the Confederate General—Pemberton or Johnston or Forrest—twice to the black child's once, else, lacking that once in three, the black one would not play at all.

Not the tall man, he was still the hunter, the man of the woods; and not the slave because he was free now; but that Mexican cotton seed which someone had given the Natchez doctor clearing the land fast now, plowing under the buffalo grass of the eastern prairies and the brier and switch-cane of the creek- and river-bottoms of the central hills and deswamping that whole vast flat alluvial Delta-shaped sweep of land along the Big River, the Old Man: building the levees to hold him off the land long enough to plant and harvest the crop: he taking another foot of scope in his new dimension for every foot man constricted him in the old: so that the steamboats carrying the baled cotton to Memphis or New Orleans seemed to crawl along the sky itself.

And little steamboats on the smaller rivers too, penetrating the Talla-hatchie as far up as Wylie's Crossing above Jefferson. Though most of the cotton from that section, and on to the east to that point of no economic return where it was more expedient to continue on east to the Tombigbee and then south to Mobile, went the sixty miles overland to Memphis by mule and wagon; there was a settlement—a tavern of sorts and a smithy and a few gaunt cabins—on the bluff above Wylie's, at the exact distance where a wagon or a train of them loaded with cotton either starting or resuming the journey in the vicinity of Jeffer-son, would have to halt for the night. Or not even a settlement but rather a den, whose denizens lurked unseen by day in the brakes and thickets of the river bottom, appearing only at night and even then only long enough to enter the tavern kitchen where the driver of the day's cotton wagon sat unsuspecting before the fire, whereupon driver wagon mules and cotton and all would vanish: the body into the river probably and the wagon burned and the mules sold days or weeks later in a Memphis stockyard and the unidentifiable cotton already on its way to the Liverpool mill.

At the same time, sixteen miles away in Jefferson, there was a pre-Snopes; one of the tall men actually, a giant of a man in fact: a dedi-cated lay Baptist preacher but furious not with a furious unsleeping dream of paradise nor even for universal Order with an upper-case O, but for simple civic security. He was warned by everyone not to go in there because not only could he accomplish nothing, he would very likely lose his own life trying it. But he did go, alone, talking not of gospel nor God nor even virtue, but simply selected the biggest and boldest and by appearance anyway the most villainous there and said to him: 'I'll fight you. If you lick me, you take what money I have. If I lick you I baptise you into my church': and battered and mauled and gouged that one into sanctity and civic virtue then challenged the next biggest and most villainous and then the next; and the following Sun-day baptised the entire settlement in the river, the cotton wagons now crossing on Wylie's handpowered ferry and passing peacefully and unchallenged on to Memphis until the railroads came and took the bales away from them.

That was in the seventies. The Negro was a free farmer and a political entity now; one, he could not sign his name, was Federal marshal at Jefferson. Afterward he became the town's official bootlegger (Mississippi was one of the first to essay the noble experiment, along with Maine), resuming—he had never really quitted it—his old allegiance to his old master and gaining his professional name, Mulberry, from the huge old tree behind Doctor Habersham's drugstore, in the gallery-like tunnels among the roots of which he cached the bottled units of his commerce.

Soon he (the Negro) would even forge ahead in that economic rivalry with Snopes which was to send Snopes in droves into the Ku Klux Klan—not the old original one of the war's chaotic and desperate end which, measured against the desperate times, was at least honest and serious in its desperate aim, but into the later base one of the twenties whose only kinship to the old one was the old name. And a little money to build railroads with was in the land now, brought there by the man who in '66 had been a carpet-bagger but who now was a citizen; his children would speak the soft consonantless Negro tongue as the children of parents who had lived below the Potomac and Ohio Rivers since Captain John Smith, and their children would boast of their Southern heritage. In Jefferson his name was Redmond. He had found the money with which Colonel Sartoris had opened the local cottonfields to Europe by building his connecting line up to the main railroad from Memphis to the Atlantic Ocean—narrow gauge, like a toy, with three tiny locomotives like toys too, named after Colonel Sartoris's three daughters, each with its silver-plated oilcan engraved with the daughter's christian name: like toys, the standard-sized cars jacked up at the junction then lowered onto the narrow trucks, the tiny locomotive now invisible ahead of its charges so that they appeared in process of being snatched headlong among the fields they served by an arrogant plume of smoke and the arrogant shrieking of a whistle—who, after the inevitable quarrel, finally shot Colonel Sartoris dead on a Jefferson street, driven, everyone believed, to the desperate act by the same arrogance and intolerance which had driven Colonel Sartoris's regiment to demote him from its colonelcy in the fall elections after Second Manassas and Sharpsburg.

So there were railroads in the land now; now couples who had used to go overland by carriage to the River landings and the steamboats for the traditional New Orleans honeymoon, could take the train from almost anywhere. And presently pullmans too, all the way from Chicago and the Northern cities where the cash, the money was, so that the rich Northerners could come down in comfort and open the land indeed: setting up with their Yankee dollars the vast lumbering plants and mills in the southern pine section, the little towns which had been hamlets without change or alteration for fifty years, booming and soaring into cities overnight above the stump-pocked barrens which would remain until in simple economic desperation people taught themselves to farm pine trees as in other sections they had already learned to farm corn and cotton.

And Northern lumber mills in the Delta too: the mid-twenties now and the Delta booming with cotton and timber both. But mostly booming with simple money: increment a troglodyte which had fathered twin troglodytes: solvency and bankruptcy, the three of them booming money into the land so fast that the problem was how to get rid of it before it whelmed you into suffocation. Until in something almost resembling self-defense, not only for something to spend it on but to bet the increment from the simple spending on, seven or eight of the bigger Delta towns formed a baseball league, presently raiding as far away—and successfully too—for pitchers and short-stops and slugging outfielders, as the two major leagues, the boy, a young man now, making acquaintance with this league and one of the big Northern lumber companies not only coincidentally with one another but because of one another.

At this time the young man's attitude of mind was that of most of the other young men in the world who had been around twenty-one years of age in April, 1917, even though at times he did admit to himself that he was possibly using the fact that he had been nineteen on that day as an excuse to follow the avocation he was coming more and more to know would be forever his true one: to be a tramp, a harmless possessionless vagabond. In any case, he was quite ripe to make the acquaintance, which began with that of the lumber company which at the moment was taking a leisurely bankruptcy in a town where lived a lawyer who had been appointed the referee in the bankruptcy: a family friend of the young man's family and older than he, yet who had taken a liking to the young man and so invited him to come along for the ride too. His official capacity was that of interpreter, since he had a little French and the defuncting company had European connections. But no interpreting was ever done since the entourage did not go to Europe but moved instead into a single floor of a Memphis hotel, where all—including the interpreter—had the privilege of signing chits for food and theatre tickets and even the bootleg whiskey (Tennessee was in its dry mutation then) which the bellboys would produce, though not of course at the discreet and innocent-looking places clustered a few miles away just below the Mississippi state line, where roulette and dice and blackjack were available.

Then suddenly Mr Sells Wales was in it too, bringing the baseball league with him. The young man never did know what connection (if any) Mr Wales had with the bankruptcy, nor really bothered to wonder, let alone care and ask, not only because he had developed already that sense of *noblesse oblige* toward the avocation which he knew was his true one, which would have been reason enough, but because Mr Wales himself was already a legend in the Delta. Owner of a plantation measured not in acres but in miles and reputedly sole owner of one of the league baseball teams or anyway most of its players, certainly of the catcher and the base-stealing shortstop and the .340 hitting outfielder ravished or pirated it was said from the Chicago Cubs, his ordinary costume seven days a week was a two- or three-days' beard and muddy high boots and a corduroy hunting coat, the tale, the legend telling of how he entered a swank St Louis hotel in that costume late one night and demanded a room of a dinner jacketed clerk, who looked once at the beard and the muddy boots but probably mostly at Mr Wales's face and said they were filled up: whereupon Mr Wales asked how much they wanted for the hotel and was told, superciliously, in tens of thousands, and—so told the legend—drew from his corduroy hip a wad of thousand dollar bills sufficient to have bought the hotel half again at the price stated and told the clerk he wanted every room in the building vacated in ten minutes.

That one of course was apocryphal, but the young man himself saw this one: Mr Wales and himself having a leisurely breakfast one noon in the Memphis hotel room when Mr Wales remembered suddenly that his private ball club was playing one of its most important games at a town about sixty miles away at three oclock that afternoon and telephoned to the railroad station to have a special train ready for them in thirty minutes, which it was: an engine and a caboose: reaching Coahoma about three oclock with a mile still to the ball park: a man (there were no taxis at the station at that hour and few in Mississippi anywhere at that time) sitting behind the wheel of a dingy though still sound Cadillac car, and Mr. Wales said:

'What do you want for it?'

'What?' the man in the car said.

'Your automobile,' Mr Wales said.

'Twelve fifty,' the man said.

'All right,' Mr Wales said, opening the door.

'I mean twelve hundred and fifty dollars,' the man said.

'All right,' Mr Wales said, then to the young man: 'Jump in.'

'Hold up here, mister,' the man said.

'I've bought it,' Mr Wales said, getting in too. 'The ball park,' he said. 'Hurry.'

The young man never saw the Cadillac again, though he became quite familiar with the engine and caboose during the next succeeding weeks while the league pennant race waxed hotter and hotter, Mr Wales keeping the special train on call in the Memphis yards as twenty-five years earlier a city-dwelling millionaire might have hacked a carriage and pair to his instant nod, so that it seemed to the young man that he would barely get back to Memphis to rest before they would be rushing once more down the Delta to another baseball game.

'I ought to be interpreting, sometime,' he said once.

'Interpret, then,' Mr Wales said. 'Interpret what this goddamn cotton market is going to do tomorrow, and we can both quit chasing this blank blank sandlot ball team.'

The cotton seed and the lumber mills clearing the rest of the Delta too, pushing what remained of the wilderness further and further southward into the V of Big River and hills. When the young man, a youth of sixteen and seventeen then, was first accepted into that hunting club of which he in his hierarchial time would be Master, the hunting grounds, haunt of deer and bear and wild turkey, could be reached in a single day or night in a mule-drawn wagon. Now they were using automobiles: a hundred miles then two hundred southward and still southward as the wilderness dwindled into the confluence of the Yazoo River and the big one, the Old Man.

The Old Man: all his little contributing streams levee-ed too, along with him, and paying none of the dykes any heed at all when it suited his mood and fancy, gathering water all the way from Montana to Pennsylvania every generation or so and rolling it down the artificial gut of his victims' puny and baseless hoping, piling the water up, not fast: just inexorable, giving plenty of time to measure his crest and telegraph ahead, even warning of the exact day almost when he would enter the house and float the piano out of it and the pictures off the walls, and even remove the house itself if it were not securely fastened down.

Inexorable and unhurried, overpassing one by one his little confluent feeders and shoving the water into them until for days their current would flow backward, upstream: as far upstream as Wylie's Crossing above Jefferson. The little rivers were dyked too but back here was the land of individualists: remnants and descendants of the tall men now taken to farming, and of Snopeses who were more than individualists: they were Snopeses, so that where the owners of the thousand-acre plantations along the Big River confederated as one man with sandbags and machines and their Negro tenants and wagehands to hold the sand-boils and the cracks, back here the owner of the hundred or two hundred acre farm patrolled his section of levee with a sandbag in one hand and his shotgun in the other, lest his upstream neighbor dynamite it to save his (the upstream neighbor's) own.

Piling up the water while white man and Negro worked side by side in shifts in the mud and the rain, with automobile headlights and gasoline flares and kegs of whiskey and coffee boiling in fifty-gallon batches in scoured and scalded oil-drums; lapping, tentative, almost innocently, merely inexorable (no hurry, his) among and beneath and between and finally over the frantic sandbags, as if his whole purpose had been merely to give man another chance to prove, not to him but to man, just how much the human body could bear, stand, endure; then, having let man prove it, doing what he could have done at any time these past weeks if so minded: removing with no haste nor any particular malice or fury either, a mile or two miles of levee and coffee drums and whiskey kegs and gas flares in one sloughing collapse, gleaming dully for a little while yet among the parallel cotton middles until the fields vanished along the roads and lanes and at last the towns themselves.

Vanished, gone beneath one vast yellow motionless expanse, out of which projected only the tops of trees and telephone poles and the decapitations of human dwelling-places like enigmatic objects placed by inscrutable and impenetrable design on a dirty mirror; and the mounds of the predecessors on which, among a tangle of moccasins, bear and horses and deer and mules and wild turkeys and cows and domestic chickens waited patient in mutual armistice; and the levees themselves, where among a jumble of uxorious flotsam the young continued to be born and the old to die, not from exposure but from simple and normal time and decay, as if man and his destiny were in the end stronger even than the river which had dispossessed him, inviolable by and invincible to, alteration.

Then, having proved that too, he—the Old Man—would withdraw, not retreat: subside, back from the land slowly and inexorably too, emptying the confluent rivers and bayous back into the old vain hopeful gut, but so slowly and gradually that not the waters seemed to fall but the flat earth itself to rise, creep in one plane back into light and air again: one constant stain of yellow-brown at one constant altitude on telephone poles and the walls of gins and houses and stores as though the line had been laid off with a transit and painted in one gigantic unbroken brush-stroke, the earth itself one alluvial inch higher, the rich dirt one inch deeper, drying into long cracks beneath the hot fierce glare of May: but not for long, because almost at once came the plow, the plowing and planting already two months late but that did not matter: the cotton man-tall once more by August and whiter and denser still by picking-time, as if the Old Man said, 'I do what I want to, when I want to. But I pay my way.'

And the boats, of course. They projected above that yellow and liquid plane and even moved upon it: the skiffs and skows of fishermen and trappers, the launches of the United States Engineers who operated the Levee Commission, and one small shallow-draught steamboat steaming in paradox among and across the cotton fields themselves, its pilot not a riverman but a farmer who knew where the submerged fences were, its masthead lookout a mechanic with a pair of pliers to cut the telephone wires to pass the smokestack through: no paradox really, since on the River it had resembled a house to begin with, so that here it looked no different from the baseless houses it steamed among, and on occasion even strained at top boiler pressure to overtake like a mallard drake after a fleeing mallard hen.

But these were not enough, very quickly not near enough; the Old Man meant business indeed this time. So now there began to arrive from the Gulf ports the shrimp trawlers and pleasure cruisers and Coast Guard cutters whose bottoms had known only salt water and the mouths of tidal rivers, to be run still by their salt water crews but conned by the men who knew where the submerged roads and fences were for the good reason that they had been running mule-plow furrows along them or up to them all their lives, sailing among the swollen carcasses of horses and mules and deer and cows and sheep to pluck the Old Man's patient flotsam, black and white, out of trees and the roofs of gins and cotton sheds and floating cabins and the second storey windows of houses and office buildings; then—the salt-water men, to whom land was either a featureless treeless salt-marsh or a snake- and alligator-infested swamp impenetrable with trumpet vine and Spanish moss; some of whom had never even seen the earth into which were driven the spiles supporting the houses they lived in—staying on even after they were no longer needed, as though waiting to see emerge from the water what sort of country it was which bore the economy on which the people—men and women, black and white, more of black than white even, ten to one more—lived whom they had saved; seeing the land for that moment before mule and plow altered it right up to the water's receding edge, then back into the river again before the trawlers and cruisers and cutters became marooned into canted and useless rubble too along with the ruined hencoops and cowsheds and privies; back onto the Old Man, shrunken once more into his normal banks, drowsing and even innocent-looking, as if it were something else besides he who had changed, for a little time anyway, the whole face of the adjacent earth.

They were homeward bound now, passing the river towns, some of which were respectable in age when south Mississippi was a Spanish wilderness: Greenville and Vicksburg, Natchez and Grand-and Petit Gulf (vanished now and even the old site known by a different name) which had known Mason and one at least of the Harpes and from or on which Murrell had based his abortive slave insurrection intended to efface the white people from the land and leave him emperor of it, the land sinking away beyond the levee until presently you could no longer say where the water began and earth stopped: only that these lush and verdant sunny savannahs would no longer bear your weight. The rivers flowed no longer west, but south now, no longer yellow or brown, but black, threading the miles of yellow salt marsh from which on an offshore breeze mosquitoes came in such clouds that in your itching and burning anguish it would seem to you you could actually see them in faint adumbration crossing the earth, and met tide and then the uncorrupted salt: not the Gulf quite yet but at least the Sound behind the long barrier of the islands—Ship and Horn and Petit Bois, the trawler and cruiser bottoms home again now among the lighthouses and channel markers and shipyards and drying nets and processing plants for fish.

The man remembered that from his youth too: one summer spent being blown innocently over in catboats since, born and bred for generations in the north Mississippi hinterland, he did not recognize the edge of a squall until he already had one. The next summer he returned because he found that he liked that much water, this time as a hand in one of the trawlers, remembering: a four-gallon iron pot over a red bed of charcoal on the foredeck, in which decapitated shrimp boiled among handsful of salt and black pepper, never emptied, never washed and constantly renewed, so that you ate them all day long in passing like peanuts; remembering: the predawn, to be broken presently by the violent near-subtropical yellow-and-crimson day almost like an audible explosion, but still dark for a little while yet, the dark ship creeping onto the shrimp grounds in a soundless sternward swirl of phosphorus like a drowning tumble of fireflies, the youth lying face down on the peak staring into the dark water watching the disturbed shrimp burst outward-shooting in fiery and fading fans like the trails of tiny rockets.

He learned the barrier islands too; one of a crew of five amateurs sailing a big sloop in off-shore races, he learned not only how to keep a hull on its keel and moving but how to get it from one place to another and bring it back: so that, a professional now, living in New Orleans he commanded for pay a power launch belonging to a bootlegger (this was the twenties), whose crew consisted of a Negro cook-deck-hand-stevedore and the bootlegger's younger brother: a slim twenty-one or -two year old Italian with yellow eyes like a cat and a silk shirt bulged faintly by an armpit-holstered pistol too small in calibre to have done anything but got them all killed, even if the captain or the cook had dreamed of resisting or resenting trouble if and when it came, which the captain or the cook would extract from the holster and hide at the first opportunity (not concealed really: just dropped into the oily bilge under the engine, where, even though Pete soon discovered where it would be, it was safe because he refused to thrust his hand and arm into the oil-fouled water but instead merely lay about the cockpit, sulking); taking the launch across Pontchartrain and down the Rigolets out to the Gulf, the Sound, then lying-to with no lights showing until the Coast Guard cutter (it ran almost on schedule; theirs was a job too even if it was, comparatively speaking, a hopeless one) made its fast haughty eastward rush, going, they always like to believe, to Mobile, to a dance, then by compass on to the island (it was little more than a sandspit bearing a line of ragged and shabby pines thrashing always in the windy crash and roar of the true Gulf on the other side of it) where the Caribbean schooner would bury the casks of green alcohol which the bootlegger's mother back in New Orleans would convert and bottle and label into scotch or bourbon or gin. There were a few wild cattle on the island which they would have to watch for, the Negro digging and Pete still sulking and refusing to help at all because of the pistol, and the captain watching for the charge (they couldn't risk showing a light) which every three or four trips would come—the gaunt wild half-seen shapes charging suddenly and with no warning down at them as they turned and ran through the nightmare sand and hurled themselves into the dinghy, to pull along parallel to the shore, the animals following, until they had tolled them far enough away for the Negro to go back ashore for the remaining casks. Then they would heave-to again and lie until the cutter passed back westward, the dance obviously over now, in the same haughty and imperious rush.

That was Mississippi too, though a different one from where the child had been bred; the people were Catholics, the Spanish and French blood still showed in the names and faces. But it was not a deep one, if you did not count the sea and the boats on it: a curve of beach, a thin unbroken line of estates and apartment hotels owned and inhabited by Chicago millionaires, standing back to back with another thin line, this time of tenements inhabited by Negroes and whites who ran the boats and worked in the fish-processing plants.

Then the Mississippi which the young man knew began: the fading purlieus inhabited by a people whom the young man recognised because their like was in his country too: descendants, heirs at least in spirit, of the tall men, who worked in no factories and farmed no land nor even truck patches, living not out of the earth but on its denizens: fishing guides and individual professional fishermen, trappers of muskrats and alligator hunters and poachers of deer, the land rising now, once more earth instead of half water, vista-ed and arras-ed with the long leaf pines which northern capital would convert into dollars in Ohio and Indiana and Illinois banks. Though not all of it. Some of it would alter hamlets and villages into cities and even build whole new ones almost overnight, cities with Mississippi names but patterned on Ohio and Indiana and Illinois because they were bigger than Mississippi towns, rising, standing today among the tall pines which created them, then tomorrow (that quick, that fast, that rapid) among the stumpy pockage to which they were monuments. Because the land had made its one crop: the soil too fine and light to compete seriously in cotton: until people discovered that it would grow what other soils would not: the tomatoes and strawberries and the fine cane for sugar: not the sorghum of the northern and western counties which the people of the true cane country called hog-feed, but the true sweet cane which made the sugar house molasses.

Big towns, for Mississippi: cities, we called them: Hattiesburg, and Laurel, and Meridan, and Canton; and towns deriving by name from further away than Ohio: Kosciusko named after a Polish general who thought that people should be free who wanted to be, and Egypt because there was corn there when it was nowhere else in the bad lean times of the old war which the old women had still never surrendered, and Philadelphia where the Neshoba Indians whose name the country bears still remain for the simple reason that they did not mind living in peace with other people, no matter what their color or politics. This was the hills now: Jones County which old Newt Knight, its principal proprietor and first citizen or denizen, whichever you liked, seceded from the Confederacy in 1862, establishing still a third republic within the boundaries of the United States until a Confederate military force subdued him in his embattled log-castle capital; and Sullivan's Hollow: a long narrow glen where a few clans of families with North Ireland and Highland names feuded and slew one another in the old pre-Culloden fashion yet banding together immediately and always to resist any outsider in the pre-Culloden fashion too: vide the legend of the revenue officer hunting illicit whiskey stills, captured and held prisoner in a stable and worked in traces as the pair to a plow-mule. No Negro ever let darkness catch him in Sullivan's Hollow. In fact, there were few Negroes in this country at all: a narrow strip of which extended up into the young man's own section: a remote district there through which Negroes passed infrequently and rapidly and only by daylight.

It is not very wide, because almost at once there begins to the east of it the prairie country which sheds its water into Alabama and Mobile Bay, with its old tight intermarried towns and plantation houses columned and porticoed in the traditional Georgian manner of Virginia and Carolina in place of the Spanish and French influence of Natchez. These towns are Columbus and Aberdeen and West Point and Shuqualak, where the good quail shooting is and the good bird dogs are bred and trained—horses too: hunters; Dancing Rabbit is here too, where the treaty dispossessing them of Mississippi was made between the Choctaws and the United States; and in one of the towns lived a kinsman of the young man, dead now, rest him: an invincible and incorrigible bachelor, a leader of cotillions and an inveterate diner-out since any time an extra single man was needed, any hostess thought of him first.

But he was a man's man too, and even more: a young man's man, who played poker and matched glasses with the town's young bachelors and the apostates still young enough in time to still resist the wedlock; who walked not only in spats and a stick and yellow gloves and a Homburg hat, but an air of sardonic and inviolable atheism too, until at last he was forced to the final desperate resort of prayer: sitting after supper one night among the drummers in the row of chairs on the sidewalk before the Gilmer Hotel, waiting to see what (if anything) the evening would bring, when two of the young bachelors passing in a Model T Ford stopped and invited him to drive across the line into the Alabama hills for a gallon of moonshine whiskey. Which they did. But the still they sought was not in hills because these were not hills: it was the dying tail of the Appalachian mountain range. But since the Model T's engine had to be running fast anyway for it to have any headlights, going up the mountain was an actual improvement, especially after they had to drop to low gear. And coming from the generation before the motor car, it never occurred to him that coming back down would be any different until they got the gallon and had a drink from it and turned around and started back down. Or maybe it was the whiskey, he said, telling it: the little car rushing faster and faster behind a thin wash of light of about the same volume that two lightning bugs would have made, around the plunging curves which, the faster the car ran, became only the more frequent and sharp and plunging, whipping around the nearly right-angle bends with a rock wall on one hand and several hundred feet of vertical and empty night on the other, until at last he prayed; he said, 'Lord, You know I haven't worried You in over forty years, and if You'll just get me back to Columbus I promise never to bother You again.'

And now the young man, middleaged now or anyway middleaging, is back home too where they who altered the swamps and forests of his youth, have now altered the face of the earth itself; what he remembered as dense river bottom jungle and rich farm land, is now an artificial lake twenty-five miles long: a flood control project for the cotton fields below the huge earth dam, with a few more outboard-powered fishing skiffs on it each year, and at last a sailboat. On his way in to town from his home the middleaging (now a professional fiction-writer; who had wanted to remain the tramp and the possessionless vagabond of his young manhood but time and success and the hardening of his arteries had beaten him) man would pass the back yard of a doctor friend whose son was an undergraduate at Harvard. One day the undergraduate stopped him and invited him in and showed him the unfinished hull of a twenty-foot sloop, saying, 'When I get her finished, Mr Bill, I want you to help me sail her.' And each time he passed after that, the undergraduate would repeat: 'Remember, Mr Bill, I want you to help me sail her as soon as I get her in the water:' to which the middleaging would answer as always: 'Fine, Arthur. Just let me know.'

Then one day he came out of the postoffice: a voice called him from a taxicab, which in small Mississippi towns was any motor car owned by any footloose young man who liked to drive, who decreed himself a taxicab as Napoleon decreed himself emperor; in the car with the driver was the undergraduate and a young man whose father had vanished recently somewhere in the West out of the ruins of the bank of which he had been president, and a fourth young man whose type is universal: the town clown, comedian, whose humor is without viciousness and quite often witty and always funny. 'She's in the water, Mr Bill,' the undergraduate said. 'Are you ready to go now?' And he was, and the sloop was too; the undergraduate had sewn his own sails on his mother's machine; they worked her out into the lake and got her on course all tight and drawing, when suddenly it seemed to the middle-aging that part of him was no longer in the sloop but about ten feet away, looking at what he saw: a Harvard undergraduate, a taxi-driver, the son of an absconded banker and a village clown and a middleaged novelist sailing a home-made boat on an artificial lake in the depths of the north Mississippi hills: and he thought that that was something which did not happen to you more than once in your life.

Home again, his native land; he was born of it and his bones will sleep in it; loving it even while hating some of it: the river jungle and the bordering hills where still a child he had ridden behind his father on the horse after the bobcat or fox or coon or whatever was ahead of the belling hounds and where he had hunted alone when he got big enough to be trusted with a gun, now the bottom of a muddy lake being raised gradually and steadily every year by another layer of beer cans and bottle caps and lost bass plugs—the wilderness, the two weeks in the woods, in camp, the rough food and the rough sleeping, the life of men and horses and hounds among men and horses and hounds, not to slay the game but to pursue it, touch and let go, never satiety—moved now even further away than that down the flat Delta so that the mile-long freight trains, visible for miles across the fields where the cotton is mortgaged in February, planted in May, harvested in September and put into the Farm Loan in October in order to pay off February's mortgage in order to mortgage next year's crop, seem to be passing two or even three of the little Indian-named hamlets at once over the very ground where, a youth now capable of being trusted even with a rifle, he had shared in the yearly ritual of Old Ben: the big old bear with one trap-ruined foot who had earned for himself a name, a designation like a living man through the legend of the deadfalls and traps he had wrecked and the hounds he had slain and the shots he had survived, until Boon Hogganbeck, the youth's father's stable foreman, ran in and killed it with a hunting knife to save a hound which he, Boon Hogganbeck, loved.

But most of all he hated the intolerance and injustice: the lynching of Negroes not for the crimes they committed but because their skins were black (they were becoming fewer and fewer and soon there would be no more of them but the evil would have been done and irrevocable because there should never have been any); the inequality: the poor schools they had then when they had any, the hovels they had to live in unless they wanted to live outdoors: who could worship the white man's God but not in the white man's church; pay taxes in the white man's courthouse but couldn't vote in it or for it; working by the white man's clock but having to take his pay by the white man's counting (Captain Joe Thoms, a Delta planter though not one of the big ones, who after a bad crop year drew a thousand silver dollars from the bank and called his five tenants one by one into the dining room where two hundred of the dollars were spread carelessly out on the table beneath the lamp, saying: 'Well, Jim, that's what we made this year.' Then the Negro: 'Gret God, Cap'n Joe, is all that mine?' And Captain Thoms: 'No no, just half of it is yours. The other half belongs to me, remember.'); the bigotry which could send to Washington some of the senators and congressmen we sent there and which would erect in a town no bigger than Jefferson five separate denominations of churches but set aside not one square foot of ground where children could play and old people could sit and watch them.

But he loves it, it is his, remembering: the trying to, having to, stay in bed until the crack of dawn would bring Christmas and of the other times almost as good as Christmas; of being waked at three oclock to have breakfast by lamplight in order to drive by surrey into town and the depot to take the morning train for the three or four days in Memphis when he would see automobiles, and the day in 1910 when, twelve years old, he watched John Moissant land a bicycle-wheeled aileronless (you warped the whole wing-tip to bank it or hold it level) Bleriot monoplane in the infield of the Memphis race-track and knew forever after that someday he too would have to fly alone; remembering: his first sweetheart, aged eight, plump and honey-haired and demure and named Mary, the two of them sitting side by side on the kitchen steps eating ice cream; and another one, Minnie this time, grand-daughter of the old hillman from whom, a man himself now, he bought moonshine whiskey, come to town at seventeen to take a job behind the soda counter of the drug store, watching her virginal and innocent and without self-consciousness pour Coca-Cola syrup into the lifted glass by hooking her thumb through the ring of the jug and swinging it back and up in one unbroken motion onto her horizontal upper arm exactly as he had seen her grandfather pour whiskey from a jug a thousand times.

Even while hating it, because for every Joe Thoms with two hundred silver dollars and every Snopes in a hooded nightshirt, somewhere in Mississippi there was this too: remembering: Ned, born in a cabin in the back yard in 1865, in the time of the middleaged's great-grand-father and had outlived three generations of them, who had not only walked and talked so constantly for so many years with the three genera-tions that he walked and talked like them, he had two tremendous trunks filled with the clothes which they had worn—not only the blue brass-buttoned frock coat and the plug hat in which he had been the great-grandfather's and the grandfather's coachman, but the broad-cloth frock coats which the great-grandfather himself had worn, and the pigeon-tailed ones of the grandfather's time and the short coat of his father's which the middleaged could remember on the backs for which they had been tailored, along with the hats in their eighty years of mutation too: so that, glancing idly up and out the library window, the middleaged would see that back, that stride, that coat and hat going down the drive toward the road, and his heart would stop and even turn over. He (Ned) was eighty-four now and in these last few years he had begun to get a little mixed up, calling the middleaged not only 'Master' but sometimes 'Master Murry,' who was the middleaged's fa-ther, and 'Colonel' too, coming once a week through the kitchen and in to the parlor or perhaps already found there, saying: 'Here's where I wants to lay, right here where I can be facing out that window. And I wants it to be a sunny day, so the sun can come in on me. And I wants you to preach the sermon. I wants you to take a dram of whiskey for me, and lay yourself back and preach the best sermon you ever preached.'

And Caroline too, whom the middleaged had inherited too in his hierarchial turn, nobody knowing anymore exactly how many more years than a hundred she was but not mixed up, she: who had forgotten nothing, calling the middleaged 'Memmy' still, from fifty-odd years ago when that was as close as his brothers could come to 'William'; his youngest daughter, aged four and five and six, coming in the house and saying 'Pappy, Mammy said to tell you not to forget you owe her eighty-nine dollars.'

'I wont,' the middleaged would say. 'What are you all doing now?'

'Piecing a quilt,' the daughter answered. Which they were. There was electricity in her cabin now, but she would not use it, insisting still on the kerosene lamps which she had always known. Nor would she use the spectacles either, wearing them merely as an ornament across the brow of the immaculate white cloth—headrag—which bound her now hairless head. She did not need them: a smolder of wood ashes on the hearth winter and summer in which sweet potatoes roasted, the five-year-old white child in a miniature rocking chair at one side of it and the aged Negress, not a great deal larger, in her chair at the other, the basket bright with scraps and fragments of cloth between them and in that dim light in which the middleaged himself could not have read his own name without his glasses, the two of them with infinitesimal and tedious and patient stitches annealing the bright stars and squares and diamonds into another pattern to be folded away among the cedar shavings in the trunk.

Then it was the Fourth of July, the kitchen was closed after breakfast so the cook and houseman could attend a big picnic; in the middle of the hot morning the aged Negress and the white child gathered green tomatoes from the garden and ate them with salt, and that afternoon beneath the mulberry tree in the back yard the two of them ate most of a fifteen-pound chilled watermelon, and that night Caroline had the first stroke. It should have been the last, the doctor thought so too. But by daylight she had rallied, and that morning the generations of her loins began to arrive, from her own seventy and eighty year old children, down through their great- and twice-great-grandchildren—faces which the middleaged had never seen before until the cabin would no longer hold them: the women and girls sleeping on the floor inside and the men and boys sleeping on the ground in front of it, Caroline herself conscious now and presently sitting up in the bed: who had forgotten nothing: matriarchial and imperial, and more: imperious: ten and even eleven oclock at night and the middleaged himself undressed and in bed, reading, when sure enough he would hear the slow quiet stockinged or naked feet mounting the back stairs; presently the strange dark face—never the same one of two nights ago or the two or three nights before that—would look in the door at him, and the quiet, courteous, never servile voice would say: 'She want the ice cream.' And he would rise and dress and drive in to the village; he would even drive through the village although he knew that everything there will have long been closed and he would do what he had done two nights ago: drive thirty miles on to the arterial highway and then up or down it until he found an open drive-in or hot-dog stand to sell him the quart of ice cream.

But that stroke was not the one; she was walking again presently, even, despite the houseman's standing order to forestall her with the automobile, all the way in to town to sit with his, the middleaging's, mother, talking, he liked to think, of the old days of his father and himself and the three younger brothers, the two of them two women who together had never weighed two hundred pounds in a house roaring with five men: though they probably didn't since women, unlike men, have learned how to live uncomplicated by that sort of sentimentality. But it was as if she knew herself that the summer's stroke was like the throat-clearing sound inside the grandfather clock preceding the stroke of midnight or of noon, because she never touched the last unfinished quilt again. Presently it had vanished, no one knew where, and as the cold came and the shortening days she began to spend more and more time in the house, not her cabin but the big house, sitting in a corner of the kitchen while the cook and houseman were about, then in the middleaging's wife's sewing room until the family gathered for the evening meal, the houseman carrying her rocking chair into the dining room to sit there while they ate: until suddenly (it was almost Christmas now) she insisted on sitting in the parlor until the meal was ready, none knew why, until at last she told them, through the wife: 'Miss Hestelle, when them niggers lays me out, I want you to make me a fresh clean cap and apron to lay in.' That was her valedictory; two days after Christmas the stroke came which was the one; two days after that she lay in the parlor in the fresh cap and apron she would not see, and the middleaging did indeed lay back and preach the sermon, the oration, hoping that when his turn came there would be someone in the world to owe him the sermon which all owed to her who had been, as he had been from infancy, within the scope and range of that fidelity and that devotion and that rectitude.

Loving all of it even while he had to hate some of it because he knows now that you dont love because: you love despite; not for the virtues, but despite the faults.

[*Holiday*, April 1954; the text printed here has been taken from Faulkner's typescript.]

The Singing River

RUTH E. BASS

Mississippi is rich in place names that reflect the language of Native Americans and the influences of the French, English, and Spanish settlers: Rolling Fork, Anguilla, Hernando, Pontchatoula, Pocohontas, Gautier, and Atchafalaya, to name a few. Here a worker for the Works Progress Administration (WPA) put in writing for the folklore collection the legend of how the Singing River on the Gulf Coast got its name.

THE MOST WIDELY circulated and best known legend connected with the Gulf Coast is the story of the singing river. In 1699 Bienville claims to have heard the mysterious music that is still heard from time to time near Pascagoula, where the river runs into the Bay. Many attempts have been made to solve the mystery of the source of the music and legend has explained it in several different ways. When the music is heard it seems to come from both air and water and to envelope the listener in a sound that has been compared to the hum of a swarm of bees, the humming of telegraph lines or an Aeolian harp. Some authorities claim that the sound is produced by a species of fish but this had never been satisfactorily proved. The music does not come at certain times or seasons. It may be heard at one place a few evenings then not heard again for several years. Sometimes it is heard best on the bay and at other times up the river or on the bayou. One story of the music as told by some of the fishermen on the bay is that Captain Kidd used to bury his stolen treasures on a certain small island that was entirely washed away by a hurricane. The treasure was carried into the bay by the Mermaids who still guard it. The music is the singing of the these mermaids. Many old negroes claim to have heard mermaids singing on the Pascagoula River and even on the Leaf River. Another legend is that a long long time ago the Biloxi Indians called themselves "children of the sea," claimed that they had originally come up from the blue waters of the Gulf, and worshipped a Sea-maiden. When the white men came among the Biloxis, they went about with a cross and persuaded the Indians to give up their worship of the Sea-maiden in favor of the White Man's God. The Sea-Maiden was a jealous goddess and one night the priest was awakened by a sound of singing and of rising waters. He went out and saw the waters of the bay had risen up into a great wave that almost reached the clouds. On the top of the great wave, high against the moon stood the Sea-Maiden singing:

"Come to me, children of the sea.
Neither book, nor bell, nor cross
Shall hold you from your queen."

Then as the priest watched he saw the Indians fling themselves into the water and swim toward the Sea-Maiden. When they neared the great wave it descended with a roar and engulfed the entire tribe. On his deathbed this priest said that this thing had happened because he, himself, was not in a true state of grace and that if a priest would row to the spot where the singing of the Sea-Maiden was still heard and drop some Holy Water into the bay, all the souls at the bottom would be saved, though that priest himself would be immediately swallowed up by the waves. No priest has yet carried this Holy Water to ransom the souls of the Biloxis so the sad music still haunts the bay, rising through the waters on still nights, from the caves where they still worship the Sea-Maiden.

The best known and most widely accepted story of the Singing River is the legend of the Pascagoulas. This legend which is given at length in the History of Jackson County is as follows: The Pascagoula tribe of Indians was at one time strong and powerful but constant wars with the Biloxis and other enemies depleted the tribe until at last only a remnant was left. This remnant led by their loved chief, Altama, at last found itself surrounded by their bitter enemies the Biloxis and in danger of being taken into captivity. To escape this fate the entire tribe joined hands and singing a tribal song waded into the river, reached deep water and were carried, still clinging together and still singing, out into the bay. The souls of these Pascagoulas can still be heard singing from the waters in which they perished.

FROM

Deep'n as It Come

PETE DANIEL

In 1927 the great flood reminded people on both sides of the Mississippi River of their limitations. As Professor Pete Daniel notes, it was the year Lindbergh reached Paris, the year the first talking movie, The Jazz Singer, *came out, the year Babe Ruth hit sixty home runs—and the year that the Army Corps of Engineers proclaimed they could prevent floods. On April 21, at Mound Landing, Mississippi, and at Pendleton, Arkansas, when the torrents of rain backed up all the tributaries and the Ohio River began flowing upstream, the levees broke. Says Daniel, "The contradictions of sorrow and humor, helplessness and bravery, courage and fear, humility and pride, death and salvation, despair and hope, calm and panic—all reveal the human dimension of the flood disaster." In the following account, Daniel, a professor of history and author of* The Shadow of Slavery, *captures the words of the survivors from his careful research in newspapers, magazines, letters, official reports, reminiscences, and speeches (from chapter 2, "Crevasse").*

IN THE VERNACULAR of the people who live along the Mississippi River, a *crevasse* is a break in the levee. That single word carried dread, often panic, for water twenty feet above the land level bursts out across the fields, sweeping all before it. The April 21 crevasse at Mound Landing, Mississippi, about eighteen miles north of Greenville, sent shock waves through the entire area.

When the levee broke early in the morning, men were frantically tossing sandbags on top of it, trying to keep the river harnessed. Many workers were killed when it collapsed; no one will ever know how many. At first the press reported hundreds, but later the figures were reduced; no accurate count could be made, for the confusion was too great. Charlie Williams of Greenville was there directing the high-water fight; he said that the levee "just seemed to move forward as if 100 feet of it was *pushed out* by the river." At that very moment General Alexander G. Paxton was in Greenville, talking on the phone to the levee workers at Mound Landing. " 'We can't hold it much longer,' " the general recalled hearing. "Then followed three words that I shall remember as long as I live—'There she goes.' "[1]

It was as if the flood had struck last week instead of nearly fifty years ago. Cora Lee Campbell sat on her front porch in Greenville, some eighteen miles south of Scott, where she had lived in 1927. "They was working on that levee, and it was real pitiful, and they were working on it with them there sacks, trying to daub 'em and everything. It was on, I think, Thursday morning that I got up, and I walked across that long bridge, and I just did make it back across. See, the Lord just was with me. A lady sent for me to come, Miss Anne, to come over to her home; she had something for me. That was in Scott, over in Scott. I runned over there; by the time I got across that long bridge, that bridge done this-away, parted, right in the middle.

"And so I run and run and run, and when I got home the bells was ringing, the whistles was blowing, and, oh, it was a terrible time. I picked this boy, Roosevelt Campbell, Jr., up on my hip to run, and his teeth was agoing br-br-br-br, thataway, you know, and made it to the levee. And when we made it to the levee, chile, them there bubbles was just boiling, boiling, boiling, boiling. That water was deep'n as it come.

"We stayed on the levee three nights and two days, and we didn't have nowhere to lay down. There was a lot of folks on the levee, my father and this child Roosevelt Campbell, my husband, his father, and all the rest of the other people around us. We made little bitty little houses, just big enough for a child to get in, and I laid down there on a army blanket that I raised this child in and the water just come up on me, and I had to take him and lay him in my breast to keep him dry, from getting chilled. It didn't do me no good. Then, in three days a boat come and it took us to Rosedale, and the boat it like to sunk, oh Lord, it was a time. The boat like to sunk, they was so many peoples on the boat, and then they was some people was so ill and mean till they didn't want to get on the boat."[2]

T. H. "Buck" Pryor of Jonesboro, Arkansas, was on the boat that picked up the refugees at Scott. His recollection, written to Mississippi Educational Television after seeing a recent special program on the flood, adds a significant footnote to the rescue of the Scott refugees. "We went up river and docked at the break at Scott, Miss. There were about 300 people on the Levee. Dr. Douglas [S. W. Douglas] and I were on the upper deck when the Captain lowered the gangplank and we saw him walk up the gangplank to be met by two big men, each with a gun on his hip. We could not hear the conversation but we saw the Captain dejectedly turn and come back to the ship.

"Dr. Douglas picked up his Black Bag and said, 'Follow me'—I did. The Captain told Dr. Douglas that the two big men with guns said that they were not going to let us take those people off the Levee.

"Dr. Douglas brushed the Captain aside, strode up the gangplank and he was then met by these two men with guns on hips. I was right behind him—and *scared*.

"The doctor said—and I hope I can repeat verbatim but it's been a long time ago and you will please excuse the language but am trying to repeat Dr. Douglas—*verbatim*—I think he said—'Apparently you two gentlemanly sons-of-bitches are in charge here and you have told the Captain that we are not going to be permitted to minister to these people—now I come here by authority of the American Red Cross and the God of all creation—if either of you has guts enough to pull the gun you carry please start now or get out of my way and I don't believe either of you has the guts';—those two gun-carrying Mississippi fellows stood aside—we went on the Levee—we found the sick and infirm—we loaded all on the Barges and left those two 'gun-carrying' fellows there all alone."[3]

After the river broke out at Mound Landing, it spread across the Mississippi Delta. The water did not race across the land as one pictures a flood gushing through a mountain valley (the Johnstown flood often comes to mind); rather, it moved at a pace of some fourteen miles a day. Everyone who saw the water and heard it had that image branded in their minds forever, for it had the eeriness of a full eclipse of the sun, unsettling, chilling.

Whether in Mississippi or in other flooded areas, the description varied little. Louise Cowan of Greenville, who kept a journal during the flood, wrote down a planter's impression of the approaching water. "Standing on the veranda of his handsome home he saw the flood approach in the form of a tan colored wall seven feet high, and with a roar as of a mighty wind." East of Greenville in Leland, Edwin Bagley, who was fourteen years old in 1927, recalled the water rolling to Deer Creek, pouring over the bank into the creek, filling it, and creeping onward. "Talk about a distressing sound," he said, "people screaming, dogs barking, and the sound of that water, like a stream of water in a mountain."[4]

At Metcalfe, only four miles out of Greenville, Fred Chaney was already in a boxcar, his home for the duration of the flood. "At nine o'clock we could hear the rustle of waters in the woods a mile North of our box car haven," he wrote in his reminiscences of the flood. "It sounded not unlike the rising rush of the first gust of wind before an oncoming storm and a shiver shot up and down my spine as the rustling noise grew louder and its true significance plumbed the depths of my mind. Before I reached the railroad track the water was swirling around my feet! From somewhere out of the night rose the piercing wail of a negro woman's hysterical scream."[5]

In Greenville, General Paxton remembered April 21 vividly. "It was about as wild a day as I have experienced in all my life," and that included three wars. "I have never seen anything equal to it. The fire whistle was blowing repeatedly and people were swarming down the streets in throngs. Pandemonium broke out everywhere." Across the river in Arkansas City, Grady F. Jones reported a similar experience. "All the cattle was lowing, all the dogs barking, every rooster crowing, babies crying, women screaming and all hurrying to the high places."[6]

Greenville residents knew the flood was on its way, but they hoped that the protection levee around the town would keep the water out. At the same time they feared another break in the main levee along the river. It was the tension of not knowing if the protection levee or the main levee would hold, not knowing exactly how or at what time the water would reach town, that made the night of April 21 so tense in Greenville.

NOTES

[1] Alexander Gallatin Paxton, *Three Wars and a Flood* (n.p., n.d.), p. 24; copy in Mississippi Levee Commissioners Office, Greenville.

[2] Interview with Cora Lee Campbell, Greenville, May 17, 1975.

[3] T. H. "Buck" Pryor to Mississippi Educational Television, Apr. 25, 1974; in possession of Henry Kline II, Mississippi Educational Television Network, Jackson.

[4] Louise Henry Cowan, "Overflow in Greenville, 1927," Louise Henry Cowan Papers, William Alexander Percy Library, Greenville; interview with Edwin Bagley, Greenville, May 21, 1975.

[5] Fred Chaney, "A Refugee's Story," Fred Chaney Papers, Mississippi Department of Archives and History, Jackson.

[6] Paxton, *Three Wars*, p. 24; Camden (Ark.) *Evening News,* May 2, 1927.

On the Gulf

ELIZABETH SPENCER

*Elizabeth Spencer was born in Carrollton, Mississippi, in 1921. She is
the author of such diverse books as* Light in the Piazza, *set in Italy,*
The Voice at the Back Door, *about race relations in Mississippi, and,
more recently,* The Night Travelers, *which takes place in North Carolina. On being asked about her life in Montreal, Canada, where she and
her English husband, John Rusher, lived for many years, Spencer said,
"You can't really know what it is to be southern unless you know what
it is not to be southern." The following is from her introduction to* On
the Gulf, *"An Opening to the Sea." The book is illustrated with work
by Mississippi artist Walter Anderson. Through rich sensory detail, Spencer evokes the excitement of a trip to the Mississippi Gulf Coast.*

IF I COULD HAVE one part of the world back the way it used to
be, I would not choose Dresden before the fire bombing, Rome before
Nero, or London before the blitz. I would not resurrect Babylon, Car-
thage or San Francisco. Let the leaning tower lean and the hanging
gardens hang. I want the Mississippi Gulf Coast back as it was before
Hurricane Camille.

All through my childhood and youth, north of Jackson, up in the
hills, one happy phrase comes down intact: "the coast." *They've just been
to the coast . . . they're going to the coast next week . . . they're fishing at the
coast . . . they own a house at the coast . . . let's go to the coast. . . . When? For
spring holidays? next week? . . . Now!*

What was magical about it? In the days I speak of, it did not have a
decent beach. Strictly speaking, it was not even a sea coast. The islands
that stood out in the Gulf—Horn Island, Ship Island, Cat Island and
the rest—took the Gulf surf on their sandy shores: what we called "the
coast" was left with a tide you could measure in inches, and a gradual
silted sloping sea bottom, shallow enough to wade out in for half a mile
without getting wet above the waist. A concrete sea wall extended for
miles along the beach drive, shielding the road and houses and towns
it ran past from high water that storms might bring, also keeping the
shore line regular. Compared to the real beaches of Southern California, or Florida, or the Caribbean islands, all this might seem not much
to brag about: what was there beside the sea wall, the drive along it, the

palms and old lighthouses, the spacious mansions looking out on the water, with their deep porches and outdoor stairways, their green lattice work, their moss hung oaks and sheltered gardens, the crunch of oyster gravelling side roads and parking lots . . . why was this so grand?

Well, it wasn't "grand," let that be admitted. Natchez was grand. New Orleans had its seductive charms securely placed in a rich Creole history. Still, nothing gave Mississippians quite the feeling of our own Gulf Coast.

We came down to it driving through plain little towns, some pretty, some not, went south of Jackson through Hattiesburg. The names come back: Mendenhall, Magee, Mount Olive, Collins, Wiggins, Perkinston. Somewhere in there was D'Lo, curiously pronounced Dee-Lo. In all of these, people of an Anglo-Saxon sameness in names and in admirable qualities, were pursuing life patterns thought out so long ago they could never be questioned since. A day or two to piece the relationships together and anyone from Carrollton or Winona or Pickens or Vaiden could pick up the same routine of life there as in the ancestral home.

But soon there was the thrilling smell of salt on the breeze increasing until suddenly there was Gulfport and straight ahead the harbor with its big ships at rest and to either side the long arms of the beach drive stretching east to Biloxi, west to Pass Christian and Bay St. Louis. There were names foreign to our ears, the mystery of these almost foreign places, easy in their openness, leaning toward the flat blue water, serene beneath the great floating clouds. That first thin breath of sea air had spread to a whole atmosphere. There was no place where it wasn't.

What to do in a car crowded with friends on holiday from school but drive straight to the water's edge and sit there breathless, not knowing which way to go first, but ready to discover.

I must have come there first with girls from around home, or friends from college in Jackson. Someone would have borrowed the family car. Occasions blur into one long sighing memory of live oaks green the year round, and the pillared white houses the trees sheltered, set along the sweep of beach drive, boxes of salt water taffy to chew on, and little screened restaurants advertising SHRIMP! ALL YOU CAN EAT FOR $1. Gumbo, too, "made fresh every day." Jax beer. Prohibition lingered for a long time inland, but the coast never paid it much attention. Names alone would tell you that they wouldn't. French and Spanish were here from the first, but Poles and Yugoslavs and Czechs had come long ago to work in the fishing industries, while the French traded and the Spanish built ships. But we wouldn't have thought of looking up their history. It was the feeling those names breathed that stirred us: Ladnier, Saucier, Legendre, Christovich, Benachi, Lameuse, Lopez, Toledano. Religion here was foreign, too: churches like Our Lady of the Gulf stood proclaiming it, with a statue of the Virgin in the wide paved entrance court, and a bare but graceful façade, facing boldly out to sea. Those who ran the restaurants, and went out in the shrimp boats, worshipped here, as did no doubt the men who waded the shallow water at night with flambeaux blazing, spears ready for flounder, and the women, too, who sat talking through the long afternoons on latticed porches. We learned that annually at Biloxi, before the shrimp boats go out to their deep sea fishing grounds, an outdoor mass is held to bless the fleet. It is a great occasion, and one of general rejoicing. These were ancient ways. Above, the white clouds mounted high, the gulls on broad white wings soared and tacked, tilting into the wind. The pelicans stroked toward land in flawless formation. Mid-afternoon in spring. Intense heat had not yet taken over, but a stillness came on, a sense of absolute suspension. The camellias were long finished, the azaleas, lingering, but past their height. Magnolia blooms starred dark green branches. Jasmine breathed in the back gardens. The moss hung breezeless. Time stood still.

We were used to staying at the Edgewater Gulf, a wonderful hotel between Gulfport and Biloxi. Its grounds were ample. I remember a cool lobby of gently turning ceiling fans, plants in white recesses, and rooms designed each with a long entrance passage facing on the sea, drawing a constant breeze through latticed doors. Parting admonitions—"Don't talk to strangers," "Be careful where you swim," "Be sure to call Sally the minute you get there"—may have sounded in our ears for a while on the way down, but vanished after Gulfport. Yet I cannot recall any serious mischief we ever got ourselves into.

Mosquito Blues

DOROTHY SHAWHAN

Born in Tupelo and reared in Verona, Mississippi, Dorothy Shawhan received her B. A. degree from Mississippi University for Women, an M. A. degree from Louisiana State University, and an M. F. A. degree from George Mason University. A professor of English and chair of the Division of Languages and Literature at Delta State University, Shawhan published her first novel, Lizzie, *in 1995. The following essay, originally published in* Delta Scene *magazine in 1983, traces the history and development of the winged insect of the Culicidae family, better known as the mosquito. Using references ranging from the Oxford English Dictionary to Faulkner, Shawhan presents an unrelenting aspect of Mississippi's terrain.*

HAWAII HAS tarantulas, Texas has rattlers, Florida alligators, Minnesota black flies, and even Eden had a snake. You're whistling Dixie if you don't admit that in the Delta we have our own special reason to sing the blues—the mosquito.

In almost any Delta scene the mosquito plays a key role. I've seen them change a genteel garden party into a leg-slapping, foot-stomping, arm-waving blood bath; I've heard a single mosquito buzz sleeping households into hysterics in the middle of the night; I've watched neighbors virtually disappear from the community because a mosquito swarm took up right outside the kitchen door.

Ask any Deltan the disadvantages in living here, and chances are 100 to 1 that a mosquito will turn up somewhere in the answer. But if you're planning to move to get away from them, good luck. The only place on planet Earth from which mosquitos haven't been reported is the Antarctic (and that could be because there's nobody there to report). Even the North Pole has a mosquito problem. Not surprising when you consider the 2,600 species loose in the world, all of which I believe are represented in the Delta, or might as well be.

Oldtimers say mosquitoes weren't always this bad around the Delta. The rice, they say, the rice fields are bringing them in like flies. Suggest that to a farmer, though, and they'll act like you've attacked Mom, apple pie, and Chevrolet. It's running water in those rice fields, they say, and mosquitoes won't breed in fresh running water.

Well, I don't know, but mosquitoes aren't famous for being choicy about their breeding places. They can breed in fresh or salt water (some need only seven days from egg to adult). In Trinidad they breed in bromeliads. They've been found flourishing in steamy hot alkaline pools around a volcano in Uganda and in tanks of hydrochloric acid in India. Compared to those, a Delta rice field must be paradise.

Mosquitoes will bite anything that moves almost—not just people but dogs, cattle, birds, even reptiles. But only the female bites; she needs the blood to mature her eggs and make more mosquitoes. Despite their bloodthirsty reputations, mosquitoes are allegedly vegetarians who feed on nectar and plant juices, though I've never seen them do it.

If you're a person mosquitoes love to bite, you may or may not want to know it's because of your body odor. Somehow the way you smell turns them on. Experts say that mosquitoes will have as hosts only those who smell right.

While most of what mosquitoes dispense in the Delta is aggravation, time was when they wiped out whole populations of towns, devastated herds, and brought economic ruin. Through history mosquitoes have been at the center of medical, social, political, and economic issues all over the world. They spread such plagues as yellow fever, encephalitis, malaria, and heart worms for dogs. Obviously with a record like that, there ought to be a law against them and, as it turns out, there is.

Mosquitoes have been against the law in this country for years. Mississippi's mosquito abatement laws go back to 1928, but our mosquitoes haven't got the word yet. For those who want to keep up with the latest in legislation, the National Mosquito Control Association puts out an official publication called *Mosquito News.*

Seems we've tried almost every kind of control—getting rid of the breeding places, invoking the help of the dragonfly, mosquito fish, and purple martin, and even releasing genetically incompatible males. In Cleveland we have the mosquito truck, which comes trailing streams of insecticide about 6 p.m. each summer evening. I'm sure the mosquito truck means well, but I learned, after near asphyxiation, not to have the attic fan on when it passed by.

The award for the best title of a mosquito publication goes to an Oakland, California, public information pamphlet entitled *Mosquitoes Are Unnecessary* (kind of like evil). One of this pamphlet's hottest tips is that goldfish eat mosquito eggs and larva and so are good to have around, but that goldfish will *not* leap in the air and take the mosquito on the wing. Undoubtedly.

Despite the fact that mosquitoes are illegal, they continue to bite, and worse yet to buzz. If you're like me, you'd rather be bitten than buzzed. I wouldn't mind being bitten so much if mosquitoes could just do it quietly. I can snooze through a bite, but not that terrible hum that signals the end of a good night's sleep.

It may comfort you to know that both males and females hum, so everything that buzzes may not bite. The sound is made by high wing beat frequency. The female's humming is slightly lower than the male's; she uses it to attract him.

According to a West African folk tale, that whole buzzing business began years ago when a mosquito bored an iguana half crazy with a tale about a farmer digging sweet potatoes that were as big as she (the mosquito). The iguana said he didn't have to listen to that nonsense, stuck a stick in each ear, and slithered off through the reeds.

Consequently the iguana didn't hear the python speak to him, the python took offense, decided there was a plot, and set off a chain of events that infected all of the creatures in the jungle with a bad case of paranoia.

Finally jungle life reached such a state of discord that the King of the Beasts investigated and traced the trouble back to the mosquito. But the mosquito hid out and was never brought to justice. She still suffers from a guilty conscience, though, and is always whining in people's ears to ask if everyone is still angry.

You bet they are. She should know that by now.

Another version of the buzz is in a tale by Robert Benchley about how a mosquito named Lillian explains her technique to Mother Nature. According to Lillian, mosquitoes project their voices to make their victims think they're right there about to pounce, when actually they're clear across the room. In the mosquito code, it's not enough to draw blood; the challenge is to keep the victim up half the night tormenting him. Hearing the projected buzz, the victim makes futile attempts to swat the mosquito, goes back to bed, hears it again, gets up. You know the story. Finally the mosquito zeroes in, hums in one ear, the victim swats, the mosquito circles around and bites the poor wretch's neck on the other side.

A mosquito's bite smarts no matter what we call it, and the names we usually call it are mostly unprintable. But according to the Oxford English Dictionary (OED), the word *mosquito* came into our language from the Spanish and is a dimunitive of the word *mosca*, meaning *fly*. A little fly. The earliest mention of the word as recorded in the OED is in M. Phillips, *Hakluyt's Voyage*, 1589:

> We were also oftentimes greatly annoyed with a kinde of flie . . . The Spanyards called them Musketos.

And later in G. Percy, *Purchas His Pilgrim* (1625):

> Their bodies are all painted red to keepe away the biting of Muscetos.

Maybe they were onto something we need to find out about.

The New World harbored the pests too. In records of Lewis and Clark's expedition in Missouri (1814):

> The mosquitoes have been so troublesome that it was impossible even to write without the assistance of a mosquito bier (net).

I know how that is.

The mosquito has become such a part of the folklore in the South that we tend to think of it as peculiarly our own institution. B.A. Botkin in a book called *Southern Folklore* has recorded a number of mosquito tales.

As one might expect, Texas has produced some of the biggest mosquitoes ever. Houstonians claim that their mosquitoes wear 45-inch undershirts. In Galveston town fathers include mosquitoes in the cow ordinance, while other Texans say the truth is that mosquitoes on the Texas coast are rarely bigger than an ordinary mocking bird.

Mississippi's mosquitoes are no slouches either. Ruth Bass of Hazlehurst put together some lore about them back in 1938. In one story an unfortunate traveler through the state hitched his horse by the side of a creek to go look for a ford, and when he came back the mosquitoes had "et up his horse, chawed up his saddle, and was a-pitchin' that horse's shoes to see who'd get the bridle."

An even worse predicament was that of Mississippian Bill Jenkins, who woke up one night to find himself being carried through the air by two mosquitoes. One asked the other if they should eat Bill there or hide him in the swamp for later. The other mosquito replied, "I speck we better eat him here. If we take him down to that swamp some of them big skeeters is liable to take him away from us."

From Louisiana comes this proverb in Creole dialect: *Maringouin perdi so temps quand li pique caiman.* (The mosquito loses his time when he tries to sting the alligator.)

Buzz off, in other words.

One popular belief in Southern folklore is that holding your breath while a mosquito bites you makes her unable to withdraw her bill. Then you can swat her good. Personally, I'd rather swat *before* she starts to bite.

Another favorite idea is that mosquitoes don't bite during an eclipse. My brother-in-law stood out in a mosquito swarm at 2 a.m. during the last eclipse and claimed they didn't bite him. They never do, though. Body odor.

Tall tales about the mosquito are not relegated to historical folklore; they're being created daily all around us. For example, I have a student who claims his aunt died of mosquito inhalation in her own front yard last summer.

Another student tells me that the nature of mosquitoes has changed drastically down around Anguilla. Seems they're larger than ever, black, and have yellow stripes down their backs.

Mosquitoes, one of William Faulkner's early novels, is considered a failure by the critics, and it's no wonder with a title like that. In the book Faulkner uses the mosquito as a metaphor for adults who lead meaningless lives, whose talk drones on and on, but who never really say or do anything. You know the kind.

In his epigraph to the book, Faulkner describes mosquitoes (and his characters) as "little and young and trusting" in the "sweet young spring" ("you could kill them sometimes"). But in August "they were bigger, vicious, ubiquitous as undertakers, cunning as pawnbrokers, confident and unavoidable as politicians." Isn't that the truth.

Another instance of the mosquito as controlling metaphor is in J.F. Powers short story "The Valiant Woman." Here a gentle priest, harassed for years by a domineering housekeeper, is as ineffective in getting rid of her as he is in swatting mosquitoes. In the final scene, after failing once again to free himself from the housekeeper's tyranny, he breaks a statue of St. Joseph as he swats madly at a mosquito with a rolled magazine. "What is it, Father? Are you hurt?" the housekeeper shouts outside his door.

"Mosquitoes, damn it! And only the female bites!"

"Shame on you, Father. She needs the blood for her eggs."

In a frenzy of frustration, Father throws his magazine and lunges at the mosquito with his bare hands. Is there a Deltan alive who can't identify with that scene?

When my world literature students were studying fables (Aesop, de la Fontaine), I asked them to write a fable themselves, a Delta fable creating characters from animals in the Delta to illustrate a moral. The mosquito was often the antagonist. In "The Frog and the Alligator," the writer illustrates how even the worst of enemies can become the best of friends. Al the Alligator's favorite food was frog legs until one day he was attacked by a huge mob of mosquitoes (who didn't know the Creole proverb). Fred the Frog bargained with Al saying he would eat the mosquitoes if Al would promise not to eat him and to protect him from the other gators. The arrangement worked and soon spread to the rest of the swamp where everybody, except the mosquitoes, lived happily ever after.

One of my colleagues has such a thing about mosquitoes that he rarely gets out of the house from April to October. Festoons of insect strips swing from the ceiling of his apartment like crepe paper at the junior prom. He maintains that he gets bites just *thinking* about mosquitoes and that, in fact, his worst welts are caused by mosquitoes that bite his back and that he never sees. Nobody else can see them either, he says, which fact leads him to conclude that these particular backbiters are, well, invisible. Sure they are, Bill, sure they are.

Bill also insists that if you flex your arm muscle at the exact moment that a mosquito bites your arm vein, you can explode the insect— "splatter the little sucker all over the place." (Note, though, that this works only with visible mosquitoes.)

Laying all jokes and foolishness aside, as my grandmother often said but never did, the feeling that a mosquito is sneaking up behind you to zap you on the back seems to be a common one in the Delta. Hence the furtive over-the-shoulder glances, the ghostly mosquito lights that fry in the night, the spray cans, the backs against the wall.

In our family there's nothing that sparks more intense speculation on the nature of God and man than the mosquito. "Why did God make mosquitoes?" my eight-year-old son asked as soon as we moved to the Delta, and he's wrestled with the question ever since. My three-year-old niece was heard to declare, as she battled a swarm in her sandbox, that she was mad at God because he made mosquitoes and that God is mean. And my five-year-old nephew advanced a cynical and rather terrifying hypothesis about the human race when he suggested that perhaps God made people so mosquitoes would have something to bite.

My father sometimes indirectly uses the mosquito as an example of HOW IT IS: The man who discovered that the mosquito was the carrier of yellow fever didn't get anything, but the man who invented the slot machine made millions.

Do mosquitoes build character? Are we better persons in the Delta as a result of our suffering? Can anything good come of the mosquito? Hard questions like these have yet to be resolved by native philosophers.

There are incurable optimists who try to find good even in the mosquito. They point to the food chain and the worthy birds, etc. who feed on them. They talk about mosquitoes as forces for democracy, levelers who bite people irrespective of economic and social station.

I remain unconvinced. Last summer, however, I did witness a good example of making the best of it. We were having a party in my sister's backyard when we were driven inside by, you guessed it, thousands of mosquitoes. In the process of getting in the house with all the children, we let a good number of the mosquitoes come with us.

My brother-in-law, the mosquito proof one, saw at once an opportunity to clear the house of mosquitoes and to keep the children occupied. He offered a 5-cent bounty for every dead mosquito body presented him.

Oh, the carnage that followed. The children loved the game and became increasingly competitive as the mosquitoes dwindled. "This is really primitive," one mother said to me over the uproar. "Sort of like *Lord of the Flies.*" In the heat of the competition, one young entrepreneur was caught bringing the same carcass over and over.

Even the adults got in the spirit of the thing. In the kitchen, one of Cleveland's leading citizens stood on a chair with the flyswatter, going after them. "I'm not paying you, Jim," my brother-in-law barked in alarm, seeing how handily he dispatched mosquitoes.

"I just hate the little bastards," Jim answered, voice full of emotion.

"I understand," I said, spraying Off on his ankle where three mosquitoes were chowing down.

Jim says his mother-in-law gave him a mosquito gun for his birthday. Shoot 'em, she advised. That notion appeals to me. Think of it, the mosquito might become our greatest natural resource. A whole new sport for the Delta, with obvious economic benefits. And mosquito hunters might soon free our land from its plague. Only the sissies would be left killing big things like ducks and deers. It'd take real men to shoot a mosquito at 200 yards.

PART THREE

Conflict

A Lost Heroine
of the Confederacy

B E L L E   E D M O N D S O N

Born in Pontotoc, Mississippi, in 1840, Isabella Buchanan Edmondson spent most of her formative years in Holly Springs. The following excerpts from her diaries (from the chapter "Smuggling through the Lines") reveal a little-known aspect of the Civil War—the fact that women as well as men risked their lives daily. While her two brothers were off fighting, Belle Edmondson smuggled goods under her hoop skirt to Confederate soldiers in Memphis and gathered valuable information for the troops. Throughout her diaries, she creates ironic pictures, such as her endless sewing while Yankee troops camped nearby, or her patient teaching of reading to her black servant while her brothers fought to preserve slavery. Nearly arrested in 1864 for her scouting activities, she found refuge at Waverley Plantation near West Point in Clay County (as did Caroline Seabury, whose account is also reprinted in this volume). Owned by Col. George Hampton Young, Waverley was a popular social center and, during the Civil War, it became a gathering place for Confederate leaders and sympathizers. Loretta and William Galbraith, editors of A Lost Heroine of the Confederacy, *found Edmondson's diaries at Waverley in the early 1970s.*

M O N D A Y 7 The quiet of our life was disturbed to day, by the arrival of 150 Yankees—only two came to the house. We gave them their dinner. Mr Wilson and Decatur were down in the Orchard. Helen sent for them to come and capture the Yanks, we saw the rest coming & Tate and I ran to tell them it was too great a risk. Mr W. and D. were nearly to the gate; I was never so excited. We turned them in time, the two Yanks passed while we were standing there. Mr W. and D. came to the house and spent some time with us, when Mr W. followed the Yankees. They returned about 9 o'c, on their way to Memphis. D. and Cousin F. had a run again, with the horses, but fortunately none of them came in. I have not done any work today, have suffered death with my spine. Tate and Helen at work in my room all day. I sat in Tate's room until bed time. Beulah, Laura and

Tip all in time. I amused myself reading Artemus Ward's book. We did not hear what the Yanks went for. We heard from Eddie & the boys, all safe. One of Henderson's scouts arrived. . . .

MARCH 16 Went up Street directly after Breakfast to finish a little job I forgot on yesterday. At one o'clock Mrs Fackler, Mrs Kirk & I began to fix my articles for smugling. We made a balmoral of the Gray cloth for uniforms, pin'd the Hats to the inside of my hoops, tied the boots with a strong list, letting them fall directly in front, the cloth having monopolized the back & the Hats the side. All my buttons, brass buttons, Money &c in my bosom. Left at 2 o'clock to meet Anna at Mr Barbiere's—started to walk, impossible that, hailed a hack—rather suspicious of it, afraid of small-pox. Weight of contrabands ruled—jumped in with orders for a hurried drive to Cor Main & Vance. Arrived, found Anna not ready had to wait for her until 5 o'clock, very impatient started at last. Arrived at Pickets, no trouble at all—although I suffered horibly in anticipation of trouble. Arrived at home at dusk, found Mr Wilson & Harbert, gave them late papers, and all news. Mrs Harbert here to meet her Bro, bro't Mr Wilson a letter from Home in Ky. Worn out. 8 yds Gray cloth, 2 Hats, 1 pr Boots, 1 doz. Buttons, letters &c, 2 cords, 8 tassels. Laura, Beulah & Tippie Dora all in.

WEDNESDAY 23 Tate & I went to Memphis this morning bright & early. Stoped at Mrs. Aperson's first, from there to Cousin Frazor['s home]. Tate met me at Mrs Worsham's room, we then went up street, walked until three o'clock, attended to all affairs entrusted to our care, ready to leave at half past three. All of the Yankee Cavalry moving, destination not known—could hear no particulars. Think they are going after Forrest, who we think is on his way to Kentucky. The Yankees are evidently on a great fright about something. God grant they may be defeated in all their undertakings. We came through white Pickets. I think we will not try them again—the Negroes are ten times more lenient. We came by Wash Taylor's, got two hats for Soldiers. Came through Yankee camp, if the Lord forgive me, I will never do it again. Yankee Soldier drove our horse in Nonconnah for us—seemed to be a gentleman for which we were very grateful. Found Mr Harbert awaiting our report. Mr John & Henry Nelson & Mr Harbert took tea with us. Jim & Mr Pugh completed the list for a nice Rebel meeting. Brought a great deal through the lines this eve—Yankee Pickets took our papers.

THURSDAY 24 I slept very late this morning—had breakfast in my room. I would rather have slept than have the choicest dishes from old Schwab's. Ready at last, arrived in the Parlor found Jim & Mr Pugh with the girls having a nice time. Spent the morning fixing my old Bombazine dress. Enjoyed my dinner finely. Did not stay in the Parlor very long after dinner, came to my room and prepared for a nice evening siesta with London Papers for companions. Soon fell into the arms of Morpheus, slept soundly but have had no spirit since awakening. Joanna got back from Memphis bringing Mammy to see Prince. Anna Nelson will ride her Bro's horse, through the lines to morrow. Mr Harbert came early this eve. I left them all in the Parlor—Father allows them to sit up late as he is reading the Papers. I got tired and came to my room but found it very cheerless, no fire, smoking. Laura, Beulah & Tip all asleep. Oh I am so lonely. I feel a presentiment something good is going to turn up for the Confederacy. God bless my dear Bros and bring them safe home again.

MONDAY 18 Well I expect our days of peace and quiet are over, another squad of Yanks passed. Four stoped here, staid until after dinner and went on back to Memphis. All of them except one, seemed to be a gentleman, this one was a black abolitionist, oh! how I heartily despise him. I promised to make a Confederate Flag for one of them, Mr Greer, and he promised he would not reenlist. So I have spent the evening making one, and will give it next time he comes. . . .

THURSDAY 14 Hal, Theresa and I got up very early and started for the Country, after running around first on one road and then another we finally arrived at Waverly just 7 miles above Columbus,[1] although we had traveled ten or twelve miles. We crossed the Tombigbee, rode up to Mr Young's when he came out and insisted on our getting out, until he would send and try to find out where Bro lived, failed however, but we spent the day. Fate, how strange, yet how delightful. They are a very wealthy family, a real Southern Mansion. His daughters are very accomplished, and Miss Lou is a beautiful girl. Such delightful Music, and an elegant dinner, our first peaches and Milk. We went to the Pond late this evening, to try to learn to swim. Hal would not venture, Theresa and I tried it. I did not have any confidence in myself therefore did not make much improvement. Theresa was more successful. We had a delightful drive home, found Mamie well, and good news from Forrest.

NOTES
[1] The plantation and small community that grew up around it were named for the Waverley novels of Sir Walter Scott. The name is spelled variously as Waverly and Waver-

ley. Colonel Young used the latter spelling in an 1857 letter to his daughter Lucy, while an 1856 map of Mississippi used the former version. Examples of both spellings occur in contemporary accounts. Except when quoting from sources that use the Waverly rendition, as Belle does, all references in these notes will adhere to the Waverley spelling. George Young to Lucy Young, 4 Sept. 1857; A New Map of Mississippi (Philadelphia: Desilver, 1857), Waverley Collection, MSUS, cited hereafter as WC.

Civil War Diary: 1861–1863

C Y R U S F. B O Y D

*At the age of twenty-four, Cyrus Boyd enlisted in the Fifteenth Iowa In-
fantry, serving as orderly sergeant until he accepted a commission as first
lieutenant. After he returned home to Iowa, Boyd composed his reminiscences of the Civil War based on the diary he had kept on the battlefield.
Although he was a Union soldier, his account is remarkably similar to
those written by Confederates. In his preface, Boyd compared his situation
to a spoke "in a great wheel moved by the motion of of some great invisible
power and not permitted to know why or wherefore he is expected to perform his part in the great work." The selections here are from part 3,
"Iuka to Lafayette, Tennessee; The Battle of Corinth."*

[Iuka, Mississippi]
Sept 22nd [1862]   Weather hot. . . . The green-flies are so thick here
that the earth can scarcely be seen in many spots and they hang in the
bushes like bees in swarming time

Sept 29th   Since the 22d nothing of note has transpired   The
weather continues hot   With one or two others I went to look at the
battle-field   Where the enemy cut through our lines there has been
most severe fighting   I have never seen before evidence of such a desperate contest on a small piece of ground   The fight was for the possession of an field battery and was on the crest of a hill in the timber   The
trees around are almost torn to kindling wood by the dreadful fire of
the Artillery and Musketry.   25 dead horses lay close together and
about 40 men belonging to the 5th Iowa Inft buried in *one grave*
here.   Besides numerous other graves scattered all through the
woods   Many of the 17th Iowa were killed   Saw many of the enemies
dead lying around not more than half covered   The ground in many
places was *white* as snow with *creeping worms*   The darkness of the forest
and the terrible mortality made it one of the most *horrible* places I was
ever in   Then the *silence* was oppressive   Not a sound could be heard
except once in a while the chirp of some lonely bird in the deep forest   To think of our poor fellows left to sleep in that dark wood   (But
one must not think of such things) . . .

Forced march to Corinth Mississippi

Oct 1st   We were called up at 11 oclock last night and ordered to be ready to march immediately   Got ready but did not start until day-light   Came 20 miles to-day and within 6 miles of Corinth   Cathcart received his commission yesterday and to-day took his place in the Company as 2d Lieut   Our men set fire to all the houses along the line of march to-day   I think this is wrong and should [be] stoped at once

Oct 2d   Arrived in Corinth about 10 o'clock. Went two miles west of town and camped. . . . Corinth is well fortified now and is surrounded by forts and abatis or fallen timber along all the roads.

Battle of Corinth Miss

Oct 3d   At break of day we were called up by the drums and fell into Companies thinking that the weather was hot we were going out to drill before breakfast as had been our habit in hot weather   With the whole Brigade we marched North about one mile through the woods.   Were arranged in line of battle and stacked arms and while here a detail went back to camp and brought up the breakfast   About 9 oclock rumor came that Price and Van Dorn were marching on Corinth and we should perhaps have a fight   But few believed the story.   By 10 o'clock the sound of artillery and musketry could be heard to the west about as far away as Chewalla   The noise of the guns became nearer and by 1 o'clock we could see masses of the enemy marching along the Memphis and Charleston Railroad to the west   The troops in front of us kept falling back and finaly took position in line to our right   The 11th and 13th [Iowa] were posted a little way behind us as a Reserve

We occupied a naked high ridge with nothing to protect us from the fire of the enemy   About 2 oclock we could see them advancing toward our position in line of battle   There were three distinct lines one be-hind the other and all advancing in the most deliberate manner at *bayo-nets fixed*   We could hear the commands of the Rebel Officers distinctly, but we were cautioned "not to fire until we received orders to open"   Genl Crocker and Lieut Col Belknap rode along the line and urged no man to fire until the order was given

Our men got upon one knee and had guns all cocked and ready when the front Regiments of the enemy took deliberate aim at us and the whole line fired into us and we heard the Rebel shout and *yell*   Then somebody commenced firing and we shot away in the smoke not knowing exactly where to aim as the enemy were in lower ground than we   But their first volley laid out many a man for us   Every one now took to a tree or some place to protect himself   The Rebs soon

closed upon us and came on with countless numbers   They swarmed
around on our left and fired from behind trees and logs and kept pressing forward   Our ranks became much confused and the regiments
held as a Reserve fell back toward our Camp without helping us any

The battle raged fiercely for a time and men fell in great numbers   Middlesworth the 1st Corporal in our company stood at my left
hand and a ball struck him in the abdomen and he fell with a groan—
Corp Heatley fell shot through the head and Lieut Cathcart fell dead
at almost the first fire   He had on his sword and uniform   Several of
our Company were wounded and the enemy closing in so rapidly the
whole Regiment began to fall back not having even time to pick up the
wounded but left them to their *fate*   Just as the Regt began to break
Charley Vinton came staggering along by me and asked some fellow
who passed him to help him   The man did not stop or take any notice
whatever of him and I took Charley by the arm and assisted him for
some distance   He was wounded not severely in the head but the blood
covered him all over and he looked like one mortally wounded   I left
him with a Surgeon who was trying to get some other wounded men to
an ambulance

To our left I could now see the Rebs running from tree to tree and
firing rapidly while our men were doing the same but falling back
toward the Camp   The tents had been lowered to the ground and the
volleys of bullets did not hurt them   I could see the Rebs tearing the
Sutlers tents away and going for the goods   I fired nine or ten rounds
all told and by this time everything was on the *retreat* toward Corinth
and the fireing had almost ceased in the woods   We were outside the
abatis and all the road leading in toward Corinth were crowded with
men hurrying toward the town   When we reached the timber inside
the abatis it was almost sun-down   Here we formed another line of
battle and under cover of Fort Williams   The men kept straggling in
for an hour and some did not come in at all   Sam Roberts, Henry
Hooten and Clark were missing and must have been taken prisoners   Here we lie on our arms for the night under a clear sky

Oct 4th   The enemy could be heard all night bringing up his artillery
and the rolling of wheels and the commands of the officers could be
distinctly heard   A little before daylight a Rebel shell came from a gun
in the edge of the wood and went over into the town—another soon
followed and soon the cannonade opened in good earnest   Our Fort
opened on a Rebel battery and soon silenced its fire   Several shells
came over to wake us up and a number of men in the 11th Iowa just in
rear of us were wounded.

Fort Williams contains 5, 34 and 64 pounders and she put some heavy shells over into the woods which must have made havoc among the enemy   We were warned to lie close to the ground and look out for a *charge*   Fort Robinette on our right and distant about 400 yards kept up a heavy fire upon the woods in front the enemy answering occasionally

About 10 o'clock a heavy roll of musketry was heard to the North and looking over in front of Robinette we could see thousands of gray uniforms swarming from the woods and climbing over the fallen timber   Every one came as best he could toward the works   The cannon at Robinette poured charge after charge into their ranks but they faltered not and on they came and soon reached the work[s]   The gunners stood to their pieces and many of them *fell there*   A few ran back to the rear where the Infantry lay about 200 yards from the fort.   The "Stars and bars" floated over Robinette but only for a brief time of a few seconds.   The Infantry rose from their lair and with fixed and glistening bayonets and one discharge from their muskets rushed on the victorious legions [and] with a *cheer* killed or captured all that were left   No sooner had the smoke cleared away than the second assaulting force emerged from the woods and bore down on Robinette with the most *terrific yells*   The guns from the fort loaded with grape and canister mowed them down by hundreds   But when the advance had almost reached the fort the gunners this time abandoned their pieces and ran back to the Infantry.   The Rebs headed by an officer who had come up a winding road on horseback now reached the redoubt and began climbing over its walls and some ran around the embankment and got possession of the guns and had them *turned* on our men when a long *blue* line of uniforms could be seen rising out of the grass and bushes and with a *cheer* rushed on the victorious enemy   Muskets were clubbed and many were killed with the bayonet   The ranks of the rebels melted like snow and most of them stood their ground and died in and around the little fort

It was a bloody contest and we could see men using their bayonets like pitch forks, and thrusting each other through   How glorious the old flag looked as it again floated over the works in the smoke and breath of battle

Finaly those of the enemy who did not fall or surrender started for the woods across the abatis or by the meandering roads for the shelter of the timber   It was every fellow for himself and the "devil take the hindmost"   No description is adequate to picture the gauntlet of death that these fugitives ran.   Very few reached the timber *alive*   Robinette belched forth her fearful burden of shell and grape in their rear and our fort threw in a flanking fire of heavy shell while a field battery between us and Robinette raked the bal[ance] of the ground and the Infantry poured after them a deadly rain of musket balls

With no guns and coats and hats gone I saw a scattering few reach the timber and escape from the "jaws of death"   Although they are enemies of our government and our flag I could not help but *pity* these poor fellows who thus went into *certain* and *sure destruction* here   When the smoke had cleared away we learned that the enemy had fled in confusion   They had been *cut to pieces* in the most intense meaning of that term.   Such bravery has never been excelled on any field as the useless assaults on Robinette   The prisoners tell us that Van Dorn commanded and that he was *drunk* and ordered his men to drink whiskey and *gun powder* and then ordered them to take the works at any cost *however great*

In front of Robinette lie hundreds of dead.   126 dead men lie within 40 feet of the fort.   Most of them are in the ditch surrounding   One dead man lies just on the slope of the work stiff in death with a hammer in one hand and a lot of *rat tail files* in the other   His mission had been to *spike the cannon*   They are so tightly gripped that the fingers can scarcely be opened   Several others I saw with their muskets *gripped* in their dead hands as tight as a vise could hold   Thus they perished with the most unearthly look on their dying faces   Col Rogers of a Texas Regt who led the charge lies dead with his slain horse within a few feet of the fort and his Adjt only a few yards from him   All around them were heaps of slain—principaly Texas and Arkansas men

Price, Van Dorn, Villepique and all the transmissipi troops were here and it was one last deperate effort to retrieve their losses in the Missippi Valley   But this is the worst set back they have met. . . .

Have orders to be ready to march at daylight tomorrow morning   Genl Rosecrans our commanding General came around this eve and was almost taken from his horse by the soldiers   The *wildest enthusiasm* prevailed and every man seems ready to pursue the enemy   We have had but few battles so well managed as old "Rosa" has managed this one

The dead have been burried this eve and we did not even get to see those of our Regiment as details from other Regiments burried them   Some of the enemy penetrated into the town and more than 100 were captured in the *bakeries* and *stores*   We are tired and hungry to-night and the excitement and fatigue of the two days battle and its glorious termination entitles us to a *rest*

FROM

The Civil War

SHELBY FOOTE

Born in Greenville, Mississippi, in 1916, the novelist and historian Shelby Foote had William Alexander Percy as a mentor and Walker Percy as a friend. In Foote's three-volume history of the Civil War, he brings to bear the historian's attention to research and the novelist's concern for story. Upon its completion in 1974, The Civil War won a nomination for the Pulitzer Prize. In his bibliographical note to volume 3, Foote explains that people have the misconception that all the decisive battles of the Civil War took place in Virginia, whereas "Vicksburg, for example, was as 'decisive' as Gettysburg." The following excerpt, from a chapter called "Unvexed to the Sea," describes the tense negotiations for Vicksburg's surrender between Gen. John C. Pemberton and Gen. Ulysses S. Grant (who had fought on the same side as lieutenants in the same division in Mexico). The Union had gained control of the Mississippi from Cairo to the gulf except for the four-mile stretch at Vicksburg. Located on the Mississippi River, Vicksburg was protected by its high bluffs and was crucial in determining control of the Mississippi River. After the Confederates lost Memphis in May of 1862, flag officer David G. Farragut was ordered to capture Vicksburg. When this attack failed, the Confederates regained control of 240 miles of the Mississippi River. On October 14, 1862, Pemberton, a native of Pennsylvania who had decided to fight for the South, was appointed by President Davis to resist Grant's renewed attempts to capture Vicksburg. After yet another failure to capture the city, Grant tried to bypass it by cutting canals around it. When the fourth such attempt failed, Grant decided to join forces with the army in the gulf and attack Vicksburg from the south. On May 25, 1863, Grant ordered siege operations on the city. By July 4, Confederate soldiers, who had been subsisting on pea bread and the meat of slaughtered horses, surrendered. After the fall of Vicksburg and of Port Hudson, in Louisiana, the North regained control of the Mississippi River from Cairo to the gulf, prompting President Lincoln's remark that "the Father of Waters again goes unvexed to the sea."

IT WAS INDEED a Glorious Fourth, from the northern point of view; Gideon Welles did not exaggerate in speaking wholesale of a "list of brilliant successes" scored by the Union, afloat and ashore, on this eighty-seventh anniversary of the nation's birth. For the South, however, the day was one not of glory, but rather of disappointment, of bitter irony, of gloom made deeper by contrast with the hopes of yesterday, when Lee was massing for his all-or-nothing attack on Cemetery Ridge and Johnston was preparing at last to cross the Big Black River, when Taylor was threatening to retake New Orleans and Holmes was moving into position for his assault on Helena. All four had failed, which was reason enough for disappointment; the irony lay in the fact that not one of the four, Lee or Johnston, Taylor or Holmes, was aware that on this Independence Eve, so far at least as his aspirations for the relief of Vicksburg or Port Hudson were concerned, he was too late. At 10 o'clock that morning, July 3, white flags had broken out along a portion of Pemberton's works and two high-ranking officers, one a colonel, the other a major general, had come riding out of their lines and into those of the besiegers, who obligingly held their fire. The senior bore a letter from his commander, addressed to Grant. "General," it began: "I have the honor to propose to you an armistice for several hours, with a view to arranging terms for the capitulation of Vicksburg."

Pemberton's decision to ask for terms had been reached the day before, when he received from his four division commanders, Stevenson, Forney, Smith, and Bowen, replies to a confidential note requesting their opinions as to the ability of their soldiers "to make the marches and undergo the fatigues necessary to accomplish a successful evacuation." After forty-six days and forty-five nights in the trenches, most of the time on half- and quarter-rations, not one of the four believed his troops were in any shape for the exertion required to break the ring of steel that bound them and then to outmarch or outfight the well-fed host of bluecoats who outnumbered them better than four to one in effectives. Forney, for example, though he expressed himself as "satisfied they will cheerfully continue to bear the fatigue and privation of the siege," answered that it was "the unanimous opinion of the brigade and regimental commanders that the physical condition and health of our men are not sufficiently good to enable them to accomplish successfully the evacuation." There Pemberton had it, and the other three agreed. "With the knowledge I then possessed that no adequate relief was to be expected," the Pennsylvania Confederate later wrote, "I felt that I ought not longer to place in jeopardy the brave men whose lives had been intrusted to my care." He would ask for terms. The apparent futility of submitting such a request to a man whose popular fame was based on his having replied to a similar query with the words, "No terms except an unconditional and immediate surrender can be accepted," was offset—at least to some extent, as Pemberton saw it—by two factors. One was that the Confederates had broken the Federal wigwag code, which permitted them to eavesdrop on Grant's and Porter's ship-to-shore and shore-to-ship exchanges, and from these they had learned that the navy wanted to avoid the troublesome, time-consuming task of transporting thousands of grayback captives far northward up the river. This encouraged the southern commander to hope that his opponent, despite his Unconditional Surrender reputation, might be willing to parole instead of imprison the Vicksburg garrison if that was made a condition of avoiding at least one more costly assault on intrenchments that had proved themselves so stout two times before. The other mitigating factor, at any rate to Pemberton's way of thinking, was that the calendar showed the proposed surrender would occur on Independence Day. Some among the defenders considered a capitulation on that date unthinkable, since it would give the Yankees all the more reason for crowing, but while Pemberton was aware of this, and even agreed that it would involve a measure of humiliation, he also counted it an advantage. "I am a northern man," he told the objectors on his staff. "I know my people. I know their peculiar weaknesses and their national vanity; I know we can get better terms from them on the Fourth of July than on any other day of the year. We must sacrifice our pride to these considerations."

One other possible advantage he had, though admittedly it had not been of much use to Buckner at Donelson the year before. John Bowen had known and befriended Grant during his fellow West Pointer's hardscrabble farming days in Missouri, and it was hoped that this might have some effect when the two got down to negotiations. Although Bowen was sick, his health undermined by dysentery contracted during the siege—he would in fact be dead within ten days, three months short of his thirty-third birthday—he accepted the assignment, and that was how it came about that he was the major general who rode into the Union lines this morning, accompanied by a colonel from Pemberton's staff. However, it soon developed that the past seventeen months had done little to mellow Grant in his attitude toward old friends who had chosen to do their fighting under the Stars and Bars. He not only declined to see or talk with Bowen, but his reply to the southern commander's note, which was delivered to him by one of his own officers, also showed that he was, if anything, even harsher in tone than he had been in the days when Buckner charged him with being "ungenerous and unchivalrous." Pemberton had written: "I make this proposition to save the further effusion of blood, which must otherwise be shed to a frightful extent." Now Grant replied: "The useless effusion of blood you propose stopping by this course can be ended at any time you may choose, by an unconditional surrender of the city and garrison. . . . I do not favor the proposition of appointing commissioners to arrange terms of capitulation, because I have no terms other than those indicated above."

There were those words again: Unconditional Surrender. But their force was diminished here at Vicksburg, as they had not been at Donelson, by an accompanying verbal message in which Grant said that he would be willing to meet and talk with Pemberton between the lines that afternoon. Worn by strain and illness, Bowen delivered the note and repeated the off-the-record message, both of which were discussed at an impromptu council of war, and presently—by then it was close to 3 o'clock, the hour Grant had set for the meeting—he and the colonel retraced in part the route they had followed that morning, accompanied now by Pemberton, who spoke half to himself and half to his two companions as he rode past the white flags on the ramparts. "I feel a confidence that I shall stand justified to my government, if not to the southern people," they heard him say, as if he saw already the scapegoat role in which he as an outlander would be cast by strangers and former friends for whose sake he had alienated his own people, including two brothers who fought on the other side. First, however, there came a ruder shock. Despite the flat refusal expressed in writing, he had interpreted Grant's spoken words, relayed to him through Bowen, as an invitation to parley about terms. But he soon was disabused of this impression. The three Confederates came upon a group of about a dozen Union officers awaiting them on a hillside only a couple of hundred yards beyond the outer walls of the beleaguered city. Ord, McPherson, Logan, and A. J. Smith were there, together with several members of Grant's staff and Grant himself, whom Pemberton had no trouble recognizing, not only because his picture had been distributed widely throughout the past year and a half, but also because he had known him in Mexico, where they had served as staff lieutenants in the same division. Once the introductions were over, there was an awkward pause as each waited for the other to open the conversation and thereby place himself in somewhat the attitude of a suppliant. When Pemberton broke the silence at last by remarking that he understood Grant had "expressed a wish to have a personal interview with me," Grant replied that he had done no such thing; he had merely agreed to such a suggestion made at second hand by Bowen.

Finding that this had indeed been the case, though he had not known it before, Pemberton took a different approach. "In your letter this morning," he observed, "you state that you have no other terms than an unconditional surrender." Grant's answer was as prompt as before. "I have no other," he said. Whereupon the Pennsylvanian— "rather snappishly," Grant would recall—replied: "Then, sir, it is unnecessary that you and I should hold any further conversation. We will go to fighting again at once." He turned, as if to withdraw, but fired a parting salvo as he did so. "I can assure you, sir, you will bury many more of your men before you will enter Vicksburg." Grant said nothing to this, nor did he change his position or expression. The contest was like poker, and he played it straight-faced while his opponent continued to sputter, remarking, as he later paraphrased his words, that if Grant "supposed that I was suffering for provisions he was mistaken, that I had enough to last me for an indefinite period, and that Port Hudson was even better supplied than Vicksburg." Grant did not believe there was much truth in this, but he saw clearly enough from Pemberton's manner that his unconditional-surrender formula was not going to obtain without a good deal more time or bloodshed. So he unbent, at least to the extent of suggesting that he and Pemberton step aside while their subordinates talked things over. The Confederate was altogether willing—after all, it was what he had proposed at the outset, only to be rebuffed—and the two retired to the shelter of a stunted oak nearby. In full view of the soldiers on both sides along this portion of the front, while Bowen and the colonel talked with the other four Union generals, the blue and gray commanders stood together in the meager shade of the oak tree, which, as Grant wrote afterwards, "was made historical by the event. It was but a short time before the last vestige of its body, root and limb had disappeared, the fragments taken as trophies. Since then the same tree has furnished as many cords of wood, in the shape of trophies, as 'The True Cross.' "

Capture of Jefferson Davis

JEFFERSON DAVIS

*After hearing of General Lee's surrender on April 9, 1865, Jefferson
Davis determined to leave Richmond, Virginia, and make his way south.
Overtly, it seemed, he was heeding the warnings such as those of Major
William Sutherlin that he was in grave danger, but covertly he harbored
a dream of joining troops west of the Mississippi River and marshalling
the Confederate forces of Kirby Smith. Earlier, he had refused an offer
from General Sherman for escape to Cuba or Europe. He and his wife,
Varina, had agreed that safety for both lay in their separation. Yet ironically, after traveling separately through Virginia and the Carolinas, their
parties converged near Washington, Georgia, on May 6. Mrs. Davis
tried to prevent Davis's capture by distracting Corporal George Munger
of the Fourth Michigan Cavalry. This she failed to do, but when she
stopped Davis from attacking Munger, she quite possibly prevented her
husband's death. In the following account, Davis vividly describes his
capture by the Federals on May 10. He reveals details that explain the
later popular, but erroneous rumor that he had tried to disguise himself
as a woman. He was subsequently imprisoned at Fort Monroe in Virginia.*

. . . MY HORSE and arms were near the road on which I expected
to leave, and down which the cavalry approached; it was therefore im-
practible for me to reach them. As it was quite dark in the tent, I picked
up what was supposed to be my "raglan," a waterproof light overcoat,
without sleeves; it was subsequently found to be my wife's, so very like
my own as to be mistaken for it; as I started, my wife thoughtfully threw
over my head and shoulders a shawl. I had gone perhaps fifteen or
twenty yards when a trooper galloped up and ordered me to halt and
surrender, to which I gave a defiant answer, and dropping the shawl
and raglan from my shoulders, advanced toward him; he leveled his
carbine at me, but I expected [that] if he fired, he would miss me, and
my intention was in that event to put my hand under his feet, tumble
him off on the other side, spring into his saddle, and attempt to escape.
My wife, who had been watching, when she saw the soldier aim his carbine at me, ran forward and threw her arms around me. Success depended on instantaneous action, and recognising that the opportunity

had been lost, I turned back, and, the morning being damp and chilly, passed on to a fire beyond the tent.

Our pursuers had taken different roads, and approached our camp from opposite directions; they encountered each other and commenced firing, both supposing that they had met our armed escort, and some casualities resulted from their conflict with an imaginary body of Confederate troops. During the confusion, while attention was concentrated upon myself, except by those who were engaged in pillage, one of my aides, Col. J. Taylor Wood, with Lt. Barnwell, walked off unobserved. His daring on the sea made him an object of special hostility to the Federal Government, and he properly availed himself of the possible means of escape. Col. Pritchard went over to their battle-field, and I did not see him for a long time, surely more than an hour after my capture. He subsequently claimed credit, in a conversation with me, for the forbearance shown by his men in not shooting me when I refused to surrender.

Many falsehoods have been uttered in regard to my capture, which have been exposed in publications by persons there present—by Secretary Reagan, and by the colored coachman, Jim Jones, which must have been convincing to all who desired to know the truth.

Crusade for Justice: The Autobiography of Ida B. Wells

IDA B. WELLS

Born to slaves in 1862, Ida B. Wells kept a diary from 1885 to 1887 recalling her early years of hardship. The following account (chapter 1, "Born into Slavery") reveals the hardships she suffered as a child. One of the founders of the National Association for the Advancement of Colored People (NAACP), she fought against racial discrimination in every facet of American life, from disenfranchisement to segregation. When, as editor of a small newspaper in Memphis called Free Speech, *she criticized the Memphis board of education for disparities between black schools and white schools, she was dismissed from her teaching job. She married a Chicago lawyer, Ferdinand C. Barnett, in 1895, and in Chicago she was active in organizing progressive civic clubs such as the Equal Rights Association (Era) Club. In her preface, Wells-Barnett explains that she wrote her autobiography "because there is such a lack of authentic race history of Reconstruction times written by the Negro himself."*

I WAS BORN in Holly Springs, Mississippi, before the close of the Civil War [16 July 1862]. My parents, who had been slaves and married as such, were married again after freedom came. My father had been taught the carpenter's trade, and my mother was a famous cook. As the erstwhile slaves had performed most of the labor of the South, they had no trouble in finding plenty of work to do.

My father [called Jim] was the son of his master, who owned a plantation in Tippah County, Mississippi, and one of his slave women, Peggy. Mr. Wells had no children by his wife, "Miss Polly," and my father grew up on the plantation, the companion and comfort of his old age. He was never whipped or put on the auction block, and he knew little of the cruelties of slavery. When young Jim was eighteen years old, his father took him to Holly Springs and apprenticed him to learn the carpenter's trade, which he expected him to use on the plantation.

My mother[1] was cook to old man Bolling, the contractor and builder to whom my father was apprenticed. She was born in Virginia and was one of ten children. She and two sisters were sold to slave traders when young, and were taken to Mississippi and sold again. She often told her children that her father was half Indian, his father being a full blood. She often wrote back to somewhere in Virginia trying to get track of her people, but she was never successful. We were too young to realize the importance of her efforts, and I have never remembered the name of the country or people to whom they "belonged."

After the war was over Mr. Bolling urged his able young apprentice to remain with him. He did so until election time. Mr. Bolling wanted him to vote the Democratic ticket, which he refused to do. When he returned from voting he found the shop locked. Jim Wells said nothing to anyone, but went downtown, bought a new set of tools, and went across the street and rented another house. When Mr. Bolling returned he found he had lost a workman and a tenant, for already Wells had moved his family off the Bolling place.

I do not remember when or where I started school. My earliest recollections are of reading the newspaper to my father and an admiring group of his friends. He was interested in politics and I heard the words Ku Klux Klan long before I knew what they meant. I knew dimly that it meant something fearful, by the anxious way my mother walked the floor at night when my father was out to a political meeting. Yet so far as I can remember there were no riots in Holly Springs, although there were plenty in other parts of the state.

Our job was to go to school and learn all we could. The Freedmen's Aid had established [in 1866] one of its schools in our town—it was called Shaw University then, but is now Rust College. My father was one of the trustees and my mother went along to school with us until she learned to read the Bible. After that she visited the school regularly to see how we were getting along. A deeply religious woman, she won the prize for regular attendance at Sunday school, taking the whole brood of six to nine o'clock Sunday school the year before she died. She taught us how to do the work of the home—each had a regular task besides schoolwork, and I often compare her work in training her children to that of other women who had not her handicaps. She was not forty when she died, but she had borne eight children and brought us up with a strict discipline that many mothers who have had educational advantages have not exceeded. She used to tell us how she had been beaten by slave owners and the hard times she had as a slave.

The only thing I remember about my father's reference to slave days was when his mother came to town on one of her annual visits [after slavery]. She and her husband owned and tilled many acres of land and every fall brought their cotton and corn to market. She also brought us many souvenirs from hog-killing time. On one such occasion she told about "Miss Polly," her former mistress, and said, "Jim, Miss Polly wants you to come and bring the children. She wants to see them."

"Mother," said he, "I never want to see that old woman as long as I live. I'll never forget how she had you stripped and whipped the day after the old man died, and I am never going to see her. I guess it is all right for you to take care of her and forgive her for what she did to you, but she could have starved to death if I'd had my say-so. She certainly would have, if it hadn't been for you."

I was burning to ask what he meant, but children were seen and not heard in those days. They didn't dare break into old folks' conversation. But I have never forgotten those words. Since I have grown old enough to understand I cannot help but feel what an insight to slavery they give. . . .

NOTES

[1] Her mother was Elizabeth Warrenton, of Virginia. This identification was provided in a letter to Alfreda Duster from A. J. Wells, brother of Ida B. Wells, 9 July 1941.

FROM

The Facts of Reconstruction

JOHN R. LYNCH

In 1847, John R. Lynch was born to a mother who was a slave and a father who was a wealthy planter in Concordia Parish, Louisiana. Because Patrick Lynch died before he could free his son, Lynch and his mother were ultimately sold to a purchaser in Natchez, where Lynch finally gained his freedom in 1864. Except for a few courses in night school, he was a self-educated man who was surprised to be appointed justice of the peace of Adams County, as he describes in the following selection (chapter 1, "The Part Played by Mississippi in the Early Days of Reconstruction"). Lynch went on to win a seat as a Republican in the Mississippi House of Representatives in 1869 and, in 1872, he was elected Speaker of the House. In 1873, he became the first black from Mississippi to be elected to the United States House of Representatives. A correspondent for the New York Times *noted on March 4, 1872, that, as a representative, "[Lynch] has won the admiration and respect of the entire House." Lynch was a strong supporter of public education and was instrumental in the passage of the Civil Rights Bill in 1875, a bill that, as he explained it, was about "protection in the enjoyment of public rights" for blacks rather than fostering social equality. His essays collected in* The Facts of Reconstruction, *published in 1913, show Lynch to be ahead of his time. Unlike most of his contemporaries, he viewed Reconstruction positively, a position unpopular until taken up by the revisionist school in the 1930s many years after Lynch's book was published. In the following account, Lynch explains the furor over President Grant's submission of Mississippi's rejected revision of the state constitution to a popular vote. The objection, by white and black southerners, was over a clause denying public office to previous Confederates. In 1866, when Grant made clear that the objectionable clause would be voted on separately, the ratification of the constitution took place.*

THE FIRST ELECTION held in Mississippi under the Reconstruction Acts took place in 1867, when delegates to a Constitutional Convention were elected to frame a new Constitution. The Democrats decided to adopt what they declared to be a policy of "Masterly Inactivity," that is, to refrain from taking any part in the election and to allow it to go by default. The result was that the Republicans had a large majority of the delegates, only a few counties having elected Democratic delegates. The only reason that there were any Democrats in the Convention at all was that the party was not unanimous in the adoption of the policy of "Masterly Inactivity," and consequently did not adhere to it. The Democrats in a few counties in the State rejected the advice and repudiated the action of the State Convention of their party on this point. The result was that a few very able men were elected to the convention as Democrats,—such men, for instance, as John W. C. Watson, and William M. Compton, of Marshall County, and William L. Hemingway, of Carroll, who was elected State Treasurer by the Democrats in 1875, and to whom a more extended reference will be made in a subsequent chapter.

The result of the election made it clear that if the Democratic organization in the State had adopted the course that was pursued by the members of that party in the counties by which the action of their State Convention was repudiated, the Democrats would have had at least a large and influential minority of the delegates, which would have resulted in the framing of a constitution that would have been much more acceptable to the members of that party than the one that was finally agreed upon by the majority of the members of that body. But the Democratic party in the State was governed and controlled by the radical element of that organization,—an element which took the position that no respectable white Democrat could afford to participate in an election in which colored men were allowed to vote. To do so, they held, would not only be humiliating to the pride of the white men, but the contamination would be unwise if not dangerous. Besides, they were firm in the belief and honest in the conviction that the country would ultimately repudiate the Congressional Plan of Reconstruction, and that in the mean time it would be both safe and wise for them to give expression to their objections to it and abhorrence of it by pursuing a course of masterly inactivity. The liberal and conservative element in the party was so bitterly opposed to this course that in spite of the action of the State Convention several counties, as has been already stated, bolted the action of the convention and took part in the election.

Of the Republican membership of the Constitutional Convention a large majority were white men,—many of them natives of the State and a number of others, though born elsewhere, residents in the State for many years preceding the war of the Rebellion. My own county, Adams (Natchez), in which the colored voters were largely in the majority, and which was entitled to three delegates in the convention, elected two white men,—E. J. Castello, and Fred Parsons,—and one colored man, H. P. Jacobs, a Baptist preacher. Throughout the State the proportion was about the same. This was a great disappointment to the dominating element in the Democratic party, who had hoped and expected, through their policy of "Masterly Inactivity" and intimidation of white men, that the convention would be composed almost exclusively of illiterate and inexperienced colored men. Although a minor at that time, I took an active part in the local politics of my county, and, being a member of a Republican club that had been organized at Natchez, I was frequently called upon to address the members at its weekly meetings.

When the State Constitution was submitted to a popular vote for ratification or rejection I took an active part in the county campaign in advocacy of its ratification. In this election the Democrats pursued a course that was just the opposite of that pursued by them in the election of delegates to the Constitutional Convention. They decided that it was no longer unwise and dangerous for white men to take part in an election in which colored men were allowed to participate. This was due largely to the fact that the work of the convention had been far different from what they had anticipated. The newly framed Constitution was, taken as a whole, such an excellent document that in all probability it would have been ratified without serious opposition but for the fact that there was an unfortunate, unwise and unnecessary clause in it which practically disfranchised those who had held an office under the Constitution of the United States and who, having taken an oath to support and defend the Constitution of the United States, had afterwards supported the cause of the Confederacy. This clause caused very bitter and intense opposition to the ratification of the Constitution. When the election was over it was found that the Constitution had been rejected by a small majority. This result could not be fairly accepted as an indication of the strength of the two parties in the State, for it was a well-known fact that the Republican party had a clear majority of about 30,000.

Notwithstanding the large Republican majority in the State, which was believed to be safe, sure and reliable, there were several causes that contributed to the rejection of the newly framed Constitution. Among the causes were:

First. In consequence of the bitterness with which the ratification of the Constitution had been fought, on account of the objectionable clause referred to, intimidating methods had been adopted in several counties in which there was a large colored vote, resulting in a loss of several thousand votes for the Constitution.

Second. There were several thousand Republicans both white and colored,—but chiefly colored,—who were opposed to that offensive and objectionable clause, believing the same to be unjust, unnecessary, and unwise; hence, many of that class refused to vote either way.

Third. There were thousands of voters, the writer being one of that number, who favored ratification because the Constitution as a whole was a most excellent document, and because its ratification would facilitate the readmittance of Mississippi into the Union; after which the one objectionable clause could be stricken out by means of an amendment. While all of this class favored and advocated ratification for the reasons stated, yet their known attitude towards the clause proved to be a contributary cause of the rejection of the Constitution.

The reader may not understand why there were any colored men, especially at that time and in that section, that would have any sympathy for the white men who would have been victims of this clause had the new Constitution been ratified. But if the reader will closely follow what this writer will set down in subsequent chapters of this work, he will find the reasons why there was and still is a bond of sympathy between the two races at the South,—a bond that the institution of slavery with all its horrors could not destroy, the Rebellion could not wipe out, Reconstruction could not efface, and subsequent events have not been able to change. The writer is aware of the fact that thousands of intelligent people are now laboring under the impression that there exists at the South a bitter feeling of antagonism between the two races and that this has produced dangerous and difficult problems for the country to solve. That some things have occurred that would justify such a conclusion, especially on the part of those who are not students of this subject, will not be denied.

After the rejection of the Constitution no further effort was made to have Mississippi readmitted into the Union until after the Presidential and Congressional elections of 1868. The Democratic party throughout the country was solid in its support of President Andrew Johnson, and was bitter in its opposition to the Congressional Plan of Reconstruction. Upon a platform that declared the Reconstruction Acts of Congress to be unconstitutional, revolutionary, and void, the Democrats nominated for President and Vice-President, Ex-Governor Horatio Seymour, of New York, and General Frank P. Blair, of Missouri. The Republicans nominated for President General U.S. Grant, of Illinois, and for Vice-President Speaker Schuyler Colfax, of Indiana. These candidates were nominated upon a platform which strongly supported and indorsed the Congressional Plan of Reconstruction.

On this issue the two parties went before the people for a decision. The Republicans were successful, but not by such a decisive majority as in the Congressional election of 1866. In fact, if all the Southern States that took part in that election had gone Democratic, the hero of Appomattox would have been defeated. It was the Southern States, giving Republican majorities through the votes of their colored men, that saved that important national election to the Republican party. To the very great surprise of the Republican leaders the party lost the important and pivotal State of New York. It had been confidently believed that the immense popularity of General Grant and his prestige as a brilliant and successful Union general would save every doubtful State to the Republicans, New York, of course, included. But this expectation was not realized. The result, it is needless to say, was a keen and bitter disappointment, for no effort had been spared to bring to the attention of the voters the strong points in General Grant. A vote against Grant, it was strongly contended, was virtually a vote against the Union. Frederick Douglass, who electrified many audiences in that campaign, made the notable declaration that "While Washington had given us a country, it was Grant who had saved us a country." And yet the savior of our country failed in that election to save to the Republican party the most important State in the Union. But, notwithstanding the loss of New York, the Republicans not only elected the President and Vice-President, but also had a safe majority in both branches of Congress.

One of the first acts of Congress after the Presidential election of 1868 was one authorizing the President to submit Mississippi's rejected Constitution once again to a popular vote. The same act authorized the President to submit to a separate vote such clause or clauses of said Constitution as in his judgment might be particularly obnoxious to any considerable number of the people of the State. It was not and could not be denied that the Constitution as a whole was a most admirable document. The Democrats had no serious objection to its ratification if the clause disfranchising most of their leaders were eliminated. When it became known that this clause would be submitted to a separate vote, and that the Republican organization would not insist upon its retention, no serious opposition to the ratification of the Constitution was anticipated. And, indeed, none was made.

The time fixed for holding the election was November, 1869. In the mean time the State was to be under military control. General Adelbert Ames was made Military Governor, with power to fill by appointment every civil office in the State. Shortly after General Ames took charge as Military Governor the Republican club at Natchez agreed upon a slate to be submitted to the Military Governor for his favorable consideration, the names upon said slate being the choice of the Republican organization of the county and city officials. Among the names thus agreed upon was that of the Rev. H. P. Jacobs for Justice of the Peace. It was then decided to send a member of the club to Jackson, the State capital, to present the slate to the Governor in person in order to answer questions that might be asked or to give any information that might be desired about any of the persons whose names appeared on the slate. It fell to my lot to be chosen for that purpose; the necessary funds being raised by the club to pay my expenses. I accepted the mission, contingent upon my employer's granting me leave of absence.

Natchez at that time was not connected with Jackson by railroad, so that the only way for me to reach the capital was to go by steamer from Natchez to Vicksburg or to New Orleans, and from there by rail to Jackson. The trip, therefore, would necessarily consume the greater part of a week. My employer,—who was what was known as a Northern man, having come there after the occupation of the place by the Federal troops,—not only granted me leave of absence but agreed to remain in the city and carry on the business during my absence.

When I arrived at the building occupied by the Governor and sent up my card, I had to wait only a few minutes before I was admitted to his office. The Governor received me cordially and treated me with marked courtesy, giving close attention while I presented as forcibly as I could the merits and qualifications of the different persons whose names were on the slate. When I had concluded my remarks the Governor's only reply was that he would give the matter his early and careful consideration. A few weeks later the appointments were announced; but not many of the appointees were persons whose names I had presented. However, to my great embarrassment I found that my own name had been substituted for that of Jacobs for the office of Justice of the Peace. I not only had no ambition in that direction but was not aware that my name was under consideration for that or for any other office. Besides, I was apprehensive that Jacobs and some of his friends might suspect me of having been false to the trust that had been reposed in me, at least so far as the office of Justice of the Peace was concerned. At first I was of the opinion that the only way in which I could disabuse their minds of that erroneous impression was to decline the appointment. But I found out upon inquiry that in no event would Jacobs receive the appointment. I was also reliably informed that I had not been recommended nor suggested by any one, but that the Governor's action was the result of the favorable impression I had made upon him when I presented the slate. For this, of course, I was in no way responsible. In fact the impression of my fitness for the office that my brief talk had made upon the Governor was just what the club had hoped I would be able to accomplish in the interest of the whole slate. That it so happened that I was the beneficiary of the favorable impression that my brief talk had made upon the Governor may have been unfortunate in one respect, but it was an unconscious act for which I could not be censured. After consulting, therefore, with a few personal friends and local party leaders, I decided to accept the appointment although, in consequence of my youth and inexperience, I had serious doubts as to my ability to discharge the duties of the office which at that time was one of considerable importance.

Then the bond question loomed up, which was one of the greatest obstacles in my way, although the amount was only two thousand dollars. How to give that bond was the important problem I had to solve, for, of course, no one was eligible as a bondsman who did not own real estate. There were very few colored men who were thus eligible, and it was out of the question at that time to expect any white property owner to sign the bond of a colored man. But there were two colored men willing to sign the bond for one thousand dollars each who were considered eligible by the authorities. These men were William McCary and David Singleton. The law, having been duly satisfied in the matter of my bond, I was permitted to take the oath of office in April, 1869, and to enter upon the discharge of my duties as a Justice of the Peace, which office I held until the 31st of December of the same year when I resigned to accept a seat in the lower branch of the State Legislature to which I had been elected the preceding November.

When I entered upon the discharge of my duties as a Justice of the Peace the only comment that was made by the local Democratic paper of the town was in these words: "We are now beginning to reap the ravishing fruits of Reconstruction."

A Slaveholder's Daughter

B E L L E   K E A R N E Y

*Born in 1863 in Madison, Mississippi, Belle Kearney was the daughter
of a wealthy landowner who served in the legislature and was a lieutenant in the Civil War. In her autobiography,* A Slaveholder's Daughter, *Kearney describes the drastic changes the defeat of the South brought
her family. She also reveals, as the following passage shows, the difficulties she faced regarding her desire to get involved in politics and to obtain
a law degree (from the chapter "Storms of the Soul"). Despite these obstacles, in 1923 she became the first woman in the South to be elected to the
state senate, a seat she held for two terms. In the same year, Nellie Nugent
Somerville of Greenville became the first woman to be elected to the state
house of representatives.*

O U R   H O M E   W A S headquarters not only for Methodist preachers
but as well for Democratic politicians. Every candidate for office in the
country found his way there, to mother's infinite chagrin and the un-
bounded delight of father and me. Mother often declined to appear at
the table, so I would preside and afterward go into the parlor and talk
with the visitors for hours on the situation of public affairs. The aspi-
rants were of all descriptions—from the sleek, town-bred lawyer, "out"
for the Senate, to the thin, country granger, who yearned to be a constable. They afforded me ample opportunity to learn the methods of political campaigns and to study the motives and natures of men. Often
requests were made by the different candidates for my support in a
canvass; but there were others who had little regard for a woman's assistance.

One summer when the roads were kept dusty by the continuous go-
ings to and fro of the anxious office-seekers, one of these interesting
subjects dined at our house. He was a most forlorn specimen, with
heavy, drooping eyes, straggling moustache and languid movements.
His clothes, from the disconsolate set of his collar down to his edge-
frayed trousers, draggling over his well-worn boots, gave evidence of a
long, hard race on the war path. My sympathies were so aroused that as
soon as dinner was over I followed him to the front gallery and, in a
burst of condolence, said impulsively: "Mr. F., it is my intention to
throw the whole weight of my influence to have you elected!" Looking

at me in a sleepily—quizzical fashion, he replied in a droning tone: "It had never occurred to me to ask the assistance of ladies in a political campaign. I supposed they were too busy in other matters to be interested in anything so weighty."

Then he proceeded to tell this joke: There was a great convention of women held somewhere, and a certain local society sent its delegate. When the representative returned a meeting was called that the ladies might hear her report. When this was finished she remarked that questions were "in order." A slim little woman, with a weazen face peering out from a flaring poke-bonnet, arose in the rear of the room, and in a thin, high key called out: "Sister, what sort of hats did the women wear?" Then my hopeful candidate, turning towards me more fully, with a glimmer of something in his eyes which *he* would have called humor, said: "It was my impression that *all* ladies thought more about hats and such things than politics."

It was needless to say the facetious gentleman, with the well-worn apparel and Don Quixote air, lost my support suddenly and completely.

As the days went by they found me more and more deeply immersed in reading. Father bought me translations of the Greek, Latin and Italian poets. An old physician, quite a literateur, who had recently come into the neighborhood, loaned me valuable books that we did not own. He put me under special obligations by sending Allison's "Essays" and Montesquieu's "Spirit of Laws." From other sources some of the works of Ruskin, Carlyle and Herbert Spencer came to me and found an honored place among my treasures. Although applying myself sedulously to books, I was being consumed with a feverish restlessness. My wretchedness went beyond the power of words to express. A deep-rooted desire to do something definite was always present; but every undertaking that suggested itself seemed walled off by insurmountable barriers.

Finally I concluded to study law under father, but when my intention was announced to him he discouraged it utterly, arguing that if there were in my possession the legal lore of Blackstone and the ability of a Portia it would not guarantee me the opportunity of practising in the South. No woman had ever attempted such an absurdity, and any effort on my part, in that line, would subject me to ridicule and ostracism. After this fatal ending to my aspirations, I again sought refuge in books. With no definite object ahead and with not the faintest rim of a crescent of hope above my dull horizon.

Progress of Women: A Speech to the Hypatia Club, 1898

NELLIE NUGENT SOMERVILLE

*Born in Greenville, Mississippi, in 1863, Nellie Nugent Somerville be-
came involved in politics through the suffrage movement by serving as an
officer in both state and national organizations. In 1923, Somerville and
Belle Kearney became the first women to be elected to the state legislature,
Kearney to the senate and Somerville to the house of representatives. (Somerville's daughter, Lucy Somerville Howorth, appointed to the board of
appeals of the Veteran's Administration by President Franklin Roosevelt,
is another story of activism for women's rights.) The following speech, from
a handwritten manuscript by Somerville, gives an impressive overview of
the progress of women at the time all over the world on the issues of education for women, property rights, and laws concerning the "age of consent."
At the time of this speech, Mississippi was one of the more progressive
states, having been the first to pass a law granting property rights to
women in 1839 and the first to establish a state-supported college for
women in 1884. The following speech was delivered to the Hypatia Club,
a literary organization in Greenville named for a Roman woman mar-
tyred for her attempts to reawaken reverence for the Roman gods and god-
desses in the fourth century A.D. The original of Somerville's speech has
several tantalizing "prompts" in parentheses, clearly intended to remind
her of stories she meant to tell extemporaneously. For example, in her remarks on education for women, she placed in parentheses "Ex. Mrs. Stanton," leaving the reader wondering if this was a reference to Elizabeth
Cady Stanton, who drafted the* Declaration of Sentiments *in 1848 at
the women's rights convention in Seneca Falls, New York. At the end of
the manuscript, Somerville wrote the fragment* "The New York Voice
says. . . ," *making the intended ending of her speech unclear.*

IN PRESENTING this subject much might be said in sarcasm or in
jest but sarcasm is a weapon which truth does not need and in such a
cause jesting would be a culpable waste of time. I shall ask you to consider, not that imaginary progress of women which horrifies and alarms
many good people but the real progress from former conditions to

those now existing by way of preface. In the United States, high schools were not open to girls until about the beginning of the century. In 1790 girls were permitted to go for two hours in the afternoon provided there was room on account of the absence of boys. It is also a well known fact that violent objection was made in earlier days to any education whatever for women. Many good people contended that women would neglect household duties if they knew how to read and write. These objectors have their lineal descendants in those who fear that the endowment of political rights will lead women to forget their family cares. The higher education of women began in 1833 with the founding of Oberlin college. Some universities in almost every country now admit women but all do not grant degrees. This advance was not made without great effort on the part of women. A few years ago the desire for a thorough education was considered unwomanly. Special effort was required to secure for women this opportunity to acquire professional training in any line. Every such advance has been strenuously resisted by the same class who now oppose woman suffrage. At this time women have ample facilities for medical education and in many places there are hospitals controlled entirely by women. One result of this has been the addition to evangelizing forces of women as medical missionaries. In many foreign countries no male physician is allowed access to women and the woman physician is the greatest blessing which Christian women have given to their unfortunate heathen sisters. In educational matters then the progress of women means simply that women are not ridiculed or abused for desiring an education and many opportunities are afforded them though not altogether such as are open to men. What does this objectionable phrase mean in the religious world? A few decades ago women had no large responsibilities in the management of religious affairs. The change may perhaps be well described as progress from individual work to organized work. Most denominations now have their missionary boards of woman for foreign and domestic work. Money raised is expended by these boards and through them women missionaries are sent to every part of the globe. The W.F.M.S. of M.E. church was organized in 1869. Ours in 1878. These organizations were not formed without the usual protest against women leaving home duties. The phenomenal success of these societies very plainly shows that their appeals touched some chord in the hearts of women which had never before been reached. "Woman's work for woman" furnished a pathetic and successful appeal. Curious and interesting is the legal aspect of this subject. Among savage and semi-civilized tribes woman was (and is) a mere chattel and her position sunk to the lowest depths of degradation. Among many tribes the loan of a wife or daughter was, and is, the extreme of hospitality. Many tribes were indifferent to chastity before marriage. Wives were acquired by purchase or by capture. Among the Greeks and Romans these brutal customs gradually gave way to marriage by dowry. By the later Roman law property over and above the dowry could be given to a woman and controlled by her. Later still daughters were given the right to inherit equally with sons. English common law gave a married woman's property absolutely to her husband. Roman law also gave the father absolute control of children. But here it may be said that ancient history is not pertinent. The connection is, however, close. In the last generation many women suffered from similar laws. From the time marriage by dowry was instituted in early Greece until the middle of the present century, no law was enacted to protect a wife's property from her husband's misappropriation. The first effort in this direction was made in the N.Y. Legislature in 1836, but the law was not passed until twelve years later. Many men have always bitterly opposed all efforts to enlarge the property rights of married women. As to the legal status of women at present, the right of married mothers to their children has never been generally granted. In only seven states are the father and mother on an equality in this respect. As to property rights, in every state and territory a married woman can now make a will of both real and personal property but in sixteen states the married woman has not yet secured full legal control of her wages. In Nevada a law of 1873 decrees that "her earnings are the wife's if her husband has allowed her to appropriate them to her own use and it is deemed a gift from him to her." In five states the husband has control of the wife's property and in three more the wife's control is not full. You will therefore observe that in some states wives are actually wearing their husband's clothes as sufferers under these laws.

There is one class of laws which are a blot upon our civilization. If there are among my auditors those who do not desire a share in making laws, I beg that they will inform themselves in regard the odious laws covered by the title "Age of Consent." It is a fact that in one state, Delaware, a man cannot be punished for the ruin of a girl of seven years. That being the age fixed by the law of that state as the "age of consent." In other states this age is placed at ten and on to eighteen. In 1885 Oregon was the only state in which the age was above twelve years. In 1885 Mr. W. T. Stead ventilated this subject in the *Pall Mall Gazette* and through his disclosures a wave of reform swept over the U.S. also. Be it noted that in this reform also woman suffragists have led.

The women who have gone, and still go, before state legislatures seeking change in these laws are members of organizations which advocate woman's suffrage. Consider if you please, on one hand, the false modesty which rears girls in ignorance of physical laws, and on the other, the laws which protect men in destroying the virtue of a child of seven, ten or twelve years. If these laws correctly represent the womanhood of America, then indeed am I ashamed of my sex. Great progress has been made in the industrial, educational and legal position of women but every step of the way has been hotly contested, one party contending for advancement, the other reiterating the lament that woman would lose her womanliness, forget the ties of affection, and the sanctity of homelife be destroyed, should any change be made in her position. And strangest of all it is expected that women should feel complimented by this reflection upon their stability and discretion.

Considering the past history and present conditions of women throughout the world, I have reached the conclusion that only two classes are constant in theory and practice on the woman question. The Mohammedan, who says women have no souls and were created solely for the convenience and pleasure of men. From birth to death their women are treated with contempt which is thoroughly consistent with their faith. The advocates of equal rights in every sphere of life holding that women are intellectually and spiritually equal to men, these are also consistent. Between these is the class who accord to women equally in mental and moral endowments but give them no more civil rights than a Mohammedan woman enjoys. Especially is it difficult to understand the mental processes of the reverend gentleman, who while professing reverence for women said he would rather see a saloon and a brothel on every corner than that women should have the ballot and of another who said "every woman who rides a bicycle has a personal devil."

On this point, John S. Mill said, "They are declared to be better than men," an empty compliment which must provoke a bitter smile from every woman of spirit, since there is no other situation in life in which it is the established order and considered fitting and proper that the better should obey the worse. After all what is a ballot? Simply an expression of opinion.

After Freedom

HORTENSE POWDERMAKER

*A graduate of Yale University and a professor of anthropology at Queens
College in New York, Hortense Powdermaker resided in Indianola, Mississippi, in 1932, where she conducted interviews and participated in
the lives of black people. At the time, the town was made up of about
three thousand people, a little over half of whom were black. Nearly sixty
years "after freedom" and at the time when Jim Crow laws kept the races
separate, Powdermaker applied anthropological methods she had used in
such places as Zambia, Melanesia, and New Guinea to study the blacks
and whites of "Cottonville." Mississippi was chosen because it was as yet
untouched by social studies. The final selection of Indianola was made
because of the "unusually able and intelligent education officials, white
and colored," who assured Powdermaker of their cooperation. The state
department of education, introducing her as "visiting teacher," helped
her gain access to the culture. When the book was first published in
1939, it received little notice, because another scholar, John Dollard, had
published a similar study called* Caste and Class in a Southern Town
*two years earlier. However, because Powdermaker gained unusual accep-
tance among the black women of the community, Elliott M. Rudwick
claims in the introduction to the Atheneum edition that her book "contains the superior description of the Negro subculture." This excerpt from
a chapter called "Social Contours: The Negroes" was gleaned from multi-
ple interviews with a cross-section of ninety-seven black informants.*

WITHIN THE Negro town population there is more diversity than
among the Whites, and less difference from the country dwellers. Negroes frequently shift their residence as between the country and the
town, and this in no way affects their social status. They also move more
easily from one social level to another. In background, too, there is
considerable diversity, although with less distance between extremes
than is found among the Whites of the community as a whole.

The background of slavery common to all the Negroes of Cottonville
implies a comparatively short known lineage. Few can trace it beyond
the last generation of slaves, and many family lines seem to start with
the Emancipation Proclamation. There are none who can vie with the
white aristocracy in following their ancestry back through centuries of

glamour and achievement. Among the Negroes it is the maternal rather than the paternal line of descent that is most likely to be stressed. In many cases the father and his connections are not known.

Because slavery is the background, the master often figures as part of it. Sometimes he may actually be an ancestor. Frequently he is at least an influence. He was likely to be more of a factor with house slaves than with field slaves. To a large extent the white influence is responsible for a difference often perceptible even today between descendants of house slaves and those whose parents or ancestors worked in the fields. The master would naturally choose his favorites among the slaves to be in the house where they would be near him and would be spared the heavy labor of the field. Here they enjoyed advantages that have been described in detail by historians of the pre-Civil War South. Not only were they better clothed, fed, housed, than the field slaves; in daily contact with their white masters and mistresses they learned many refinements and enjoyed a richer and more varied experience than the field laborers, who were restricted to their own class and race for all associations except in formal contacts with a white overseer. Many of the house slaves acquired some smattering of education. More women than men were employed as house slaves, and the master who took a Negro mistress often chose her from among those in the house, or had her transferred to it. Often the children of such unions would be brought up there. Thus the house slaves were on the whole the ones most likely to bequeath a light skin, a heritage that might play a considerable part in the career of their descendants.

After emancipation, the house slaves were the ones most likely to be advised and at times more actively assisted by their masters. In any case they were far better equipped to cope with the new conditions than those who had been kept in the fields. They were more ready, also, to profit by the educational opportunities opened to them just after the Civil War, when a number of well-educated Northerners, fired by missionary zeal, came south to teach the Negroes.

A few typical cases will illustrate characteristic, though by no means invariable, relations between such background and present condition.

> A very black woman does not know of any racial intermixture in her background. Her parents were field slaves on the same plantation in Alabama, and she is one of their seventeen children, nine of whom lived to grow up. The parents of sharecroppers and always very poor. When she was about ten, she was given to an aunt who had no children and who was also a sharecropper. She helped her aunt in the fields until she married. Then she worked in the fields with her husband. She had no schooling.

A brown-skinned woman whose family has a very strong tradition says that her ancestry is mixed Negro, Indian, and white. Her paternal grandparents were born in North Carolina and sold to a Mississippi planter. They were both house slaves and "when freedom came" they were by no means illiterate. Several years "after freedom" they bought a 180-acre farm on credit in one of the hill counties in the central part of the state, and worked it successfully. They laid great emphasis on education, sending their five children to the best schools available for as long as possible. On the maternal side the grandparents were also house slaves who acquired property after the Civil War. The grandfather proved to be an excellent farmer, and when he died left an estate of more than a thousand acres and about $10,000 in cash. All his eight children went through elementary school, some to high school, and two to college. Teaching and selling insurance were the occupations they followed. . . .

A fifty-year-old woman of the upper middle class shows clearly the marks of refinement often evident in descendants of house slaves. She is a small woman, with light brown skin and long kinky gray hair, who remarks with a laugh that she has such a mixture in her she sometimes doesn't know what she is. Her mother was an octoroon, whose own mother was part Indian and whose father was her white master, of Scotch-Irish blood. The mother was given her freedom by her white father, and taken into his house, where she was brought up with his white daughter. The two girls looked very much alike. The mother first married an octoroon from a neighboring plantation and had by him two very light children, with light hair. But he was a slave and was sold away. Later, she married a Negro who had Indian blood, and the informant is a product of this marriage. Her father was a renter and died when she was three or four years old. The mother then married a carpenter, also a Negro with Indian blood. He too died after a short time, and the mother supported herself by taking in extra-fine washing, such delicate dresses and laces as people would not trust to a regular laundress. The informant herself has never done farm work or cooking. She learned to sew and manicure, and supported herself by this. Her first husband was a bartender and her second a carpenter. . . .

Many Negroes in the community cannot trace their ancestry back to slavery times. . . .

A black-skinned woman of forty who takes in washing says she was born in Alabama and has no family traditions except hard work in the cotton fields. She was one of nineteen children. When she was three years old, her mother died and her father went away to work. She never saw him after that. Her mother's sisters divided up the children and she was brought up by an aunt. She worked very hard in the fields, never went to school, and cannot write at all. Her aunt's house was overcrowded and she was made to work harder than her cousins. She escaped as soon as possible through an early marriage.

The colored population of the community falls into an upper, a middle, and a lower class. The upper class includes no more than five percent of the local Negroes. The lower class is larger than this, but still a distinct minority. By far the majority of the Negroes, as of the Whites, belong to the middle class. Among the Negroes, however, there is a perceptible division into upper and lower middle class, and there is a large group on the borderline between these divisions, a "respectable" element who share certain characteristics of both. For our purposes, when a person is designated as middle-class without the qualification of upper or lower, it is to be assumed that he belongs to this borderline group.

The Negro classes are by no means to be equated with the White classes in the same relative positions. The criteria which separate them are quite different, as are their relations to the classes above and below them. Socially, the upper class, like the white aristocracy, constitutes an exclusive and revered minority. Economically, it represents on the whole a lower economic level and hence lower standards of living than are to be found among the middle-class Whites. The standard of living in the lower middle class is definitely above that of the Poor Whites, and that of the lower-class Negroes is certainly not below it. This means that there is less distance between economic extremes among the Negroes than among the Whites. . . .

The most constant class indication among the Negroes has to do with the acceptance of certain modes of behavior formerly restricted to Whites, particularly those which center in marriage and sex life, family life, education, occupation, and forms of religious worship. . . . It is the upper class that has to the greatest degree taken over both form and meaning. The middle class has adopted fewer white patterns, and it is in most cases the form rather than the meaning that has been accepted. The lower class follows the fewest, and most of those in form merely. . . .

This is clearly brought out in connection with the most adamant requirement for membership in the small upper class of Negroes in our community: namely, a rigid and even Puritanical code of sex behavior, with stern emphasis on pre-marital chastity and marital fidelity. . . .

The mere handful of people who form the upper class commands the respect of the other Negroes, and exercises an influence out of all proportion to its numbers. Its role is not without an element of consecration. It is the privileged class; but it is also the class that works to

advance the status of all the Negroes, partly by definite activities in behalf of the others, partly by the proof it offers of what the race can do
and be. Thus to an extent it actually frees the lower classes of a certain
responsibility. Those who do not wish to better themselves can relax
and enjoy life serene in the consciousness—or unconsciousness—that
these more industrious members are looking out for the racial
reputation. . . .

Education is second only to the code of sexual behavior as an index
of status, and is the chief means of advancing one's social position. The
minimum of education for a member of the upper class is high school,
and many of them have been through one of the southern Negro colleges, or have had a few years at one. Again it must be pointed out,
however, that neither this nor any other single criterion is indispens-
able. One may find a prosperous landowner who has little education
and is not impeccable in his sexual behavior, but who is nevertheless an
accredited member of the upper class. In such a case, his social peers
are well aware of his moral and intellectual deficiencies, but still accept
him perhaps because he has succeeded in reaching the rank of landed
proprietor, which formerly was reserved for the white master.

Occupation is closely connected with education and family background and the connection enhances the importance of all three. The
professional people—teachers, education officials, doctor, dentist—all
belong to the upper class. The prestige of professionals and of education in general is not unrelated to the former prohibition against professional training for Negroes, and to the contention that they lacked
ability to profit by it. The few business men are also members of the
upper class, and again mark a triumph over a former prohibition, and
over the imputation that Negroes lack the acumen to succeed in the
business world. Selling insurance carries at least as high a prestige as
teaching, and is engaged in by enterprising college graduates who are
eager to make a mark.

Because of the narrow economic margin between them, income and
the symbols of wealth do not vary markedly or consistently from class
to class. None of the upper class is very poor or is accepting charity, but
a very modest standard of living is sufficient to maintain one's upper-
class status; and even this standard can be reduced without necessarily
lowering status. Only three Negroes in town own automobiles. Two of
these cars belong to members of the upper class. The third is owned by
an ex-bootlegger who has more money than some of the upper class,
but who, because of his illiteracy, immorality, and occupation, is a member of the lower middle class. In the surrounding rural area some of

the landowners and school principals have cars, usually old ones. In each case, the automobile stands merely for one's having a certain amount of money and does not alter or even indicate the status of the owner. Yet possessions may acquire social importance. Although clothes and furniture as acquisitions mean little from this point of view, heirlooms mean a great deal, for obvious reasons. This does not imply that interest in possessions is lacking, but merely that their connection with social status is tenuous and indirect. Symbols of wealth may become important as signs of individual achievement and as sources of individual gratification. The tales of *nouveaux-riches* among the middle-class Whites can be matched by tales of *nouveaux-riches* among the middle- and even upper-class Negroes . . .

In discussing the middle class, it may be repeated that the criteria for this as well as for other Negro classes are not the same as those used for the Whites. It is the mode of behavior and the degree of acceptance of white patterns which primarily indicate class to the Negro, rather than occupation or income. . . .

The main strength of the church is the middle class. Almost everyone in it is a church member. The members of the upper middle class are the ones who really direct church affairs. The others usually belong to a church, but are less active in attendance and administration. From the middle class as a whole come the "shouters" and the loud "amens."

. . . Occupying the economic fringe, the lower class is on the whole poorer than the middle class. Many of its members have no regular work but are supported by occasional odd jobs, and relief or charity. The economic difference is not paramount, however. Some of them have more money than some of the middle class, who also can accept charity or relief without loss of status.

> A woman who receives a pension because her husband died in the World War, and who also makes a fair amount by bestowing sexual favors, is better off economically than a good many in the class above her. But because she is almost completely illiterate and a prostitute, she is not a member of the middle class. Her neighbor, who does laundry work for a living, is just as illiterate, but her promiscuous sexual affairs are carried on with some degree of privacy, and so she ranks as a member of the lower middle class.

Most of the lower class have at some time been church members and many still are, but their attendance is variable. A number of them go to church only for the revivals, or the numerous church entertainments.

Certain minor differentiae that follow class distinctions and help to define them will appear in the subsequent discussion. A few may be

mentioned here, briefly. One is wife beating, which is far more preva-
lent in the lower than in the upper classes. It is something for a woman
to boast about if her husband does not beat her, except in the upper
class, where wife beating is neither frequent nor sanctioned. The same
type of distinction applies to a jail record. For the lower class it is more
or less assumed that some member of any family will get into jail, and
when this happens it is unfortunate but not a serious disgrace. The
lower middle class may get into jail almost as often, but it is less taken
for granted. The upper middle class succeed in staying out of jail often
enough so that a jail record in a family is definitely undesirable; and
fail often enough so that absence of it is cause for pride. The upper
class regard a jail record much as the middle-class Whites would, although the stigma may be somewhat modified by the special relations
of the Negro to the law in this community. . . .

In any society, class distinctions will be reflected by social usages current at different levels. In this group, the usages which distinguish
classes have obvious relations to the basic racial distinction. This is particularly clear in the use of the social title, which white usage has
freighted with profound significance for the Negro. Members of the
upper class, particularly the women, do not address or refer to each
other by first names, but always with the social title. In company, husbands and wives refer to each other as "Mr." and "Mrs." even when
only intimate friends are present. One eminent member of the upper
class refers to his wife as "Madam." The white society of an earlier period maintained a greater formality of address than do the Whites of
Cottonville today; but social symbolism as well as social lag is strongly
evident in the rigid observance now current among upper-class Negroes. In the other classes, first names are always used between friends
who are conversing, although in the upper middle class a third person
will be referred to as "Mr.," "Mrs.," or "Miss," and a person will frequently refer to his spouse by title even when speaking to intimates. In
the lower middle class and the lower class, the name is generally used
without any title.

As in almost any society, clothing is an index of social status. The
lower classes, when they can afford it, are as up-to-date in dress as is the
upper class. There is often, but not always, an indication of economic
difference in material and workmanship. The chief distinction, however, is that women of higher social status deliberately avoid bright colors, and are offended if clerks in the stores assume that they want
something "loud." This is another instance where the usual class criteria carry additional or altered meaning and emphasis among the Ne-

groes. The upper-class Negro who dresses with quiet good taste is not only demonstrating that he possesses this attribute of breeding; he is also, and actively, repudiating the assumption that all Negroes are either slovenly or flashy, that all Negroes are alike, that *he* is to be identified with the inferior type of Negro. Every trivial act may be charged, in addition to its other significance, with this double message of disclaimer: *We* are not like that; *I* am not like them.

In this rather rough and schematic sketch of class differentiation, some factors appear to be a cause, others a result, and still others a mere concomitant of membership in a given class. . . .

FROM

The Magnolia Jungle

P. D. EAST

*P. D. East had thought he wanted to be a doctor but found his calling as
the iconoclastic editor of a country newspaper called* The Petal Paper, *
so named for the little town where it was located, across the Leaf River
from Hattiesburg. As told in* The Magnolia Jungle, *published in
1960, he was born in 1921 to an unstable mother who decided to give
him up, and was then adopted by a hard-working couple, Jim and Birdie
East, living in Columbia, in south Mississippi, at the time. East's
adopted father worked in many different lumber mills in the Piney Woods,
while his mother ran a boardinghouse. According to the statistics East
provides, from the First World War until the depression, 60 to 75 percent
of Mississippi's economy depended on the timber industry, yet the workers
realized very little profit. Having lived in dire poverty and hard times,
East developed sympathy for the underdog. In 1954, when the Supreme
Court decision of* Brown v. Board of Education *struck down the concept of "separate but equal," East found the resulting backlash against
blacks to be intolerable. When he began writing satire lampooning the
Ku Klux Klan and the White Citizens' Council in his editorials for* The
Petal Paper *called "East Side," his circulation in Petal dropped to
twenty-five. He was supported in his efforts, however, by people around
the country, especially subscribers in New York City and Los Angeles. The
following excerpt shows the involvement of Mississippi supporter,
William Faulkner, and illustrates the politics involved in keeping the
unpopular paper going (from chapter 24).*

I HAD REACHED a decision about the situation in Petal. I saw no
point in keeping an office, paying rent and other expenses connected
with maintaining it. My wife and I decided to buy a larger house, one
in which I could have a work room. We worked out a transaction
whereby we could make the down payment on a three-bedroom home
with the equity we had in our two-bedroom house, and the additional
cost of payments would still be less than office rent in Petal. We made
the move in July 1956.

As stated already, there were pleasant moments in spite of the ever-
advancing jungle. One of those pleasant memories grew out of a letter
I'd had from a professor at the University of Mississippi, in Oxford. Dr.

Josh Brass had written me saying that since he subscribed to a labor paper and other radical publications, he supposed he could stand *The Petal Paper*. In his letter he also said he and William Faulkner had discussed the possibility of forming some sort of moderate group in the state. My response to the idea was immediate; it was something I'd given thought to ever since my realization of the need for communication. In subsequent correspondence we arranged a meeting for the purpose of further discussion. Dr. Brass invited me to Oxford to meet with him and Faulkner. There was some hesitation when I thought of a meeting with William Faulkner, but the idea of a moderate group was more important than my apprehension over Faulkner. It was true that I wanted to meet Faulkner, but when I thought of the tales I'd heard about him, I had no idea what to expect; as usual, I went with a blank mind. Josh Brass filled me in on minor points: don't discuss Faulkner's work with him; don't try to force a conversation; leave him alone; he'd speak when he wanted to and not before. To follow Josh's advice was easy enough for me, since I'd not read Faulkner's works, except for his short stories. Nor was I given to forcing conversations with anyone, even though there were times when I'd wanted to do so.

I drove to Oxford on a Friday in June. The following morning Brass and I discussed conditions in the Magnolia Jungle, as well as William Faulkner. Immediately after lunch we were to pick up Faulkner at his home. I'd seen a number of Junes in Mississippi, but none had been hotter than the one in 1956. I was suffering from the heat, barely able to breathe, when we turned into the Faulkner driveway. Faulkner's home sits off a dead-end street, not visible from any approach. However, it seemed that entirely too many curious persons had found it anyway. Driving in, I felt the bottom of my car scrape the road; it was extremely rough, the ruts deep and filled with holes. "Good God," I said to Josh, "you'd think a Nobel Prize winner could afford to care for his driveway!" Josh said he thought Faulkner left it that way in order to discourage visitors. "As a matter of fact," he continued, "I wouldn't be surprised if he dug the holes in it himself."

What I expected in Faulkner I don't know. Perhaps I thought he might look a little like God, or perhaps one of the better-known archangels. I suppose it would have mattered little how he appeared, I'd still have been surprised. We parked behind Faulkner's Plymouth station wagon, about a 1950 model. Faulkner walked from around back of the house. I stood there with my mouth open. He was a small man, short, slightly inclined to be chubby, not fat. He was dressed in a sailor cap, the kind you can buy for a dollar at any variety store. A pipe was sticking in his mouth. He wore a faded, thin blue shirt and a pair of khaki pants torn off just above the knees. They'd not been cut, not those pants; they'd been torn. I can't recall his shoes, but he wasn't wearing socks. Josh introduced us. We shook hands; he was polite, courteous, and his voice was soft, but strong and clear. It was a pleasant, delightful voice. He was brown as an Indian, having spent much of the summer on his sailboat. His mustache was trimmed neatly. His eyes were dark brown, almost black, in color. His facial features were clear-cut; it was a strong, calm face. The presence of Faulkner, with his soft-spoken, quiet voice, his strong face, had the effect of making me want to keep my own voice at a moderate pitch. I felt at ease with him; his presence had an over-all tranquilizing effect on me. After I'd closed my mouth and taken note of the man, I was keenly aware of a great liking for him as a person. I couldn't help but wonder how those wild tales of Faulkner had come into being; but, of course, I realized I was always prejudiced in favor of any person I liked.

After hoisting sail, we moved out in the Sardis Reservoir, a large body of water about ten miles west of Oxford. From the time we were intro-duced at one o'clock, until around three—after the trip out to the res-ervoir, the setting of the sails and a tour around the water area—Faulkner said not one word to me. Nor had I spoken to him. For the better part of two hours the two of us sat in the stern of the boat, our knees touching, and not a sound was made. I watched him closely, observing the great patience he seemed to have, and anyone sailing a boat in June on the Sardis Reservoir, with the wind as still as death, has to have patience. After about an hour, my rump hurt. The seat was a six-inch board, and what with my standing six feet two inches high and weighing two hundred and twenty-five pounds, a six-inch board was hardly conducive to a comfortable rump.

Finally, after that long silence, Faulkner said to me: "Well, East, any-body put any dead cats on your porch lately?" The silence had been broken, and he'd broken it. I was most cautious in my conversation with Faulkner; I wasn't sure of anything about the man. Finally, I felt free to speak as I pleased, which I did, and he responded as I'd hoped. I was glad to know Bill Faulkner was human; indeed, I was happy to know he wasn't really God. After that slow, hot sail, we were preparing to return to Oxford. The car was parked near a little store, and Faulkner asked, "You want a Coke, East?" I said yes; the Cokes were opened and Faulk-ner didn't have any money with him. I paid. Upon returning home, he asked if I'd be his guest while I was in Oxford. As it was, I'd already checked into the Alumni House at the university, so I declined. Later I was to learn from Josh that I'd been honored by the invitation, that Faulkner hardly ever asked anyone to stay at his home as a guest.

At dinner that evening, and again the next day, we discussed at length the possibility of forming a "Mississippi Moderates" group. It was decided, finally, that it was impossible. Faulkner felt that we'd spend all our time fending off attacks rather than getting anything worth while accomplished. After deciding on the impossibility of the moderate-group formation, we turned to the question of what we could do to bring about some hope in what we viewed as a hopeless situation. Someone recalled that a group of students at the university had done a series of papers on the general situation. They had called them "The Nigble Papers" and had lampooned the Scotch-Irish, of whom the vast majority of Mississippians will tell you they are descendants. Copies were gathered; we considered what we could do along that line. It was finally decided that if we could let other moderates in the state know of our attempt at moderation, that in itself would be worth while; also, we saw the possibility of getting college students whose minds had not yet been closed to laugh at the stupidity around them. The publication of a paper was decided on. Faulkner suggested to me that if it were known the two of us had anything to do with it, the effectiveness would be lost. I felt inclined to agree with him again. Our plan was to print a paper about twice a year, pointing up with humor the prevailing situation in our state. I volunteered to edit and publish the first paper. What's more, I even said I'd pay for it.

And so it was that *The Southern Reposure* came into existence, having been born in Bill Faulkner's living room. I returned home, loaded with "Nigble Papers" to edit, rewrite and shape into something to appeal to college students throughout the state. Almost from the inception of the idea, I ran into trouble. After days of editing, rewriting and trying to write a suitable introduction to the paper, after checking with Faulkner on it, my printers refused to print the paper for me. One of the vice-presidents, of whom they had many, called me and said they'd decided that if it were known they did the printing it might offend someone, especially the Boy Scouts of America. I was surprised but not angry at their decision. I failed to understand it, in view of the fact that they were on the verge of bankruptcy and it was a cash printing job. There was only one thing to do about *The Southern Reposure,* and that was to get Easton King to print it for me. I went to see him. Not only would he print it, he said, but he'd help me edit the copy if I wanted him to do so. I was pleased to have his help. The project was under way.

In the meantime another minor problem arose. My paper was due out on July 5; what with the fourth being a holiday, I had agreed to go to press on the sixth. On the afternoon of July 5 the telephone rang. It was the shop in Gulfport. The vice-president who didn't want to offend the Boy Scouts said they had decided to close down the business. I was not a Boy Scout, but I was offended. Indeed, I was angry. Great God from Gulfport, I exploded, it seemed to me any business about to go broke would know it more than eighteen hours ahead of time. It was from experience that I spoke; I'd been going broke over two and one half years. I had occasion to visit Easton King once again. There was no hesitancy about his taking back my printing, and he didn't bother to complain about the short notice. The turn of events delayed the print-ing of *The Southern Reposure.*

When *The Southern Reposure* was printed, it was a tabloid, five columns in width, sixteen inches in depth, and we printed about 10,000 of them, 2,000 of which were mailed to individuals in the state. The additional copies were sent to most of the colleges, to moderates on campus whom we knew, for distribution. No one knew the source of the paper, nor did anyone know who was responsible for its appearance on campuses throughout the state. From all reports the effort was worth while. One of the most interesting sidelights on the Scotch-Irish effort was reported to me from a Baptist college located in the state. The college was a segregation stronghold, its president having justified segregation through the Scriptures and more than one faculty member having made the speaking rounds for the Citizens Councils. Our moderate contact distributed papers in two buildings; the students began to read them and to laugh. One faculty member ordered all "that trash be gathered and burned." The result was the same as such efforts have had through history: those who had had no interest in reading the paper at once made efforts to get a copy. I was told copies were selling for one dollar each on the campus. I sat back and hoped such would be the case all over the state.

Shortly after the papers were distributed I had occasion to visit with Faulkner again. "East," he said, "you did a damned good job with that paper. I've sent copies to New York." It wasn't much of a compliment, true; but coming from Bill Faulkner, and knowing he wasn't given to gab, I was most grateful for his having said it. While Faulkner never put the question to me directly, he seemed interested to know how I happened to hold my views. There it was again. That old, old question, and still I was without an answer that made sense. I had given much thought to it, and I thought about it again in the hope of giving an understandable and satisfactory answer to Faulkner.

"Bill," I answered, "I think for the simple reason that I believe in God." That's all I came up with; he made no effort to pursue the subject further, and I was glad about that.

As to *The Southern Reposure,* it amounted to a *tour de force* and nothing more. We were never able to come up with another idea. However, on the whole, I feel *The Southern Reposure* served a worth-while purpose. It is true that certain persons were offended. I was told one minister was upset because of a quote from the Bible. I inserted the quote and deliberately misquoted it in text and reference. Somehow to my mind it seemed to fit under the name across the top of the front page. It was "Know Ye the Truth and Be Ye Then Free, John 3:16." I still think it fits, especially when I consider the ever-present, teeming jungle.

In view of our desire to be anonymous, and in view of my accepting the job of getting the paper together and circulated, I decided it would be fitting to have a highly proper person as editor, publisher and crusader. That person was Nathan Bedford Cooclose, whose masthead read: "*The Southern Reposure* is published quarterly by the Solvent Publishing Company, Blue Ribbon, Mississippi, and is edited by Nathan Bedford Cooclose." With the co-operation of Faulkner and Easton King, I wrote copy for Nathan Bedford, his

PUBLISHER'S INTRODUCTION

It was late spring that my son, Ernest Chris, returned to our plantation, "The Southern Manor," and brought the worst, certainly the most disturbing, news of my entire life.

I was stretched out on my hammock in the front yard, relaxing with a cool mint julep before dinner. Ernest Chris had returned from a college near Jackson, Mississippi, which he had attended during the year. I attended the same college; so did my father and so did his father.

Never have I been so upset by any news as by that brought home by my son, Ernest Chris.

He had been a member of the U.S.D.S. (United Sons and Daughters for Segregation) at our college. My son informed me, and I confirmed it, to be sure, that the Scotch-Irish among us were a real threat, indeed, a terrible menace to our way of life.

Here are some facts I have confirmed about the Scotch-Irish in Mississippi today.

SMELL: The average Scotch-Irish smells like smoke. This is most unpleasant, and is caused by drinking a concoction known as "Uisgebeatha." This drinking causes bad breath, naturally. It is only natural that if the Scotch-Irish wanted to act civilized, as you and I, he would flavor his drink with mint. No, my friend, mint and smoke do not mix!

HABITS: The average Scotch-Irish is a repulsive and obnoxious creature who is apt, if the notion strikes him, to pull a highland fling on the main street of any one of our towns in Mississippi. They are a group who, except for the women, carry long-bladed knives to church with them. This, I assure you, is a heathen practice. In addition, they have come to expect to be served oatmeal in our finest restaurants simply because they have the required fifteen cents. Anyone with good breeding knows that oatmeal is horse food! And to top off the whole business, they eat popcorn in the movie houses. Which, of course, is not very couth, and, besides, it's damned annoying.

SPEECH: We Southerners have tried for years to keep the "r" sound out of our language, and have tried to teach the same basic good taste to the Scottrish among us. But, lo and behold, they insist on pronouncing the "r" and, what's more, they do it with a roll. They are, no matter how hard we try, still barbaric.

MORALS: You should know the low morals of the Scottrish among us! Why, indeed, they breed like turtles! Their divorce rate is outrageous! They even like the smell that is their own; therefore they don't take baths every day as you and I do. To put it mildly, the Scottrish is a trifle lax in writing checks around the first of each month. The cannot and will not accept business responsibility, no matter how hard we try. You know this to be true as well as I. In addition to their poor breeding, they are vulgar to an unbearable point. How many times have you heard one exclaim "Hoot mon" or "Begorrrrah!" How disgusting!

In view of all the above information, I have taken the only means of which I know to bring certain news and views to you; I have undertaken the publication of this little paper, *The Southern Reposure.*

I have asked myself, as surely you must have, "Do I want my young daughter to marry a windbag, highland-flinging, kilt-wearing creature whose ancestry is questionable?"

Like your answer, mine is the same: *No!*

Knowing, of course, that the best thing that could be done would be to send them back to the bogs from which they came, I offer it to you for speculation. If that fails, then, we must stick together in an all-out effort to make it clear to the Scottrish that we will treat them kind, but they *must* stay in their place.

In short, this paper proposes to maintain segregation of the Scotch-Irish, no matter what the cost!

It is a known fact that smoke and mint don't mix.

So, why try it at our expense?

Sincerely,
NATHAN BEDFORD COOCLOSE

Following his introduction, Mr. Cooclose decided to run a five-column streamer at the top of the front page, above the name plate, in which he sought to catch the eye and interest of anyone seeing his paper. The two-line streamer, actually written by Faulkner, declared: EASTLAND ELECTED BY NAACP AS OUTSTANDING MAN OF THE YEAR. He did not follow up with a news story. However, there were a number of news stories, each having to do with a phase of the Magnolia Mess. Mr. Cooclose declared his paper was a member of the Confederate Press Association; also across the bottom of the two inside pages his war cry was sounded: THE SOUTH WAS BUILT IN THE SOUTH FOR SOUTHERNERS. As to news stories, Nathan Bedford gave an impartial account of reports reaching his desk. Example:

ADDIT TRIAL REACHES CLIMAX

Addit, Mississippi (CPA)—The trial of sixteen-year-old Alexander Graham Tell, young Scotch-Irish boy hauled into court for insulting pretty Mrs. Ruby Jean Hollofield, 23, reached its climax yesterday when A. J. Elliss, prosecuting attorney, announced, "This trial may very well cast the die—either for keeping our blood pure or for mongrelizing with the Scotch-Irish. If Tell is set free, the bars are down, and the undefiled heritage of our ancestors is at an end."

Mrs. Hollofield, wife of blond young farmer Lonnie Hollofield, told the court that as she passed Tell on the street, he turned to a companion and whispered, "What a wee bonnie lassie!" She immediately reported the offense to her husband, who had Tell arrested. The boy did not deny saying this, but said he meant it merely as a compliment.

Attorney Elliss asked that the boy be given a severe prison sentence for his offense. "Such audacity and lewdness," he said, "are the norm of behavior for a people whose history includes such notorious figures as Mary, Queen of Scots and Macbeth. There can be no compromise with them."

Red-haired young Tell, wearing the plaids of his clan, is being kept under heavy guard at the county jail for fear that the citizens of Addit, among whom feeling over the incident is running very high, will throw him into the river with a horse collar around his neck.

. . . Being a reasonable and practical man, the publisher and editor felt his paper should have a few "Letters to the Editor." He called on several friends to state their views on the menace of the Scotch-Irish to the Southern way of life. There were others, but two of his friends expressed their views and concern by writing:

DEAR SIRS:

For a long time I have suspected that my little son Ignatz was being influenced by insidious propaganda. But imagine my horror when I realized the full extent of his mental pollution. Today I found, securely hidden under his mattress, a copy of *Emerson's Essays*. God alone knows what strange ideas are seething now in my child's head. The reading of Emerson can only lead to questioning, thinking and, ultimately—yes, though I shudder to say it—to an open mind. Mothers, I implore you—sooner kill your own flesh and blood than see it come to this. If your child is hiding books by Emerson, Paine, Whitman or Walt Kelly in his dresser drawers, destroy them as the un-American trash that they are.

Respectfully,
MRS. WIENER WALD, JR.

DEAR SIR:

I do not believe God wants us to mix with the Scotch-Irish, else why did he put them off on a little island by themselves? They do not want integration any more than we do. I love the Scotch-Irish, but only if they stay in the place God appointed for them. A careful reading of the Holy Bible will show you God's stand on segregation. John 22:19 and March 17:14 tell us what the Master said on the subject.

The Scotch-Irish have only been in this country two hundred years. Before that they lived in the highlands of Scotland, totally without washing machines, electric lights, automobiles, and all the other basic elements of civilization, and dressed only in the rudest sort of kilts. Furthermore, I maintain that after two hundred years they are still Scotch-Irish, and no amount of civilization will change the fact. I think I need not point out to you the basic immorality of their characters. There is hardly a one of them that does not get divorced, and eat meat on Fridays. Their music, as typified by such dances as the jig or the highland fling, is characteristically lewd and shows the primitive rhythms of the highlands from whence they came.

I have a little daughter, a sweet, cherubic little girl, and sooner would I take up arms as my grandfather did in '61 and pour out my life's blood before I would see her go to school with Scotch-Irish children. The tragic results of such a contact—perhaps someday red-haired, freckle-faced children with such names as Patrick or Andrew—would be too much for me. May the Lord take me before such a day arrives.

I am willing to grant that the Scotch-Irish have given us great men—like Andrew Carnegie or Robert Burns, for instance—but for the most part they have shamefully wasted the opportunities that our great land has given them.

Again, let me repeat: let the rabble-rousers do what they may, the Scotch-Irish were meant to till the soil: God has appointed it. (Genesis 52:2.) We are kind to them, let them keep their place.

Respectfully,
STANISLAUS WOCKINSKY

. . . I had spent well over three hundred dollars on the venture, not one cent of which I could afford. I had gotten my friend Easton to share the expense, in that he printed it at cost, possibly below. It had been fun. I'd laughed until my ulcer hemorrhaged. While confined with milk and pablum I wondered how silly, childish and immature the whole venture had been. I wondered if the cost and effort had been a complete waste. I can say frankly and honestly that I felt much better about the entire matter when contributions began to come in from various parts of the nation. Obviously we had a blabbermouth in our midst, but he'd blabbered where it helped. Not only did I feel better about the matter with the contributions arriving, but I was delighted and happy when a check from one of the great educators in the country arrived. Dr. Arthur M. Schlesinger of Harvard sent a check to help pay for *The Southern Reposure*. And Bill Faulkner? Hell, he didn't even buy the Cokes. But it was good to know he was on the same side as I. . . .

Witness in Philadelphia

FLORENCE MARS

A native of Philadelphia, Mississippi, Florence Mars knew well the land and people she came to describe after the murders of Council of Federated Organizations (COFO) workers James Earl Chaney, Andrew Goodman, and Michael Schwerner on June 21, 1964, in reaction to the civil rights movement. During the twenties and thirties, her paternal grandfather had taught her about the people as he collected payment for his medical services in mules. In 1962, after having earned her living as a freelance writer and photographer in Atlanta and New Orleans, Mars returned to Neshoba County to raise Hereford cattle and run the Neshoba County Stockyards, which she owned. When she testified before a grand jury against the Ku Klux Klan, she was harassed, threatened with financial ruin, and at one point arrested on false charges of drunken driving and put in jail. In the following passage from the chapter entitled "It's a Hoax," Mars portrays the unreal atmosphere in the town of Philadelphia after the murders, as preparations were going on for the Neshoba County Fair. Forty-four days later, the bodies of Chaney, Goodman, and Schwerner were found by the FBI in an earthen dam. In October of 1967, six Klansmen, including imperial wizard Sam Bowers, were sentenced for conspiracy to murder, a charge carrying maximum prison terms of only ten years. But, as Mars states, "The convictions were a turning point for Mississippi. This was the first time a jury in the state had returned a guilty verdict in a major civil rights case since Reconstruction, and the convictions marked the end of the long chain of widely publicized and unpunished racial killings that began after the Supreme Court decision of 1954."

IT WAS PARTICULARLY chilling to see klansmen get together in certain places near the square during the day, constantly watching the streets and talking with each other. The Steak House Cafe, on a corner one block off the square, was the central meeting place. The cafe became a private club after the Civil Rights Act was passed and then, appropriately enough, hung white sheets in the windows. As in most Mississippi restaurants Negro women did all the cooking and kitchen work and white women served the food. Men milled around outside all day long, and there was constant traffic between the Steak

House and the bowling alley located directly across the street. In addition, there were several barbershops and drugstores where a few men met at a time, often heading up to the Steak House afterwards.

My friends and I did not doubt that these men knew a murder had been committed, and that it was "theirs." Yet, they claimed as loudly as anyone that it was a hoax and probably helped convince the town that it was. At the same time, some of them made surprisingly vicious remarks such as, "I wouldn't give no more thought to killing them than wringing a cat's neck" and "I could kill them easier than I could kill Germans I didn't know."

The second indication of Klan membership was affiliation with the auxiliary police. In early 1964 the Mississippi legislature had set up machinery to form local homeguard units to assist local police in dealing with expected racial violence. Immediately after the murders an auxiliary police unit was organized at local initiative in Neshoba County. When the FBI began its investigation, the auxiliary police provided a legitimate vehicle for klansmen to get together frequently. Many men in the "goon squad" were in the auxiliary police, and though not all auxiliary policemen were members of the Klan, it was clear that a great many klansmen were members of the auxiliary police. In fact, the auxiliary was the legitimate police arm of the Ku Klux Klan. The auxiliary met openly in the National Guard Armory at night and occasionally directed traffic, sometimes having to leave work to do so.

The third indication of who belonged to the Klan came from noticing whom the FBI sought out for frequent questioning, which in a town the size of Philadelphia was impossible not to know. Also, the FBI constantly asked Ellen and me about the people they were questioning.

Finally, we picked up information through Negro friends and domestic help. It all added up to a large and powerful organization, one that almost certainly included the sheriff and his deputy. It was possible to be quite certain about the membership of certain individuals one might not ordinarily expect to be in the Klan because of accumulated circumstantial evidence. For example, the FBI asked repeatedly about the owner of an appliance shop, a man not associated with goon squad activities. Furthermore, the FBI virtually camped on his doorstep. We felt sure he was in the Klan; later, his maid told me that she had found a white robe in his closet.

When I began to realize the extent of Klan organization, and that it reached into the sheriff's office, I determined to do what I could to oppose Klan forces in the community. If the community was not to be a party to murder, it could not sanction the organization responsible for the murders. I knew the majority of the community saw the killings in racial terms: the COFO workers were the enemy and whatever happened to them was justified and deserved. However, I knew I would do what I could not only to assist the FBI but, if it was in my power, to help the civic leadership see the issue and act. I thought that despite whatever feeling they had toward COFO, a few men of influence would eventually be able to see the principle of justice involved.

FBI agents told me they were having trouble finding people who would talk with them. What puzzled agents was the attitude of Philadelphia's businessmen. Executives in the privacy of their offices were as cool and noncommittal as the man on the street. They especially wondered why the man who was generally acknowledged to be the most influential and powerful businessman in the community was not really cooperating with them.

After this conversation with the agents, I went to talk with the man they were referring to, a prominent citizen and an old family friend, who had earlier sent the telegram of protest to Walter Cronkite. I thought perhaps he had reacted with understandable civic loyalty to the insulting misnomer of the county but hadn't realized the strength and danger of the Ku Klux Klan. I thought if anyone had the courage to stand in opposition to the Klan, it was he. When I told him the FBI thought they had a Klan murder on their hands, he seemed surprised. He said he had been busy and hadn't given it as much attention as he should have but he certainly was interested and would look into it.

I said the FBI would be glad to talk to him and I was sure they could tell him more than I could. He said, "Well, that's all right. I've got some contacts of my own that I can check." I left thinking he would look into it and possibly take some action. After a few weeks I knew that he was aware of the strength of the Klan and that he had taken no action.

Several months later he told a New York *Times* reporter, "We were just the tragic victims of chance. I have never felt a guilty conscience about this thing for the simple reason that I know our people here are as good as people anywhere else. The rest of the country thinks it has been tense in Philadelphia. But we've just been free and easy—business as usual."

Throughout July the FBI investigation and search for the bodies continued. Even though the FBI was piecing together what had happened that night, without the bodies there could be no crime to prosecute. Busloads of sailors went day after day to one community and then another, making their headquarters at country stores. Residents looked on the search as an affront to the good name of their communities.

Once during this period, I happened into a store near my cattle farm. The proprietor's wife was full of enthusiastic talk about her experiences of the last few days. For one thing, she had sold out everything the day before when the search crews were in the area. However, when a group of sailors stood around the store laughing and making jokes as if she weren't there, she finally told them that Shady Grove was a community of law-abiding and God-fearing people, and said, "Y'all don't really expect to find any bodies around here do you?" She indignantly told me that some funny-talking boy had stuck his finger in her face and said, "Yes ma'am, we expect to find them pretty close to here."

In the Bethsaida community, eight miles south of Philadelphia, my great aunt, Fannie Smith, was extremely agitated by the intrusion of FBI agents who went to every house in the community, sometimes more than once. She said there had never been any trouble in that community and she knew that no one out there had anything to do with the disappearance. Aunt Fannie told me that there had been some shooting on the night of June 21, up around a well-known bootleg place a short distance south from her house, on Highway 19. But she said something was always going on up there and nobody ever paid any attention to it. The FBI ultimately found that the shots she heard were in fact the shots that had killed the boys.

As the weeks passed it began to seem less likely to many that the boys really were alive; it also seemed less likely to many that any bodies would be found in Neshoba County. However, most people continued to hang onto the hope that the disappearance was a hoax. Toward the end of July I overhead a Philadelphia matron say, in a tone she usually reserved to console the bereaved, "I believe with all my heart they are alive somewhere. We may never know it, but I believe it is so nevertheless." A proprietor in one of the stores on the square had a more realistic attitude and, at about the same time, said to me, "I just hope that if they are dead, they won't find their bodies anywhere around here." I usually didn't respond in such cases, but this time I said, "I hope they are found around here. It will be the only way to get the community to accept any responsibility for what has happened." At the time, I felt this was very important.

July passed and it began to look like, hoax or not, there would be no bodies found in the county. Preparations for the fair, held in the beginning of August, went on as usual that year. Cabins were cleaned out, repairs made, and talk turned more and more to matters concerning the fair.

A week before the fair opened the FBI moved a dragline in from Jackson onto the old Jolly Place, located about five miles southwest of Philadelphia. On Tuesday, August 4, beneath fifteen feet of dirt in a newly completed earthen dam, the FBI found the bodies of Michael Schwerner, James Chaney, and Andrew Goodman. The FBI had roughly estimated from the dam construction where the bodies might be; then, an agent, on impulse, walked fifteen paces toward the center. There, directly beneath, the bodies were found, side by side. This ended one of the most extensive searches ever conducted by the FBI. The farm belonged to Olen Burrage, the owner of a Neshoba County trucking firm who lived two miles away. He said he didn't know anybody who would kill the boys and put the bodies on his property. He also said, "I want people to know I am sorry it happened. I just don't know why anybody would kill them and I don't believe in anything like that."

The discovery shattered Neshoba County's hoax rationale and was met with silence or muted conversation. A few avoided the overwhelming evidence that this was indeed no hoax by saying that the FBI had put the bodies there. This was evidenced by the fact that the FBI knew exactly where to dig. Further, it was rumored that the dirt caked to the bodies was different from the dirt in the dam.

Early in the search the FBI had widely circulated the rumor that they would pay up to $25,000 for information leading to discovery of the bodies. After the discovery the FBI claimed that its attention had been drawn to the new earthen dam during flights over the area in a helicopter. No one believed it, and there was widespread, if quiet, speculation about who had told the FBI where the bodies were. It was rumored that a preacher who was being closely interrogated by the FBI had bought an expensive new automobile. Others suspected of having told were reported to be out of town for a few days. Any evidence of new wealth was suspect. However, people generally continued to talk about the upcoming fair, trying to act as if nothing had happened.

The klansmen were unmistakably anxious over the discovery. Activity picked up again on the streets, but without the earlier swaggering self-assurance. Men scurried to the same meeting places, but with worried looks and a greater sense of urgency. Undoubtedly they were deeply concerned about who had told the FBI where the bodies were, or even more. At first, arrests were expected, but within two weeks the fear of imminent arrest waned.

I hoped now that there would be a statement from civic leadership deploring the crime. It was past time for the county to admit what had happened and to confront and repudiate the Klan. There was no statement. I later found out that two substantial businessmen had gone to the mayor and asked if he would make a statement on behalf of the town. One of the businessmen told me the mayor remained silent a long time and then without looking at them pushed a sheet of paper across the desk, asking them to write the statement they thought he should make. Sensing that the mayor was disturbed, the businessman put the paper in his pocket and left to think about it. He said he finally decided not to write out a statement because he didn't want to put the mayor on the spot.

The following Monday, six days after the bodies were found, the Neshoba County Fair opened. As always, anticipation was great. On the weekend before families moved into the cabins that stand like a ghost town the rest of the year, and by Monday the fairgrounds were transformed into a tiny magical town.

The fair *almost* seemed the same. There were the same speakings, bands, horseraces, community exhibits, dances, sings, and carnival activities; the same crowds milled near the pavilion and sat on benches built around the oak trees, and there was the same talk about how good it was to be back. The unpleasant events of the summer were not discussed. The press, at the fair every year, was not intrusive and most fairgoers were unaware of the presence of FBI agents.

Still, there was an air of unspoken tension, greatly heightened by the bizarre presence of the auxiliary police. The full force of about fifty men patrolled the grounds wearing high boots and blue police uniforms. Their helmets rode low on their foreheads and looked like those of Nazi storm troopers. Their belts were loaded with live ammunition; a billet hung from one hip and a gun from the other. The auxiliary police made their unofficial headquarters under an oak tree by the pavilion, directly in front of our family cabin. Here they met with klansmen not in the auxiliary and together watched the crowds. Their presence was not commented on.

Terror in the Night

JACK NELSON

In Terror in the Night, *published in 1992, Pulitzer-Prize winning journalist Jack Nelson looks back at the year 1967, a time when the Ku Klux Klan in Mississippi began terrorizing Jews. This is the story of the bombing of the Jewish synagogue, Temple Beth Israel, and of the house of Rabbi Perry Nussbaum, both in Jackson, and the subsequent bombing of the Jewish synagogue in Meridian. The bombings were masterminded by imperial wizard Sam Bowers, the "mad-dog killer" Tommy Tarrants, Klansman Danny Doe Hawkins, and an elementary school teacher, Kathy Ainsworth. Nelson himself became embroiled in the conflict when his story was printed in the* Los Angeles Times. *Bowers was never caught for these activities although he served six years for his role in the Goodman-Chaney-Schwerner killings in Philadelphia. Kathy Ainsworth was killed in the shoot-out with the FBI and became a martyr for the weakened Klan. Danny Joe Hawkins joined a supermilitant racist and anti-Semitic group in Kansas City, Missouri. Tommy Tarrants served fifteen years at Parchman, where he converted to Christianity. This selection, from chapter 3, shows the terror and also the complexity of being Jewish in Jackson, Mississippi, in 1967.*

A LITTLE PAST 10:00 P.M. that night, the shock of an enormous explosion shook Al Binder's antebellum home in a fashionable section of Jackson, literally lifting him out of bed. Instantly the young lawyer was wide awake. Temple Beth Israel was only a half mile away and because of all the Klan threats against the Jewish community he immediately figured it had been bombed. He worried about Rabbi Perry Nussbaum, who often worked late in his office; he might be inside the synagogue. Binder pulled on his clothes and drove as fast as he could through the empty streets.

Joe Harris, a prominent building contractor, and his wife, Maxine, also were jarred awake. "Joe, something big blew up," she exclaimed. "You better get up and see what's going on." As he struggled to get his clothes on, she turned on the radio. At first there was music, but then a bulletin: Temple Beth Israel had been bombed.

"I knew it," Joe had said as he hurried out to his car. "The rabbi's gonna get us all killed."

Binder was the first to reach the scene. The night was dark, with a warm mist hanging in the air. The smell of dynamite stung his nose. He looked around, but saw no other cars in the parking lot and no lights shining in the synagogue. Maybe the rabbi had not worked late after all.

Police cars, ambulances and fire trucks arrived, sirens screaming. The spotlights of the emergency vehicles illuminated the building. The blast had ripped through the administrative offices and a conference room, torn a hole in the ceiling, blown out windows, ruptured a water pipe and buckled a wall. An octagonal structure dominated by a massive roof, Temple Beth Israel had been dedicated only seven months earlier. Now Binder could see smoke coming from the windows.

Scores of neighborhood residents, some in their bathrobes, were beginning to collect on the lawn. The night was so dark and foggy that people in the crowd had difficulty recognizing one another. Standing in groups of two or three, everyone spoke in whispers, as though talking aloud would violate something already defiled by what everyone assumed had been a bomb. Over and over they asked one another, "Why would anybody do such a thing?"

The crowd opened a path for Rabbi Nussbaum and his wife, Arene. The Nussbaums too had been awakened by the blast and were already dressing when FBI agent Jim Ingram, in charge of civil rights enforcement in Mississippi, called to confirm their fear that it had come from the temple. Now, nervously surveying piles of shattered glass and plaster, Arene said, "Just think what would have happened if someone had been inside there."

"This is a fear I've been living with," Nussbaum answered. Turning to a local reporter, he added, "I had intended to do some work in my study tonight, but changed my mind at the last minute and stayed home."

. . . Nussbaum not only had a difficult personality, he was still—after more than a decade in Mississippi—seen as an outsider. The rabbi himself had grown fond of the state and its people—an affection that compounded his inner conflict as the civil rights struggle intensified. But he rejected the elaborate strategies that most Jews in the South had developed for dealing with their vulnerable situation. Members of his congregation felt that he did not really understand what it meant to be a Jew in the South.

Jews had lived in Mississippi since before it joined the Union in 1817. They had fought on its side when it tried to leave the Union in 1860;

many were proud that a Jew, Judah Benjamin, had been an important figure in Jefferson Davis's Confederate government. Along with other whites, they had supported and prospered from "the peculiar institution" of slavery in its pure form before Emancipation and in its covert form afterward. Yet even when they tried to convince themselves of their acceptance by their fellow Southerners, deep down they always knew they were viewed as aliens in a land of uncompromising, militant, fundamentalist Protestantism. "Judaism may rank higher in the moral order of Bible Belt fundamentalist circles than, say, Black Christianity or Roman Catholicism, but it remains nonetheless a less-than-equal sect, an extraneous and foreign relation in an area of xenophobes," Murray Polner wrote in *Rabbi: The American Experience.*

To thrive, many Jews concluded, they had to assimilate into the dominant culture in every way possible. Becoming "200 percent Southerners," they submerged their own religious and cultural heritage, partly out of a frankly acknowledged appetite for the comfortable life and partly out of fear of the violence that never seemed far below the surface in Mississippi.

Nussbaum's predecessor, Rabbi Meyer Lovitt, who had served as spiritual leader of Jackson's Jews for twenty-five years, understood and supported this approach. He—like most of his generation of rabbis across the South—avoided controversial issues such as civil rights. He downplayed the differences between Judaism and Christianity and supported as much assimilation as circumstances would permit. Jewish holidays were observed inconspicuously, and if Jewish families wished to join the rest of the community in putting up Christmas trees, Lovitt made no objection. Maxine Harris remembered Lovitt being "just like a little Santa Claus. He'd check the Jewish houses to see who had Christmas trees and say, 'That's a nice little Hanukkah bush.' There never was any trouble with Rabbi Lovitt."

In all of the South, Jews, especially the dominant, assimilationist-minded German Jews, adopted Southern ways while not completely abandoning their old-world rituals. They went to their Reform temples on Friday nights, but they shunned Hebrew chanting and did away with bar mitzvahs. Kosher kitchens survived almost exclusively in the homes of Jews with eastern European roots, who arrived later. In *The Provincials,* Eli Evans described a not untypical Sabbath celebration in a Reform household in Anniston, Alabama. "First, Mama blessed the lights. And then, we always had our favorite Sabbath meal—oyster stew, steak, ham, or fried chicken; Mama's homemade biscuits and corn bread too; hoppin john and sweet potato pie for dessert."

Nussbaum had sought to change all that. He criticized those who put up Christmas trees. He reinstituted bar mitzvahs and other Jewish ceremonies. He embraced Zionism and Israel, both of which Southern Jews had traditionally held at arm's length. He insisted openly that Judaism was a distinct religion and not just an earlier, Old Testament form of Christianity—"the Jewish church," as many people in Jackson often called it. Altogether, in large ways and small, he made the congregation more aware of its Jewishness and he made the Jewishness more conspicuous in the larger community—neither of which the members of Temple Beth Israel welcomed.

Nussbaum's personal manner and his approach to Judaism had only compounded what bothered the congregation most about him: the rabbi was just too liberal on the race issue, and much too close to the civil rights movement for all but a few members. Assigned to congregations in the northern United States for most of his career, Nussbaum right from the start had aroused concern among Beth Israel's leaders about where he stood on race. Although he had given them a reassuring pledge never to do anything that would cause problems for the congregation, over the years he had done a series of things that caused some members to worry. They feared his activities would put a spotlight on the Jewish community, antagonize the Jackson Establishment and disturb the uneasy peace that Jews throughout the South struggled to maintain with the Christians who dominated their society.

As it turned out, the worriers were right. With Perry Nussbaum, considering his life and his nature, it could hardly have turned out otherwise.

Coming of Age in Mississippi

ANNE MOODY

Anne Moody was born in Centreville, Mississippi, in 1940, the daughter of black sharecroppers. Despite poverty and racism, she applied herself in school and sports and, by age nine, began to contribute to the family income by doing menial work. Upon discovering Moody's mastery of algebra, a white woman who employed her as a maid paid her to tutor the woman's son and his friends. Always an excellent student, Moody attended Natchez College, then Tougaloo, in Jackson, with the help of scholarships and by working as a waitress. While at Tougaloo she registered black voters through the Student Nonviolent Coordinating Committee (SNCC) and the Council of Federated Organizations (COFO) and found herself at the center of "the Movement." On May 20, 1963, civil rights leader Medgar Evers appeared on television in Jackson appealing for racial justice. He was the first black man to do so and his image on television stirred residents, blacks and whites alike. Eight days later students from Tougaloo staged a sit-in at Woolworth's lunch counter in Jackson. On June 12, Evers was murdered. The following is Moody's firsthand account of the sit-in (from part 4, "The Movement").

I HAD BECOME very friendly with my social science professor, John Salter, who was in charge of NAACP activities on campus. All during the year, while the NAACP conducted a boycott of the downtown stores in Jackson, I had been one of Salter's most faithful canvassers and church speakers. During the last week of school, he told me that sit-in demonstrations were about to start in Jackson and that he wanted me to be the spokesman for a team that would sit-in at Woolworth's lunch counter. The two other demonstrators would be classmates of mine, Memphis and Pearlena. Pearlena was a dedicated NAACP worker, but Memphis had not been very involved in the Movement on campus. It seemed that the organization had had a rough time finding students who were in a position to go to jail. I had nothing to lose one way or the other. Around ten o'clock the morning of the demonstrations, NAACP headquarters alerted the news services. As a result, the police department was also informed, but neither the policemen nor the newsmen knew exactly where or when the demonstrations would start. They stationed themselves along Capitol Street and waited.

To divert attention from the sit-in at Woodworth's, the picketing started at J. C. Penney's a good fifteen minutes before. The pickets were allowed to walk up and down in front of the store three or four times before they were arrested. At exactly 11 A.M., Pearlena, Memphis, and I entered Woolworth's from the rear entrance. We separated as soon as we stepped into the store, and made small purchases from various counters. Pearlena had given Memphis her watch. He was to let us know when it was 11:14. At 11:14 we were to join him near the lunch counter and at exactly 11:15 we were to take seats at it.

Seconds before 11:15 we were occupying three seats at the previously segregated Woolworth's lunch counter. In the beginning the waitresses seemed to ignore us, as if they really didn't know what was going on. Our waitress walked past us a couple of times before she noticed we had started to write our orders down and realized we wanted service. She asked us what we wanted. We began to read to her from our order slips. She told us that we would be served at the back counter, which was for Negroes.

"We would like to be served here," I said.

The waitress started to repeat what she had said, then stopped in the middle of the sentence. She turned the lights out behind the counter, and she and the other waitresses almost ran to the back of the store, deserting all their white customers. I guess they thought that violence would start immediately after the whites at the counter realized what was going on. There were five or six other people at the counter. A couple of them just got up and walked away. A girl sitting next to me finished her banana split before leaving. A middle-aged white woman who had not yet been served rose from her seat and came over to us. "I'd like to stay here with you," she said, "but my husband is waiting."

The newsmen came in just as she was leaving. They must have discovered what was going on shortly after some of the people began to leave the store. One of the newsmen ran behind the woman who spoke to us and asked her to identify herself. She refused to give her name, but said she was a native of Vicksburg and a former resident of California. When asked why she had said what she had said to us, she replied, "I am in sympathy with the Negro movement." By this time a crowd of cameramen and reporters had gathered around us taking pictures and asking questions, such as Where were we from? Why did we sit-in? What organization sponsored it? Were we students? From what school? How were we classified?

I told them that we were all students at Tougaloo College, that we were represented by no particular organization, and that we planned to stay there even after the store closed. "All we want is service," was my reply to one of them. After they had finished probing for about twenty minutes, they were almost ready to leave.

At noon, students from a nearby white high school started pouring in to Woolworth's. When they first saw us they were sort of surprised. They didn't know how to react. A few started to heckle and the newsmen became interested again. Then the white students started chanting all kinds of anti-Negro slogans. We were called a little bit of everything. The rest of the seats except the three we were occupying had been roped off to prevent others from sitting down. A couple of the boys took one end of the rope and made it into a hangman's noose. Several attempts were made to put it around our necks. The crowds grew as more students and adults came in for lunch.

We kept our eyes straight forward and did not look at the crowd except for occasional glances to see what was going on. All of a sudden I saw a face I remembered—the drunkard from the bus station sit-in. My eyes lingered on him just long enough for us to recognize each other. Today he was drunk too, so I don't think he remembered where he had seen me before. He took out a knife, opened it, put it in his pocket, and then began to pace the floor. At this point, I told Memphis and Pearlena what was going on. Memphis suggested that we pray. We bowed our heads, and all hell broke loose. A man rushed forward, threw Memphis from his seat, and slapped my face. Then another man who worked in the store threw me against an adjoining counter.

Down on my knees on the floor, I saw Memphis lying near the lunch counter with blood running out of the corners of his mouth. As he tried to protect his face, the man who'd thrown him down kept kicking him against the head. If he had worn hard-soled shoes instead of sneakers, the first kick probably would have killed Memphis. Finally a man dressed in plain clothes identified himself as a police officer and arrested Memphis and his attacker.

Pearlena had been thrown to the floor. She and I got back on our stools after Memphis was arrested. There were some white Tougaloo teachers in the crowd. They asked Pearlena and me if we wanted to leave. They said that things were getting too rough. We didn't know what to do. While we were trying to make up our minds, we were joined by Joan Trumpauer. Now there were three of us and we were integrated. The crowd began to chant, "Communists, Communists, Communists." Some old man in the crowd ordered the students to take us off the stools.

"Which one should I get first?" a big husky boy said.

"That white nigger," the old man said.

The boy lifted Joan from the counter by her waist and carried her out of the store. Simultaneously, I was snatched from my stool by two high school students. I was dragged about thirty feet toward the door by my hair when someone made them turn me loose. As I was getting up off the floor, I saw Joan coming back inside. We started back to the center of the counter to join Pearlena. Lois Chaffee, a white Tougaloo faculty member, was now sitting next to her. So Joan and I just climbed across the rope at the front end of the counter and sat down. There were now four of us, two whites and two Negroes, all women. The mob started smearing us with ketchup, mustard, sugar, pies, and everything on the counter. Soon Joan and I were joined by John Salter, but the moment he sat down he was hit on the jaw with what appeared to be brass knuckles. Blood gushed from his face and someone threw salt into the open wound. Ed King, Tougaloo's chaplain, rushed to him.

At the other end of the counter, Lois and Pearlena were joined by George Raymond, a CORE field worker and a student from Jackson State College. Then a Negro high school boy sat down next to me. The mob took spray paint from the counter and sprayed it on the new demonstrators. The high school student had on a white shirt; the word "nigger" was written on his back with red spray paint.

We sat there for three hours taking a beating when the manager decided to close the store because the mob had begun to go wild with stuff from other counters. He begged and begged everyone to leave. But even after fifteen minutes of begging, no one budged. They would not leave until we did. Then Dr. Beittel, the president of Tougaloo College, came running in. He said he had just heard what was happening.

About ninety policemen were standing outside the store; they had been watching the whole thing through the windows, but had not come in to stop the mob or do anything. President Beittel went outside and asked Captain Ray to come and escort us out. The captain refused, stating the manager had to invite him in before he could enter the premises, so Dr. Beittel himself brought us out. He had told the police that they had better protect us after were were outside the store. When we got outside, the policemen formed a single line that blocked the mob from us. However, they were allowed to throw at us everything they had collected. Within ten minutes, we were picked up by Reverend King in his station wagon and taken to the NAACP headquarters on Lynch Street.

After the sit-in, all I could think of was how sick Mississippi whites were. They believed so much in the segregated Southern way of life, they would kill to preserve it. I sat there in the NAACP office and thought of how many times they had killed when this way of life was threatened. I knew that the killing had just begun. "Many more will die before it is over with," I thought. Before the sit-in, I had always hated the whites in Mississippi. Now I knew it was impossible for me to hate sickness. The whites had a disease, an incurable disease in its final stage. What were our chances against such a disease? I thought of the students, the young Negroes who had just begun to protest, as young interns. When these young interns got older, I thought, they would be the best doctors in the world for social problems.

Before we were taken back to campus, I wanted to get my hair washed. It was stiff with dried mustard, ketchup and sugar. I stopped in at a beauty shop across the street from the NAACP office. I didn't have on any shoes because I had lost them when I was dragged across the floor at Woolworth's. My stockings were sticking to my legs from the mustard that had dried on them. The hairdresser took one look at me and said, "My land, you were in the sit-in, huh?"

"Yes," I answered. "Do you have time to wash my hair and style it?"

"Right away," she said, and she meant right away. There were three other ladies already waiting, but they seemed glad to let me go ahead of them. The hairdresser was real nice. She even took my stockings off and washed my legs while my hair was drying.

There was a mass rally that night at the Pearl Street Church in Jackson, and the place was packed. People were standing two abreast in the aisles. Before the speakers began, all the sit-inners walked out on the stage and were introduced by Medgar Evers. People stood and applauded for what seemed like thirty minutes or more. Medgar told the audience that this was just the beginning of such demonstrations. He asked them to pledge themselves to unite in a massive offensive against segregation in Jackson, and throughout the state. The rally ended with "We Shall Overcome" and sent home hundreds of determined people. It seemed as though Mississippi Negroes were about to get together at last.

FROM

So the Heffners Left McComb

HODDING CARTER

During the long, hot summer of the civil rights movement in 1964, Mc-Comb had more than its share of violence. As Pulitzer Prize-winning journalist Hodding Carter said, "The very name McComb was a hissing." In these brief passages from chapter 1, we see the ostracism and consequent exile suffered by the Heffners for befriending two Council of Federated Organizations (COFO) workers and inviting them to a supper of hot tamales. After being harassed, seeing the family dog poisoned, and having Red Heffner's office lease for his insurance company abruptly canceled, the Heffners were forced to move to Jackson and later to Washington, D.C. The mention of Carla's letter refers to one written by their then seventeen-year-old daughter to her parents from New York describing her own awakening of conscience about racism.

SIX DOZEN FROZEN hot tamales can scarcely be thought of as a collective instrument of personal disaster. For Albert W. Heffner, Jr., whom friends in McComb, Mississippi, and elsewhere call Red, and his wife, Mary Alva, better known as Malva, they were. On the night of July 17, 1964, they served the hot tamales to the wrong people, to wit, two young white civil rights workers, one an ordained minister.

Red and Malva purchased the tamales at Doe's in Greenville, Mississippi, at the end of a glorious 4th of July weekend complete with a Delta wedding and three days of fun. On the way home they bought them there because Doe's regionally famous tamales lean strongly to garlic and Red and Malva like garlic.

This story is principally that of forty-two-year-old Red and Malva who is forty but doesn't look it. They had lived in McComb for ten years before the sharing of these tamales made them refugees from McComb and the state of Mississippi. It concerns, too, their seventeen-year-old daughter Carla and Malva's nineteen-year-old daughter, Jan Nave, who was Miss Mississippi for 1963–64 and whose GI father was killed in the Battle of the Bulge a month before Jan was born.

The tale also has to do with the overwhelming majority of the 8000 white residents of McComb, all bound together in a unity spawned of fear. McComb is a community of 13,000 souls in Southwest Mississippi's Pike County. . . .

An incontrovertible fact about frozen hot tamales that have been thawed and heated is that they have to be eaten soon or thrown away. And there they were, six dozen of them and just Red and Malva to undertake to consume them. It was natural for Red to think of inviting the personable young minister, who was expected later anyhow for a meeting with the Smiths and themselves, to help eat the hot tamales, which would otherwise go to waste. So the Heffners asked Don to come early and he accepted. Don asked if he could bring someone else and Red agreed instinctively. The someone was Dennis Sweeney, the SNCC staff worker from Stanford. They came right over and the four of them sat down before the big platter of tamales.

Only seconds after the last tamales had been eaten and just as the Smiths were coming in the front door, Carla telephoned again from New York to tell her parents of her latest adventures in the big city.

In the course of the conversation Malva told Carla that Don—whom she had met by telephone three nights earlier—and a friend, named Dennis Sweeney, were there and had been sharing in Doe's hot tamales. Later in the conversation, Carla repeated the name Dennis Sweeney, asking if she hadn't seen his picture in the *Enterprise-Journal.*

So it was that Dennis' full name was spoken twice. In the light of immediately subsequent events, it would appear probable that someone else was listening in.

After Malva had cleared the table, everyone settled down in the den to discuss the hoped-for meeting between the mayor, the chief of police, and Don. It is extraordinary that to this day Red and Malva can't figure out why they were concerning themselves so greatly with trying to create an element of understanding in their tense little city.

"It was more than one thing," Red said months later when McComb was only a part of their past. "The disappearance of those boys in Philadelphia was the shocker. I didn't want to have any more kids killed in Mississippi. But there was more to it than that. Carla's letter from New York was part of it. So was the meeting at the vicarage. Probably most of all it was how reasonable everything Don McCord said seemed to be. And don't forget I was worried about the image of my town. You don't get new industries by burning houses of God and beating up people. It just seemed the right thing to do at the time."

About ten minutes later the telephone rang again. Malva answered. A woman's voice asked: "Can I speak to Dennis Sweeney?"

Assuming the caller was someone from COFO headquarters, Malva handed Dennis the receiver.

As Dennis related it afterward, the voice asked him how the civil rights work was coming along. He answered: "Pretty well, I guess," trying to think who the caller might be. The voice then asked if he were a friend of the Heffners. Having met them for the first time only a short hour or so before and having partaken of their favorite dish, which, not being a garlic lover, he had not particularly liked, he answered tentatively, "Yes, I guess so." But by now a wary combat veteran after several weeks in McComb, he recognized the danger in continuing the conversation and explained to his caller that he didn't want to talk further until the speaker identified herself. The anonymous caller hung up.

Dennis rejoined the group and everyone talked about the mysterious queries and wondered how his presence at the Heffners' was known. Don said no one at headquarters would have told an outsider where Dennis was because no worker ever disclosed the whereabouts of another unless he was satisfied of the good intent of the inquirer.

Although they did not know it at first, automobiles were already beginning to encircle the house, which stood on a corner atop a small rise. Because of the corner's steep incline and sharp turn, any automobile ascending the street automatically shifts into second gear. Soon the collective lower notes became audible to those in the house, even over the hum of the air-conditioner. Red's curiosity was only casual at first, but the others were almost immediately disturbed by the sudden buildup of traffic in a residential area. However, no one looked out and the conversation went on.

Some ten minutes later the telephone rang again. This time the speaker identified himself as D. B. Dekle, a resident of Carroll Oaks and a business acquaintance of Red's, who was manager of a McComb funeral home and a one-time insurance agent. The two men occasionally talked shop, but neither had ever been in the other's home. Dekle asked Red: "Whose car is that in front of your house?"

"My first thought was to tell him it's none of your business, D.B.," Red says. "But I knew how upset our town already was and I didn't want to make things any worse. So I very carefully explained who was there, made reference to the editorial about the meeting the day before, and told him we were now discussing the possibility of a similar meeting with city officials. Dekle seemed satisfied with the explanation. All he said was OK."

Obviously nervous now because of the second phone call, Don and Dennis decided to leave. Before going, Don telephoned the FBI headquarters in the Holiday Inn Motel and for their information told them of the strange sequence of telephone calls. He said that someone must have monitored the Heffners' phone to discover Dennis' presence. He then gave Red the FBI telephone number in case he should want it. Colton offered to follow the COFO car out of the neighborhood.

Red opened the front door. Now those inside discovered why the sound of motors had increased. Ringing the corner, with their headlights trained on the house, eight to ten automobiles were parked, their engines running. Red told himself that after the people in the waiting automobiles saw him they would realize there was no need for the demonstration. Practically blinded by the headlights, he led the way down the front walk. The COFO workers' car was partially blocked by one of the cars surrounding the house, but the Smiths' was not. Colton and Angela got in their automobile, which was parked behind Dennis', and Colton backed up a few feet to give Dennis room to turn around in the driveway, as the Heffners watched in the glare of the headlights. Colton U-turned in the street so as to be immediately behind Don and Dennis and the four drove away from Carroll Oaks. The waiting automobiles fell in behind them.

After the Philadelphia disappearances, most COFO cars in Mississippi had been equipped with two-way radios. So were the various COFO headquarters to which they were attached. By radio, Don and Dennis now arranged that they should be met at the Church of the Mediator by an escort from their headquarters. By the time the pair reached the church, two carloads of workers had already arrived. They were able to get the license numbers of some of the trailing automobiles from Carroll Oaks to turn over to the FBI. Back in the house, Red telephoned the FBI and reported the incident. The agent who answered told him it was a matter for the local police, which it was, as the FBI has no authority to intervene in local police matters. When Red telephoned police headquarters, the desk sergeant who answered said he would send someone to check on the safety of the COFO workers and that the police would come by his house.

No policeman turned up at the Heffner home. So after waiting half an hour Red got out his shotgun and loaded his .38 automatic and put it in a trousers pocket. The pistol, rarely handled, was in one drawer and, as a safety measure, the clip was in another. But which drawer neither Malva nor Red could remember. It took some while to find the two parts and put them together. Then the tense couple crossed the street to the home of their long-time neighbors and good friends, Peter and Helen Hallin.

Pete Hallin, formerly of Jamestown, New York, is executive vice-president of Croft Metal Products, fabricators of aluminum windows and doors, and a man who, because of the firm's economic importance to McComb, is reasonably safe from community pressures. The Hallins offered the Heffners a drink and over it they discussed the disturbing events of the night. Before the Heffners left the Hallins', another friend and neighbor, Norwood Prestridge, dropped in. The next day he told Helen Hallin that as he walked across her yard to his own home next door a policeman had drawn up in a patrol car and commented to him that the folks in Carroll Oaks were sure out to get the Heffners. But no policeman came to the Heffners' home.

Meanwhile, a troubled Chief Guy had driven to COFO headquarters in his pajamas, robe, and bedroom slippers to ask if anyone wanted to prefer any charges. There was nothing to charge anyone with.

The Heffners turned out their lights and watched automobiles returning to the homes in their neighborhood. Red tried to telephone D. B. Dekle, but his phone didn't answer.

This is how it started. The start was also the beginning of the finish for the Heffners. But they didn't know it then.

Mississippi: The Fallen Paradise

WALKER PERCY

Walker Percy was a second cousin to William Alexander Percy, author of Lanterns on the Levee. *Born in 1916 in Birmingham, Alabama, Walker was thirteen when his father committed suicide. After his mother was killed in a car accident a few years later, Will Percy formally adopted him and his two brothers, and he was brought up in "Uncle Will's" Greenville home, a gathering place for artists and writers. After graduating from the University of North Carolina, Percy attended the College of Physicians and Surgeons at Columbia University, where he received an M. D. degree in 1941. While interning at Bellevue Hospital in New York, he contracted tuberculosis, a turning point in his life. During his convalescence in the Adirondacks, he began to write. In 1961, his first novel,* The Moviegoer, *was published, and in the following year, it won the National Book Award. His next novel,* The Last Gentleman *(1966), was a semiautobiographical work in which the most significant scene was set in Greenville. In addition to his six published novels, Percy's serious essays on subjects ranging from Catholicism to semiotics have been collected in such works as* The Message in the Bottle, Lost in the Cosmos, *and* Signposts in a Strange Land. *In "Mississippi: The Fallen Paradise," published in 1965, Percy analyzes race relations during the treacherous times in Mississippi after the University of Mississippi riot in 1962 and on the heels of the 1964 Civil Rights Bill. He also captures the subtleties of class attitudes, seldom fully articulated.*

A LITTLE MORE than one hundred years ago, a Mississippi regiment dressed its ranks and started across a meadow toward Cemetery Ridge, a minor elevation near Gettysburg. There, crouched behind a stone wall, the soldiers of the Army of the Potomac waited and watched with astonishment as the gray-clads advanced as casually as if they were on parade. The Mississippians did not reach the wall. One soldier managed to plant the regimental colors within an arm's length before he fell. The University Grays, a company made up of students from the state university, suffered a loss of precisely one hundred per cent of its members killed or wounded in the charge.

These were good men. It was an honorable fight and there were honorable men on both sides of it. The issue was settled once and for all, perhaps by this very charge. The honorable men on the losing side, men like General Lee, accepted the verdict.

One hundred years later, Mississippians were making history of a different sort. If their record in Lee's army is unsurpassed for valor and devotion to duty, present-day Mississippi is mainly renowned for murder, church-burning, dynamiting, assassination, night-riding, not to mention the lesser forms of terrorism. The students of the university celebrated the Centennial by a different sort of warfare and in the company of a different sort of General. It is not frivolous to compare the characters of General Edwin Walker and General Lee, for the contrast is symptomatic of a broader change in leadership in this part of the South. In any event, the major claim to fame of the present-day university is the Ole Miss football team and the assault of the student body upon the person of one man, an assault of bullying, spitting, and obscenities. The bravest Mississippians in recent years have not been Confederates or the sons of Confederates but rather two Negroes, James Meredith and Medgar Evers.

As for the Confederate flag, once the battle ensign of brave men, it has come to stand for raw racism and hoodlum defiance of the law. An art professor at Ole Miss was bitterly attacked for "desecrating" the Stars and Bars when he depicted the flag as it was used in the 1962 riot—with curses and obscenities. The truth was that it had been desecrated long before.

No ex-Mississippian is entitled to write of the tragedy which has overtaken his former state with any sense of moral superiority. For he cannot be certain in the first place that if he had stayed he would not have kept silent—or worse. And he strongly suspects that he would not have been counted among the handful, an editor here, a professor there, a clergyman yonder, who not only did not keep silent but fought hard.

What happened to this state? Assuredly it faced difficult times after the Supreme Court decision of 1954 and subsequent court injunctions which required painful changes in customs of long standing. Yet the change has been made peacefully in other states of the South. In Georgia before the 1965 voting bill was passed by Congress, over 39 per cent of Negroes of voting age were registered to vote. In Mississippi the figure was around 6 per cent.

What happened is both obvious and obscure. What is obvious is that

Mississippi is poor, largely rural, and has in proportion the largest Negro minority in the United States. But Georgia shares these traits. Nor is it enough to say that Mississippi is the state that refused to change, although this is what one hears both inside and outside the state. On the contrary, Mississippi has changed several times since the Civil War. There have been times, for example, when dissent was not only possible but welcome. In 1882 George Washington Cable, novelist and ex-Confederate cavalryman, addressed the graduating class at the University of Mississippi:

> We became distended—mired and stuffed with conservatism to the point of absolute rigidity. Our life had little or nothing to do with the onward movement of the world's thought. We were in danger of becoming a civilization that was not a civilization, because there was not in it the element of advancement.

His address was warmly received by the newspapers of the region. It is interesting to speculate how these remarks would be received today at Ole Miss, if indeed Cable would be allowed to speak at all.

Two significant changes have occurred in the past generation. The most spectacular is the total defeat of the old-style white moderate and the consequent collapse of the alliance between the "good" white man and the Negro, which has figured more or less prominently in Mississippi politics since Reconstruction days. Except for an oasis or two like Greenville, the influential white moderate is gone. To use Faulkner's *personae*, the Gavin Stevenses have disappeared and the Snopeses have won. What is more, the Snopeses' victory has surpassed even the gloomiest expectations of their creator. What happened to men like Gavin Stevens? With a few exceptions, they have shut up or been exiled or they are running the local White Citizens' Council. Not even Faulkner foresaw the ironic denouement of the tragedy: that the Compsons and Sartorises should not only be defeated by the Snopeses but that in the end they should join them.

Faulkner lived to see the defeat of his Gavin Stevens—the old-style good man, the humanist from Harvard and Heidelberg—but he still did not despair because he had placed his best hope in the youth of the state. Chick Mallison in *Intruder in the Dust,* a sort of latter-day Huck Finn, actually got the Negro Lucas Beauchamp out of jail while Gavin Stevens was talking about the old alliance. But this hope has been blasted, too. The melancholy fact is the Chick Mallisons today are apt to be the worst lot of all. Ten years of indoctrination by the Citizens' Councils, racist politicians, and the most one-sided press north of Cuba has produced a generation of good-looking and ferocious young bigots.

The other change has been the emigration of the Negro from Mississippi, reducing the Negro majority to a minority for the first time in a hundred years. At the same time great numbers of Negroes from the entire South were settling in Northern ghettos. The chief consequence has been the failure of the great cities of the North to deal with the Negro when he landed on their doorstep, or rather next door. Mississippi has not got any better, but New York and Boston and Los Angeles have got worse.

Meanwhile there occurred the Negro revolution, and the battle lines changed. For the first time in a hundred and fifty years, the old sectional division has been blurred. It is no longer "North" versus "South" in the argument over the Negro. Instead there has occurred a diffusion of the Negro and a dilution of the problem, with large sections of the South at least tolerating a degree of social change at the very time Northern cities were beginning to grumble seriously. It seems fair to describe the present national mood as a grudging inclination to redress the Negro's grievances—with the exception of a few areas of outright defiance like north Louisiana, parts of Alabama, and the state of Mississippi.

Words Without Meaning

It is only within the context of these social changes, I believe, that the state can be understood and perhaps some light shed upon a possible way out. For, unfavorable as these events may be, they are nevertheless ambiguous in their implication. The passing of the moderate and the victory of the Snopeses may be bad things in themselves. Yet history being the queer business that it is, such a turn of events may be the very condition of the state's emergence from its long nightmare.

During the past ten years Mississippi as a society reached a condition which can only be described, in an analogous but exact sense of the word, as insane. The rift in its character between a genuine kindliness and a highly developed individual moral consciousness on the one hand, and on the other a purely political and amoral view of "states' rights" at the expense of human rights led at last to a sundering of its very soul. Kind fathers and loving husbands, when they did not themselves commit crimes against the helpless, looked upon such crimes with indifference. Political campaigns, once the noblest public activity in the South, came to be conducted by incantation. The candidate who hollers nigger loudest and longest usually wins.

The language itself has been corrupted. In the Mississippi standard version of what happened, noble old English words are used, words like *freedom, sacredness of the individual, death to tyranny,* but they have subtly changed their referents. After the Oxford riot in 1962, the Junior Chamber of Commerce published a brochure entitled *A Warning for Americans,* which was widely distributed and is still to be found on restaurant counters in Jackson along with the usual racist tracts, mammy dolls, and Confederate flags. The pamphlet purports to prove that James Meredith was railroaded into Ole Miss by the Kennedys in defiance of "normal judicial processes"—a remarkable thesis in itself considering that the Meredith case received one of the most exhaustive judicial reviews in recent history. The "warning" for Americans was the usual contention that states' rights were being trampled by federal tyranny. "Tyranny is tyranny," reads the pamphlet. "It is the duty of every American to be alert when his freedom is endangered."

Lest the reader be complacent about Mississippi as the only state of double-think, the pamphlet was judged by the *national* Jay Cees to be the "second most worthy project of the year."

All statements become equally true and equally false, depending on one's rhetorical posture. In the end even the rhetoric fails to arouse. When Senator Eastland declares, "There is no discrimination in Mississippi," and, "All who are qualified to vote, black or white, exercise the right of suffrage," these utterances are received by friend and foe alike with a certain torpor of spirit. It does not matter that there is very little connection between Senator Eastland's utterances and the voting statistics of his home county: that of a population of 31,020 Negroes, 161 are registered to vote. Once the final break is made between language and reality, arguments generate their own force and lay out their own logical rules. The current syllogism goes something like this: (1) There is no ill-feeling in Mississippi between the races; the Negroes like things the way they are; if you don't believe it, I'll call my cook out of the kitchen and you can ask her. (2) The trouble is caused by outside agitators who are communist-inspired. (3) Therefore, the real issue is between atheistic communism and patriotic God-fearing Mississippians.

Once such a system cuts the outside wires and begins to rely on its own feedback, anything becomes possible. The dimensions of the tragedy are hard to exaggerate. The sad and still incredible fact is that many otherwise decent people, perhaps even the majority of the white people in Mississippi, honestly believed that President John F. Kennedy was an enemy of the United States, if not a communist fellow-traveler.

How did it happen that a proud and decent people, a Protestant and Anglo-Saxon people with a noble tradition of freedom behind them, should have in the end become so deluded that it is difficult even to discuss the issues with them because the common words of the language no longer carry the same meanings? How can responsible leadership have failed so completely when it did not fail in Georgia, a state with a similar social and ethnic structure?

The answer is far from clear, but several reasons suggest themselves. For one thing, as James Dabbs points out in his recent book *Who Speaks for the South?*, Mississippi was part of the wild west of the Old South. Unlike the seaboard states, it missed the liberal eighteenth century altogether. Its tradition is closer to Dodge City than to Williamsburg. For another, the Populism of the eastern South never amounted to much here; it was corrupted from the beginning by the demagogic racism of Vardaman and Bilbo. Nor did Mississippi have its big city which might have shared, for good and ill, in the currents of American urban life. Georgia had its Atlanta and Atlanta had the good luck or good sense to put men like Ralph McGill and Mayor Hartsfield in key positions. What was lacking in Mississippi was the new source of responsible leadership, the political realists of the matured city. The old moderate tradition of the planter-lawyer-statesman class had long since lost its influence. The young industrial interests have been remarkable chiefly for their discretion. When, for example, they did awake to the folly of former Governor Barnett's two-bit rebellion, it was too late. And so there was no one to head off the collision between the civil-rights movement and the racist coalition between redneck, demagogue, and small-town merchant. The result was insurrection.

Death of an Alliance

The major source of racial moderation in Mississippi even until recent times has been, not Populism, but the white conservative tradition with its peculiar strengths and, as it turned out, its fatal weakness. There came into being after Reconstruction an extraordinary alliance, which persisted more or less fitfully until the last world war, between the Negro and the white conservative, an alliance originally directed against the poor whites and the Radical Republicans. The fruits of this "fusion principle," as it is called, are surprising. Contrary to the current mythology of the Citizens' Councils, which depicts white Mississippians throwing out the carpetbaggers and Negroes and establishing our present "way of life" at the end of Reconstruction, the fact is that Negroes enjoyed considerably more freedom in the 1880s than they do now. A traveler in Mississippi after Reconstruction reported seeing whites and Negroes served in the same restaurants and at the same bars in Jackson.

This is not to say that there ever existed a golden age of race relations. But there were bright spots. It is true that the toleration of the Old Captains, as W. J. Cash called them, was both politically motivated and paternalistic, but it is not necessarily a derogation to say so. A man is a creature of his time—after all, Lincoln was a segregationist—and the old way produced some extraordinary men. There were many felicities in their relation with the Negro—it was not all Uncle Tomism, though it is unfashionable to say so. In any case they lost; segregation was firmly established around 1890 and lynch law became widespread. For the next fifty years the state was dominated, with a few notable exceptions, by a corrupt Populism.

What is important to notice here is the nature of the traditional alliance between the white moderate and the Negro, and especially the ideological basis of the former's moderation, because this spirit has informed the ideal of race relations for at least a hundred years. For, whatever its virtues, the old alliance did not begin to have the resources to cope with the revolutinary currents of this century. Indeed the world view of the old-style "good" man is almost wholly irrelevant to the present gut issue between the Negro revolt and the Snopes counterrevolution.

For one thing, the old creed was never really social or political but purely and simply moral in the Stoic sense: if you are a good man, then you will be magnanimous toward other men and especially toward the helpless and therefore especially toward the Negro. The Stoic creed worked very well—if you were magnanimous. But if one planter was just, the next might charge 80 per cent interest at the plantation store, the next take the wife of his tenant, the next lease convict labor, which was better than the sharecropper system because it did not matter how hard you worked your help or how many died.

Once again in recent years dissent became possible. During the depression of the 1930s and afterward there were stirrings of liberal currents not only in the enthusiasm for the economic legislation of the Roosevelt Administration but also in a new awareness of the plight of the Negro. Mississippi desperately needed the New Deal and profited enormously from it. Indeed, the Roosevelt farm program succeeded too well. Planters who were going broke on ten cent cotton voted for Roosevelt, took federal money, got rich, lived to hate Kennedy and Johnson and vote for Goldwater—while still taking federal money. Yet there was something new in the wind after the war. Under the leadership of men like Hodding Carter in the Delta, a new form of racial moderation began to gather strength. Frank Smith, author of the book

Congressman from Mississippi, was elected to Congress. Described by Edward Morgan as "a breath of fresh air out of a political swamp," Smith was one of the few politicians in recent years who tried to change the old racial refrain and face up to the real problems of the state. But he made the mistake of voting for such radical measures as the Peace Corps and the United Nations appropriation, and he did not conceal his friendship with President Kennedy. What was worse, he addressed mail to his constituents with a Mr. and Mrs., even when they were Negroes. Smith was euchred out of his district by the legislature and defeated in 1962 by the usual coalition of peckerwoods, super-patriots, and the Citizens' Councils.

But the most radical change has occurred in the past few years. As recently as fifteen years ago, the confrontation was still a three-cornered one, among the good white man, the bad white man, and the Negro. The issue was whether to treat the Negro well or badly. It went without saying that you could do either. Now one of the parties has been eliminated and the confrontation is face to face. "I assert my right to vote and to raise my family decently," the Negro is beginning to say. His enemies reply with equal simplicity: "We'll kill you first."

Yet the victory of the Snopeses is not altogether a bad thing. At least the choice is clarified. It would not help much now to have Gavin Stevens around with his talk about "man's struggle to the stars."

The old way is still seductive, however, and evokes responses from strange quarters. Ex-Governor Ross Barnett was recently revealed as mellow emeritus statesman in the old style, even hearkening to the antique summons of noblesse oblige. A newspaper interview reported that the Governor was a soft touch for any Negro who waylaid him in the corridor with a "Cap'n, I could sho use a dollar." The Governor, it was also reported, liked to go hunting with a Negro friend. "We laugh and joke," the Governor reminisced, "and he gets a big kick out of it when I call him Professor. There's a lot in our relationship I can't explain." No doubt, mused the interviewer, the Governor would get up at all hours of the night to get Ol' Jim out of jail. It is hard to imagine what Gavin Stevens would make of this new version of the old alliance. Unquestionably something new has been added. When Marse Ross dons the mantle of Marse Robert, Southern history has entered upon a new age. And perhaps it is just as well. Let Governor Barnett become the new squire. It simplifies matters further.

Public vs. Private

Though Faulkner liked to use such words as "cursed" and "doomed" in speaking of his region, it is questionable that Mississippians are very different from other Americans. It is increasingly less certain that Minnesotans would have performed better under the circumstances. There is, however, one peculiar social dimension wherein the state does truly differ. It has to do with the distribution, as Mississippians see it, of what is public and what is private. More precisely it is the absence of a truly public zone, as the word is understood in most places. One has to live in Mississippi to appreciate it. No doubt it is the mark of an almost homogeneous white population, a Protestant Anglo-Saxon minority (until recently), sharing a common tragic past and bound together by kinship bonds. This society was not only felicitous in many ways; it also commanded the allegiance of Southern intellectuals on other grounds. Faulkner saw it as the chief bulwark against the "coastal spew of Europe" and "the rootless ephemeral cities of the North." In any case, the almost familial ambit of this society came to coincide with the actual public space which it inhabited. The Negro was either excluded, shoved off into Happy Hollow, or admitted to the society on its own terms as good old Uncle Ned. No allowance was made—it would have been surprising if there had been—for a truly public sector, unlovely as you please and defused of emotional charges, where black and white might pass without troubling each other. The whole of the Delta, indeed of white Mississippi, is one big kinship lodge. You have only to walk into a restaurant or a bus station to catch a whiff of it. There is a sudden kindling of amiability, even between strangers. The salutations, "What you say now?" and "Yall be good," are exchanged like fraternal signs. The presence of fraternity and sorority houses at Ole Miss always seemed oddly superfluous.

One consequence of this peculiar social structure has been a chronic misunderstanding between the state and the rest of the country. The state feels that unspeakable demands are being made upon it while the nation is bewildered by the response of rage to what seem to be the ordinary and minimal requirements of the law. Recall, for example, President Kennedy's gentle appeal to the university the night of the riot when he invoked the tradition of L. Q. C. Lamar and asked the students to do their duty even as he was doing his. He had got his facts straight about the tradition of valor in Mississippi. But unfortunately, the Kennedys had no notion of the social and semantic rules they were up against. When they entered into negotiations with the Governor to get Meredith on the campus, they proceeded on the reasonable assumption that even in the arena of political give and take—*i.e.*, deals—words bear some relation to their referents. Such was not the case. Governor Barnett did not doublecross the Kennedys in the usual sense. The double cross, like untruth, bears a certain relation to the truth. More serious, however, was the cultural confusion over the word "public." Ole Miss is not, or was not, a public school as the word is usually understood. In Mississippi as in England a public school means a private school. When Meredith finally did walk the paths at Ole Miss, his fellow students cursed and reviled him. But they also wept with genuine grief. It was as if he had been quartered in their living room.

It is this hypertrophy of pleasant familial space at the expense of a truly public sector which accounts for the extraordinary apposition in Mississippi of kindliness and unspeakable violence. Recently a tourist wrote the editor of the Philadelphia, Mississippi, newspaper that, although he expected the worst when he passed through the town, he found the folks in Philadelphia as nice as they could be. No doubt it is true. The Philadelphia the tourist saw is as pleasant as he said. It is like one big front porch.

A Place to Start

How can peace be restored to Mississippi? One would like to be able to say that the hope lies in putting into practice the Judeo-Christian ethic. In the end, no doubt, it does. But the trouble is that Christendom of a sort has already won in Mississippi. There is more church news in the Jackson papers than news about the Ole Miss football team. Political cartoons defend God against the Supreme Court. On the outskirts of Meridian a road sign announces: "The Largest Percentage of Churchgoers in the World." It is a religion, however, which tends to canonize the existing social and political structure and to brand as atheistic any threat of change. "The trouble is they took God out of everything," said W. Arsene Dick of Summit, Mississippi, founder of Americans for the Preservation of the White Race. A notable exception to the general irrelevance of religion to social issues is the recent action of Millsaps College, a Methodist institution in Jackson, which voluntarily opened its doors to Negroes.

It seems more likely that progress will come about—as indeed it is already coming about—not through the impact of the churches upon churchgoers but because after a while the ordinary citizen gets sick and tired of the climate of violence and of the odor of disgrace which hangs over his region. Money has a good deal to do with it too; money, urbanization, and the growing concern of politicians and the business community with such things as public images. Governor Johnson occasionally talks sense. Last year the Mayor and the business leaders

of Jackson defied the Citizens' Councils and supported the token deseg-
regation of the schools. It could even happen that Governor Johnson,
the man who campaigned up and down the state with the joke about
what NAACP means (niggers, alligators, apes, coons, possums), may
turn out to be the first Governor to enforce the law. For law enforcement, it is becoming increasingly obvious, is the condition of peace. It
is also becoming more likely every day that federal intervention, perhaps in the form of local commissioners, may be required in places like
Neshoba County where the Ku Klux Klan has been in control and law
enforcement is a shambles. Faulkner at last changed his mind about
the durability of the old alliance and came to prefer even enforced
change to a state run by the Citizens' Councils and the Klan. Mississippians, he wrote, will not accept change until they have to. Then perhaps
they will at last come to themselves: "Why didn't someone tell us this
before? Tell us this in time?"

Much will depend on the residue of good will in the state. There are
some slight signs of the long overdue revolt of the ordinary prudent
man. There must be a good many of this silent breed. Hazel Brannon
Smith, who won a Pulitzer Prize as editor of the Lexington *Advertiser,*
recently reported that in spite of all the abuse and the boycotts, the
circulation of the paper continues to rise. The Mississippi Economic
Council, the state's leading businessmen's group, issued a statement
urging compliance with the 1964 Civil Rights Act and demanding that
registration and voting laws be "fairly and impartially administered for
all." In McComb several hundred leading citizens, after a reign of terror which lasted for a good part of 1964, demanded not only law and
order but "equal treatment under the law for all citizens."

It may be that the corner has been turned. Mississippi, in the spring
of 1965, looks better than Alabama. But who can say what would have
happened if Martin Luther King had chosen Greenwood instead of
Selma? Mississippi may in fact *be* better just because of Selma—though
at this very writing Ole Miss students are living up to form and throwing
rocks at Negroes. Nor can one easily forget the 1964 national election.
The bizarre seven-to-one margin in favor of Senator Goldwater attests
to the undiminished obsession with race. It would not have mattered if
Senator Goldwater had advocated the collectivization of the plantations
and open saloons in Jackson; he voted against the 1964 Civil Rights Bill
and that was that.

Yet there is little doubt that Mississippi is even now beginning to feel
its way toward what might be called the American Settlement of the
racial issue, a somewhat ambiguous state of affairs which is less a solu-

tion than a more or less tolerable impasse. There has come into being an entire literature devoted to an assault upon the urban life wherein this settlement is arrived at, and a complete glossary of terms, such as alienation, depersonalization, and mass man. But in the light of recent history in Mississippi, the depersonalized American neighborhood looks more and more tolerable. A giant supermarket or eighty thousand peole watching a pro ball game may not be the most creative of institutions, but at least they offer a *modus vivendi*. People generally leave each other alone.

A Southerner may still hope that some day the Southern temper, black and white, might yet prove to be the sociable yeast to leaven the American lump. Indeed he may suspect in his heart of hearts that the solution, if it comes, may have to come from him and from the South. And with good reason: the South, with all the monstrous mythologizing of its virtues, nevertheless has these virtues—a manner and a grace and a gift for human intercourse. And despite the humbuggery about the perfect love and understanding between us white folks and darkies down in Dixie, whites and blacks in the South do in fact know something about getting along with each other which the rest of the country does not know. Both black and white Southerner can help the country a great deal, though neither may choose to do so; the Negro for fear of being taken for Uncle Tom, the white from simple vengefulness: all right, Yankee, you've been preaching at us for a hundred years and now you've got them and you're making a mess of it and it serves you right. It may well come to lie with the South in the near future, as it lay with the North in 1860, to save the Union in its own way. Given enough trouble in New York and Chicago, another ten years of life in the subways and urine in the streets, it might at last dawn on him, the Southerner, that it is not the South which is being put upon but the *country* which is in trouble. Then he will act as he acted in 1916 and 1941.

Some day a white Mississippian is going to go to New York, make the usual detour through Harlem, and see it for the foul cheerless warren that it is; and instead of making him happy as it does now, it is going to make him unhappy. Then the long paranoia, this damnable sectional insanity, will be one important step closer to being over.

FROM

This Little Light of Mine

KAY MILLS

In her biography of Fannie Lou Hamer, Kay Mills writes that Hamer was "born into that old Mississippi but died in the new." Born the youngest of twenty children in Montgomery County, Mississippi, in 1917, Fannie Lou Townsend's family moved to Sunflower County in 1919 to work on a plantation owned by E. W. Brandon. By the time she was thirteen, Fannie Lou was picking two to three hundred pounds of cotton a day. That hard life led to later strength when she decided, despite harassment, to register to vote. In 1963, Hamer was brutally beaten in Winona, Mississippi, while working with the Student Nonviolent Coordinating Committee (SNCC). She is best known for her speech on behalf of the Mississippi Freedom Democratic Party at the Democratic National Convention in Atlantic City in 1964 in which she said, "I'm sick and tired of being sick and tired." The title of her biography was taken from her favorite song, "This Little Light of Mine," popularized by Pete Seeger during the civil rights movement. The following passage describes Hamer's funeral in Ruleville, Mississippi, in 1977 (from chapter 17, "Go Home to My Lord and Be Free").

THE TRAVELING, the speaking, and the singing had ended for Fannie Lou Hamer. Now others would travel to Ruleville to speak and sing in her honor. Hundreds of people gathered for her funeral at the Williams Chapel Baptist Church. It was, by all accounts, a day on which the movement reassembled and could have rekindled its fires. But the activists of the 1960s were pulled in too many different directions in the 1970s, so the moment passed, if indeed it had existed at all. Some of those who had worked with Mrs. Hamer had gone into government—national, state, or local. Others had become lawyers out of state, or teachers, or social workers, all with their own lives. Others had grown increasingly militant and separatist. Even when they had worked in the state, they had agreed on little beyond their overriding abhorrence of the white supremacist system, so why start agreeing now? Mrs. Hamer, representing the grass-roots people, had been a keystone, a unifying force. "None of the others could command so much respect," said her farm co-op ally, Ron Thornton.

On the day of the funeral, United Nations Ambassador Andrew

Young landed in a government plane at the Indianola airport. Assistant Secretary of State Hodding Carter arrived. Michigan Congressman Charles Diggs attended, as did Vernon Jordan of the National Urban League, Dorothy Height of the National Council of Negro Women, and activist Ella Baker. Stokely Carmichael, in Memphis for a speech, showed up, as did H. Rap Brown, both former Student Non-Violent Coordinating Committee leaders. Austin Scott, who had covered the civil rights movement and who reported on Mrs. Hamer's funeral for the *Washington Post,* marveled in print that the small Delta town had never seen a funeral quite like it. "People denounced only 15 years ago as 'outside agitators' and 'troublemakers' were here today as honored guests."

Mississippi highway patrol officers directed traffic. Hundreds of local people—people who didn't have the big names of Young or Hodding Carter or Carmichael—couldn't get into the packed church for the services, and some of the activists felt that Mrs. Hamer's real friends were ignored. The overflow crowd was accommodated at a separate memorial service at Ruleville Central High School. . . .

Wearing an open-collared shirt and showing his old fire, Stokely Carmichael strode to the lectern to speak. "Why do we come to pick out Mrs. Hamer?" Some people who live do bad things and others are happy when they die; some live indifferent lives so no one knows when they die. But others give their blood and sweat, he said, and "these are the ones we come to honor."

. . . Dorothy Height spoke about the women from the Wednesdays in Mississippi group who had come together to support those who, like Mrs. Hamer, had participated in the history-making events of the summer of 1964. Ella Baker, who had been the behind-the-scenes intellectual to Mrs. Hamer's out-front galvanizer, talked about how Mrs. Hamer not only spoke about the movement's ideas and ideals but lived them. Vernon Jordan remembered the 1964 Mississippi Freedom Democratic Party convention in Jackson. It occurred the same summer that the three civil rights workers had disappeared in Neshoba County, and there was considerable fear in the air. Mrs. Hamer, he recalled, led the singing of "Ain't Gonna Let Nobody Turn Me Around." He, too, had been afraid, especially because he had to drive from Jackson to Memphis alone after that meeting. "After I heard Mrs. Hamer sing, I was not afraid."

Among those who had the most fear had been white Mississippians. "I think history will say that among those who were freed more totally and earlier by her were white Mississippians who were finally freed, if they had the will to be free, from themselves, from their history, from their racism, from their past," said Hodding Carter as he looked out over Mrs. Hamer's casket at the mourners. Tears seemed to well in his eyes as he added: "And I know that there's no way for us who have been freed to adequately thank those who freed us except to try also to continue the work which Mrs. Hamer and so many of you began, are continuing and will continue in the future. I'm glad I had a chance to be here. I'm gladder yet that I can say that I am from here because of Mrs. Hamer and because of many of you."

After the Tougaloo College choir sang, Andrew Young, who had gone to Winona to free Mrs. Hamer and the others from jail in 1963, read from Isaiah and from Revelation in the Bible. He said that the first time he had heard of Mrs. Hamer was when Willie Peacock, Sam Block, and James Bevel would write about how they would get together and sing spirituals with the people in the Delta. They relied heavily on freedom songs because they didn't have the nerve to talk to people about "redishing" to vote. But Mrs. Hamer had the nerve, and she had to leave the Marlow plantation because of it. Bevel called Young, he remembered, to ask whether they could scrape up $50 to haul her furniture into town. Most of the black people in Ruleville then didn't want to have anything to do with her. Fifteen years later, Young said, people from the U.S. government had come to pay their respects to Mrs. Hamer. "She literally, along with many of you, shook the foundations of this nation, and everything I learned about preaching, politics, life and death, I learned in your midst. The many people who are now elected officials would not be where they are had we not stood up then. And there was not a one of those that was not influenced and inspired by the spirit of this one woman, Mrs. Hamer."

Young, who had been appointed to his UN job by fellow Georgian Jimmy Carter, recalled an evening waiting for the 1976 election results. By 3:00 A.M., they still hadn't heard from Hawaii or Mississippi. When he thought it might hinge on Mississippi, he thought, "Lord, help us." But "when they said that Mississippi went our way, I knew then that the hands that had been pickin' the cotton had finally picked the President. Yet the picking of the President is just one more step along the way. For picking a President and not having picked a single black elected official in Sunflower County can't be considered a victory. . . . Memorializing Fannie Lou Hamer abroad and not carrying on her work at home is to betray everything she lived and stood for." When Young finished speaking, he led a hand-clapping version of "This Little Light of Mine." The services were over.

PART FOUR

Social Fabric

FROM

The Jesuit Relations and Allied Documents

FATHER LE PETIT

The French built Fort Rosalie in Natchez in 1716 and sent Jesuit missionaries like Father Le Petit to convert the Natchez Indians to Catholicism. When these attempts failed, war broke out. In his letters to his superior, this one dated July 12, 1730, Father Le Petit described and tried to justify the battle of 1729 against the Natchez tribe. In the process, he gave a detailed description of the Natchez religious practices, some of which included human sacrifice.

THIS NATION OF Savages inhabits one of the most beautiful and fertile countries in the World, and is the only one on this continent which appears to have any regular worship. Their Religion in certain points is very similar to that of the ancient Romans. They have a Temple filled with Idols, which are different figures of men and animals, and for which they have the most profound veneration. Their Temple in shape resembles an earthen oven, a hundred feet in circumference. They enter it by a little door about four feet high, and not more than three in breadth. No window is to be seen there. The arched roof of the edifice is covered with three rows of mats, placed one upon the other, to prevent the rain from injuring the masonry. Above on the outside are three figures of eagles made of wood, and painted red, yellow, and white. Before the door is a kind of shed with folding-doors, where the Guardian of the Temple is lodged; all around it runs a circle of palisades, on which are seen exposed the skulls of all the heads which their Warriors had brought from the battles in which they had been engaged with the enemies of their Nation.

In the interior of the Temple are some shelves arranged at a certain distance from each other, on which are placed cane baskets of an oval shape, and in these are enclosed the bones of their ancient Chiefs, while by their side are those of their victims who had been caught themselves to be strangled, to follow their masters into the other world. Another separate shelf supports many flat baskets very gorgeously painted, in which they preserve their Idols. These are figures of men and women made of stone or baked clay, the heads and the tails of extraordinary serpents, some stuffed owls, some pieces of crystal, and some jaw-bones of large fish. In the year 1699, they had there a bottle and the foot of a glass, which they guarded as very precious.

In this Temple they take care to keep up a perpetual fire, and they are very particular to prevent its ever blazing; they do not use anything for it but dry wood of the walnut or oak. The old men are obliged to carry, each on in his turn, a large log of wood into the enclosure of the palisade. The number of the Guardians of the Temple is fixed, and they serve by the quarter. He who is on duty is placed like a sentinel under the shed, from whence he examines whether the fire is not in danger of going out. He feeds it with two or three logs, which do not burn except at the extremity, and which they never place one on the other, for fear of their getting into a blaze.

Of the women, the sisters of the great Chief alone have liberty to enter within the Temple. The entrance is forbidden to all the others, as well as to the common people, even when they carry something there to feast to the memory of their relatives, whose bones repose in the Temple. They give the dishes to the Guardian, who carries them to the side of the basket in which are the bones of the dead; this ceremony lasts only during one moon. The dishes are afterward placed on the palisades which surround the Temple, and are abandoned to the fallow-deer.

The Sun is the principal object of veneration to these people; as they cannot conceive of anything which can be above this heavenly body, nothing else appears to them more worthy of their homage. It is for the same reason that the great Chief of this Nation, who knows nothing on the earth more dignified than himself, takes the title of brother of the Sun, and the credulity of the people maintains him in the despotic authority which he claims. To enable them better to converse together, they raise a mound of artificial soil, on which they build his cabin, which is of the same construction as the Temple. The door fronts the East, and every morning the great Chief honors by his presence the rising of his elder brother, and salutes him with many howlings as soon as he appears above the horizon. Then he gives orders that they shall light his calumet; he makes him an offering of the first three puffs which he draws; afterwards raising his hand above his head, and turning from the East to the West, he shows him the direction which he must take in his course.

There are in this cabin a number of beds on the left hand at entering: but on the right is only the bed of the great Chief, ornamented with different painted figures. This bed consists of nothing but a mattress of canes and reeds, very hard, with a square log of wood, which serves for a pillow. In the middle of the cabin is seen a small stone, and no one should approach the bed until he has made a circuit of this stone. Those who enter salute by a howl, and advance even to the bottom of the cabin, without looking at the right side, where the Chief is. Then they give a new salute by raising their arms above the head, and howling three times. If it be anyone whom the Chief holds in consideration, he answers by a slight sigh and makes a sign to him to be seated. He thanks him for his politeness by a new howl. At every question which the Chief puts to him, he howls once before he answers, and when he takes his leave, he prolongs a single howl until he is out of his presence.

When the great Chief dies, they demolish his cabin, and then raise a new mound, on which they build the cabin of him who is to replace him in this dignity, for he never lodges in that of his predecessor. The old men prescribe the Laws for the rest of the people, and one of their principles is to have a sovereign respect for the great Chief, as being the brother of the Sun and the master of the Temple. They believe in the immortality of the soul, and when they leave this world they go, they say, to live in another, there to be recompensed or punished. The rewards to which they look forward, consist principally in feasting, and their chastisement in the privation of every pleasure. Thus they think that those who have been the faithful observers of their laws will be conducted into a region of pleasures, where all kind of exquisite viands will be furnished them in abundance that their delightful and tranquil days will flow on in the midst of festivals, dances, and women; in short, they will revel in all imaginable pleasures. On the contrary, the violators of their laws will be cast upon lands unfruitful and entirely covered with water, where they will not have any kind of corn, but will be exposed entirely naked to the sharp bites of the mosquitoes, that all Nations will make war upon them, that they will never eat meat, and have no nourishment but the flesh of crocodiles, spoiled fish, and shell-fish.

. . . One of the principal articles of their Religion, and particularly the servants of the Great Chief, is that of honoring his funeral rites by dying with him, that they may go to serve him in the other world. In their blindness they willingly submit to this law, in the foolish belief that in the train of their Chief they will go to enjoy the greatest happiness.

To give an idea of this bloody ceremony, it is necessary to know that as soon as an heir presumptive has been born to the great Chief, each family that has an infant at the breast is obliged to pay him homage. From all these infants they choose a certain number whom they destine for the service of the young Prince, and as soon as they are of a competent age, they furnish them with employments suited to their talents. Some pass their lives in hunting, or in fishing, to furnish supplies for the table; others are employed in agriculture, while others serve to fill up his retinue. If he happens to die, all these servants sacrifice themselves with joy to follow their dear master. They first put on all their finery, and repair to the place opposite to the Temple, where all the people are assembled. After having danced and sung a sufficiently long time, they pass around their neck a cord of buffalo hair with a running knot, and immediately the Ministers appointed for executions of this kind, come forward to strangle them, recommending them to go to rejoin their master, and render to him in the other world services even more honorable than those which had occupied them in this.

• The principal servants of the great Chief having been strangled in this way, they strip the flesh off their bones, particularly those of their arms and thighs, and leave them to dry for two months, in a kind of tomb, after which they take them out to be shut up in the baskets which are placed in the Temple by the side of the bones of their master. As for the other servants, their relatives carry them home with them, and bury them with their arms and clothes.

. . . Each year the people assemble to plant one vast field with Indian corn, beans, pumpkins, and melons, and then again they collect in the same way to gather the harvest. A large cabin situated on a beautiful prairie is set apart to hold the fruits of this harvest. Once in the summer, toward the end of July, the people gather by order of the great Chief, to be present at a grand feast which he gives them. This Festival lasts for three days and three nights, and each one contributes what he can to furnish it; some bring game, others fish, etc. They have almost constant dances, while the great Chief and his sister are in an elevated lodge covered with boughs, from whence they can see the joy of their subjects. The Princes, the Princesses, and those who by their office are of distinguished rank are arranged very near the Chief, to whom they show their respect and submission by an infinite variety of ceremonies.

The great Chief and his sister make their entrance in the place of the assembly on a litter borne by eight of their greatest men: the Chief holds in his hand a great scepter ornamented with painted plumes, and all the people dance and sing about him in testimony of the public joy. The last day of this Feast he causes all his subjects to approach, and makes them a long harangue, in which he exhorts them to fulfill all their duties to Religion; he recommends them above all things to have a great veneration for the spirits who reside in the Temple, and carefully to instruct their children. If any one has distinguished himself by some act of zeal, he is then publicly praised. Such a case happened in the year 1702. The Temple having been struck by lightning and reduced to ashes, seven or eight women cast their infants into the midst of the flames to appease the wrath of Heaven. The great Chief called these heroines, and gave them great praises for the courage with which they had made the sacrifice of that which they held most dear; he finished his panegyric by exhorting the other women to imitate so beautiful an example in similar circumstances.

The fathers of families do not fail to carry to the Temple the first of their fruits, their corn and vegetables. It is the same even with presents which are made to this Nation; they are immediately offered at the gate of the Temple, when the guardian, after having displayed and presented them to the spirits, carries them to the house of the great Chief, who makes a distribution of them as he judges best, without any person testifying the least discontent.

FROM

Border Romances

W. GILMORE SIMMS

Simms hailed from Charleston, South Carolina, and wrote about it in such works as The Yemassee, *set in the Low Country. He also wrote extensively about other places in the South. According to scholar Mary Ann Wimsatt, "His writing exhibits qualities that mark southern literature from its beginnings: a sense of time and history, a love of southern landscape, a respect for southern social institutions, and a firm belief in class stratification and enlightened upper-class rule." In this piece, chapter 1, "Court Season," from* Border Romances *(1885), he describes that most venerable of southern institutions, court day, in Raymond, Mississippi. One of the more amusing observations he makes is the contrast of New Yorkers and their "jostling" habits with the people of Raymond, where such behavior was a "dangerous experiment." The courthouses of Mississippi are generally known to be the center of activity, and, in the old days, as Simms notes, they were often the setting for violence.*

COURT SEASON

THE LITTLE TOWN of Raymond, in the state of Mississippi, was in the utmost commotion. Court-day was at hand, and nothing was to be heard but the hum of preparation for that most important of all days in the history of a country-village—that of general muster alone excepted. Strange faces and strange dresses began to show themselves in the main street; lawyers were entering from all quarters—"saddlebag" and "sulky" lawyers—men who cumber themselves with no weight of law, unless it can be contained in moderately-sized heads, or valise, or saddle-bag, of equally moderate dimensions. Prowling sheriff's officers began to show their hands again, after a ten or twenty days' absence in the surrounding country, where they had gone to the great annoyance of simple farmers, who contract large debts to the shopkeeper on the strength of crops yet to be planted, which are thus wasted on changeable silks for the spouse, and whistle-handled whips for "Young Hopeful" the only son and heir to possessions, which, in no long time, will be heard best of under the auctioneer's hammer. The population of the village was increasing rapidly; and what with the sharp militia colonel, in his new box coat, squab white hat, trim collar and high-heeled boots, seeking to find favor in the regiment against the next election for supplying the brigadier's vacancy; the swaggering planter to whom certain disquieting hints of foreclosure have been given, which he can evade no longer, and which he must settle as he may; the slashing overseer, prime for cockfight or quarter-race, and not unwilling to try his own prowess upon his neighbor, should occasion serve and all other sports fail; the pleading and impleaded, prosecutor and prosecuted, witnesses and victims—Raymond never promised more than at present to swell beyond all reasonable boundaries, and make a noise in the little world round it.

Court-day is a day to remember in the West, either for the parts witnessed or the parts taken in the various performances; and whether the party be the loser of an eye or ear, or has merely helped another to the loss of both, the case is still the same; the event is not usually forgotten.

The inference was fair that there would be a great deal of this sort of prime brutality performed at the present time. Among the crowd might be seen certain men who had already distinguished themselves after this manner, and who strutted and swaggered from pillar to post, as if conscious that the eyes of many were upon them, either in scorn or admiration. Notoriety is a sort of fame which the vulgar mind essentially enjoys beyond any other; and we are continually reminded, while among the crowd, of the fellow in the play, who says he "loves to be contemptible." Some of these creatures had lost an eye, some an ear; others had their faces scarred with the strokes of knives; and a close inspection of others might have shown certain tokens about their necks, which testified to bloody ground fights, in which their gullets formed an acquaintance with the enemy's teeth, not over-well calculated to make them desire new terms of familiarity. Perhaps, in most cases, these wretches had only been saved from just punishment by the humane intervention of the spectators—a humanity that is too often warmed into volition, only when the proprietor grows sated with the sport. All was crowd and confusion. At one moment the main street in Raymond was absolutely choked by the press of conflicting vehicles. Judge Bunkell's sulky hitched wheels with the carriage of Colonel Fishhawk, and 'Squire Dickens' bran new barouche, brought up from Orleans only a week before, was "staved all to flinders"—so said our landlady—"agin the corner of Joe Richards' stable." The 'squire himself narrowly escaped the very last injury in the power of a fourfooted beast to inflict, that is disposed to use his hoofs heartily—and, bating an abrasion of the left nostril, which diminished the size, if it did not, as was the opinion of many, impair the beauty of the member, Dickens had good reason to congratulate himself at getting off with so little personal damage.

These, however, were not the only mishaps on this occasion. There were other stories of broken heads, maims, and injuries; but whether they grew out of the unavoidable concussion of a large crowd in a small place, or from a great natural tendency to broken heads on the part of the owners, it scarcely falls within our present purpose to inquire. A jostle in a roomy region like the west, is anything but a jostle in the streets of New York. There you may tilt the wayfarer into the gutter, and the laugh is against the loser, it being a sufficient apology for taking such a liberty with your neighbor's person, that "business is business and must be attended to." Every man must take care of himself and learn to push with the rest, where all are in a hurry.

But he brooks the stab who jostles his neighbor where there is no such excuse; and the stab is certain where he presumes so far with his neighbor's wife, or his wife's daughter, or his sister. There's no pleading that the city rule is to "take the right hand"—he will let you know what the proper rule is to give way to the weak and feeble—to women, to age, to infancy. This is the manly rule among the strong, and a violation of it brings due punishment in the west. Jostling there is a dangerous experiment, and for this very reason, it is frequently practised by those who love a row and fear no danger. It is one of the thousand modes resorted to for compelling the fight of fun—the conflict which the rowdy seeks from the mere love of tumult, and in the excess of over-heated blood.

If there was a sensation among the "arrivals" at Raymond, there was scarcely less among the residents. The private houses were soon full of visiters, and the public of guests Major Mandrake's tavern was crammed from top to bottom and this afflicting dispensation led to the strangest disruption of anciently adjusted beds and bedsteads. Miss Artemisia Mandrake, for example, was compelled to yield her cushions to a horse-drover from Tennessee, and content herself with such "sleeps" as she could find in an old arm-chair, that stood in immemorial dust in a sort of pigeon-roost garret. It was to this necessity, we may be permitted to say in this place, that she for ever after ascribed her rheumatism, and a certain awry contraction of the muscles of the neck, which, defeating her other personal charms, was not inaptly assumed, by the damsel her-self, to have been the true cause of her remaining, up to the time of this writing, an unappropriated spinster. Major Mandrake has certainly had excellent reason to repent his cupidity.

The rival tavern of Captain Crumbaugh was in equally fortunate condition with that of the major. They were both filled to overflowing by midday, and after that you could get a bed in neither for love nor money. And yet the folks continued to arrive; folks of all conditions and from all quarters; in gig and sulky, or on horseback; some riding in pairs on the same donkey—and not a few short-petticoated damsels, led by curiosity, from the neighboring farms, and mounted in like manner, on battered jades, whose mouths, ossified by repeated jerks, now defied the strenuous efforts by which the riders would have sent them forward with some show of life and spirit, as they emerged from the forests into the crowded thoroughfare.

"Well, there's a heap of folks still a-coming, and where in the world they'll find a place to lie down in to-night, is a'most past my reckoning. I'm sure the major ha'n't got another bed left, high nor low; and as for the captain, I heard him tell Joe Zeigler an hour ago, that all was full with him. Yet, do look, how they are a-coming. Can't you look, Jack Horsey, if it's only for a minute. You hav'n't got no more nateral curiosity than—"

"Shut up, Bess, you've got enough for both of us. What's it to me, and what's it to you, where the folks sleep? Let them sleep where they can; there'll be no want of beds where there's no want of money. If they have that, the captain and the major will take good care that they have every opportunity to spend it. As for you, go you and see after the poultry; court-time is a mighty bad season for chickens; they die off very sudden, and the owner is not always the wiser of the sort of death they die. Push, Bess, and see if you can forget for awhile the business of the two taverns."

The good wife was silent for a space, but this was the only acknowledgment which she condescended to yield her stubborn and incurious husband. She did not leave her place at the window, but continued to gaze with the satisfaction of a much younger person, at the throng in the thoroughfare, as it received additions momently from every new arrival. At length the stir appeared to cease—the carriages to disappear; horses vanished in the custody of bustling ostlers, and their riders, making amends for the day's abstinence, on a dry road, might be seen, in great part, at the bar-room of the major or the captain, washing away the dust from capacious throats by occasional draughts of whiskey or peach brandy.

FROM

Mississippi Mayhem

W. G. BARNER

*As writer W. G. Barner vividly points out, the University of Mississippi
and Mississippi State University have been earnest rivals in the game of
football since the first game was played in 1901. In* Mississippi Mayhem, *published in 1982, he traces the history of the rivalry. As he states
in his introduction, "Other schools feud all season. Ole Miss and State
feud all the time." John Vaught, who holds the record for coaching the
most games at Ole Miss, told a reporter for the* Jackson Daily News *in
1979, "This is a big game because the whole state is watching. No one
straddles the fence over this one. You love one team and hate the other."
Columnist Walter Stewart, writing for the* Commercial Appeal *in
Memphis, called the rivalry "the maelstrom of mayhem [that] combines
the tragic overtones of Russian drama with comedy straight out of Gilbert
and Sullivan." The following excerpt, from the chapter "But First We
Argue," describes the struggle to set up the first game between the rivaling
teams in 1901. After that momentous kickoff, the rest was history.*

THE FEUDIN' started early.

The fightin' came late.

In fact, it appeared that feuding was about all the University of Mississippi and the Mississippi Agricultural and Mechanical College would do
in football.

The University organized its first football team in 1893. A&M started
in 1895. And while letters doubtlessly followed letters, the teams didn't
agree to a playing date until 1901.

And then it was sort of a casual, while-we're-both-in-the-same-neigh-
borhood kind of thing. Mississippi was en route home from opening
Alabama's season in Tuscaloosa when it stopped off in Starkville to play.
A&M was just back home from its own season opener two days previously against Christian Brothers College in Memphis.

There was no great pre-game whoopla. No fierce, fire-in-the-eye
buildup. They simply met—an inevitable event that both had delayed
long enough.

And that started it all—the fuss, the furor that has gone on, unabated
between these two with all the fever and fervor of an old family feud.
Kind of a "cousinly" combat.

Football in 1901 was still a relatively new game, especially in the South. Although it had been 32 years since Princeton and Rutgers played the first intercollegiate football game, the sport was just catching on. Yet it already was pushing baseball in popularity.

Dr. Alexander L. Bondurant of the University's classics department had observed the game of football in the East and introduced it to a group of athletes at Mississippi. By the time of the first meeting with A&M in 1901, Mississippi had built an 18-14 record.

At A&M, class competition was the first real taste of football. The next year an agriculture student, W. M. Matthews of Harrisburg, Texas, organized the first school team.

It was Matthews, as quarterback, captain and manager, who was given the honor of selecting the team colors the night before the first game. "Maroon and white," he said, without hesitation.

For Mississippi, Dr. Bondurant chose the cardinal red of Harvard and the Navy blue of Yale. ". . . it was well to have the spirit of those two good colleges," he wrote years later.

Oddly, each school played its first football game against the same opponent—Southwest Baptist University (now Union University). Mississippi entertained SWBU in Oxford on Nov. 11, 1893 and took a 56-0 victory. Two years later, on Nov. 16, 1895, A&M traveled to Jackson, Tenn., to absorb a 21-0 defeat at the hands of these same Baptists.

A&M continued on through the '95 and '96 seasons but without victory. Years later the team manager said that the University had promised A&M a game during the Aggies' first season but didn't come through.

A Yellow Fever epidemic in 1897 delayed the opening of both schools, and football was cancelled. The University resumed the sport in '98. But interest lagged at A&M until 1901 when I. D. Sessums, an alumnus who was professor of military science and a devout advocate of football, revived interest. He enticed L. B. Harvey, a halfback at Georgetown College in Kentucky, to enroll as player-coach.

And Sessums got what others couldn't—a game with the University.

1901 was the University's 53rd year, and enrollment was 257. A&M, in its 23rd year, had 517. The population of Mississippi was 1.5 million. The new capitol had just been started. There were over 4,100 cotton gins in the state.

The Aggies had never won a game, nor scored a single point, at that time. A scoreless tie with CBC in that year's season opener was the only measure of success. Mississippi had opened with Memphis University School, a 6-0 victory on campus, followed by a 41-0 defeat at Tuscaloosa.

Athletic competition was not entirely new between A&M and University. They already had played four games in baseball since 1892, with the Aggies holding a 2-0-2 advantage.

But that was baseball. This was football. The first!

It was a warm, fall afternoon. Monday, October 28, 1901—cotton pickin' time in predominantly agricultural Mississippi. Excitement had to run high as the cadet corps of the military-minded A&M College marched out to the Starkville Fairgrounds where a gridiron had been laid out in the infield of the race track. The site is believed to have later been incorporated into the MSU Campus.

Game time was set for 3:30 in what the A&M newspaper called "the championship of the state".

Captain of the home-field Aggies was right tackle J. C. Mahoney, at 200 pounds an unusually large player for the football of that day.

Captain for Mississippi was right end Fred W. Elmer. His team had two coaches in 1901. William Sibley, a Virginia graduate who had difficulty in getting enough players out for practice that fall, left unexpectedly, though it is not known at what point in the season. Daniel S. Martin, a 1900 graduate of Auburn, came in to finish the schedule.

Game officials were Fountain Cocke of Columbus, listed as "umpire", and W. S. Davis, an A&M student, referee.

Like many other teams of the day, uniforms were mostly catch as catch could: baseball uniforms or thick shirts with turtle neck collars, or whatever was available. Games were extremely tough—head-to-head combat with no padding and no helmets. Players often let their hair grow long, and the "football topknot" was a style many of the ladies admired.

And so they were primed: two football teams composed mostly of Mississippians—old in hate, new in rivalry. Ready for their first game.

But, first, more feuding.

The game was delayed 40 minutes, the *College Reflector* of A&M reported, while the teams squabbled over N.E. (Billy) Green's being in the lineup. No reason was given, but a check with the admissions office at Mississippi State indicates that Green was a transfer student who played on the UM team the previous season.

"The University men seemed to realize," the *Reflector* analyzed, ". . . that they were destined to be defeated and wanted us to give them everything. After we agreed to take Green out, they kicked against Harris (left end F. D. Harris), saying he was from Chattanooga, and was being paid to play, and a number of other things—all of which are false."

However, Harris was eventually approved, and, belatedly, A&M kicked off. The first A&M-Mississippi game was underway!

The UM fullback who took the kickoff was downed before he reached the center of the field.

Within two minutes, A&M had a touchdown. After Mississippi fumbled, the Aggies made "several good gains," the *Reflector* reported, "then Harvey bucked center for four yards . . . and the first touchdown".

The Aggies' first touchdown in history! You probably could hear the cadets' cheers in Starkville, a mile away. Harvey also "kicked goal," and it was 6-0. In those days a touchdown counted five points.

Also, according to the rules, the scoring team received the kickoff after the touchdown. That led to another A&M score.

Tackle R. S. Wilson returned the kick 40 yards to the Mississippi 50 yard line (fields were 110 yards long, and the 55 was midfield). H. H. Pearson gained 15, Wilson five. Mahoney bucked for 10 yards, then Harvey galloped around right end for 18 but fumbled when Captain Elmer hit him. However, Pearson snapped up the loose ball and burst the remaining two yards for the touchdown. Harvey missed the goal after, and it was 11-0.

After the University got the ball on a fumble, Stone and Elmer picked up 15 yards. But when Mississippi failed to gain the required five yards in three downs, the ball went over to A&M.

With substitutes mixed in with regulars, the Aggies drove downfield for another touchdown. Carrying were Harris, Mahoney, Pearson, J.R. Ricks and H.L. Bush. Harvey hit right end, broke loose and galloped 30 yards for the score, then ran the point after. It was 17-0 at the half.

Football games were divided into two *equal* halves in the early years. But not this one. Haranguing at the start had consumed so much time that darkness cut the second half to just six minutes.

The abbreviated half began with a 55-yard Aggie drive that stalled. It was followed by a 55-yard run by the University when Elmer snatched up a fumble. But that drive, too, stalled. When the ball went over, the official called time, because of darkness. A&M had its first football victory.

From this game, A&M went on to complete a 2-2-1 season, beating Meridian Athletic Club 11-5 and losing to Tulane 24-6 and Alabama 45-0. The University closed with a 2-4 season, whipping Southwest Baptist University 17-0 and losing to LSU 46-0 and Tulane 25-11.

Football in Mississippi—and rivalry, too—was here to stay.

That same season also gave America the first of the great spectacles known as bowl games. On Jan. 1, 1902, Michigan beat Stanford 49-0 in the Tournament of Roses, which in time became the Rose Bowl, fore-runner of well over a dozen other post-season games.

Starkville and Oxford weekly newspapers failed to mention the college teams in the early years. But the daily papers, in response to a growing interest in football, began carrying more. The first A&M-University game was reported in one-paragraph stories in both the *Commercial Appeal* in Memphis and the *Times-Picayune* in New Orleans. In time, papers generally referred to University teams as Mississippi or Oxford. A&M was either Starkville or Farmers.

But student newspapers were using heavier nicknames, as witness the aftermath of the first A&M-University game.

A&M's *College Reflector* charged, "The University boys . . . played the dirtiest game of ball that we have seen. They would do anything to put our men out, so long as the referee was not looking."

Shot back the *University of Mississippi Magazine*, ". . . to one who has never indulged in any exercise more violent than a game of 'antny over' or the milking of the patient cow, football seems a brutal sport. Our bucolic friend of the Agricultural College should confine himself to mumble-peg and townball."

Thus the editorial feuding followed as naturally as athletic rivalry. And both continue still, without letup.

Logging Time

AGNES G. ANDERSON

*This previously unpublished manuscript, set down from Agnes "Sissy"
Grinstead Anderson's vivid memory, describes logging in Gautier on the
Mississippi Gulf Coast and much more. The story, which took place in
1914 or 1915, involves Theodore Dubose Bratton, the second bishop of
the Episcopal Diocese of Mississippi, the loggers, Lou and Henry, their
oxen, Star and Spot, and Sissy and her sister, Pat. It all started when
the bishop set about one summer to build log cabins for the overflowing
needs of the ten Bratton Children, as well as for the Grinstead girls who
lived next door at Oldfields in Gautier on the Gulf Coast. Anderson
remembers with delightful detail not only the fascinating process of logging, but also the making of coal, Lou's drawing of the ox, a violent
game of croquet, and the mysterious disappearance of the bishop's hat.*

THAT SUMMER the bishop spent a lot of time talking to Daddy
about log cabins. He said his children were getting big and the cottage
at Fair Havens was too small. They read everything they could lay their
hands on about log building and went together in the run-about, with
the bishop's mare, Kitty, between the shafts, all the way to Vancleave to
see an old pioneer cabin still standing close to the river crossing at
Wade. They would have taken us along, but Maman* thought it was too
far in the hot August weather, and the roads were too uncertain.

The "bishop" was Theodore Dubose Bratton, second bishop of the
Episcopal Diocese of Mississippi. His summer place was next to Oldfields Plantation on the west. What a wealth of happiness its presence
there brought to us. We loved the bishop like family with a completely
uncomplicated love, which, I now realize, was because he loved us in
the same way. We used to think he was a little mixed up because he
called us daughter, just as he did his own daughters, but we loved it.
More than fifty years later and long after his death, I was to hear a
venerable retired bishop of South Carolina characterize him by saying,
"Oh, there was a man whose tongue was dipped in love."

The bishop's desire for log cabins can be well understood when you

---

* According to her daughter, Mary Pickard, Anderson called her mother Maman in
the French manner with the accent on the second syllable.

realize that he had six children of his own, three boys and three girls, and that the second Mrs. Bratton had four of her own, two boys and two girls. The cabins were named, long before the trees were cut, "Old Maid's Roost" and "Bachelor's Retreat." If there were enough trees, the bishop was to have a tiny "castle" of his own. The trees were to be cut immediately, while "the sap was still high," according to the old-timers. This would render them less liable to the assaults of insects and weather. They were to be taken from a very thick grove of second-growth saplings on the northwest corner of the bishop's property. Once cut and hauled to location, they would have the six months till spring to "cure," stacked up like tepees in the sun.

And now began a happy time for us. A timber cutter from Vancleave came down. He brought two sawyers—strange, shy, brown-skinned men, whose kinky hair was blond and glinting instead of the expected black, and whose eyes shone blue and a little vacant against their dark skin. These men camped among the trees with their splendid team of oxen. Star was a cream-colored beast with a white whorl like an expanding galaxy on his ponderous forehead. Spot was rust black with white spots. We soon came to know that, in spite of their great strength, they were the most docile beasts on earth.

Star was Pat's favorite, as she was, quite naturally, attracted by the best. Spot was mine, and he may not have equalled Star, but I came to love him so that I cried for three nights after he went back to Vancleave. . . .

The timber man went through the whole forest with his cutters. He marked each tree to be cut with one stroke of a sharp little axe or hatchet. We saw the little clear beads of sap on the lip of the cut.

"Pure blood," said Pat, from the depths of her beautiful imagination.

We knew how to gather the hardened resin from the big trees that had been turpentined, and we used it as chewing gum when it was well hardened. It took a great deal of chewing to make it smooth and cohesive, and the taste was so astringent that it wrinkled our noses. . . .

The cutters used cross-cut saws and axes. They felled a tree down a narrow corridor so exactly that it never touched its neighbors. Shivering, it sank down and lay sighing softly after its crash upon the earth. Then the axe blades honed and the tree's bare trunk, stripped of branches, lay dead upon the ground. The cutters were brothers, named Henry and Lou.

Henry gave all the commands to Star and Spot. I don't remember ever hearing Lou speak, except for a sort of fascinating mumble in his throat which told Henry if he was going too fast or too slow and told Star and Spot that he loved them. He did, too; you could tell it by the way he wheeled those two great beasts into position, side by side, then lifted on their great wooden yoke. Henry said it was made of hickory. The curved pieces, which came up under their necks and pinched their dew-laps, had to be soaked for days before they would become pliable enough to bend double. They fitted into holes in the yoke with just enough spring to hold tight. When I was older I saw timbering opera-tions where the ox teams numbered eight and ten beasts, but the magic of Star and Spot and the bishop's few small trees never was equalled.

The heavy metal chains were fastened by hooks to the trees and like traces to the yoke. Then Henry cracked his miracle of a whip. "Hup, ah, gee, haw now, whoa" and the trees were snaked out as if they were able to wriggle and bend. The whip would give one loud crack at the start and flick about a bit, never touching, while the journey was accom-plished. The first long slim tree out was fitted into the crotches of two convenient brothers at the building site. Subsequent trees were piled against it, first one side, then the other, a magnificent long tepee or tunnel.

Pat said it was a "lodge house." She had been reading "Hiawatha." I think that there were five or six of these "lodge houses" before Henry and Lou got out the last tree. Now we were sure they would go. No indeed, every branch, every piece of bark was cleared from the loved grove. "The bugs get in if we leave dead wood," said Henry.

We were allowed to ride the fragrant loads of branches to a site far out beyond the county road. There Henry and Lou built a coal kiln. Every scrap was used, even the needles, for kindling. Lou did most of the work. He made a circle on the ground with a shallow trench around it. He showed us a sun-dew eating a tiny brown moth and a crawfish at home under its castle of dirt balls, but he did not speak. Lou was a wonderful person, almost as wonderful as Star and Spot, who stood patiently under their yoke chewing continually on their unending cuds.

Lou built that coal kiln as if he were one of the ancient pyramid builders. In the very center of the big circle he made a small circle. Tiny slivers of fat pine filled that circle with kindling-size bits, needles, and cones, but always there was an opening at the top that went straight down to the ground. Around this he would set the wood. It was sunk into the ground so that it stood slanting inward. The whole circle was filled in this way, then covered with dirt and clay. Another layer of wood was added to the top of this, and then a little smaller, and so on to the top, which rose about twenty feet. It was a magical dirt lodge house.

Lou climbed nimbly, barefooted, to the top, scratched a match on the seat of his pants and dropped it down into the hole. Down he came and, sitting on his heels, watched the top of the kiln. Sure enough, we saw it against the far blue summer sky, a little wisp of smoke. We thought we had seen it as soon as Lou did, but I think he waited for us before he held up his two hands in a gesture of triumph.

"She burns," shouted Henry and burn she did. For days and days her pyre of smoke rose into the summer sky. We got so used to it that we didn't even notice it anymore. One day Pat suddenly said, "Where's the kiln smoke?"

"I don't smell it."

Daddy laughed. "There hasn't been any smoke for days. The kiln is curing and Lou will be after that coal before long."

Sure enough, one coolish October day when we were out by the pond sampling wild persimmons, we heard the distant crack of the bull-whip. We flew up to the house and asked for permission to ride our horse, Betty, out to the kiln. It was granted and we were carried slowly, at Betty's own leisurely rate, out to the kiln. There were Lou, Star, Spot, and Henry. We slid down Betty's neck. Pat, being an excellent horse-woman, remembered to keep a tight hold on Betty's reins. She tied her to a fence post at the clearing fence, and we fairly tumbled across the county road to our friends.

"Did you come to get the coal?"

"Oh, Lou, I didn't know you had coal. How's Star? How's Spot? Hello, Henry. Will it be good coal?"

"We kin hope," said Henry.

Star and Spot were hitched to a two-wheeled homemade dump cart. They were still chewing their cuds. They looked at us, and a shiver went down both beasts' flanks as their tails rose in unison and flicked the deer flies from their sides.

"Oh," we squealed excitedly, "they know us."

Lou somehow fastened the tree hooks in strategic spots in the kiln and fastened the chains to the yokes. "Hup," said Henry, when suddenly the kiln came tumbling down. Betty reared and whinnied and we scattered, jumping and bumping. Henry and Lou, Star and Spot, all laughed.

From the cart Henry and Lou removed a great pile of old feed sacks, the burlap bag of that day—sometimes frayed from many uses, strong, rough, and woven just tight enough to hold the grain. Henry and Lou each had a sack and they gave Pat and me one together. We picked up the pieces of coal all morning, filling all the sacks. Henry fastened one of the five sacks on Betty's back for a present, but Lou, scratching where the center of his circle had been, handed us each a long, slender bit of coal like a pencil. There was one for him, too, and we watched, fascinated, while he showed us how to use them. On the weathered boards of the cart's side, he drew a glorified ox, a mixture of Star and Spot, and round its neck, instead of a yoke, a garland of flowers hung. Many years later, introduced for the first time to Minoan frescoes and cave paintings, I thought of Lou. Now the two hitched the oxen to their cart, cracked the whip, and trudged off north on the dusty county road. We waved and waved long after they were out of sight and sound. Leading Betty, we trudged off south at the edge of Molly's Causeway, where we picked some bright swamp maple leaves and stuck them gaily in Betty's bridle.

We stopped for a while at the far gate, white and clean in the bright air. Later Daddy found that the NO TRESSPASSING sign, lettered there by one of the field workers, had been faithfully copied with all of its difficult S's on the board below and there were scrawls on the third board that were never properly interpreted. We went straight to Granny with our charcoal. We knew how much she would love it.

Granny was an artist as well as being the most loving and knowledgeable person in the world when it came to the fascinations of natural things. She brought out her "block," which was not charcoal paper but something that she used for water colors. Quick as a flash, a little vignette of Jack, the fox terrier, appeared on the paper. She was so thrilled with it that she put away both pieces after each of us had had a chance to use it on a sheet of paper.

"Oh, Lou," we told him later. "We knew your coal was magic. Granny said it was as fine as the finest French charcoal."

All that winter the bishop's logs cured. Daddy would tramp over about once a week and turn them. Pat and I went there to play occasionally during the winter. But the lodges were cold and dark and very damp, so we slowly relinquished them, especially after a thousand-legger [centipede] fell onto the sleeve of my coat one afternoon as I was going out.

When at last we were sure of spring, the bishop arrived one day. He stayed for dinner, of course. Before dinner Daddy, Pat, Mr. Ladnier, Mr. Seymour, the bishop, and I worked hard on the cabins. The bishop had them all sketched out. Now he staked their shapes upon the ground and measured out the walls with string. The two big cabins were exactly alike. There were two rooms with recessed entrances and, at the back of the recess, a bathroom. The single cabin was just a room, square and plain.

When we came back after dinner the Ladniers had sawed a dead cypress, which had washed up on our beach, into suitable lengths for foundations. They were placed with great care along the bishop's string markers. From that day until Old Maid's Retreat was finished we had our beings right there. We watched the careful notching of the logs and were even called upon to mount up and jump a log into place now and then. This was great fun.

Sometimes the notches were a fraction too tight. One of the men would boost us up, and we would run along the log holding his hand and jump hard at the point. Our success would signal a buzz of congratulations and we would feel our importance. The spaces between the logs was often quite wide, and we delighted in being able to peer through.

"Chinking" was the next step in the building operation and we were even more intrigued by it. Gray moss, which at that time hung in funereal manner from almost every tree, was harvested for use in the chinking. Most of these workmen lived in one- or two-room cabins, heated by fireplaces with outside chimneys made of clay and moss, so they knew how to mix the two to make a strong chinking material. We were allowed to poke and smooth as much as we pleased. Years later, when the cabins were torn down, I remember getting a great thrill when I saw my fingerprints, tiny in comparison, all along the chinking of some of the logs. . . .

The girls were terribly attractive. What a time the second Mrs. B. had. The bishop, lost in a cloud of benignity, paid no attention, and Little Mother, as she was called, partly in reference to her size and partly as an endearment, took our her frustrations on the croquet balls. The court was laid out beneath the bishop's biggest oak and was almost completely in shade. Many a championship tournament ended with Granny and Little Mother, hatted and gloved, battling each other to the death. Given the force and vindictiveness with which those two used their Rover balls, no one had a chance against them. I suppose their concentration was the thing that made them able to become "Rovers" so quickly.

As I remember it, if you completed the course yet failed to hit the last stake, you became an invulnerable "Rover." You could interfere in any action, with the only worry being that you had to get back to the final stake and hit it before anyone else did, in order to win. That must account for the glinting eye and the terrific shot. Sometimes from the other end of the court, or its outer boundaries, that shot sailed across miles of ground and hit the stake with a resounding thump.

The bishop, in his sweaty work clothes and swinging his "lazy boy" to keep down the weeds, would sometimes have to jump to get away from a ricochetting ball. Soaked from his path-cutting, in hat and clothes he would take a shower at Bachelor's Retreat. Then he would spread his clothes on the grass to dry, including the old straw hat.

Therein hangs a tale—a sin of mine, which jumped into my head for years whenever I said the general confession. Perhaps it still does when I go to church with an undisciplined mind. Mrs. Bratton enlisted Pat's and my aid in carrying out, not only a theft, but a destroying. She reached the point where she felt in her bones a crying out of feeling that she could no longer allow the bishop to wear that hat. He contended that it was perfectly clean. Did he not wash it upon his own head after every wearing? It had lost none of its style. It was the only comfortable hat he had.

She contended that it was bedraggled, smelled to high heaven, the straw was mildewed and frayed, and the ribbon rusty. Observing it sitting upon the grass, dried by the sun, we were forced to agree, not with the bishop, but with his wife. Besides, we had heard Granny and Maman tch-tching over the bishop's headgear and Mammy, even, muttering, "T'aint fitter, t'aint fitter." Naturally, when Little Mother asked us to watch for our chance to steal it, we were ready.

I remember Pat dancing up to her one morning, "He's down on the pier. He forgot his hat."

"Dere 'tis. Yondah on da grass," Mammy said. She often lapsed into "Mammy talk" under stress.

"Get it," said Little Mother.

"Little Mother, we got it."

A bit of kerosene, a match, and poof! Suddenly the bishop's hat was gone, but, such is the work of the Almighty, that at that particular moment a strange sound was heard out on the road. It was the noise made by Mr. Henry Gautier's Model T. . . . A boy came running with a yellow paper. Our eyes were as big as saucers, for he held a telegram.

"Mr. Henry say if de bishop hurry, we kin flag down numbah 4 at Lewis Crossing."

"Run," shrieked Mrs. Bratton. "Get the bishop."

We rushed for the pier. A fluff of white ash sprayed from beneath my right foot. I didn't feel the burn until hours later.

"Come quick! Come quick!" Pat howled, and we turned, wheeling behind the bishop before we touched the pier. He was ready. A "special" member of the diocese had passed away. The family needed him.

"Where's my hat?" he asked, emerging from the house in his shantung suit, clerical collar and all.

"Get a new one in Jackson," screamed Mrs. Bratton. "There isn't time to look."

Sure enough, we could hear, borne on the east wind, the faint sound of No. 4 blowing for the river bridge. The bishop leapt into the Ford and was carried, hatless, away. . . . The bishop wore a fine Panama straw thereafter. It did not look new. Perhaps it had belonged to the departed. Mrs. Bratton made him wear a cloth cap when working.

I still puzzle over God's ways of dealing with his erring children, and can only conclude that His tongue, too, is "dipped in love."

F R O M

You Live and Learn. Then You Die and Forget It All

WILLIAM FERRIS

This unusual book, published in 1992, is folklorist William Ferris's re-
cord and preservation of the spoken stories of mule trader Ray Lum. Lum
was born on the Big Black River near Vicksburg in 1891. He grew up
in hard times, when trading food and goods was not unusual, and had
become an expert in horse and mule trading by the time he was nineteen.
He traded primarily in the Mississippi Delta, Tennessee, Texas, and in
parts of the Southwest from the 1920s until his death in 1976. Lum
was known over most of the South and Southwest for his courtliness, his
canniness with animals, and his ability to tell stories. In her foreword to
the book, Eudora Welty writes: "Indeed, the mule trader has undoubtedly
helped to form our great oral tradition in the South. William Ferris, valu-
able folklorist, practiced discoverer and custodian of our living records,
has seen in this life story an illuminating account of our not-so-long-ago
past. It is all the more enhanced by being, as well, a reflective record of a
friend."

In the following selection from the chapter "When Mules Played Out,"
Lum reveals some of the secrets of mule trading.

IF YOU COME in green to a mule sale, you wouldn't know what the
auctioneer had on the carpet.[1] But if you was a mule man buying mules,
you had to understand. You can't be a yokel. You got to be awake. Let's
have a little auction here:

> *Order in the court!*
> *It's a rare mule we've got here, boys, a rare mule.*
> *I've got a hundred-thirty.*
> *Will you give me five?*
> *A hundred thirty-five.*
> *If you boys want to bid on him,*
> *Just don't stand there.*
> *Those mules are not plentiful.*
> *This one shown,*
> *I don't know where you'll find the next one.*
> *You know how high mules are?*

None of you know.
You don't know until they are sold.
What do you want to give?
A hundred thirty-six.
Now eight.
Now nine.
Nine.
Speak now or hold your peace forever and eternity.
Nine.
Get in there if you want to.
If I never cock another pistol.
I got a hundred thirty-eight.
Thirty-nine.
Come on if you want to.
Hundred thirty-eight.
Thirty-nine.
Will you give nine?
Sold to Willie Jones for a hundred thirty-eight dollars.

You bought it too cheap, you son-of-a-gun. Arrest that man over there. He just give a hundred thirty-eight dollars for the mule. Oooh, some people are so tight. So young to be so tight. God forgive them, for they know not what they do. Well, I hope you get two hundred for him when you sell him.

I've auctioned, and I've seen auctions all over the world. I seen them in Chicago and St. Louis. St. Louis had the best ring men and the best auction in the world for a while. Then it moved about.

One time Fort Worth was the biggest auction.

Another time Memphis was the biggest auction.

Another time St. Louis was the biggest auction.

And then Chicago had the biggest auction.

That thing moved around in cycles. That's the way it done. And when tractors come, the auctions faded out. They was like mule traders. They didn't die. They just faded away.

It's been a long time since I sold a mule. Been a long time since I sold anything. But I always say it's not a man's age that stops him, it's his health.

The last big sale I made was in Birmingham, and I had a load of registered horses there. . . .

While I was selling, the boy that had been to auction school come to me and said, "Mr. Lum, they won't buy a pitching horse."

"Is that so? They won't buy a bucking horse? Well, we'll see about that." I had six pitching horses that had cost fifty dollars a piece. I said, "Folks, out in Texas a good bucking horse is worth lots of money. These are some horses they almost bought to go to England, but they didn't pitch hard enough. They didn't want them unless they was sunfishers. You know a sunfisher puts his back where his belly is and you ain't going to stay on him. Well, these horses wasn't good enough to be sunfishers."

So this first horse come in, and Squire sat down on him. He sat on this horse like he was glued to him. He bent with the horse and never was in danger of being throwed, and that horse would holler. God Almighty, I never heard a horse bellow like that before. This little woman bought the horse for three hundred and fifty dollars. That was one of the horses the boy said wouldn't bring nothing.

Every mule man carried a walking stick or a whip, you know. He didn't hit the mule with the whip. He'd just crack it, and the mule would move. My brother Clarence is a good hand with a whip, and he looks graceful doing it. A whip'll last him three or four years. He never hits the mule with his whip. Another fellow I knew, he'd wear out a whip every week. That's the difference in people.

A lot of people don't want their mules hit. I learned that early in life. I found out people like you better when you respect their stock. . . .

Some mules are sensitive around the ears. This one is. When that bit hits his mouth, he'll lay his ears right on back. A lot of mules are thataway. If you take his ear and twist it, you can go and do anything you want with him. You just got to have more sense than the mule.

This mule right here is about ten years old. That's close to her age. You go by how broad the teeth are across the back. The older they get, the sharper they get across the back. Now you got it. This mule is awful gentle. You can do anything you want with her. Come here, gal. She's already shod, and she's gentle. That's about as pretty a mule as you'll see. No, you won't have any trouble with her. When the bit hits her mouth, she'll go right on. That's a good mule. Get up, good lady. She'll keep herself fat off what a chicken knocks out of his trough. That will be an easy-kept mule, don't you see, easy-kept.

When you want to mouth a horse, just pull his top lip up. If his teeth are broad like this, he's young. . . . When he gets about seven years old, his teeth will look like my middle finger right here. When he gets about eight years old it will look kind of like this little finger here. The older he gets, the sharper his teeth get. You tell a horse's age by his teeth.

I remember one time I saw a fellow, and he was pulling a horse's mouth open and looking down his throat. So I said, "I've been feeding him oats."

"I'm looking to see how old he is."

"And you're looking down his throat?"

"Yeah."

"Uh huh." Well, you find a man like that, and you can tell him anything you want. . . .

There was a man here at the barn yesterday with a horse thirty-five years old. He rides him every day. I asked him, "How old do you think your horse is?"

"I think he is about seven or eight years old."

I had already mouthed him. I just went on and left it that way. Let sleeping dogs lie. You can't tell folks about horses.

You know how to tell if a horse is blind? Clap your hands and if he throws up one ear, he's blind on that side. If he's blind in one eye, he'll try to see out of that ear. I remember Old Uncle Dan MacBroom come in once and tied his horse in the stall. I knew he had a screw 'cause when I slapped my hands, both his ears come up. I knew then he was blind in both eyes. I traded with him, and in about an hour or two I swapped him off to somebody else. . . .

The worse cheating ever I got, a doctor come up with a pretty horse, and I traded for him. When he left, I found a plug in his windpipe, and there was a big hole in his neck. I forget who I traded him to. I got every kind of snide,[2] but that didn't matter. I didn't pay no attention to that. . . .

When you go to buy a horse, don't get one that's too fat. What was it the man said, "A lean hound for a long chase." That's right. You run a potbellied horse, and he'll give out, but take one that looks like a racehorse, and you can ride him all you want to. Just talk to him once in a while, give him a little air and give him a quart of oats, and it'd be the same as giving that potbellied son-of-a-bitch a bushel.

Another thing I never wanted was a big horse. I remember a man wanted a big horse once, and I bought him one in St. Louis. That horse was nearly eighteen hands high, a freak of nature. He just kept growing tall, don't you see, like some people. So I shipped him on to the man I was buying for, and that man phoned me up and called me everything on earth. "I'll never let you buy another horse for me as long as you live. What do you expect me to do with that long, tall son-of-a-bitch you sent me?"

"Drown the son-of-a-bitch! Drown him!"

"Well," the man said, "there ain't enough water. Hell, there ain't a creek or a river that's deep enough to drown him."

Yeah, he ought to have been chloroformed, put to sleep. Get his head out of the feed sack. Good God, good for nothing!

Mules are like Maxwell House coffee. They're good till they drop. Yeah, mules was the backbone of the country, and George Washington bred the first mule. Yes, sir, his bread was done.

You had to have a mule to farm with if you was going to plow. In slavery time a hundred years ago, they didn't have nothing to farm with but mules. They used the mule to build the South, don't you know. Stop and think about it. Mules built the railroads and the levees. They protected us from the river.

They used to say mules is like whiskey. As long as they drink whiskey, they'll make it, and long as they work mules, they'll raise them. I believe that's really true. Long as they drink it, they'll make it, and long as they work them, they'll raise them. So it works both ways.

A man with six or seven acres, all he needs is one mule to work that land. He don't need a tractor. The time is coming when they won't be using big tractors for little farms. If you can't afford to buy a tractor to work five or six acres, you can get you a little mule.

There's a lot of people that'll buy a little mule to plow their crop. The world's not going to stop if they can't get tractors. I've seen it good, and I've seen it bad. But it's not going to stop. It's going to keep right on going. It could be that those bygone days will come back. That's the way I see it. It could be that you'll run out of gas all over the world, and then you'll haul every damn thing with mules again. It's possible.

We don't know how much gas is down under the ground. We don't know whether it's going to last. It could quit. History repeats, they say. I don't like to predict anything bad, but it could happen. If we run out of gasoline, we'll go back to mules. Farmers got to go on. Lots of people now don't know a damn thing about mules, but they can learn.

Time changes, and the time will come when it will be profitable to raise mules. Up in the Delta where they use tractors on big farms, they wouldn't give you a nickel for a mule. But out in these hills where they got just five or ten acres, they still work mules.

What animal is it that you can do away with every one of them, and in a period of time there'll be more? Don't be ashamed if you don't know. I guess I've asked a thousand lawyers, bankers, and doctors, and none of them knew. You don't know the answer even though I been talking about them. If you do away with all of them, in a period of time there'll be more.

Some folks'll holler, "Chickens."

They figure a chicken's got eggs and would go to hatching. Well, I never did consider a chicken an animal. Now what would you say that was?

It's a mule. Mules don't breed. They don't cross. There's two ways to get a mule. If you take a jack and a mare horse and put them together, you get a mule. That's what you call a jack screw. If you breed a saddle mare with a jack, you'll get a mule that'll ride awful good. It'll take after its mother. It'll have more of the mare in it than it has the jack.

Now then, if you want to go the other way, you put a jenny under a stud horse and get a henny. A henny is a mule with little short ears. A cross with a jack and a mare is a different cross from a stud and a jenny, don't you see. You make a different cross.

. . . One of these days I'm going up to Mule Day in Columbia, Tennessee. Every year at Columbia they have a thousand pretty girls riding a thousand pretty mules. Here's the mule, and here's the girl, and they ride bareback, don't you know. It must be a pretty sight to see. If you don't like to look at the girls, look at the mules. You'll have all kinds.

And a damn mule colt, they like to play, you know. If you have two or three mule colts around, and you got a calf in the same pasture, you better get them separated. They don't belong in there together. The mule colts will be playing and will just grab the calf by the neck and throw him over the fence.

A fellow asked another one, "What is a mule?"

"Oh, it's one of those hard tails."

They call them hard tails. You know, you shave a mule's tail. If you don't shave it, he'll have a long, bushy tail just like a horse. They shave the tail so they don't have a lot of hair dragging around in the harness.

I knew more mules named "Maud" than anything else. They'd call a matched team Maud and Annie. "Whoa, Annie, whoa. Gee, Maud." Gee was to your right when you were plowing, and haw was to your left.

If I can get my hands on a mule's jaw, I can tell how old he is. I don't care how dark it is, all I want to do is get my hand on his jaw. The jawbone of an old mule gets sharp. It's wide just like your thumb here when he's young, and when he gets twenty years old, it gets real narrow. And a jack's jaw is the same way.

The jawbone of an ass goes back to the Bible. Methuselah took the jawbone of the ass and whipped off so many thousand of those fellows, don't you know. I remember seeing in the Bible about the jawbone of an ass, and I thought a lot about that old dry bone. You know, if a good stout man got ahold of it, he could whip an awful lot of them. That Methuselah must have been awful strong.

NOTES
[1] *On the carpet:* In the auction ring; being sold.
[2] *Snide:* A defective animal.

Sacred Space

T O M   R A N K I N

In Sacred Space, *published in 1993, photographer and folklorist Tom
Rankin conveys through words and pictures the dignity and beauty of
lakes, churches, and cemeteries—sacred spaces for African-Americans of
the Mississippi Delta. After the Civil War, black churches were centers for
racial identity, places that offered relief from racial discrimination, and,
later, where protests were organized. Under the pastoring of Reverend
Tom Bronner, New Bethel Church at Gunnison was one such sacred
space. Another was Stamps Lake on Perthshire Plantation, home of the
artist and sculptor Emma Lytle, who has rendered the outdoor baptisms
held there in nearly life-sized oils. The following account, in which we
learn how Reverend Bonner was called to preach in the late 1920s, is
taken from Rankin's piece "On Praying Ground."*

T R A D I T I O N A L   O U T D O O R   baptisms represent perhaps the
quintessential transformation of an existing place into a sacred space.
Though the number of outdoor baptisms in bayous, lakes, and rivers
has declined in recent years—the natural bodies of water having been
supplanted by churchyard and indoor baptismal pools—some congregations are holding on to the traditional practice because of its history
and the symbolic relationship with the original baptism of Jesus by John
the Baptist in the River Jordan. Reverend Tom Bronner of Gunnison,
for example, held firmly to the tradition of baptizing in Stamps Lake
on Perthshire Plantation, the place where he himself had been baptized
in his teens. He continued to take candidates for baptism to the very
same spot on the lake each August until his death in 1989.

Reverent Bronner's own religious life had begun near Stamps Lake,
where he had been instructed by his preacher to find "a praying
ground, go to that praying ground and pray and ask God" for forgiveness. His preacher instructed him to go to his chosen place daily until
the Lord spoke to him. He did that for two weeks, going to the same
place "under a pecan bush on the bogue bank" [bank of a creek or
stream] each day. Some sixty years later Reverend Bronner remembered that he "had been there so many times it was clean where I had
been there praying, begging God to bless my soul." In his chosen sacred spot under that pecan bush he found God.

He described receiving his divine call to preach close by his old praying ground near the sharecropper's house where he lived:

> I was living at Perthshire. On the bogue bank, we called it. And I was on my way home on a dirt road beside a canal ditch that led into the bogue where I lived. And I was walking, stepping. Now it didn't slip up on me, the Lord had been worrying me a long time about preaching. And I talked to God like I'm talking to you. I said, "I ain't gonna preach."
>
> But something was within me, was, just like I'm talking to you, saying, "I mean for you to preach."
>
> I say, "I ain't got sense enough to preach. You get after someone else. Let me do what I'm doing." [I'm] talking to God.
>
> As I was stepping I got paralyzed. The Lord knows I'm telling you the truth. I couldn't move. I had my same mind, I had my same eyes. I could see my same person sitting on the bogue. I couldn't lift my feet. I said, "Lord." I couldn't, but I tried. While I was standing there talking back to God he was talking to me. I could hear the voice saying, "I say preach."
>
> I said, "No, I ain't."
>
> And I stood there arguing with God about what I wasn't going to do. It looked like I come to my sense. I said, "Well, if you let me go home, I'll preach." And my legs started walking. I walked up to the house.
>
> I know it. There are two things I know. I know I've been converted. And I know I've been called to preach. Them two things. Ain't much I know. But those two things I'm sure of.

With the certainty of his calling, Reverend Bronner led the New Bethel Church at Perthshire for over fifty years. In each of those years, after the annual revival held in August because that was the traditional "lay by" time when the cotton was too tall for laborers to work so they had time off until picking season, he took his church members to Stamps Lake for the annual baptism. Large crowds gathered—many more than attended the preceding church service—to watch the time-honored outdoor ritual. . . .

At Tom Bronner's last baptism, in 1989, he was very feeble and moved slowly with his cane, accepting a helpful hand from numerous people as he walked into the church and up to his chair behind the pulpit for the service that would precede the trip to the lake. He quoted from Scripture to his church members: "As Jesus say, 'Go in the hedges and highways and compel them to come.' But not with a gun, but with a good life. You can compel people to come to Jesus. The way is open there for anybody that is willing to be saved. Jesus said when he was here, 'He that believeth and are baptized shall be saved.' I don't believe that he was playing when he said those words. So we're going to the lake very pleased and very happy to have one to be baptized. Amen."

Sacred Harp Sings

W. B. ALLISON

*Allison, a researcher for the Works Progress Administration, describes a
service at Liberty Church in Duffee, near Meridian, on June 14, 1936.
The music called sacred harp, also known as shape-note singing, was a
system originating in colonial New England and developed by William
Little and William Smith in* The Easy Instructor, *published in Philadelphia in 1801. One of the successors to that songbook,* The Sacred
Harp, *published in 1844 by two masters from Georgia, B. F. White and
E. J. King, is the basis for the continuation of the tradition today in six
southern states. Devotees in Oxford, Mississippi, for instance, have been
celebrating shape-note singing since 1981 under the direction of George
W. Boswell and Warren Steel. According to Steel, the singers originally
"used four distinctive note heads to indicate the four syllables denoting
tones of a musical scale* (fa, sol, la *and* mi) *then employed in vocal
instruction, making unnecessary the pupil's need to learn and memorize
key signatures." Today most teachers use a seven-shape system. Many
well-known hymns, such as* "Amazing Grace" *and* "How Firm a
Foundation," *have their origin in shape-note singing. Here Allison describes not only the singing but also the little church in the woods and
the traditional dinner on the grounds.*

''OLD SACRED HARP SINGINGS,'' of common occur-
rence in the comparatively early days of this region, were almost abandoned for a considerable period but in more recent years have been
revived with great fervor. So marked is their return to popularity in the
rural districts that, during the early summer, a singing is held at some
church within the territory contiguous to Meridian on practically every
Sunday and some residents of the city, devotees of the older sacred
music, make a practice of attending them all.

The name is derived from that of the song book or hymnal in general use, i.e., the "Sacred Harp", a very old collection (a revision dated
1902 is generally accepted as few of the original books survive). "The
Harp" and "Old Harmony" (Christian Harmony, published in 1873)
are considered the only books appropriate for use at a real "Old Harp"
singing.

The old Liberty Church, three miles from Duffee, Newton County, has for a number of years held as an annual event, a Harp singing, on the second Sunday in June, and, as the traditions and conventions are there carefully observed, their latest service may be considered as typical. Liberty Church is situated in an oak grove on top of a fairly high hill, allowing, on one side, an extensive view, but enclosed by woods on three sides, and, from it, a path descends steeply through the woods to a fine spring. The age of the church is uncertain but a former member states that he moved into the community and, with his wife, attended services there in 1871. The building is small, about twenty-five by forty feet, but, so great is the interest through the country round that a crowd of more than five hundred persons of all ages gathered to attend the service. The singing started at ten o'clock and continued without pause until twelve, when a recess was taken and, for an hour, the invariable bountiful dinner was the center of attraction. At one o'clock the singers reassembled and continued with strong voices and unflogging zeal until nearly four o'clock.

There is no instrumental accompaniment. The singing is led by two, three or even four co-leaders who sound the key note and sing a chord in unison. The entire song is then run through in chorus, "by note," after the method of the old country singing schools, now a thing of the past. That is, instead of using the words, each note is sung by syllable as—

mi   fa   sol   sol   sol

Thereafter the number is sung through, words and music in the usual way but the complete formula is observed with each selection. The leaders are almost without exception most capable conductors who know their books by heart, after calling and singing through number after number from either book without so much as a glance at it. All parts are carried with the utmost accuracy and fervor, and it is indeed beautiful to see the rapt expression which comes upon the faces of many of the singers to whom music is truly a voice of and to the soul.

FROM

Once Upon A Time When We Were Colored

CLIFTON TAULBERT

In this his first book, Clifton Taulbert tells about growing up in Glen Allan, Mississippi, during the forties and fifties. Taulbert deliberately uses the designation "colored" to signify the time period he describes. In his introduction, he notes the many changes since his childhood: " 'Colored' people were now 'black,' soap operas had replaced quilting bees in their homes, and the schools their children attended were now integrated." Although his family was poor financially, Taulbert reverently recalls the values passed on to him by his great-grandfather, "Poppa," his great-grandmother, "Ma Pearl," the great-aunt who raised him, "Ma Ponk," and his mother, Mary, who became a teacher. Cotton chopping, hog killing, minstrel shows, and fish fries accompanied by the singing of the great Muddy Waters are all part of the world he describes. At the center of that world was the church—its people, rituals, and songs (from chapter 8, "Some Glad Morning, Some Glad Day, I'll Fly Away").

IT WAS CLOSER to our hearts than our homes—the colored church. It was more than an institution, it was the very heartbeat of our lives. Our church was all our own, beyond the influence of whites, with its own societal structure.

Even when colored people moved north, they took with them their church structure. The Baptist church, of which my family was a part, had (and has) a big network under the auspices of the National Baptist Convention. A small colored Baptist church in Glen Allan, Mississippi, and a large colored Baptist church in Saint Louis, Missouri, had the same moderator, used the same Sunday-school books, and went to the same conferences. And whether north or south, large or small, the colored church was a totally black experience.

Ma Ponk made sure I was regularly immersed in the colored-church world. As early as I remember, I spent my Sundays, both night and day, attending church with Ma Ponk. No matter the hard workweek, we all looked forward to Sunday when we would dress in our best and meet our friends.

Sunday morning came in easy and Ma Ponk would let me sleep late. The smell of hotcakes and homemade pork sausages fried in lard would float through the house. Ma Ponk only had to call once.

When I got to the kitchen Ma Ponk would be moving around the black iron stove in her starched white dress. She was on the Mothers' Board of the church, and as a church mother, she was required to wear white to Sunday services. Ma Ponk made sure her dress was hand starched and washed in rainwater to ensure that extra whiteness. She was careful not to get any spots on her dress as she skillfully turned the hotcakes and brewed her Maxwell House drip coffee. . . .

She began to pin up her hair. She had extra long silky black hair, but she felt it was unchristian to wear it down, so she would plait her hair into long braids and wrap those braids around her head. Finally to ensure her hairpins held safely, she would wrap her head in a white scarf.

In white shoes, silk stockings, starched white dress and her white scarf, Ma Ponk was ready for church. Ma Ponk's parents and grand-parents were founding members of Saint Mark's Missionary Baptist Church and she was considered one of the leaders. It was the fourth Sunday, Pastoral Day, and our little colored neighborhood was all abuzz as the gravel roads were filled with people dressed in their best, laughing and joking on the way to the sanctuary, our church.

Pastoral Sunday was the one day a month when our official elected pastor would be there to deliver the message. Other Sundays, he would be at one of the other churches he served, and Saint Mark's would have to make do with a pinch hitter. It was no great honor to be asked to speak on those off Sundays, because everybody knew that the crowd would be small and the offering (from which preachers were paid) would be low. People who felt the call to preach and positioned themselves to fill in on off Sundays were called jackleg preachers, because they had no churches of their own.

Today, however, there would be no jackleg preacher. . . . Women in their white dresses and black Sunday hats and men in their Sunday suits with their best brightly colored ties and shined shoes were shaking each other's hands, hugging and kissing the children as we took our turns climbing the steps into the main sanctuary.

Today, field hands were deacons, and maids were ushers, mothers of the church, or trustees. The church transformed the ordinary into an institution of social and economic significance. A hard week of field work forgotten, the maid's aprons laid to rest, and the tractors in the shed, these colored men and women had entered a world that was all

their own. Rough hands softened with Royal Crown grease were positioned to praise. As a young boy, I sat quietly in my seat and waited for
the services to start. The church was designed for us children to be seen
and not heard, and if by chance we talked or got caught chewing gum,
Miss Nola or one of the ever-present ushers would take a long control
stick and crack us on the head. The church rules were strict, and the
ushers made sure nothing interfered with the high spirit of the service.

While the ushers proceeded to order the crowd, three of the deacons
would place their chairs in front of the altar, for they were charged with
starting the service. As I watched the activity of the church, my eyes fell
on Mother Luella Byrd. Mother Byrd was not only head of the Mothers'
Board, but basically in charge of the church. There she sat, dressed in
white with her black cape draped over her shoulders, her arms folded
and her face set. Once Mother Byrd had taken her position, God could
begin to move. Ma Ponk reluctantly paid homage to Mother Byrd, but
under her breath she could be heard saying, "Byrd acts like she owns
Saint Mark's."

And it was true; Mother Byrd was without question the matriarch of
the church. Not only was she an influencing and stabilizing factor for
Saint Mark's, but her demand for perfection and self-respect and her
high hopes for the colored race will always be with me. She was slightly
overweight and walked with her left foot turned outward. When she
walked, her hands would be clasped behind her back, and whatever the
day, she was dressed as if she were in charge.

Mother Byrd was known for her Easter program which was a must
for all the children of the church. We were expected to know our parts
to perfection. Securing a commitment from the parents, she would give
us our speeches one month in advance and hold practices weekly. Our
limited resources never bothered her, only spurred her on to pull out
of us the best she knew to be there. For her, Saint Mark's Missionary
Baptist Church was Washington Cathedral and we, her pupils, were the
cream of the crop. With determination, she'd take our unorganized
minds, lack of ambition, and bad grammar and create a top-quality program. Mother Byrd had no formal education herself, but she encouraged us to work hard and get an education. She was a proponent of
black pride long before it became fashionable as she tuned out our
excuses and channeled our efforts.

Every Sunday morning, Mother Byrd was seated front and center at
Saint Mark's by the time the singing began. As the song "I'll Fly Away"
rang throughout the building, she rocked back and forth while the congregation rocked from side to side. While they sang, Elder Thomas

began to preach. The singing and the preaching would blend and build together to a fever pitch. Elder Thomas, like an athlete at peak performance, paced the front of the church and preached until he was covered with sweat and the entire congregation was caught up in the spiritual fervor. . . .

Quartet singers represented more than colored harmonizing; they were examples of the good life. If those singers happened to have come from Memphis, our excitement could not be contained. You see, we knew that all the really good singers lived in Memphis. If the singers were coming from Memphis, Saint Mark's wasn't good enough for them. They would sing at Mount Zion Baptist Church. . . .

I remember the Sunday after church at Saint Mark's when Ma Ponk and her friend Miss Doll decided we'd go to the big quartet singing at Mount Zion. Every colored person in Glen Allan wanted to be part of the Mount Zion singing. Ma Ponk didn't wear white because tonight she would not be on the mothers' bench. Tonight, she dressed in her best, a multi-colored jersey dress, and wore her black straw hat. I wore my one good outfit, my brown gabardines and a plaid shirt.

The Memphis singers, usually all men, were role models of sorts for the young colored males and objects of fantasy for the women. These singers were dressed in the latest northern fashions, and their hair was ironed to their heads. Their shiny straightened hair would glisten under the exposed sixty-watt bulbs. The women idolized them, and the young black males would come out in droves.

According to Ma Ponk, you couldn't get these people out for real church, but at a singing they'd take up good seats and the Christians would have to stand. There they'd be, the young male field hands dressed in gabardines and nylon puckered shirts. The more fortunate ones wore suits and pointed-toe shoes. For the women, this singing brought out more fishnet and taffeta material than any other event. Their hair would be tightly curled and pressed to their heads, held in place by rhinestone combs. . . .

And the singers would sing until their clothes were dripping with perspiration and their guitar strings were begging for mercy. Once the singing got going good, they'd rip off their ties and coats and throw them to the crowd. We were all enthralled by the Memphis sound. Even Ma Ponk, not known for unnecessary emotion, would rock back and forth while making sure her hands remained tightly folded. Mount Zion hosted all the Memphis singing stars of those years, even the late great Sam Cooke. . . .

F R O M

Drums of the Toli

R O B E R T   L .   H A R D E E

Top athletes at the Neshoba County Fair, held in Philadelphia, Missis-
sippi, are the Choctaw Indians with their annual stickball games. The
bloodiest football games pale in comparison to these dead-earnest contests,
where one can lose not only his dignity and pride but a beaver pond—or
even a wife. The Mississippi Choctaws were not legally recognized by the
federal government as a tribe until 1918. According to Hardee, the sto-
ries in his book describing these Choctaw games "range in locale all the
way from Bogue Homa reservation, three miles east of Sandersville,
Miss., north to the big Choctaw Central School in Neshoba county—and
even beyond to the historic Nanih Waiyah mound in central Mississippi.
They extend in time from the war-torn Forties to the similarly turbulent
years of the late Sixties" (from the section "Rough and Rugged").

W H A T   I S   T H E roughest game played in America?

The query takes in a lot of territory and the burden of proof would seem incalculable—but Choctaw Indians living in a cluster of central Mississippi counties (Neshoba, Newton, Winston and Leake) think they've got the answer.

Their entry for top rating among wild and frenzied athletic contests would be stickball. The one historic rule is that the stick-carried ball must not be touched or moved with the hands. The chief of the ball game (mingo toli) has authority to warn against "unnecessary rough-ness"—but a runner may be blocked, tackled, tripped, thrown or ridden to the dust with seldom a peep from the big boss of the tilt.

Also, an opposing player can dislodge the ball from the grip of the carrier with a hefty swing of his two sticks. In short, if anybody is looking for a limb-battering sport scarcely hampered by restraints, this is it.

The square sticks, 30 inches long, are carved from select hickory, thinned to a quarter-inch thickness at the ends, turned back into an oval contour and bound and laced with buckskin or goat hide. The ball, somewhat larger than one used for golf, is shaped tightly with cord or strips of cloth strengthened with an interlacing of deerskin. It fits hand-ily into the cup-shaped ends of the sticks.

The playing field is 100 yards long. Anchored firmly at each end is a two-inch-thick pine or hardwood goalpost eight inches wide and twelve feet high.

Signal for the game to begin is a sort of "grand march" of the two teams (15 players on each) onto the field, each led by a colorfully-garbed drummer beating a brisk rhythm. The teams are identified by their suits of royal blue, crimson or orange. The full-cut home-sewn suits, similar to baseball togs but of lighter-weight cloth, are embellished by broad stripes down the sides of the sleeves and pants.

With guards stationed downfield and at each goal, the remaining players form a circle at the 50-yard line. Here the referee (chief of the ball game) tosses up the sphere. The combatants pounce upon the ball with their sticks. The clash of hickory against hickory assails the stands. Soon somebody darts out of the milling huddle and heads for his goal—but how he maneuvers the ball into his sticks as they are banged and battered from all sides is one of the puzzles of the game.

The sphere can be advanced by running or passing. The ball is so difficult to catch with a pair of sticks that if a receiver snags one in 50 passes, he is doing well.

The player scores (one point) by tapping his sticks (with the ball enclosed) against the goal. He has to bull his way through a swarm of guards to get there. Or, with luck that almost never happens, he can fling the ball and hit the post for a tally.

Advancing to scoring position is scarcely less difficult. The ball may be lost to charging adversaries and retrieved a half dozen times before a marker can be made.

Fleet runners who would make a football scout's blood pressure rise can fade away from a pack of pursuers in their dash for the tall plank. But, most often, speed comes to an abrupt halt when agile goalpost guards throttle the thrust.

Stickball is a low-scoring affair. A big game at the Choctaw Indian Fair in Neshoba County wound up with a combined Standing Pine-Red Water team on top with a 5-3 win over Bogue Chitto.

In all the moves and counter moves, the referee is scarcely heard from except when he calls a "dead ball" landing among spectators or too far afield. He also steps in when a fight is brewing, asking the would-be assailant: "What do you want to do—get out or keep playing?" Usually, the irate player's temper cools and he stays in.

Actually, a player seldom leaves the game for any reason at all. If he's in the lineup to begin with, he stays in. Playing barefoot, unpadded and without helmet, he would seem to have as promising a chance to come out unscathed as if he had been caught in a stampeding herd of buffaloes. Yet the perplexing thing is that, despite vicious body-bruising contacts and precipitous bone-risking falls, an injury rarely sends a player to the sidelines and almost never to a hospital.

Other than being fortunate for the participant, one happy result is that the spectator can watch the tilt with virtually no frustrating time-outs to stop the action. The game proceeds apace, interrupted only by brief pauses between quarters.

The quarters are usually 15 minutes long. Acutely aware of the discomfort of heat, the Indians shorten the periods if the temperature soars above 90. No time is given to a half-time show of any sort.

To be sure, the Indians of today take their sports without getting worked up like white fans. But a player suddenly upended always draws a chorus of laughs from the stands.

Indeed, nobody up there hollers himself hoarse to urge good old Bogue Chitto to travel northward to the glory goal. There are no mini-skirted cheerleaders to kindle the fighting spirit of the young braves. Instead, there are two drummers, Bob Henry and Carson Jackson, beating a never-changing rhythm (like the Morse code of two dots and a dash) during the length of the game.

Also, Baxter York sits at a microphone high in a booth and gives the play-by-play in flawless English with an occasional switch to the Choctaw tongue to assure his tribesmen he hasn't defected. Without benefit of spotters, York identifies the players. For example, seeing a runner streaking down the field, he comments: "That boy can run! He's a Mingo." Or: "John Levi Bell took a shot (made a pass at the goal) and missed."

Nobody can pinpoint the time that stickball began. In a book printed in 1775, Bernard Romans speaks of "broken limbs and dislocated joints" suffered by players of this game. Deaths sometimes resulted.

Nevertheless, violence apparently was forgiven. In fact, this seemed to be the only occasion when the Choctaw tradition of "a life for a life" was ignored. Jugs of liquor, calculated to soothe ruffled feelings, were passed around at the end of the game.

But this spirit of forgiveness and camaraderie appeared to have been lost in later years. The games seemed to afford good chances to renew old feuds and start new ones.

Sometimes the early games amounted to more than sportive combat. Such a game between the Choctaws and Creeks was reported in a manuscript by Henry S. Halbert as taking place circa 1790. The tilt was supposed to settle ownership of a beaver pond on Noxubee River. A battle followed anyway, so apparently the melee on the field proved no substitute for weapons of war to resolve disputes.

Later games were less significant but more festive. An all-night dance would precede a tilt played between villages.

Spirited betting would take place before the game got under way the next day. Among items the braves wagered were skins, furs, trinkets, knives, dresses, blankets, pots, kettles, guns, dogs, horses—even their wives and themselves, for a time.

Though stimulating, the betting was no cure for tired limbs. Yet by mid-morning, still weary from the night's reveling, the teams—40 men on each—would line up on a dusty prairie. Since the winner had to score 16 points, reaching that mark could require an all-day battle.

In one era, the women themselves took up the game. They figured if they were sinewy enough to cultivate the corn while the men hunted and fished, stickball would offer no physical hurdle for them.

They left no heritage of feuds—but the men continued to anger one another and trade punches on the field. In the late 19th Century, not convinced that her man could always land a solid blow, the Choctaw woman would run up and down the sidelines carrying sticks she could hand to him—just in case. But today,—beaded, beribboned and full-skirted—she has withdrawn to the stands in full, festive dress.

Unlike the resplendent attire of the current stickball warrior, the early combatant wore a breechcloth around his waist with a simulated tail of white horsehair attached. A similar "mane" also hung from a band around his neck. These symbols of speed gave way later to coon and squirrel tails sewed to the seat of the player's pants.

What about the future of this ancient game? Some observers thought it would be on its way out in the present decade when the veterans in their 40s and 50s became too winded and worn to play.

But, with very few exceptions, the old guard has been replaced by teen-agers, as fleet as the wind. What's more, little boys' stickball has been inaugurated and given a place on the fair program.

So it looks as if the venerable sport, far from hobbling around on crutches, has received a new infusion of vigor.

A Creature in the Bay of St. Louis

BARRY HANNAH

Born in Meridian, Mississippi, in 1942, Barry Hannah grew up in the country near Forest, then in Pascagoula and Clinton. Hannah received a B. A. degree from Mississippi College and an M. F. A. from the University of Arkansas. He has been writer-in-residence at many colleges, including Clemson University, Middlebury College, and the University of Iowa; he currently teaches at the University of Mississippi. He is the award-winning author of such novels as Geronimo Rex, The Tennis Handsome, Airships, *and* Bats Out of Hell. *Here, in a personal reminiscence about the town of Bay St. Louis, which first appeared in* Sports Afield *(September 1994), he celebrates the great southern sport of fishing.*

W E W E R E O U T early in the brown water, the light still gray and wet. My cousin Woody and I were out wading on an oyster shell reef in the Bay. We had cheap baitcasting rods and reels with black cotton line, at the end of which were a small bell weight and croaker hook. We used peeled shrimp for bait. Sometimes you might get a speckled trout or flounder, but more likely you would catch the croaker. A large one weighed half a pound. When caught and pulled in, the fish made a metallic croaking sound. It is one of the rare fish who talk to you about their plight when they are landed. My aunt fried them crispy, covered in cornmeal, and they were delicious, especially with lemon juice and ketchup.

A good place to fish was near the pilings of the St. Stanislaus school pier. The pier gate was locked, but you could wade to the pilings and the oyster shell reef. Up the bluff above us on the town road was a fish market and the Star Theater, where we saw movies.

Many cats, soft and friendly and plump, would gather around the edges of the fish market, and when you went to the movies, you would walk past three or four of them who would ease against your leg as if asking to go to the movie with you. The cats were very social. In their prosperity they seemed to have organized into a watching society of leisure and culture. Nobody yelled at them because this was a small coastal town where everybody knew each other. Italians, Slavs, French, Methodists, Baptists and Catholics. You did not want to insult the cat's owner by being rude. Some of the cats would tire of the market offerings and come down the bluff to watch you fish, patiently waiting for their share of your take or hunting the edges of the weak surf for dead crabs and fish. You would be pulling in your fish, and when you looked ashore, the cats were suddenly alert. They were wise. It took a hard case not to leave them one good fish for supper.

That night, as you went into an Abbott and Costello movie, which cost a dime, that same cat you had fed might rub against your leg, and you felt sorry it couldn't go into the movie house with you. You might be feeling comical when you come out and see the same cat waiting with conviction as if there were something in there it wanted very much, and you threw a jujube down to it on the sidewalk. Jujubes were pellets of chewing candy the quality of vulcanized rubber. You chewed several during the movie, and you had a wonderful syrup of licorice, strawberry and lime in your mouth. But the cat would look down at the jujube, then up at you as if you were insane, and you felt bad for betraying this serious creature and hated that you were mean and thoughtless. That is the kind of conscience you had in Bay St. Louis, Mississippi.

This morning we had already had a good trip as the sun began coming out. The croakers swam in a burlap sack tied to a piling and under water. The sacks were free at the grocery, and people called them croaker sacks. When you lifted the sack to put another croaker in, you heard that froggy metal noise in a chorus, quite loud, and you saw the cats on shore hearken to it, too. We would have them with french fries, fat tomato slices from my uncle's garden and a large piece of sweet watermelon for supper.

It made a young boy feel good having the weight of all these fish in the dripping sack when you lifted it, knowing you had provided for a large family and maybe even neighbors at supper. You felt to be a small hero of some distinction, and ahead of you was that mile walk through the neighborhood lanes where adults would pay attention to your catch and salute you. The fishing rod on your shoulder, you had done some solid bartering with the sea; you were not to be trifled with.

The only dangerous thing in the Bay was a stingaree, with its poisonous barbed hook of a tail. This ray would lie flat, covered over by sand like a flounder. We waded barefoot in swimming trunks, and almost always in a morning's fishing you stepped on something that moved under your foot and you felt the squirm in every inch of your body before it got off you. These could be stingarees. There were terrible legends about them, always a story from summers ago when a stingaree had whipped its tail into the calf of some unfortunate girl or boy and buried the vile hook deep in the flesh. The child came dragging out of the water with this 20-pound brownish black monster the size of a garbage can lid attached to his leg, thrashing and sucking with its awful mouth. Then the child's leg grew black and swelled horribly, and they had to amputate his leg, and that child was in the attic of some dark house on the edge of town, never the same again and pale like a thing that never saw light; then eventually the child became half-stingaree and they took it away to an institution for special cases. So you believed all this most positively, and when a being squirmed under your foot, you were likely to walk on water out of there. We should never forget that when frightened, a child can fly short distances, too.

The high tide was receding with the sun clear up and smoking in the east over Biloxi, the sky reddening, and the croakers were not biting so well anymore. But each new fish would give more pride to the sack, and I was greedy for a few more since I didn't get to fish in the salt water much. I lived four hours north in a big house with a clean lawn, a maid and yard men, but it was landlocked and grim when you compared it to this place of my cousins's. Much later I learned his family was nearly poor, but this was laughable even when I heard it, because it was heaven: the movie house right where you fished and the society of cats, and my uncle's house with the huge watermelons lying on the linoleum under the television with startling shows like *Lights Out!* from the New Orleans station. We didn't even have a television station yet where I lived.

I kept casting and wading out deeper, toward an old creosoted pole in the water, where I thought a much bigger croaker or flounder might be waiting. My cousin was tired and red-burnt from the day before in the sun, so he went to swim under the diving board of the Catholic high school 100 yards away. They had dredged a pool. Otherwise the sea was very shallow a long ways out. But now I was almost up to my chest, near the barnacled pole where a big boat could tie up. I kept casting, almost praying toward the deep water around the pole. The lead and shrimp would plunk and tumble into a dark hole, I thought, where a special giant fish was lurking, something too big for the croaker shallows.

My grandmother had caught a seven-pound flounder from the sea wall years before and she was still honored for it, my uncle retelling the tale of her whooping out, afraid but happy, the pole bent double. I wanted to have a story like that about myself. The fish made Mama

Hannah so happy, my older cousin said, that he saw her dancing to a band on television by herself when everybody else was asleep. Soon—I couldn't bear to think about it—in a couple of days they would drive me over to Gulfport and put me on a bus for home, and in my sorrow there waited a dry red brick school within bitter tasting distance. But even that would be sweetened by a great fish and its story.

It took place in no more than half a minute, I'd guess, but it had the lengthy rapture and terror of a whole tale. Something bit and then was jerking, small but solid, then it was too big, and I began moving in the water and grabbing the butt of the rod again because what was on had taken it out of my hands. When I caught the rod up, I was moving toward the barnacled pole with the tide slopping on it, and that was the only noise around. I went in to my neck in a muddier scoop in the bottom, and then under my feet something moved. I instantly knew it was a giant stingaree. Hard skin on a squirming plate of flesh. I was sorely terrified but was pulled past even this and could do nothing, now up to my chin and the stiff little pole bent violently double. I was dragged through the mud, and I knew that the being when it surfaced would be bigger than I was.

Then, like something underwater since Europe, seven or eight porpoises surfaced, blowing water in a loud group explosion out of their enormous heads, and I was just shot all over with light and nerves because they were only 20 feet from me and I connected them, the ray and what was on my hook into a horrible combination beast that would drag out children who waded too far, then crush and drown them.

The thing pulled with heavier tugs, like a truck going up its gears. The water suddenly rushed into my face and nose. I could see only brown, with the bottom of the sun shining through it.

I was gone, gone, and I thought of the cats watching on a shore and said good-bye, cat friends, good-bye, cousin Woody, good-bye, young life. I am only a little boy and I'm not letting go of this pole—it is not even mine; it's my uncle's. Good-bye, school, good-bye, Mother and Daddy. Don't weep for me; it is a thing in the water cave of my destiny. Yes, I thought all these things in detail while drowning and being pulled rushing through the water, but the sand came up under my feet and the line went slack; the end of the rod was broken off and hanging on the line. When I cranked in the line, I saw that the hook, a thick silver one, was straightened. The vacancy in the air where there was no fish was an awful thing, like surgery in the pit of my stomach. I convinced myself I had almost had him.

When I stood in the water on solid sand, I began crying. I tried to stop, but when I got close to Woody, I burst out again. He wanted to know what had happened, but I did not tell him the truth. Instead I told him I had stepped on an enormous ray and its hook had sliced me.

When we checked my legs, there was a slice from an oyster shell, a fairly deep one I'd gotten while being pulled by the creature. I refused treatment and was respected for my close call the rest of the day. I even worked in the lie more and said furthermore that it didn't matter much to me if I was taken off to the asylum for stingaree children; those were just the breaks.

It wasn't until I was back in the dreaded schoolroom that I could even talk about the fish. My teacher doubted it, and she in goodwill told my father, congratulating me on my imagination. My father thought that was rich, but then I told him the same story, the creature as heavy as a truck, the school of porpoises, and he said that's enough. You didn't mention this when you came back.

No, and neither did I mention the two cats when I walked back to shore with Woody and the broken rod. They had watched all the time, and I knew it, because both of them stared at me with big, solemn eyes, a lot of light in them, and it was with the beings of fur that I entrusted my confidences then, and they knew I would be back to catch the big one, the singular monster, on that line going tight into the cave in water, something thrashing on the end, celebrated above by porpoises.

I never knew what kind of fish it was, but I would return and return to it the rest of my life, and the cats would be waiting to witness me and share my honor.

Families

WYATT COOPER

Born in 1927, Wyatt Cooper grew up in a large family on a farm in Pleasant Grove, Mississippi, near Quitman. There he experienced the joys, sorrows, trials and successes of a large rural family. This book is a legacy to his two sons and to his readers, an effort to preserve the sense of an extended family. Cooper juxtaposes descriptions of his early life in Mississippi with vignettes of his later time in New York, where, living with his wife, Gloria Vanderbilt, he worked as an actor, editor, and writer. He tells of his son Anderson, for instance, showing off his new pet snake to bellmen and of both boys giving a downhome greeting to visitors Alfred Lunt and Lynn Fontaine. This excerpt, from the chapter entitled "Mostly a Matter of Roots," recounts a custom familiar to all Mississippians—a trip to the family graveyard.

FARTHER INTO THE forest, beyond the ruins of the grist mill, and reached only by tracing the almost obliterated evidence of an old wagon road, was the family graveyard, already at that time unused for at least a generation.

I went there once, in a large group called together by a relative named Kanzadie Walker (she had been a Wyatt) for the purpose of erecting a tombstone on somebody's grave. I believe you could then write away somewhere and get a free tombstone for veterans of the Civil War and Kanzadie had done that for long-dead Uncle Rob Somebody— whether Cooper, Wyatt, Flowers, Bull, or Boykin, I do not remember. We made the journey to Grandpa's in Lee Dearman's school bus, a festive load of us, and at Grandpa's we had to leave the bus and continue the remaining couple of miles on foot with several brawny youths taking turns at stumbling along bearing the marble tombstone horizontally between them, while I, with Dwayne, Namon, Naomi, and others of my age, ran, in our excitement, ahead of the party and then back again, making elongated circles like impatient puppies. ("Don't get close to that Dwayne, Namon, and Naomi," my mother had admonished me that morning. "Half that family's had TB and it's catching.")

Chattering and laughing, our group invaded the deep integrity of the woods like an intruding army of alien creatures, the noise of our approach preceding us in sharp, crackling waves, unsettling the summer calm, setting off a squawking of blue jays, a cawing of crows, a disturbance of decades of peace. Kanzadie, she of the monumental and complacent bulk, maintained the lead; she was the general, the mover, the one who had caused the event to take place, and, along the way, she exercised her familiarity with the dead. "Aunt Maggie went in the 'flu epidemic of '97,' and it was consumption that took Aunt Jessie," and "Grandpa Bull was away back in them swamps ahunting—you know how he loved to hunt—when he fell dead and it took them four days to find him."

We came upon the cemetery unexpectedly and without warning. Suddenly, in the deep shadows of the tall trees and from the dense growth of bushes, there emerged directly in our path a white marble angel with wings outspread almost as if in protest. The spaces of its eyes were dark growths of fungus; on its shoulders and along the backs of its wings was an accumulation of years of fallen pine straw, and dead and rotting leaves. Spiders nested in the open mouth, and from its streaked and time-stained whiteness, it seemed to utter a soundless cry of outrage. Unseen and unsung, for seasons without number, it had stood its silent sentinel, through heat and cold, disdaining rain and lightning and thunder, and, after all this time, it seemed no more native to the place—it bore no more relation to the spirits of those people of a raw and unschooled race whose graves it guarded—than it did all those years ago when some ancestor—even Kanzadie did not know who—had had it hauled here, like the piano, from some city where ships came and went. One wondered how it had come about; one wondered by what impulse toward grandiosity, by what expression of hopeful prosperity, by what sense of dynastic necessity, by what sudden surge of religious feeling, or by what unlikely gesture toward beauty, our unknown progenitor had been propelled into the transaction of purchase by which this exotic product of a distant land, carved into being by foreign hands, came to be transported here to last out its eternity in endless exile.

Behind and around it the wilderness had taken over; tangles of briars, huckleberry, ferns, and masses of undergrowth completely hid the rusty iron fence that had once enclosed the lot, the fence that still stood but only to crumble at the touch.

Kanzadie took charge and issued orders. We had come armed with hoes, rakes, axes, and other implements for clearing land, and, while the privileged young among us climbed and played about, the men set to work. There was disagreement about where some graves were, but any question was settled by Kanzadie, and it was right that it should be so for she was an authority on burials.

"Here's Great-Grandma Boykin," she would say of a gray moss-covered stone, the carving on which was no longer decipherable, and "I remember Aunt Bett was put next to her and Cousin Willis was put right next to Aunt Bett," and "No, Emmett, you're wrong. That couldn't be where Uncle Rob is, because that's where they buried that little chap of Caroline's. I remember it was right down from Grandpa's feet. Used to be a wooden cross over it that Granddaddy Flowers made," and "Just over there, where that big oak is now, that's where they buried that little nigra of Uncle Press's that drowned at the grist mill."

My father showed me where his Great-Grandfather Beryl Boykin was buried. I asked to see his grave, because that grandfather had been murdered, knocked in the head with a singletree by a rebellious slave, who was then tied to a tree and burned, allegedly by the other slaves.

Papa, less impressed by Kanzadie's encyclopedic recall than I was, was certain that we'd placed the new Confederate tombstone over quite the wrong person (over Caroline's baby, actually), but he didn't think it was worth quarreling over. "Never mind," he said to me, when I worried about it, "it made Kanzadie happy, and it don't make a damned bit of difference to Uncle Rob."

Interview with Mrs. Arwin Deweese Turner

C H A R L O T T E   C A P E R S

While serving as director for the Mississippi Department of Archives and History from 1955 to 1969, Charlotte Capers conducted a series of interviews with people attending the Neshoba County Fair. She was a gifted interviewer, able to draw colorful details and facts from those with whom she talked. About Capers, Eudora Welty has said: "She favors the spontaneous, she enjoys the immediate response, the give-and-take of conversation, in which she is a virtuoso." The following conversation with a longtime Neshoba County Fair-goer on July 28, 1971, gives the flavor of this traditional event, often called "Mississippi's giant houseparty." Held in Philadelphia, the fair attracts over seventy thousand people annually; they come to hear state and local politicians wrangle, watch horse racing, and participate in nightlong songfests. Those lucky enough to own cottages spend the week.

Capers: This is Arwin Deweese Turner at the Deweese cabin at the Neshoba County Fair. She's going to tell us what's cooking at the fair.

Turner: Well, I would say we have about nine dozen ears of fried corn and about two gallons of butter beans and a big pile of peas, twenty pounds of turkey breast and two large hams, ready sliced to go. Then we have other—we have eggplant casserole and another casserole, I can't even remember what. We have three large cakes, caramel is preferred by most people.

Capers: What are the others?

Turner: Caramel and plain and what was that? Heavenly hash cake, chocolate pound and two kinds of pies.

Capers: What kind of pies?

Turner: Runny chocolate and pecan pie.

Capers: How about that marvelous looking bread?

Turner: I'd say about fifty muffins, equivalent of fifty muffins of cornbread and some rolls, of course. And anything to drink that you might like. We hope we can please.

Capers: Well, I'm very easy to please in that area.

Turner: Well, it's wonderful for you to be here, and we hope we have the ingredients to feed the crowd. We also will have, of course, relishes, tomatoes, sliced cucumbers and little goodies like that. . . .

Capers: Well, do you enjoy, do you really look forward like they did in the old days to coming out here, or does it get to be a chore? It looks like a lot of hard work.

Turner: With everybody working—and we love to have company so much—we prepare for probably a hundred people a day, and, if they don't come, we're disappointed. After you've fixed all that food, it's a great disappointment if they don't come, so we love having people. And they're always welcome.

Capers: Well, it's just wonderful to be here. Now, this Deweese cabin, how long has it been here? It's one of the older cabins.

Turner: We've had one, this is probably the second or third, and it's been remodeled since—I'm not going to tell my age, but I'm sure we've had it around forty or fifty years, at least fifty years.

Capers: Well, have you always had overnight company out here?

Turner: Anybody. We have beds for about, I'd guess, fifteen to twenty. The children particularly love it at night. Then, of course, there's dancing and all the entertainment under the pavillion and the grandstand.

Capers: Do you have the all-night hymn sing they used to have?

Turner: They have old songs from about midnight till three. That's about the hour that takes place. So you have to stay up to get in on the real activities in the middle of the night. But it's no trouble out here, you can't sleep much anyway. We've had very cool weather this time, but awfully muddy. That's been bad. But the people have been wonderful.

Capers: Do you live in Philadelphia?

Turner: Yes, we all do.

Capers: Tell me about your father. Did he come to Philadelphia, or was he already here?

Turner: He was a lumberman from the beginning, you see, as a young man. Then he established the A. Deweese Lumber Company. In '66 we sold out to Weyerhaeuser. It's Deweese Operation, Weyerhaeuser-Deweese Operations. My father was, of course, a great lover of people, and I hope we've inherited it. We feel like we did.

Capers: I can insert this comment. You're the most warm and cordial and hospitable people I know.

Turner: Well, we appreciate that. We do hope that everybody will feel welcome to come. We don't particularly have to know the people, just so they come and enjoy the day. We love to feed them and refresh them and have them with us.

Capers: Just marvelous. Let me ask you one more thing, Arwin. Was your father a native of this part of the country?

Turner: Oh, yes.

Capers: He was born. . . .

Turner: In this county.

Capers: Do you know where his father came from? We're interested in tracing the migration of families.

Turner: I think North Carolina was originally his family [home]. In fact, there are a good number of Deweeses in Philadelphia, Pennsylvania. There are some real interesting facts—I never have studied it. There is a very prominent doctor whose portrait hangs in the museum in Philadelphia, Pennsylvania, a Doctor Deweese who was of the early lineage. I get all this mail, but I'm not very good about answering it. People are real interested, you know.

Capers: Let me ask you, you're a third generation Mississippian? You and Martha?

Turner: Yes.

Capers: Would you name the members of your family? Your mother and father, what were their names?

Turner: Ab Deweese and Mattie Deweese.

Capers: What was her maiden name?

Turner: She was Wyatt. We have lost three wonderful brothers, Dewitt, Edwin and Pete. Tom is the only boy left, but there are three girls. Martha Wilkinson of Jackson, Lib Neilson of New Orleans and I'm the third.

Capers: I'm sure you have thousands of grandchildren.

Turner: I have a great-grandchild, thank you. We have worlds of grand-children.

Capers: Well, thank you, Arwin, and I appreciate it.

Turner: Charlotte, the reason my grandmother lived to be ninety-one was that she fixed a little toddy early in the morning and sipped it all day. She drank whiskey, she dipped snuff and ate pork three times a day.

Capers: It cut her down.

Turner: It cut her down to ninety-one. I tell everybody that's the reason she died so young.

Capers: All those bad habits.

Turner: Everything. . . .

Fridays with Red: A Radio Friendship

B O B   E D W A R D S

Baseball sportscaster Walter Lanier "Red" Barber was born in 1908 in Columbus, Mississippi. When he was ten, his father, a railroad engineer, accepted a job with the Atlantic Coast Line and moved his family to Sanford, Florida. Barber began his career as sports announcer at the University of Florida in 1930 and became a feature on National Public Radio in 1979. This memoir was written by Morning Edition *host Bob Edwards, who worked with Barber for many years over the airwaves. As the following chapter, "Barberisms," illustrates, Barber, who was brought up reading Greek and Roman mythology, was capable of sophisticated literary allusions as well as the downhome folk expressions such as "sitting in the catbird seat" for which he became famous. When Jackie Robinson broke the color barrier in major league baseball, Barber's nonchalance positively affected others' attitudes towards blacks playing in professional games.*

A RED BARBER BROADCAST was a piece of Americana, and artists in other fields paid tribute. At various times, Red was the announcer on radio shows featuring the big bands of Sammy Kaye and Woody Herman. Woody's "herd" played a number called "Red Top" in honor of Red Barber.

For the higher of brow, there was a musical composition Red and I discussed on my thirty-ninth birthday, May 16, 1986:

> BOB: Forty-five years ago today, WOR in New York first played *A Symphony in D for the Dodgers* by Robert Russell Bennett. And you figure into this history a little later that summer. You narrated it at a performance at the Lewis-Ohn Stadium by the Philharmonic Symphony Orchestra, Wilhelm Steinberg conducting.
>
> RED: Well, for goodness sake, you sure dig up the most interesting data. And I remember that sitting on the very front row was Larry MacPhail, who was running the Dodgers, and I thought he would just break all the buttons on his vest.
>
> BOB: MacPhail figures in the third movement, the scherzo, in which MacPhail goes a-hunting for a star pitcher. He offers to trade Prospect Park

and the Brooklyn Bridge even for Bob Feller, but the Cleveland management says no in the form of a big E-flat minor chord.

RED: Well, this is very intriguing. Robert Russell Bennett was not only a composer—he was conducting his own orchestra at that time on WOR and on
the Mutual network—but also he was a marvelous orchestrator. To identify
him better, he orchestrated *South Pacific*. And he was a baseball fan. He
used to like to bring his grandson to Ebbets Field, and I would leave seats
for them. And in narrating it, I was the voice in the fourth movement.
And Robert Russell said over the air, he said, "Now, of course, Beethoven
used a whole . . . chorus in his . . . symphony. But we're going to have to
settle for Red Barber."

We finally located a recording of Bennett's symphony and played a
bit of the fourth movement on the air. Accompanying Bennett's music
is Red's description of a Dolph Camilli home run over Mel Ott's head.
Brooklyn won the "game," 2–1, and I observed that this was odd since
Bennett was a Giants fan. But Red pointed out that he, the Dodger
announcer, had something to do with writing that script.

Red appreciated good music and good literature. John Bunzel of the
Hoover Institution saw Red reading Arnold Toynbee on the beach at
Chappaquiddick in 1960. Toynbee as a beach book? Bunzel also in-
formed me of a couple of literary references in Red's play-by play:

One afternoon he described a game in which the shortstop kicked away two
ground balls before making a good play on a third—at which Red declared,
"Like the Ancient Mariner, he stoppeth one of three!" (Here is the beginning of Coleridge's poem: "It is an ancient mariner/And he stoppeth one
of three./ By the long gray beard and glittering eye,/ Now wherefore stop-
p'st thou me?" The Mariner has stopped one of three men going to a wedding.)

On another occasion, a Dodger leadoff man hit a double and then remained rooted there while the next three batters grounded out, unable even
to advance him to third. At which Red intoned, "They left him languishing
there like the Prisoner of Chillon!" Now there was a more arcane reference,
though Byron's "Sonnet on Chillon" and "Prisoner of Chillon" were also
read in high schools.

Red Barber made genuine contributions to the language. Etymolo-
gists loved him, and some dictionaries still cite him as a reference
source. A distant relative of the poet Sidney Lanier, Red loved the
printed and spoken word. He expanded and celebrated the language,
and left it enriched as a result.

"Rhubarb," for example, was Red's word for an argument. He called
Ebbets Field "the rhubarb patch" because there were so many argu-

ments there. If two great rivals were about to meet, he would predict, "There'll be blood on the moon." If a team was getting a bunch of hits, he would say they were "tearin' up the pea patch." Other announcers might say a lopsided game was "in the bag." Red was more specific: he would have it "tied up in a croker sack." On the other hand, a close game might be "tighter than a new pair of shoes on a rainy day." A graceful infielder could be "movin' easy as a bank of fog," but watch out for that pitcher "wild as a hungry chicken hawk on a frosty morning." Pitchers might not be good hitters, but Freddie Fitzsimmons was "no slouch with the willow." A ball hit back to the pitcher would get a "come back little Sheba." If there was trouble fielding the ball, it might be because the ball was "slicker than oiled okra." Billy Cox had an arm so strong "he could toss a lamb chop past a hungry wolf." A runner employing a strategic slide "swung the gate" on the fielder trying to make the tag. "That was a wild game with the Cardinals last week—ooh, that one was full of fleas." After a home run, Tommy Henrich had a grin "big as a slice of watermelon." And look at Big Johnny Mize, who "swings that big bat as if it weighed no more than a dried turkey feather." When Jackie Robinson shook hands with Joe Louis, "photographers sprang up around them like rain lilies after a cloudburst."

Kenneth Kattzner, a *Morning Edition* listener in Washington, D.C., sent me some more. A high-scoring game had "developed into a ringtailed, double-jointed doozy." "There's no action in the Dodger bullpen yet, but they're beginning to wiggle their toes a little." "This situation is as ticklish as the moment just before you are about to sneeze."

In April of 1982, listener Ken Pearson wrote from Brockton, Massachusetts, asking that Red explain something he said after the fourth game of the 1947 World Series. This was the game in which Yankee pitcher Bill Bevens took a no-hitter into the ninth inning, only to lose the game by giving up a double to Dodger pinch hitter Cookie Lavagetto.

RED: . . . I just sort of caught my breath and without thinking about it, Bob, I said, "Well, I'll be a suck-egg mule." Ed Murrow was then in charge of news and special events for CBS, and he was my superior there. He had hired me to be director of sports following Ted Husing. And he said to me later . . . , "You know, I think that is the perfect way to use rhetorical emphasis." And he had me come on his news program that night and explain it. And, Bob, I don't know how to explain it except that when you are doing something such as you and I are doing, live radio without any preparation, no script, you are just concentrating on the event, concentrating on your work, and something just comes out. In fact, later in that series, when DiMaggio hit what looked like a home run and Gionfriddo caught it against the left-center-field bullpen gate, I said, "Oh, doctor." And people have remembered that. And I hadn't planned it. It just came out.

That's what you do in ad-lib broadcasting. When you realize that, things just suddenly come out of your subconscious. . . . When you're talking in front of an open microphone, it sometimes frightens you. I know that that's one of the reasons many, many years ago, when I started broadcasting, I made a resolution that I would never say a word in private, a profane word or a foul word, that I could never say on a microphone, because I didn't want any speech habits to get to where maybe sometime, in an unguarded moment, I might say something.

Some of Red's expressions have become clichés now—"high on the hog," "walkin' in tall cotton," "liftin' the ox-cart out of the ditch," "scraping around the bottom of the pickle barrel," "hollerin' down the rain barrel." Sammy Kaye would grouse during rehearsal "as cross as a bear with a boil in his nose." When the sponsor's executives visited the show, the ad agency men "would swarm around them like bees on a busted sugar barrel." Red seemed to have an endless supply, and he came by them honestly. His father was a storyteller with a great sense of humor. His mother was an English teacher who wouldn't let her children use bad grammar. They were the perfect parents to produce a well-read man who could tell funny stories with perfect grammar. Red felt his principal job was to report the truth, but he also knew he should be entertaining. The man who nearly joined a minstrel show had a flair for show biz.

And Red himself became part of English literature when he was featured in a James Thurber short story published in *The New Yorker*. The title of the story, "The Catbird Seat," was Red's most famous phrase, an expression he often used on the air. Red first heard the term at a penny-ante poker game in Cincinnati during the Depression. Red kept raising the bet, not knowing that another player, Frank Koch, was holding a pair of aces. Raking in the pot, Koch announced he had been "in the catbird seat all the while," and he thanked Red for making all those raises. Red said he was entitled to use the expression because he had paid for it. So when a baseball team had a comfortable lead, Red would say the team was "sittin' in the catbird seat."

In the Thurber story, a character uses many of Red's expressions, and Thurber wrote that the character picked them up by listening to Red Barber on the radio. Through this character, one master storyteller paid tribute to another. But the story of the story doesn't end there. Here's how Red told the tale during an NPR talk show on April 4, 1990:

RED: . . . when I came to New York and started using those expressions over the radio, James Thurber would listen. And then he got the idea of doing "The Catbird Seat" for *The New Yorker* magazine. I had never met Mr. Thurber, and he never called and asked permission or anything else. And then a couple of years after that, I wanted to write a column for the *New York Journal American* . . . and I found out that I couldn't use the title "The Catbird Seat." And also I saw in *Variety* that they were going to make a motion picture out of "The Catbird Seat," and I sent word to Mr. Thurber that that was gettin' the goose a little far from the gander. I understand that he got furious, and he had said he wanted to meet me sometime. And after I had remonstrated about his use of my language, he got mad. My daughter teaches English at LaGuardia Community College in New York. From time to time that story has come up and she's had certain students say to her, "Miss Barber, shouldn't your father be ashamed to steal that material from Thurber?" . . . When H. Allen Smith decided to write a book about a cat that owned a ball club and was going to name that cat Rhubarb, at least H. Allen called and asked, "Do you mind if I use that word 'rhubarb'?" I said, "Of course not, I'd be very pleased." But I never heard from Thurber.

It's a wonder that Thurber never wrote "The Saga of the Suck-Egg Mule."

America's Dizzy Dean

CURT SMITH

*Born in Lucas, Arkansas, in 1931, Jay Hanna (Dizzy) Dean grew up
to become one of the greatest pitchers in baseball. He pitched for the St.
Louis Cardinals and the Chicago Cubs from 1932 to 1941. He and his
brother Paul (Daffy) pitched two victories each for St. Louis in the World
Series against the Detroit Tigers in 1934. In 1941, after an arm injury
failed to heal, Dean turned to sports announcing and became famous for
his colloquialisms, such as "the runner slud into third." He was elected
to the National Baseball Hall of Fame in 1953. Curt Smith, prize-winning author and former reporter for the Rochester (New York)* Democrat & Chronicle, *describes in the epilogue to his biography Dean's
funeral in Wiggins, Mississippi, in 1974.*

HATTIESBURG FADED and the Gulf Coast neared. Biloxi lay
thirty miles to the south and east, New Orleans ninety miles to the west.
Route 49 yielded and a side road appeared. Past fields and lumber the
highway weaved, past the timber and beef which lent the region growth,
the garages marked by mud, past the pine cones and mangled sheds,
the flowers splashed by hues of purple and blue. This was home country, Mississippi, sweltering yet reposed. The furies had raged a decade
earlier, intolerance luring counter bigotry, violence the nation's wrath.
The years since then had wrought a groping, tentative calm; unrest and
quiet still grappled, each bidding for the other's soul.

Remnants, marred and aging, flanked the winding road. Perched
above adjacent structures was a water tower; houses bathed beneath the
sun beyond. A freight yard towered as the village drew close; near its
center a box car was marooned. "Illinois Central," the deserted vessel
read, "Main Line of Middle America." A feed plant and ice cream shop
lined the road's leftmost curb; the Fowler Hotel, almost abandoned,
adorned its right. Magnolia Drive remained the major street. The railroad terminal still stood. Train tracks split the hamlet's heart. Wiggins
had changed little since Ol' Diz took leave.

Now, as twenty, fifty, a hundred years before, the South took refuge
in its separate culture, the folkways had borne incessant turmoil—in
literature and mores, in idiom and commerce, in the pride and poignancy its embattled station caused. Diz had clasped this culture, and

downhome cronies, and Wiggins guideposts as well—the post office where daily he received his mail; the furniture store where he autographed baseballs for Jimmy Davis, owner and long-time friend; the bank which he frequented with maddening occurrence. "Man, that Wiggins," Diz often said, "they got lots of good ol' boys down there." Most of Dean's old guard had since departed—Ed Taylor, financier, to Texas, Boyce Holleman, lawyer, to Gulfport, Miss., Jack McHenry, local entrepreneur, to illness which warped his strength. Few of Dean's friends lingered, left to sample the timeless ambience Wiggins continued to uphold.

Wiggins was a decent locale, its people agreed. "A God-fearing, church-going Baptist town," Jimmy Davis exclaimed. Wiggins was sober and restrained; seat of Stone County, Mississippi's smallest, it barred even the private exchange of whiskey and beer. Wiggins was also patriotic; war had deeply scarred the town. Service was respected, the flag held high, protest dismissed as obstinate and wrong. And, more than one newcomer added, Wiggins was wary, too, cautious of progress, of the slow sweep of change. "I know all small towns have faults, and Wiggins is no different," a recent transplant said. "It's closer than close-knit. But towns like this also have virtues—that's why some people stay here five, maybe six decades." Wiggins loved the native South, and America, and values, sainted landmarks, besieged but holy.

Wiggins loved Ol' Diz, too, said most, even those who questioned its complacent curb. "He'd come into town ever' morning," a resident of Pine Avenue, the business street, said. "Always had on a brilliant Hawaiian shirt, like it was flowed from the islands that day. He'd go to the post office, the bank, poke his head into stores, say hello to everybody, help 'em when he could." Death glorifies one's past; that must surely be true of Diz. Townfolk remembered his gruff, unflagging presence ("loud, not offensive"), his empathy for the common soul ("he'd be talking to a banker. Even before he was done, he'd come over and talk to me"), his penchant for charity—different from what Bud Blattner had ascribed. Mentioned were Dizzy's ventures, solely pioneered and publicly unknown—endeavors with impoverished youth, paying for vacations in New York, financing their flight from Wiggins and back; covert aid for former ballplayers, their career over and bankroll deplete; an offer to underwrite construction of Wiggins' First Baptist Church. "Diz didn't glorify these things," a Magnolia Drive inhabitant said. "He didn't go out seeking a lot of headlines. Like when he wanted to build the church. He didn't have to do it, but that's what he wanted. No strings attached. That tells you what kind of a man he was." Town officials declined Dizzy's bid; his money came from Falstaff beer. "Beer was wrong, you know. That tells you what kind of emotions run through Wiggins."

Diz? Jimmy Davis reflected. Diz was a winner. "He'd bet you five cents and fight just as hard as he would for fifty thousand dollars," said Davis, reclining in his dark cluttered office, feet upon the desk. "When he lost, he'd pay up quick. 'Fast pay makes fast friends,' Diz would roar, but he almost always won." Bulky, bespectacled, comfortable in a self-made way, Davis was early bequeathed with Ol' Diz's favor. "We had about seven or eight of us. We ate together, socialized together, befriended each other and praised Ol' Diz."

. . . "Seriously," he said, frowning, "Diz was not a religious person in the strictest sense. But inwardly, he was very moral. His attitude toward children and his fellow man—you can't beat his behavior toward them. And after all," he paused, groping as his wife approached, "that's what it's all about." But what of Dean the hustler, the man whose behavior often wavered, inwardly or out? Had Wiggins stripped away the duality? Had the hobo triumphed for good? "Oh, Diz, would win fifty dollars on blackjack," Davis whistled. "And he still loved to gamble. But he'd turn right around and buy you a fifty-dollar dinner." Here, as in Lucas, the sensitive side prevailed.

Conflicting truths tore at one's sleeve. Wiggins need not be kind to Dizzy Dean. The town reaped no profits from his past; no longer could he enrich its locals. Yet its praise seemed genuine, prompted less by deliberate intent than affection and concern. Now, as in life before, Diz was clutched to Wiggins' self-styled rustic breast. "I remember once," said a young village belle, "I was bicycling with a friend down in front of Dizzy's house. And he was sitting out on his front porch, just his underwear on. Did he run when he saw us! Embarrassed? You bet. But he was always looking to have a good image for us, for the town."

So Diz was accepted, ushered into Wiggins' 'closer than close-knit' heart. Why, though, was he so infatuated in return, so magnanimous toward a town which could not further his career, nor multiply his wealth, nor link him with influential peers? Often before, while Diz played the simple, well-meaning clown, he seemed less than harmless beneath, less than delighted with the surface role he must cradle and mold. Dean sulked at Frisch, bullied Blattner, served as benevolent despot to Kirby and Reese. Roaming Wiggins streets, however, he played the elder statesman and comic laureate, wholly at ease with both. Childless, his admirers from afar more numerous than friends, Diz had strayed from Bradenton to Dallas to Phoenix and back South, no real kinship present except for his wife. Wiggins aborted Dean's caravan, the restless soul coming home at last. Perhaps, one mused, the wanderer had yielded to constancy and peace; only here, with Diz's fall from network fame concluded, nothing now to be gained from his friendship, no self-serving favors to be wrung, only here could he sense these people with him, with him because they loved him, and sense himself complete.

He was an old-fashioned man, his values born in an earlier, more unruffled time. These people were his friends, more so than the plastic allies of the past; he enjoyed them because he trusted them, because they liked "the big ol' ox," in Reese's vivid phrase, because he shed his bravado, the image which the nation knew, and found that Wiggins reveled in what lay behind—the small-town innocent whose innocence sufficed.

"He grew to like it here," Ovin Hickman, a retired barber, said. "He found people who talked to him, who appreciated him for what he was. And always glad to talk to little people, not important people, people like me," people less little than neglected and abused. Life greeted Dizzy Dean with hardship, poverty his early, accustomed curse. Poor once himself, Diz became, in Wiggins, a tribune of the poor, the unsung, the slightly soiled, an itinerant sojourner turned squire from Bond.

I left Jimmy Davis and turned upstreet. It was altogether probable, one supposed, that neither Dean's foes nor allies ever wholly knew Ol' Diz. Neither honored what the other prized—Dizzy's capacity for charity, for spite, for fleeting malice and more lasting largesse, for the clashing emotions which altered his career. Neither grasped fully his ideals or duality, the crudity and compassion, the flights of meanness and pervasive good. Both denied the diversity of this deeply textured man. Yes, I remembered Reese saying, Ol' Diz had been insufferably complex. "Who can sort out the conflicts?" he said quietly. "Even those who knew Diz didn't know all the parts. All we know is what Diz left us. A lot of fine memories for a lot of fine folks."

"I cain't never thank him enough," Ella Mae Robertson, of Booneville, Arkansas, once had said. "That Ol' Diz, even for poor people like me, he made life fun again, he made life grand." Here in Wiggins, amid encircling Southern woods, this gentle man named Diz reaped the harvest of his years, and left what he had lived—a touch of the American Dream. . . .

PART FIVE

Body and Soul

George E. Ohr

GARTH CLARK

As historian and ceramics dealer Garth Clark notes in this monograph, George Ohr was called the first American artist-potter because of the risks he took in pushing his clay forms to their limit. Born in Biloxi, Mississippi, in 1857, Ohr was not fully appreciated as an artist until, long after his death in 1918, a family friend, Bobby Davidson Smith, reintroduced his work at the Gulf South Ceramics Show in 1965 and 1967. Called "the mad potter," Ohr created scandals and hid behind a mask of eccentricity, which finally resulted in his dismissal as instructor at Sophie Newcomb College. He once said, "I am the apostle of individuality, the brother of the human race, but I must be myself, and I want every vase of mine to be itself." Sporting a moustache over two feet long, Ohr said in an autobiographical essay published in Crockery and Glass Journal *(December 12, 1901), "I've had some fun in my 44 years, running away from danger and getting caught with open arms every time." But as Clark states, serious recognition of Ohr's work is growing steadily.*

THE FIRST OF THE artist-potters in the United States, and arguably the finest, is the Biloxi potter George E. Ohr (1857–1918). Present day recognition of Ohr's historical importance has been slow in coming for an intriguing reason. Ohr believed that he was an artist, way ahead of his time, and decided not to sell his more serious work. In all he kept 6,000 pieces, comprising a major portion of his oeuvre and had these packed away in a warehouse, awaiting a generation that could appreciate his genius, "when the work may be purchased by the nation." In fact the scenario proved to be a little more mercantile. The hoard of Ohr pots was discovered by a New York antiques dealer, James W. Carpenter. He commissioned a fascinating monograph on Ohr from Robert Blasberg and put the objects on sale. It was the first public display for most of the pieces and this body of work has begun to alter attitudes about Ohr. Until recently he was known by a few pieces in public and private collections. The curious quality of these pieces, together with a fragmentary knowledge of Ohr's bizarre life, had led to his being dismissed as an eccentric regional potter.

The work shown by Carpenter illustrated the development and logic of Ohr's clay handling, revealing him to be an artist of substance and prophecy. For not only was he the first American artist-potter in chronological terms, but he was also the first stylistically, working with an insouciance and energy that was not to resurface until the Abstract Expressionist and Funk movements after World War II.

Ohr was one of the first potters to tear away at the boundaries of decorative and fine art, or what John Coplans terms "the hierarchy of materials." This is implicit in his turning away from the seductive, controlled surface concerns of Victorian decorative art and plunging into the esthetics of risk. He pushed the expressionist qualities of clay to its plastic limit, dealt with form on a level of poetic anthropomorphism, and played a capricious and satiric game with function. In his double-spouted teapot (Collection of the Smithsonian Institution) one sees Ohr employing the utilitarian object as a contextural idea and not a functional reality. In these and many other areas Ohr is the true prophet of American clay, even down to the spirit of machismo, exhibitionism, and the workshop circuit that he employed to gain an audience for his work. Ohr neatly sidestepped the trap of European mannerism into which other pioneers such as Adelaide Robineaux and Charles Fergus Binns became embroiled. He left behind a wealth of objects that even after seventy years pertinently confront and challenge the concerns of the ceramic arts today.

Ohr was the son of a Biloxi blacksmith, a trade which he later took up himself. After spending some of his youth in New Orleans, working on various jobs, he was offered a job as an apprentice potter by a family friend, Joseph Meyer. He joined Meyer around 1885, and as soon as he had acquired the rudiments of the craft, Ohr left on a two-year, sixteen state tour of the nation's potteries, returning to Biloxi to set up a pottery with capital of twenty six dollars. His first pottery burnt down in 1893 and was rebuilt the following year. The new building became a landmark in Biloxi and was even featured in European-made souvenir plates for the town.

It would appear that Ohr initially made moulded wares of rather elaborate forms with naive relief decoration of riverboats and rustic scenes. His forte became the throwing wheel, where he showed an extraordinary skill. He would throw vulnerably thin vase forms to a point where they became nearly impossible to control. Then, just as they were on the point of collapse he would "wring the neck of his pots", as Blasberg so evocatively termed it, ruffle the lips or pummel, fold, wrinkle, twist and dent the forms. This treatment, the wrinkling and ruffling of forms, was not unknown in Victorian decorative art, particularly in

glass. But the effect achieved was carefully controlled and effetely decorative. Ohr's handling of the clay by contrast was furiously gestural, im-
buing his forms with an expressionist energy unusual in his day. To the
forms would be added his distinctive tendril-like handles which would
repeat the movement and fluidity of the form.

In glazing his forms, Ohr always showed restraint. He dabbled with
some success in flambé rouge and other histrionic glaze effects popular
at the turn of the century, but never succumbed to the glaze-chemistry
addiction that blinded the judgment of his contemporaries. He also
produced some decorative glazes such as a mottled glaze that gave the
appearance of tortoiseshell, as well as several metallic glazes. But he
most frequently used a monochrome glaze or a silky transparent lead
glaze. It is somewhat ironic that Ohr was appreciated in his day for his
glazes and not his forms. Edwin Atlee Barber, one of the best turn-of-
the-century ceramic historians valued Ohr's work, but stated that the
forms were only occasionally artistic and that "the principal beauty of
his ware consists of the glazes."

Ohr enjoyed recognition of a kind in his day. He exhibited at the
major fairs alongside the more dignified members of the ceramic arts
community and at the 1904 St. Louis Exposition, won an award for the
most original art pottery. Charles Binns appreciated his work and would
lecture to his students at Alfred University on the beauty and genius of
Ohr's work. Nonetheless, Ohr felt, and with some justification, that his
work was not fully appreciated. Certainly it is difficult to divine whether
Ohr's early fame came from his pots or his frequently outrageous "stunting", as it was termed. Ohr was as much a performer as a potter.
Whereas most art potteries were content to have their work shown unat-
tended in glass cases at the fairs, Ohr made a policy of accompanying
his work. At the fairs he would demonstrate his throwing skills under
large banners that read "I am the greatest potter in the world—Let any
man prove otherwise". This exhibitionism turned into street theatre
when Ohr became deeply religious and concerned with social justice.
One Mardi Gras season in Biloxi saw Ohr on a float in his nightshirt
with a huge wooden cross. Placards stated that certain doctors, lawyers
and civic leaders were not prepared to carry the people's cross. But
the community took the protest to be sacrilegious. A more private and
intriguing form of stunting was Ohr's interest in trick photography,
usually featuring the Ohr "twins". This paralleled a strain of surrealism
in his pottery as seen in the poetic and erotic "vagina" pots he created,
and which possibly contributed to Ohr's abrupt dismissal from Sophie
Newcomb College, where he worked for a short time under Joseph

Meyer. So that he would not be forgotten by the girls of the college, Ohr left behind a plaster of his muscular throwing arm for use in the life drawing classes!

In 1909, Ohr vowed he would never throw another pot, closed his pottery (or Pot-Ohr-Ree, as he preferred to call it) and became a Cadillac dealer. He acquired a motorcycle and became a familiar sight spluttering through the streets of Biloxi with this long moustache (it was over two feet long from tip to tip) trailing in the breeze behind him.

But one should be careful not to let Ohr's taste for eccentricity overwhelm. One of the most insightful observations about Ohr's behaviour was contained in a letter from Dr. Paul E. Cox to Robert Blasberg, describing Cox's first meeting with Ohr. At first Ohr was rather rude to his visitor, as Cox had just been employed in the ceramic department of Newcomb College and Ohr was still smarting from his dismissal. But later he became more relaxed:

"Then he sat on the edge of the bed blinking his black eyes at me. Finally he said, 'You think I am crazy, don't you?' I replied that Meyer had told me about him and that I did not think he was crazy. (I still don't.) With that George stopped his act and remarked, 'I found out long ago that it paid me to act this way.'"

It was a touching and telling confession. It suggests that Ohr used his buffoonery to hide the intense conviction he felt for his work, preferring a notoriety as a Southern curiosity to total rejection as an artist, which might have been the fate had Ohr presented his work without the trappings that he chose. A serious recognition of his work is now growing and while the nation has not erected a temple to his work, as Ohr anticipated, he is being collected by some of the most discerning collectors of contemporary art in the United States.

FROM

Father of the Blues

W. C. HANDY

Born in 1873 in Florence, Alabama, W. C. Handy first responded to the haunting power of the blues in a deserted train station in Tutwiler, Mississippi, in 1903. As Handy tells us in this passage from his 1941 autobiography (from chapter 6, "Mississippi Mud"), the unknown musician was playing what would become known as the "Yellow Dog Blues." But Handy did not decide to become a blues composer until later, after the astonishing reaction to a "native band" at a dance in Cleveland, Mississippi. Handy, who lived for a time in Clarksdale, was quite partial to the Delta and the Deep South. He said, "Every time I put by enough money for a trip to Europe, I end up by purchasing a ticket to one of the more remote sections of the deep South, knowing fully in my mind that Europe and its environs carry no such rich traditions and inspirational fertility as are embodied in this section of our America." In 1914, after he wrote "St. Louis Blues," he was established as "father of the blues," and the city of Memphis named a park in his honor.

SUMMER RETURNS. A blistering sun beats down upon a gang of black section hands during the late nineties. They are working down in Mississippi, laying the railroad tracks for the Yazoo Delta line between Clarksdale and Yazoo City. Their hammers rise and fall rhythmically as they drive the heavy spikes and sing "Dis ole hammer killed John Henry, won't kill me. Dis ole hammer killed John Henry, won't kill me." A locomotive, following the progress of the men, is steaming idly on the track. The letters "Y. D." are painted boldly on its coal car.

A traveling salesman comes up the embankment, mops the sweat from his face, shifts a chaw of tobacco from one bulging red cheek to the other, and says:

"Hey, boy. What in tarnation does that there Y. D. stand for?"

A Negro straightens up, rubs the kink out of his back and begins to scratch his head in obvious puzzlement.

"H'm," he ventures slowly. "Yaller Dawg, I reckon."

The stranger's eyes twinkle. He cackles softly and walks on down the track. "Yaller Dawg," he repeats under his breath. "That's pretty cute, hanged if it ain't. Yaller Dawg. Gee whiz, that's a good one." The Yazoo Delta R. R. was christened The Yellow Dog.

This story was circulated and the idea spread until one branch of the Yazoo Delta was known as the North Dog. For reasons equally suggestive, the fast, direct train from Clarksdale to Greenville was known as the Cannon Ball, while its slow-time, round-about companion between those points was called the Peavine. Negroes had nicknamed all these roads.

During my last year with Mahara's Minstrels I little guessed that I would shortly know every foot of these lines by heart. At no time did I even dream that the Mississippi delta would presently become my stamping grounds, but that is exactly how it worked out, and I know now that it was the best thing that could ever have happened to me.

The year was 1903, and the outfit was in Michigan when the decision was made. A Michigan town had offered me an opportunity to direct its municipal band, composed of white musicians, and I was slowly making up my mind to accept. While this decision was pending, I received a letter which contained an offer to direct a colored Knights of Pythias band in Clarksdale, Mississippi. There was little comparison between the two propositions, as I saw it. The Michigan thing was miles ahead, more money, more prestige, better opportunities for the future, better everything I thought. Yet, for no good reason that I could express, I turned my face southward and down the road that led inevitably to the blues.

Perhaps my friend Jim Jordan turned the trick. A former pupil of mine in the Corinth, Mississippi, band, Jim actually sold the Delta city to me. Earlier, it seems, he had sold me to the town folks. I bowed to his persuasion and gave my word to the managers of the Southern band. A few days later a cashier's check, drawn on the Planters Bank and signed by an S. L. Mangham, came to cover my expenses to Clarksdale. I stuffed the check into my pocket, having no immediate need for it, and began packing my duds.

In Clarksdale a few days later I entered the Planters Bank. A guard directed me to the cage of the assistant cashier and there I saw something I had never seen before in all my travels. A Negro stood at the window of that Southern white bank handling foreign and domestic drafts. Still blinking and wondering whether or not I was awake, I approached the window. "I have no one to identify me," I apologized, slipping the check through the cage.

He gave me a suave smile. "My name is your endorsement," he said quietly. "You will find it on the other side."

He was S. L. Mangham, assistant cashier. More important still, he was a clarinet player in the band I had come to direct. The local businessmen and bank officials called him Stack; they swore by him, coming and going. Whatever Stack promised, they said, he delivered. I found that he was held in equal favor by the band. Stack never left the platform when we played for dances. He never took a drink, and he never got excited. Nothing upset him. I cannot recall ever having seen his name or picture in a newspaper, yet Stack was a power in the town. He remained with the bank for thirty years and until it closed its doors. Mangham developed a peculiar type of paralysis and had to wear an iron truss to keep his head from turning around backwards, but now the truss is not necessary.

The band which I found in Clarksdale and the nine-man orchestra which grew out of it did yeoman duty in the Delta. We played for affairs of every description. I came to know by heart every foot of the Delta, even from Clarksdale to Lambert on the Dog and Yazoo City. I could call every flag stop, water tower and pig path on the Peavine with my eyes closed. It all became a familiar, monotonous round. Then one night at Tutwiler, as I nodded in the railroad station while waiting for a train that had been delayed nine hours, life suddenly took me by the shoulder and wakened me with a start.

A lean, loose-jointed Negro had commenced plunking a guitar beside me while I slept. His clothes were rags; his feet peeped out of his shoes. His face had on it some of the sadness of the ages. As he played, he pressed a knife on the strings of the guitar in a manner popularized by Hawaiian guitarists who used steel bars. The effect was unforgettable. His song, too, struck me instantly.

Goin' where the Southern cross' the Dog.

The singer repeated the line three times, accompanying himself on the guitar with the weirdest music I had ever heard. The tune stayed in my mind. When the singer paused, I leaned over and asked him what the words meant. He rolled his eyes, showing a trace of mild amusement. Perhaps I should have known, but he didn't mind explaining. At Moorhead the eastbound and the westbound met and crossed the north and southbound trains four times a day. This fellow was going where the Southern cross' the Dog, and he didn't care who knew it. He was simply singing about Moorhead as he waited.

That was not unusual. Southern Negroes sang about everything. Trains, steamboats, steam whistles, sledge hammers, fast women, mean bosses, stubborn mules—all become subjects for their songs. They accompany themselves on anything from which they can extract a musical sound or rhythmical effect, anything from a harmonica to a washboard.

In this way, and from these materials, they set the mood for what we now call blues. My own fondness for this sort of thing really began in Florence, back in the days when we were not above serenading beneath the windows of our sweethearts and singing till we won a kiss in the shadows or perhaps a tumbler of good home-made wine. In the Delta, however, I suddenly saw the songs with the eye of a budding composer. The songs themselves, I now observed, consisted of simple declarations expressed usually in three lines and set to a kind of earth-born music that was familiar throughout the Southland half a century ago. Mississippi with its large plantations and small cities probably had more colored field hands than any other state. Consequently we heard many such song fragments as *Hurry Sundown, Let Tomorrow Come,* or

> Boll Weevil, where you been so long?
> Boll Weevil, where you been so long?
> You stole my cotton, now you want my corn.

Clarksdale was eighteen miles from the river, but that was no distance for roustabouts. They came in the evenings and on days when they were not loading boats. With them they brought the legendary songs of the river.

> Oh, the Kate's up the river, Stack O' Lee's
>   in the ben',
> Oh, the Kate's up the river, Stack O' Lee's
>   in the ben',
> And I ain't seen ma baby since I can't tell when.

At first folk melodies like these were kept in the back rooms of my mind while the parlor was reserved for dressed-up music. Musical books continued to get much of my attention. There was still an old copy of Steiner's *First Lessons in Harmony,* purchased back in Henderson for fifty cents. While traveling with the minstrels I had bought from Lyon and Healy a copy of Moore's *Encyclopedia of Music.* For a time books became a passion. I'm afraid I came to think that everything worth while was to be found in books. But the blues did not come from books. Suffering and hard luck were the midwives that birthed these songs. The blues were conceived in aching hearts.

I hasten to confess that I took up with low folk forms hesitantly. I approached them with a certain fear and trembling. Like many of the other musicians who received them with cold shoulders at first, I began by raising my eyebrows and wondering if they were quite the thing. I had picked up a fair training in the music of the modern world and

had assumed that the correct manner to compose was to develop sim-
ples into grandisimos and not to repeat them monotonously. As a director of many respectable, conventional bands, it was not easy for me to
concede that a simple slow-drag and repeat could be rhythm itself. Neither was I ready to believe that this was just what the public wanted. But
we live to learn.

My own enlightenment came in Cleveland, Mississippi. I was leading
the orchestra in a dance program when someone sent up an odd request. Would we play some of "our native music," the note asked. This
baffled me. The men in this group could not "fake" and "sell it" like
minstrel men. They were all musicians who bowed strictly to the authority of printed notes. So we played for our anonymous fan an old-time
Southern melody, a melody more sophisticated than native. A few moments later a second request came up. Would we object if a local colored band played a few dances?

Object! That was funny. What hornblower would object to a time-out
and a smoke—on pay? We eased out gracefully as the newcomers entered. They were led by a long-legged chocolate boy and their band
consisted of just three pieces, a battered guitar, a mandolin and a worn-
out bass.

The music they made was pretty well in keeping with their looks.
They struck up one of those over-and-over strains that seem to have no
very clear beginning and certainly no ending at all. The strumming
attained a disturbing monotony, but on and on it went, a kind of stuff
that has long been associated with cane rows and levee camps. Thump-
thump-thump went their feet on the floor. Their eyes rolled. Their
shoulders swayed. And through it all that little agonizing strain persisted. It was not really annoying or unpleasant. Perhaps "haunting" is
a better word, but I commenced to wonder if anybody besides small
town rounders and their running mates would go for it.

The answer was not long in coming. A rain of silver dollars began to
fall around the outlandish, stomping feet. The dancers went wild. Dollars, quarters, halves—the shower grew heavier and continued so long
I strained my neck to get a better look. There before the boys lay more
money than my nine musicians were being paid for the entire engagement. Then I saw the beauty of primitive music. They had the stuff the
people wanted. It touched the spot. Their music wanted polishing, but
it contained the essence. Folks would pay money for it. The old conventional music was well and good and had its place, no denying that, but
there was no virtue in being blind when you had good eyes.

That night a composer was born, an *American* composer. Those country black boys at Cleveland had taught me something that could not possibly have been gained from books, something that would, however, cause books to be written. Art, in the high-brown sense, was not in my mind. My idea of what constitutes music was changed by the sight of that silver money cascading around the splay feet of a Mississippi string band. Seven years prior to this, while playing a cornet solo, Hartman's *Mia,* on the stage in Oakland, California, I had come to the conclusion, because of what happened in this eleven minute solo, that the American people wanted movement and rhythm for their money. Then, too, the Broadway hits, *Yankee Grit* and *Uncle Sammy*—two-steps in six-eight time that we featured in Mississippi—did not have this earthy flavor.

Once the purpose was fixed I let no grass grow under my feet. I returned to Clarksdale and began immediately to work on this type of music. Within a day or two I had orchestrated a number of local tunes, among them *The Last Shot Got Him, Your Clock Ain't Right,* and the distinctly Negroid *Make Me a Pallet on Your Floor.* My hunch was promptly justified, for the popularity of our orchestra increased by leaps and bounds. But there was also another consequence. Bids came to us to play in less respectable places. We took these in our stride on the grounds that music, like joy, should be unconfined. Moreover there was money to be made, and who were we to turn up our noses?

FROM

Biedenharn Heritage: 1852–1952

EMY-LOU BIEDENHARN

Emy-Lou Biedenharn's 1962 memoir about her father, Joseph Bieden-harn, includes this chapter, called "Son, Go into the Nickel Business," which tells the story of the man who had the idea in 1894 to bottle Coca-Cola. Joseph's father, Herman, was a second-generation German who immigrated from a small village near Hamburg to this country in 1852. After exploring and living for a while in parts of Louisiana, Herman finally settled in Vicksburg, Mississippi, married, and had seven sons and a daughter. A cobbler, he was much in demand both during and after the Civil War. He and his brother opened a confectioner's shop, which young Joe soon would run. The good advice of his father to find an affordable product inspired Joe Biedenharn to bottle Coca-Cola. Only then could everyone in the rural Mississippi countryside enjoy "the holy water of the American South" created by an Atlanta pharmacist named John S. Pemberton. Emy-Lou Biedenharn gained recognition in her own right as an opera singer with a contralto voice.

IN THIS ERA of pioneering greatness, or rather what Joe Bieden-harn called the "green and growing years," it was his father who guided and encouraged each individual member of the family. His most re-membered advice was, "Son, go into the nickel business. Everybody's got a nickel. People will spend a nickel, but they will hold on to a dime."

Joe was twenty-eight years old when he first put Coca-Cola into a bottle, and sent two cases to Mr. Candler in Atlanta. He did not know it then, but from that moment he was in the nickel business. His brothers were right along with him. Will, now twenty-one, had been with Joe through thick and thin since their Uncle Henry died seven years before. Of course, in 1894 the younger Biedenharn boys were still in school. Harry was finishing high school at seventeen; Laurie was fifteen; Her-mie, thirteen; Ollie was eleven, and Albert had barely started school at seven. Nevertheless these seven brothers, even to the youngest, were working together in the confectionery business. After school the younger boys were behind the counters selling sugar cookies, five for a nickel; a bag of jelly beans for a nickel; licorice sticks, five for a nickel, fountain Coca-Cola, a nickel a glass, and now, a new excitement, a bottle of Coca-Cola for a nickel.

Joe felt the urgency to go on the road in order to sell his new nickel beverage to new people in new territory. This tall, eager young salesman worked his Mississippi territory with horse and buggy. He traveled long, dusty country roads where chickens scratched in the dust on hot summer afternoons. The iron rims of his buggy wheels grated on the hard clay ruts, while Joe let his old mare jog along at her own even pace.

On these trips he carried an old-fashioned horn with a rubber ball similar to ones used on early automobiles. As he approached the country stores, he squeezed forth a humorous "honk, honk." "Here's Uncle Joe," the children would call out, scurrying from all sides to gather in a tight bunch around his buggy. To each child he gave a jawbreaker, licorice stick, or a handful of jelly beans. With the gift of candy came squeals of laughter and teasing and tasting and talking, all at the same time.

Once inside the stores the country folk, like the children, gathered around Joe Biedenharn. They, too, called him Uncle Joe as he graciously greeted them by patting them on the back saying, "Now Neighbor have some of my candy and a cool drink on me while you tell me about your crops." Again he would say, "Partner, let's have some cold sarsaparilla pop passed around while I tell you about my new bottled beverage called Coca-Cola."

When the commissaries were full of Negro farmhands Joe Biedenharn treated them all to pop and candy. You could hear the old darkies say, "Mr. Joe sho' got a pleasing way 'bout him, no pickings or choosing with him, he jes treats everybody alike."

. . . Joe told tall-tales with dashing flavor, accented by his delightful sense of humor. . . .

The people of the South, young, old, white and black, came to associate contagious laughter and good humor with all the Biedenharns as they became accustomed to their teasing manner, mobile features, and vigorously expressive gestures. With such stalwart individualism Coca-Cola sales showed a steady and rapid increase. . . .

By 1940, each six-foot Biedenharn loved to tell his own sons and daughters that the secret of each success stemmed from their father's wise advice, "Sons, go into the nickel business. Everybody's got a nickel."

In One Lifetime

VERNA ARVEY

This memoir by Verna Arvey about her husband, William Grant Still, a world-renowned composer, was published in 1984. Arvey was a pianist and accompanist who became, as this passage from chapter 2 shows, Still's collaborator, librettist and then his wife. Born in 1895 at the country plantation named Piney Woods near Woodville, Mississippi, Still was considered black although he was of mixed ethnic descent. He studied music at Oberlin College and became a composer at a time when such an occupation was unlikely for someone of his racial makeup. As a black man, Still broke the color barrier many times. When his Afro-American Symphony *was performed in Rochester, New York, Still became the first black to attain this achievement. He was also the first black to conduct the Los Angeles Philharmonic, which he did in 1936. Arvey, a Russian Jew, recounts later in the book the reactions to their mixed marriage in Los Angeles, where they lived, which consisted of hostility from some and surprising acceptance from others. When in 1975 Opera/South, in Jackson, Mississippi, held the premier performance of Still's* Bayou Legend, *Gov. Bill Waller commended Still as a "distinguished Mississippian." Mississippi Educational Television filmed the production and brought it to national television. About this event, Arvey says, "Interesting that the success we had long coveted came in the Deep South, when the 'liberal' north was not open to us at all."*

THE YOUNG NEGRO composer about whom I had written in high school had been asked to supply part of the libretto for the opera William Grant Still had planned to write as the first work on his Guggenheim Fellowship. He talked about it so enthusiastically that by the time Still arrived in Los Angeles on May 22, 1934, a veritable fever of excitement had been worked up among his friends. Many of us were on hand to greet the composer soon after he came to town—not only the legitimate friends, but also the hangers-on, the baskers-in-reflected-glory, the wakers-up-at-all-hours-of-the-night with requests for entertainment, and the consumers of other people's liquor. The latter four categories were soon made unwelcome, for the composer had come to the West Coast with a great hunger to work and with a job to do. He intended to do it.

Now, for the first time, I saw a real composer at work. He would accept or initiate an assignment with enthusiasm, then agonize until the form, themes and treatments were clearly outlined in his head. After he started putting things down on paper, he would go slowly (just a few measures a day), but steadily every day. He would be alternately uplifted (thanking God for his inspiration), or downcast (sure that he was being unworthy of the help he had been receiving). At some point in the creation, he usually decided it was no use—he just couldn't go on with it—but then he would pick up where he had left off and bring the composition to a logical conclusion, at which point he would decide it was terrible, not fit to be performed, and he wouldn't change his mind until it had been played, until the audience had approved it and until he could hear it objectively. It took him over twenty years to approve his own *Festive Overture,* even after it had won an important prize and had been applauded by audiences and critics alike. He just didn't care for it, he said, until he heard Izler Solomon conduct it. Then an astonished look came over his face and he decided that it did sound good, after all.

As the months came and went, it became apparent that composing wasn't all there was to being a composer. Letters arrived, a lot of them. All had to be answered. People requested biographical information, photographs, program notes, speeches, material for theses, and so on. If a composer were to take time out for all of this, he would have neither time nor energy left for composing; it was a problem that had to be solved. It seemed to me that my own talents might be of use here, so I volunteered to handle the public relations and promotional side of the work. Still (who by then was called Billy by his West Coast friends) agreed, so I started to work. In addition to the secretarial and literary aspects of my labors, I often played over what he had written when his day's composing was over, because, although he could find his notes and chords on the piano, he was still far from being a performing artist on that instrument. I also included some of his music in my own piano recitals, often lecturing about him and his compositions in the process.

He paid me for all this, but not very much, since he was keeping only fifteen dollars a week for himself and sending the major part of his Guggenheim Fellowship money for the support of his family in the East. He did this despite the absence of a court order requiring him to do so. He continued to send money until the last of the children came of age.

The Guggenheim Fellowship was renewed for another year. After a brief period, Billy requested and received a Rosenwald Fellowship which also was renewed. This gave him four worry-free years, and he made the most of them.

The opera he had come to write was *Blue Steel,* based on a story by Still's friend, Carlton Moss. This was full of beautiful melodies, lush harmonies and stirring choruses. After finishing it, he decided it was not strong enough as a drama and put it aside. He was therefore delighted when Langston Hughes offered him a libretto on the life of Jean Jacques Dessalines of Haiti. Still had previously asked some of the Negro poets for opera libretti, but they had not responded. Langston himself had written this first as a play, and had then offered it to Clarence Cameron White for a possible musical setting, but White had turned it down in favor of another poet's libretto on the same subject. So now Langston proposed what was to become *Troubled Island,* and he made a trip to the West Coast to outline the work.

After he had completed the script, Langston left Los Angeles for Spain, and then Billy was really upset. From time to time, changes in the script became necessary, but he could not reach his librettist to discuss them and had to rely on his own judgment. At last, a major change had to be made at the end of the second act. New lines had to be written to fit the music and the new turn in the drama. After an exchange of many letters, during which he received the new melodic line and made an effort to fit appropriate words to it, Langston wrote that I would have to do it because he couldn't. I was apprehensive of course, because this was all strange to me. However, I worked and worried for days until the missing text was finally supplied.

Now we both knew that I could write words to fit music. Thereafter I wrote libretti for all of his operas and other vocal works. It was a more comfortable arrangement than collaborating with someone at a distance. It also allowed Billy free rein in composing, for I followed his music far more often than he followed my texts.

Some months after he came to Los Angeles on the first Fellowship, Still made a trip to Chicago to see the second performance of his ballet, *La Guiablesse* at the Chicago Opera. This time Ruth Page (who had danced the leading role before) gave the part to a newcomer, Katherine Dunham. The program included works by two American composers, both of whom were on hand for the performance. Still was happy when the rehearsal went well. His good humor left him at performance time, when the conductor stood up and beat time in silence for a number of measures. No music came out, though the ballet was supposed to open with a trumpet solo. After the performance, it was discovered that when the music was passed out to the orchestra, the trumpet's part was missing, so the trumpeter had no music to play. When the parts were returned to Still later on, the trumpet part was among them.

The other composer's work went flawlessly, in rehearsal and in performance. In later years, we were to hear of many such incidents of sabotage of other composer's works, but this was Still's first. He was pleased, though, that in spite of the disheartening opening, the rest of the ballet went off well and was received warmly by the audience.

During this period, Mrs. Claire Reis, always a friend and champion of American composers, commissioned from Still a new work for the League of Composers to be introduced by Eugene Goossens and the Cincinnati Symphony Orchestra. With his typical enthusiasm, Still turned out two works instead of one, and let Goossens take his choice. These were *Dismal Swamp* and *Kaintuck'*, the latter dedicated to me, and both for piano and orchestra. Goossens decided on *Kaintuck'* for geographical reasons. Cincinnati is almost a Kentucky town. He called it a "grand piece of tone painting." He said he placed no importance on the "fetish of first performances," so another pianist and I presented it first, for two pianos, in a Los Angeles Pro Musica concert. Howard Hanson also played it in Rochester, along with *Dismal Swamp*.

After *Afro-American Symphony* appeared in print, thanks to Fischer's diligent promotion, it was played with increasing regularity. Sir Hamilton Harty, to whom I had mentioned Still's music when I interviewed him at the Hollywood Bowl, broadcast it in London and wrote that it had created a great deal of interest. Karl Krueger, a cherished friend whom Still had met in Hollywood through the intervention of Isabel Morse Jones of the Los Angeles *Times,* gave inspired performances of it with several symphony orchestras in this country and abroad, and later twice recorded it in its entirety, the last time for his Society for the Preservation of the American Musical Heritage. It had its first performance with the New York Philharmonic Orchestra; and in Chicago it was played under the baton of Hans Lange. It was a success everywhere.

Many of the Still performances were so far away that it was financially out of the question to travel to hear all of them. So it was not until Lt. Benter and the United States Navy Symphony Orchestra broadcast the *Afro-American Symphony* over the NBC Network that I actually heard one of these major compositions in its orchestral form, having been limited until then to more or less inadequate piano reductions.

Now it burst on me in all its glory: rich, emotional, and at the same time spiritually satisfying. I had just noted a controversy in some American magazines over who could be considered a genuine American composer. All sorts of names had been offered, but none had been convincing. Suddenly, I wondered what all the shouting was about. Here was their American composer, truly a product of our own soil, both himself and the music he created. Why were none of the frantic journalists aware of him?

But they were not, so I felt especially honored when one early morning, around two or three o'clock, I was awakened out of a sound sleep at my home by the ringing of the telephone. It was Billy. He said that he had just gotten the theme for the second movement of his *G Minor Symphony,* and wanted me to hear it. He put the telephone as near the piano as possible and played the theme. It struck me then, as it has ever since, as being one of the most lofty and inspired symphonic themes I had ever heard.

Possibly Still's symphonic music received its greatest North American publicity when Leopold Stokowski played the fourth movement of the *Afro-American Symphony* on his cross-country tour with the Philadelphia Orchestra, for this tour was advertised extensively. Contrary to the general impression of Stokowski as a temperamental, flamboyant individual, we found him to be thoughtful and quite meticulous. When he studied a score he studied every bit of it. He even took note of Billy's concluding phrase on every score: "With humble thanks to God, the Source of inspiration." In one of his letters there was this paragraph: "I am so interested to see that you dedicate these works to the source of inspiration. How mysterious and yet how definite is this source! It is strange how many people seem to be so far away from it, and not to have any contact with it."

Dreams and Visions

THEORA HAMBLETT

Born in Paris, Mississippi, in 1895, Theora Hamblett grew up on a farm and became a county school teacher. She later moved to Oxford, Mississippi, where she supported herself as a seamstress and by renting rooms to students. A self-taught artist, she describes in Dreams and Visions, *published in 1975, the sources of some of the paintings in her collection of over three hundred works. Many of her paintings depict, in vibrant colors, scenes from rural life, such as a worker in a wagon going up a hill to the gin, or girls dancing around a cottonwood tree. One of her paintings,* The Vision, *was purchased by the Museum of Modern Art in New York. Her tiny brushstrokes evoke her work as a seamstress. As Hamblett reveals in the following passage, "Dream Preceding the Childhood Games Paintings," dreams were often the inspiration for such subjects as children playing at their games.*

Dream Preceding the Childhood Games Paintings

For three or four summers I had tried to paint "Heaven's Descent to Earth," then I began to wish for another engrossing subject matter for painting. I dreamed a very impressive dream with the words "Paint your dream." The dream had several indoor scenes. I knew how to paint landscapes, but not indoor scenes.

Three or four years passed. One day when planning a landscape to paint, I wondered what real life scene to put with the landscape I'd planned. I had painted very few landscapes without animal life of some kind on it. Something seemed to tell me to draw a scene of children playing "Drop the Handkerchief." I did. It gave me a great thrill of joy. That was in 1966.

When telling a friend about my joy over painting a children's game, she brought one of her books of children's games to me to refresh my memory. I had played many of those games as a child in school and when teaching in the rural schools back in the 1920's and 1930's. I spent my summers in summer school where during three different summers I was enrolled in physical education classes in which these games were played.

After painting around forty of the children's games, I recalled that dream of several years before. In the last scene of that dream, I was going to teach mountain children. As I awoke, I could feel myself playing and singing games with children.

The dream began with my working in a meat factory one afternoon. Everything went fine that afternoon. All I had to do was carry cut meat back to the packing room. The next morning I was back on the job, trying to do the same work as the afternoon before. The meat cutters would not let me carry their cut meat. When I asked for their meat, they said they had none. Then I went to another meat cutter's table to see if he had some cuts for me to carry to the packers. While I was at the other table, the cutters at the first table carried their meat to the packing room. When I went back to the first table, the cutters at the second table carried their cut pieces back to the packers. I became utterly confused and went to the head boss.

He said "I have work down this hallway you can do."

I started down the hall with him. We had only gone a few steps when he threw his left arm around my shoulder. When I tried to get away from him, he threw his right arm around me, held me fast, as we continued down the hall.

A man and woman stepped out into the hall just in front of us. They stopped and began talking to us. My boss' arms dropped from around me. While he and that couple were talking, I peeped into the room they came from and saw an outside door on the other side of the room.

I darted into that room and out the outside door, then into an alleyway. I began running. The alleyway led into a main street. Down that main street I ran and ran. Stores and houses disappeared. I came to a small stream of water, crossed it, and kept running and began ascending a hill which became a very high one.

I began to come to myself, and remembered that I could stop at the first house and call Mama to let her know where I was and that I had money to meet present expenses.

When I came to a mountain home, I stopped to phone Mama. They had a community phone, so they had to make the connections for me to talk. While they were doing that, I heard a group of children and went back to the porch to see them. The children were running towards the house. When they were near enough, I asked them why they were not in school, for it was a weekday. They must have answered, "We don't have a teacher for our school."

As I awoke, my feelings went out to them. I was saying I could teach them. As I thought about it, I could see and feel myself singing and playing games with those children.

In those days, girls just out of high schools competed for the chance to teach in the many one-teacher schools in the rural communities. Some girls liked that work while others did not. Frequently, girls went to the larger towns or cities to try to work instead of teaching in the one-teacher schools. I can imagine the girl of my dream refusing to teach in a one-teacher school and going to a large town or city instead to find work.

But God had other plans for her. He struck her dumb when on her second day of work. He gave her a way of escape and led her into the field of work where she could do the most good. Nothing but God's Holy Spirit and guidance could give anyone the strength and spiritual urge to stay on one subject for painting until he had painted over two hundred and seventy-five paintings of children's games. That dream gave me so much thrill that I was able to keep painting until I had mastered my own way or technique for landscapes. Then that inner voice or spirit told me what subject matter to put on the landscapes. Only that Divine Spirit could produce over a hundred paintings of one subject, folk games, played by children.

My Husband, Jimmie Rodgers

C A R R I E   R O D G E R S

Carrie Williamson Rodgers promised her husband that if he didn't live to do it, she would write his long-proposed book for him. After his death at the age of thirty-six, she did so. Her biography is an important record of the life of "the father of country music." Born in Pine Springs, Mississippi, in 1897, as described in this passage (chapter 4), Rodgers became a railroad section hand on the Mobile & Ohio Railroad in 1911. He married Carrie Williamson in Meridian in 1920 (his second marriage). He was dissatisfied with everything he did—working for the railroads, driving trucks, pumping gas—until he began to sing. In 1961, he was the first performer to be elected to the Country Music Hall of Fame. Diagnosed with tuberculosis in 1924, Rodgers primed his singing voice with bonded whiskey before each recording. In 1933, after having recorded twelve numbers at a New York studio, he succumbed to the disease. His body was brought home to Meridian by train, a tribute to the subject of so many of his songs. Among his most famous songs were "The Singing Brakeman," "T for Texas," and "Miss the Mississippi."

> "I'll eat my breakfast here—
> "And my dinner in New Orleans—."

The railroad yards! They were "home" to the section foreman's little boy.

Powerful black monsters belching fire and smoke; smoke white, chiffon-blue, blue-black; smoke shot through with crimson and gold. The cheery rattle and clank of gaily drunk box cars and flats. The jauntily curt "whoo-whoo"! as the "hoghead"—perhaps small Jimmie's favorite engineer, acknowledged the yard-conductor's signaling arm.

Steel rails often slippery with rain, ice, fog, dew—but always silver. The crunch of cinders. The smelly whiff of creosoted ties. Hurrying figures. Lounging figures. Men "rough and rowdy"; but men with jovial, weathered faces and great generous hearts. Men in stout blue overalls and jackets; tight peaked caps on their heads. Gray heads, black, red, bald, brown. Men with blue bandanas knotted around their leathery necks. Each man wearing the inevitable trainman's "watch and chain."

Great engines puffing, snorting; suddenly spitting out hot steam. Great steel hearts throbbing with eagerness to be heading out; or sighing contentedly, their day's work done, as they headed in.

Too, there were arrogant Pullman trains flashing on to distant, glamorous cities. Or creeping along carefully—humbly obeying the signals of some lowly blue-garbed figure; or—dusty and weary—submitting gratefully to the clean-up gang; the repair crew.

Small Jimmie Rodgers loved it all. The hurrying noisy days. Magically colorful, throbbing nights. And always, throughout the yards, men in blue tapping their shoulders, jerking their thumbs, whirling their arms, beating their fists together—or slapping their middles.

If at night, lanterns swinging in half-arcs, grand full arcs; jiggling smartly up and down, or slowly sidewise. Signals!

At fourteen, the small son of Aaron Rodgers knew them all; knew every signal of this queer deaf and dumb language. At fourteen he could laugh gleefully, right along with the oldsters, at the new brakie high on a box car, alert for relayed signals, who suddenly twisted the wheel and called out eagerly: "Go eat. O. K. Suits me fine!" Jimmie knew as well as the most experienced trainman that the relayed signal, two smart slaps on the head-brakeman's middle, meant they were heading for track eleven.

At fourteen Jimmie knew the rule-book better than some preachers know their Bible; although it is doubtful if he had ever, up to that time, seen even the outside cover of the rule-book. Still, Jimmie knew all the answers.

When a fireman asked him: "What makes up a train crew, Jimmie?" the boy answered readily, brown eyes twinkling:

"Hoghead, swellhead, two empty heads and a baked head," which slang of the yards meant engineer, fireman, two brakemen and the conductor. On occasion he would, just as readily, refer to the conductor as "the brains," and to the fireman as "the tallow pot."

He could repeat, and laugh at, the greenhorn brakie's definition of a "fixed signal". "A brakeman on top of a box car, dark night, lights out—and a cinder in his eye."

Long after he was forced to give up railroading because of failing health, when we'd be driving somewhere alone and neared a street signal, Jimmie would hark back to his railroad days, and call out alertly, if weakly: "Yaller board, Mother"—"red board" or "clear board—step on it."

Then, at fourteen, or thereabouts, Jimmie Rodgers became, to his huge delight, a real-for-sure railroad man; assistant foreman to his father. Shortly afterward he got a job as a real brakeman! His first job was on a work train, but very soon his older brother Walter, already long in the service of the rails, got him on as a regular on the New Orleans and Northeastern, from Meridian to New Orleans.

He had by then lost his baby chubbiness and was stretching upward, becoming a tall, husky young fellow. Long since his baby curls had turned to rich dark brown.

His railroad card shows fourteen years of service. During those years he played various roles on many roads; call-boy, flagman, baggage-master, brakeman.

Flagging passenger trains gave him a chance to wear a neat uniform. Always meticulous about his personal appearance, his erect bearing delighted his bosses. Nearly always it was Jimmie who was called when some very special train was due; a train bearing officials of the road, or some notable—like General Pershing.

But—"I crave to cover distance"—so, as freight brakeman, young Jimmie Rodgers thought he was doing fine. He was going places, seeing things, doing things. Carefree, happy always, when answering a call he reached first for banjo, mandolin or ukelele. When he wasn't "riding the decks" singing, testing his lungs against the rumbling, swaying box cars, he spent his time in the waycar plinking darkey melodies to admiring crew buddies. He didn't suspect, then, that often those older men deliberately shifted many of his duties to their own shoulders, thus leaving the young brakie free to plink away to his heart's content—and their delight.

His voice was full-throated now; but his singing no better, perhaps, than the average young fellow's. But he was gaining confidence. The crews heartily enjoyed his rollicking ballads of the railroads, his plaintive crooning of plantation melodies, songs of hills and rivers, as well as countless barroom ditties. He was railroad man—and minstrel. And the war was on and troop trains were being rushed madly here, there, everywhere.

It has been said that he answered his country's call during those terrifying times of 1917–1918 by serving in the navy. Jimmie Rodgers served his country by doing what was required of all railroad men; by attending to his trainman's duties. For the railroads had requested the government to exempt all trainmen.

Full crews, experienced railroaders were sorely needed to work troop trains and long trains of supplies and equipment being rushed to ports and training camps. It was impressed on the minds of all trainmen that theirs was a highly important branch of the army. So Jimmie Rodgers did his bit by "going high" on the tops of lurching box cars in sun, wind, rain, sleet, snow; by relaying signals, twisting the wheel, pulling pins; helping speed Uncle Sam's trains on their way.

And a pal of Jimmie's, Sammy Williams, told his sweetheart good-bye and went to France—to be killed in action.

So before the war was over Jimmie found time to pick out words and air to his first composition, a sentimental song. If grammar, punctuation and spelling were faulty—tenderness and emotion were not. When the world heard this first song of Jimmie's the world approved in no uncertain manner; even though there was in it no hint of what would later be called "his sentimental ballads which trail off into a mournful yodel."

From the first his railroad buddies liked the song, and the young fellows in Meridian who were his boon companions liked it. With banjo, guitar, uke, they hung around the all-night places or strolled the streets playing and singing Jimmie's song along with "Sweet Adeline" and other sentimental ballads.

But it was not until some ten years later that the world heard—and approved of it.

"He said good-bye little darling—to France I must go—they took him away to this awful German war—The third one wrote by his captain—My darling dear was dead—But I keep all his letters—I'll keep his gold rings too—."

Big Bill Blues

WILLIAM BROONZY

*Bill Broonzy, the blues artist, was born in Scott, Mississippi, in the
1890s. The exact date of his birth is not clear, because, like many black
men at the time, he added years to his age either to get a job or to join the
military. One of seventeen children, Broonzy's hard life was made bearable by music, whiskey, women, storytelling, and a sense of humor. From
life in the cotton fields of Mississippi and Arkansas and the coal mines
of Kentucky, Broonzy found his way to Chicago and then to Carnegie
Hall in New York in 1939. In his autobiography, published in 1955,
Broonzy recaptures some of the great moments of his long musical career,
which began with a fiddle he made out of a cigar box when he was ten.
"What is a blues singer?" he asks. Then he answers facetiously, "I say
he's just a meal ticket for the man or woman who wears dollar-signs for
eyes." Music critics, however, have long recognized Broonzy's greatness.
Heavily influenced by W. C. Handy, he and other native Mississippians,
such as Charley Patton, Muddy Waters, Howlin' Wolf, and later B. B.
King, were instrumental in creating the blues we know today. In this
selection, Broonzy, who died in 1958, gives the background for one of
his most famous songs (from the chapter entitled "My Songs").*

I WROTE A SONG in 1945 titled *Black, Brown And White*. I tried
RCA Victor, Columbia, Decca and a lot of little companies, but none of
them would record it. They wanted to hear it, and after I had played
and sung it they would refuse.

'And why do you want to record such a song?' they would ask. 'Nobody would buy it.'

'What's wrong with it? I would like to know. What I say is just about
the way the working Negro is treated in this country on all jobs in the
South, in the North, in the East and in the West, and you all know it's
true.'

'Yes,' they would say to me, 'and that is what's wrong with that song.
You see, Bill, when you write a song and want to record it with any
company, it must keep the people guessing what the song means. Don't
you say what it means when you're singing. And that song comes right
to the point and the public won't like that.'

I kept on trying it anyway. When I came to France in 1951 I told Mr

Hugues Panassié about it. He asked me why and I played it to him. He said:

'Yes, I like it. Do you want to record it?'

'Well I've been trying for six years but no company would record it for me.'

'Before you leave France it will be recorded,' he said.

And so it was, on September 21 of that same year, and released soon after. I carried a copy back with me to the States and I played it to them. 'We like the music,' they said, 'but not the words.'

One day I got a letter from the Mercury Recording Company that told me to get ready with about eight songs for a recording session. That was in January 1952. I recorded *Black, Brown And White* that time, but it hasn't been released. Of course I know that the Mercury Company recorded it because of Mr John Hammond. I played it to him once in 1946. Him and Alan Lomax both liked it. Mr Hammond said to me:

'Bill, that's a good song you've got there, why don't you record it?'

'I've tried nearly all the companies, but they don't like it.'

He smiled and said: 'They will.' So that's why it has been finally recorded in the States, too.

Of course there's nothing wrong with the song but the Negroes don't like it because it says: *If you's black, git back.* And I don't blame them because we all Negroes in the USA have been getting back all of our lives and we's tired of getting back. But this song doesn't mean for a Negro to get back, it just tells what has happened on jobs where Negroes go.

I remember once I went to an employment office and everybody had to get a number and get in line. Then you had to wait until your number was called. I stayed in line for about five hours. There was about fifty of us in this line and only two Negroes, me and a Negro woman.

After they had called the white men and women, one of the managers came out and said to me and the Negro woman:

'Sorry but we don't hire any Negroes today and don't know when we will.'

So this woman walked away and I said to her:

'Let's catch the street car.'

'I ain't got street car fare,' she told me, 'I've spent my last seven cents to come out here. I was so sure of getting a job because the ad in the newspaper said they wanted fifty women and I did see but about fifteen women there. So I stayed in line.'

'You's a Negro,' I said to her.

'The paper just said women.'

'You's a Negro,' I said again.

'But I'm a woman, and I know it because I've got five children and my husband got gassed in 1918 in the army.'

'You's still a Negro, and I am too, so we have to get back, can't you see what I mean?'

'I knew about it in the South, but not in the North.'

'And where are you now?'

'I'm in Chicago.'

'It's the same in New York,' I told her. 'All over the USA it's the same soup, but it's just served in a different way.'

. . . One of the verses I sing is about me and a man working together—a white man of course.

I was working in a foundry. I was a moulder there for seven years and I showed all the other moulders there how to put up a mould, how to cut their sand and how to put a pattern in the mould, because I was an all around man. When the boss would get a new pattern he would always call me and I would make anything he gave me.

So one day he called me in the office and said: 'Bill, take this man and show him how to make a mould.'

So I learned him how to make moulds and we worked together for a year. One day he asked me where I was living and he came home with me. We had been stopping and getting drinks together every pay day so far, but that day we bought a bottle of whisky and went to my house. We had a meal together and then started drinking. He got drunk and started to call me a fool.

'What do you mean, I'm a fool?'

'Just this,' he said, and he laid the stub from his cheque on the table. 'That's what I mean, my friend, let me see yours.'

So I laid mine on the table.

'Your cheque is of fifty dollars and mine is for a hundred. Can't you see you's a fool? You's my boss and have learned me everything I know and I get twice as much as you do. You's been working here for seven years and haven't got a raise.'

'Yes I have, when I started here seven years ago I was getting twenty-five dollars a week.

He laughed and said:

'When I started one year ago I was getting fifty-five dollars a week and now after you learned me to mould I get a hundred dollars a week.

Don't you see you's a fool. You know more about moulding than the man who owns the place.'

Of course he was Polish and hadn't been in the US for long. The next year he was my boss, and when he started to lay off, all the Negroes were laid off first.

So you can see what I mean by *if you's black git back*. And it happens in other parts of the world too, just in a little different way. . . .

The white man has a million dollars and I just have seven thousand dollars in the bank and a job paying sixty dollars a week. I'll pay six thousand dollars for a Cadillac, a hundred and ten dollars for a suit, forty-five dollars for a hat, forty dollars for my shoes. I'll spend all the money I have just trying to dress, ride and look like the white man. I'll get the brightest Negro woman I can so she'll look white. I'll straighten my hair and try to go in places where I'm not wanted. They tell me:

'We don't serve Negroes in here.'

I get mad because I think I look like a white man with my hair straightened, that hundred-and-ten-dollar suit, my Cadillac and a yellow woman who's hair is just as straight as a white one's.

So why don't they want me in here? I have American money and I pay tax. Is it because I'm black? Oh well, remember that song that Louis Armstrong sings called *Black And Blue:*

> *I can't hide what's on my face.*

In every place I go, all the people I meet of different races is glad to say and to be from where they was born. But me, when anybody asks me if I'm from Mississippi, I'll say yes but I'm mad and don't like to talk about it, because I was born poor, had to work and do what the white man told me to do, a lot of my people were mobbed, and lynched and beaten. The ones who owned something, the white man wanted his wife or his best horse, he had to give it up. For everything I raised on my farm, the white man was setting his price; he paid me what he wanted to give and I had to take it. So when I went to the North I tried to be like him and I got me a white woman and a big car. Some time I'd have no money to buy gas but I'd pawn my watch or my ring, so the other Negroes could see Big Bill's car and white woman. I did have the white woman because I wanted her, not to hurt anyone. I just wanted to be and act like a white man. I had a black wife at home, and in the South the white man had a white wife and a Negro woman, children by them both, and in no place he went had he to get back for nobody, and everybody liked him. So that's the reason why I tried to play and do things like him.

Even a half-white Negro was treated better than a black Negro. So I straightened my hair, changed my way of talking and walking, always trying to do things like a white man so I wouldn't have to get back. But since I've been in other parts of the world and seen that I'm not the only black man in the world and that all the other black people in the world like and love each other, it's different.

The American Negroes, they make fun out of each other. If you's from a different State in the USA, if your hair is frizzy and you's real black, all the northern Negroes who have their hair straightened and know the town, instead of trying to show me how to act and do, they'll just laugh and call me a Mississippi Negro and they don't seem to know that if their hair is straight it's just because their mother cheated on their father with a white man who's their real father.

When I came to the North I did not just come there to get a white woman or just to be with one to get back at the Negro woman, because she could have a white man in Mississippi, and I could walk down the street beside or on the same side of the street as a white woman. But lots of times I would wonder why a white man would kill me if he'd seen me with a white woman. What is it she's got that my Negro woman ain't got? He has a white woman and he has a Negro woman, too. So I came to the North and tried it. I tried everything I had seen him do, then I would go home and look in my looking-glass and I could still see Mississippi, and the next morning when I got up my hair would be gone back home and I'd have to straighten it again. And in a lot of places that I would take that white woman, she would go in there to get food and drinks for me and her because they don't allow Negroes, but I didn't care because I was in a big fine car like a white man, I had a white woman and she could get anything I could pay for. So I was happy. She would come back and say that the bill was ten dollars and it wasn't but three dollars, I would just say:

'OK, darling, let's ride around in the park.'

I tried everything not to be made to get back. I changed everything. I even learned to play my guitar differently and sing different songs. So I found out that a white woman, fine clothes, a big car and straightened hair, a change of walking and talking don't hide what's on your face and so, if you's black in the USA you've got to git back, git back. . . .

White woman, white dog and red car don't help any and I think that loving one another is the best way. Let's try it.

FROM

Allison's Wells: The Last Mississippi Spa 1899–1963

HOSFORD LATIMER FONTAINE

Allison's Wells was the inspired revival of a mineral spa inherited by Hosford Latimer Fontaine from her grandparents. To keep his wife from crying every time she heard "I'll Take You Home Again, Kathleen," John Fontaine, an advertising executive in Boston, was finally persuaded to bring her home to Mississippi in 1938. In this afterword to her memoirs, Hosford Fontaine reflects on the rich experience of the arts colony at Allison's Wells, which she directed from 1948 to 1963. A place for artists to carry out serious study under such masters as Karl Wolfe or Andrew Bucci, it was also an experience in first-class fun, Mississippi style. As Charlotte Capers said, it was a place where the plumbing was "independent," where two sets of newlyweds could find themselves mistakenly assigned to the same room, or where wide-eyed first-time participants might find themselves shelling peas or darning linen.

ALLISON'S HAD A certain charm and warmth, which warmed your heart and for the most part the servants made each guest feel that they were special. This was true from the time of my grandfather, Sam W. Wherry. Every employee was a person to him as well as for my father, Douglass Latimer, my sister Thelma, who also operated the Wells, with my brother Douglass C. Latimer during the depression and Doug fed the tenants then.

As I tell you about the employees who made that warmth, I feel very close to them. They were special. The feeling of welcome was in the air whether you came for fun to recuperate from illness or to sober up with the sulphur baths and the Allison's water. You could not drink alcohol with the Allison's water. . . .

Glenn Clark, the evangelist, said, "The reason home-cooked meals were the best was because they were cooked with love." Undoubtedly the reason Allison's was noted for its fine cuisine—love with knowledge and concern.

Another brief return to the past. My father Douglass Colquhoun Latimer had so many friends. Two of the closest were Luther Ellis, a traveling salesman, and Jed Powers of Franklin, near Lexington, who added so much to the night life of the Wells—midnight parties, hay rides, horseback riding, and one of the midnight supper delicacies was chicken wiggle served by the white coated waiters.

In the midst of the busy, happy years in the East—nine in Boston—would come real nostalgia. When I would hear on the radio, "Take Me Home Again Kathleen," I would burst into tears and John and son John would laugh at me. So when we came home in 1938, it was as though I had always known that we would. It brought back the memory of childhood and young ladyhood filled with happiness, dancing, tennis, playing dolls and many dates—and no problems—and a loving mother and father and family.

Perhaps Allison's had a real essence of values—the True Value of Life—sharing and caring and treating everyone as a person. Perhaps that is why even though Allison's has been gone since 1963—over 20 years—it is still breathing, but not with sorrow, but with emphasis on living life to the fullest.

One thing that gave the resort character were the guests who came from far and near, as Will Britton, the dean of cotton on Front Street, a poet, a close friend and the last president of The Allison Art Colony. His book was Front Street, a delight. Will was at the Wells when a dinner party was given for Eudora Welty to honor her for "Ponder Heart." This was at the King and Queen's table—a very special occasion. His last wish before dying was to return for one farewell visit. . . .

One fact that gave the resort character was the quality of the guests who came from far and near. Informal parties were given by the writers group with Charlotte Capers often there. We met first at the retreat or in the winter by the long fire in the living room. Eudora Welty entertained her friend Elizabeth Bowen, a writer, with a small group one night, just to enjoy good conversation, peace and quiet and being waited on with interest—and the from-scratch dinner.

One of the real highlights of the Art Teas to honor an artist was the one that was given for John Faulkner, of Oxford—Bill Faulkner's brother, whom we went to Ole Miss with and one of husband John's close friends and my dancing partner at the Red & Blue dance at school. John and Dolly Faulkner were our weekend guests and the tea was a real brilliant one with the largest group of friends coming to renew friendship with John whom they had known in Canton as the driver of The American Express during the WPA days. John's paintings were a dip into the past—sophisticated primitives. He was brilliant, entertaining, and the friends had a great time with crumpets and tea to follow.

There was a feeling about Allison's, which made you feel at home and welcome. So much so that many guests enjoyed sharing in the many activities. Shelling peas and stringing beans, weeding the pool as they lounged in the sun. As I was enroute to the pool for another swim, John's cousin, Mrs. Darden from Rolling Fork, Mississippi, said, "Hosford I won't shell the peas, but if you give me those yard wide Nottingham linen napkins I will darn them." And she did—with the worst ones having our name on them.

It would have been impossible for me to leave Allison's even with my husband John's death on Labor Day 1962, but it was taken out of my hands. As I was enroute to New Orleans and La Font at Pascagoula for a brief vacation before Howard Goodson was to have a midwinter Art Colony term, it came with a rush.

A telegram on the train around Brookhaven—Allison's was burning—I had only been away one hour and a half—unbelievable. The shock, the loneliness on the street there while I waited for the next fast train back to Jackson where my brother Doug and my son John III met me and drove me to Allison's. All was gone, still burning, only the pavilion left. There I was with a small suitcase. All else gone, jewelry, china, paintings—over 200 of John's and 25 of mine—as well as two exhibitions hanging in the dining room and living room.

The picture shows Allison's gone—Alladin, our dog and my sons—Goodbye to the past and on to the future—only happy memories left. Yes, it is a busy happy life sharing the wonders and cares of the new and old friends—not enough time to do everything.

Mississippi Artist: A Self-Portrait

KARL WOLFE

The artist Karl Wolfe was known primarily for his light-filled oil por-
traits. He was born in Brookhaven, Mississippi, in 1904 and reared,
along with his six siblings, in nearby Columbia. According to this excerpt
from the first chapter, "Genesis," of his 1979 autobiography, as a boy he
worked at his father's logging camp; when he graduated from high school,
at sixteen, he went to work at a sawmill. After finishing Soulé business
school in New Orleans, he was determined to become an artist and finally
got his break when he received a scholarship to the Chicago Art Institute.
During his career of fifty years, he made over seven hundred portraits
and at least a thousand other paintings. He and his wife, Mildred, also
an artist, were important presences at the art colony Allison's Wells near
Canton, where Wolfe taught painting.

IN A FEW MONTHS I'll have been painting in Jackson for fifty
years—half a century of doing what I want to do most and where I want
to do it. People seem to marvel that I made a go of it. Perhaps they
underestimate both me and Mississippi. When I think of my work, two
thousand pieces perhaps, in places meaningful to Mississippians, I'm
glad I never underestimated either. How it began and what it's been
like is what this book is about.

I was born in a house that had no screens, no electricity, no telephone,
and very little plumbing. There was a privy outside, and we slept with
yards of mosquito netting draped over our beds. With the post office in
our block, we were near the center of the town, which may have had
four or five thousand souls, and living without so many things that seem
necessary now was not odd then. In 1904 we had not dreamed of radio,
television, or even movies in Brookhaven, Mississippi. The Wright
brothers had gotten something called an aeroplane barely off the
ground, and in 1908 when I was four I saw an automobile, very likely
the first one in town.

The Illinois Central ran through Railroad Park in the middle of town—a park with grass and flowers and benches for people to sit on while they watched to see who got off and who got on the trains that stopped several times a day. But there was more to do than watch the trains. The Opera House always seemed busy. When there was no amateur theatrical, with everybody in town either on stage or in the audience, a stock company might stop off on its way to New Orleans.

And parades! Did we celebrate Mardi Gras? After sixty-five years memories get tangled. Was the Shriner's Parade a separate affair? Do I really recall being a small boy lifted onto an elephant's neck or riding between the humps of a camel? Not a camel at all but two men walking lumpily disguised as one. Did I wear a fez? My uncle, who had no children, was mayor, and I was often his mascot. Japanese-kimonoed girls under a pergola dripping wisteria still cross my vision. They were on a float that must surely have won a prize. But when a real circus came to town all local efforts seemed puny, and the circus did come—every fall.

Opposite the post office was my grandfather's store, a Mecca filled with magic for kinder. Before there was a bank in Brookhaven, people brought their savings to this quiet man to keep in his small iron safe, which stood by the pickle barrel. I only know what he was like from stories and faded photographs, but I wonder if his kind has vanished from the earth. Behind the store was his house and garden with arched hedges, brick walks, goldfish pool, grape arbor, ducks, pigeons, rabbits, and, in a bed next to the fence, red lilies that people walked blocks to admire. The Opera House next to his garden filled out the block. My uncle managed it, which is one reason our family got to see everything.

Inside grandfather's house were pillows with ruffles, matting on the floors, rugs, books, whatnots, and furniture gilded by my aunt. Too cumbersome for anything but the parlor floor were *Paradise Lost* and *Paradise Regained,* with Gustave Dore's dire illustrations. When the pictures got too scary we glanced behind us where Dresden figurines in porcelain lace too delicate to touch danced on the whatnot. It was a beautiful world to live in.

When I came down with scarlet fever and was quarantined with my mother in our own house for six weeks, the confinement may have been hellish for her, but for me it could not have been more enchanting. I was four and entertained constantly. Together we filled scrapbooks with beautiful things, and once a live hen walked on the sickroom floor, a real sunbonnet on her head. She was not red like the storybook hen but speckled black and white, which made her no less enchanting; her bonnet was red, she was alive, and I had my mother all to myself.

Miss McVoy was music teacher at Whitworth College for Women.

That she persuaded great artists like Galli-Curci and Schumann-Heinck to perform in Brookhaven seems a miracle. She did, though, and music seemed everywhere taken seriously. We were taught to read it in primary school. There was also an art teacher who gave second-grade students a sprig of goldenrod in a glass to draw with wax crayons. My drawing won first prize. From that moment I was an artist.

Sixty-five years later, Brookhaven looks like it has just been scrubbed and painted white. The business part of town with narrow streets straight as rulers reminds me of a chessboard set for a game. A church occupies many a strategic corner, the Baptist, the biggest, curiously surmounted by five domes. On the corner next to our house was the Jewish synagogue; it is still there, small, wooden, painted white, its dark purplish windows shaped like mosques. On the other side of us lived the Decelles with nine Catholic children; Henry Decelle and I were inseparable. Across the street were the McDorns, Catholic and wealthy, with twelve children and a burro from a silver mine in Colorado. The mine proved a fake, and Mr. McDorn who had persuaded his friends to invest in it, sold everything he had to reimburse them.

Keep going out Church Street and you run into what we called Silk Stocking Avenue, now a period piece. Under tall, straight oaks are medium-sized houses, every one old and in good repair—friendliness, charm, cordiality are still here. How many front yards did I play in?

Long ago, they called Brookhaven Homeseekers' Paradise, and back in town near the railway station a signboard still stands, freshly painted, proclaiming this legend. But for me this paradise was lost forever when we moved away.

I was a vulnerable ten-year-old when we moved to Columbia, Mississippi, and I found it impossible not to hate the town. The Illinois Central Railroad ran a straight line through Brookhaven, tying together the country from New Orleans to Chicago. A mainline railroad connection made a tremendous difference in the cultural development of a small town. No passenger trains came through Columbia.

In 1914 most dwellings in Columbia had been built from one unimaginative plan; two rooms and a hall in front, the hall opening onto a back porch, along one side of which were the other rooms. The raw wood interiors of houses seldom saw paint or paper, and if there were wallpaper almost certainly it covered bedbugs. Till the house my Dad bought burned we fought the bedbug scourge. If we left our front gate open, there were larger pests. Goats, cows, horses, mules would crowd the front porch, eating ferns and dropping manure. An artesian well at the center of town watered all livestock, which frequently blocked the entry of stores on Main Street. Manure was everywhere, and copulation among the beasts was a common sight, and though natural, it was unedifying if you were in the company of some nasty minded male, young or old, whose remarks could turn heaven sour. Nobody told us anything else, and a blank young mind revolted, especially the mind of a youngster who loved his mother more than anything on earth.

How my mother made me proud of helping her, I don't know. Perhaps some unconscious communication reminded us both that her care had saved me from scarlet fever only half a dozen years before. At the age of ten I was splitting and bringing in the wood burned in kitchen and fireplaces. Two years later I tended the hogs we butchered in fall and ate all winter till we were sick of pork. Each spring my mother and I made heroic attempts at gardening and rejoiced when a stock law was finally passed forcing owners to pen up all their animals, at which time we doubled our efforts. Today when spring comes, Columbia is inundated with azalea blooms—a blaze of color. But when we first moved there, no bloom could be seen except camellia japonicas which even now I don't like.

Two kinds of people were drawn to Columbia by J. J. White's sawmill; mill hands, who lived in mean houses near their work, and men with office jobs. The white-collar people settled close to the boss man, and nearby Hugh White built his own Presbyterian church, with only seventy-five members. My sister was faithful to the Ladies Aid Society for years, and long ago, when every individual did not assume he must own an automobile, she was bothered because some of the ladies had to walk to meetings. She tried to rig a schedule whereby ladies who owned cars would give carless ladies a ride. More and more the schedule got balled up, till one lady with a car offered a suggestion she thought would solve everything. It was put to a vote and passed unanimously: "Ladies with cars can ride, ladies without can walk."

I think my mother deliberately chose not to live on the same street with the Hugh Whites and their kin. She was a proud woman and a strong one, bearing children, she said, "as easily as a healthy animal." She may have been the first woman in Mississippi to serve on a school board, which she did conscientiously and soberly. Mother was also brave. One winter night when my dad was away, she and my sisters and I were sitting close to the fireplace when an odd sound came from one of the long windows that opened onto the front porch. We couldn't see out, because the blinds were closed, but from the noise we believed someone might be raking a stick across them, making a sort of corrugated rattle, slow and deliberate.

"Who is it?" asked my mother in a calm voice. There was no answer and no pause in the rhythmic stroking.

"What do you want?" she demanded a little louder. No answer. The noise went on. My heroine got a pistol from a drawer. She went to the front door, which had narrow strips of glass on either side with no blinds. It was quite dark outside and nothing could be seen.

"If you don't stop that noise I'll shoot." The sound continued. Mother placed the end of the pistol barrel against the glass and pulled the trigger. Years later the little round hole was still there. At the gun's report the raking noise stopped, but only for a short time. We watched from the bedroom as she checked the front door latch and listened intently. Then deliberately, even calmly, the raking began again.

"It can't be a human," murmured my goddess to herself, and as she unlocked the door, we children crowded behind her. We all looked out. It wasn't human. A child's picture book had been left near the edge of the porch. Somebody had left the gate open and our private dairy, Bessie, had got into the front yard. Maybe she was hungry, but while she chewed the book with bovine deliberation her horns got entangled in the front end of a rocking chair. The motion of her chewing made the back of the chair stroke the blind. We forgave her.

As a child I could not have named another quality my mother possessed. Now, however, I know she had *aspiration,* a rare quality in Columbia, Mississippi, in those days, it seemed to me.

FROM

Local Color

PECOLIA WARNER

Pecolia Warner was a quiltmaker born in 1901 near Bentonia, Missis-
sippi, and reared in Yazoo City. Having lived in New Orleans, Chicago,
and Washington, D. C., she once declared she liked Mississippi best be-
cause "here in Mississippi, you can sit out on your porch at night and
cool off." Strongly influenced by her mother's church-going, hard-working
values and the camaraderie she saw at quilting bees, she decided as a
little girl that she would one day be a quilter, too. Deriving from the West
African textile tradition, the string quilts she designed were made from
long, thin strips of leftover material. As scholar Maude Wahlman points
out, "The pattern, called Spider Leg by Pecolia Warner's mother, is the
oldest one known for Afro-American quilters." Long thought of as a craft,
quilting has begun to be regarded as art, especially since the Smithsonian
Institution hung a quilt by Harriet Powers, a woman from Georgia born
into slavery in 1836. Because of the improvisation involved, quiltmak-
ing has been compared to jazz. Though its popularity among rural people
has diminished, quilting continues in places like Tutwiler, Mississippi,
where, under the direction of Catholic nuns, women gather to make and
sell quilts in the African-American tradition. This chapter, called "Peco-
lia Warner," is part of a compilation about folk art edited by William
Ferris. It presents Warner's own description of quiltmaking.

IF I JUST GET down to it, you know, it don't take me no time to
piece up a quilt. If I take a notion to finish something I can soon get
through with it. Some of them I can put up in just a day—like that
Rocky-Road-To-California. Or the Bear's Foot. But that Little Star, now
it took me a good bit to piece that one up, because it's in such little-
bitty pieces. Now it's tedious and it takes patience, piecing up them
little pieces like that. Took me a good while to piece it. But that's a
fancy quilt, see.

But you can sit down and make them string quilts real quick. For a
string quilt, I just commence to piecing up blocks out of strings—
they're scraps, you know, I have from sewing, and some that other people save for me. Like that Six Strips quilt I made, that ain't nothing but
a lot of strings sewn together. That way you won't throw away any pieces.
See, when you get a box full of strings, you got about five or six quilts.

With string quilts you ain't got nothing to throw away. You ain't got nothing to waste. Just like when my husband Sam was in the hospital, I pieced up four string quilts. Just going back-and-forth down there to see him I did that.

A lot of these patterns—some of the different designs of these fancy quilts—that I've done pieced up, I got them out of a quilt book. See, I borrowed this book of patterns from my sister-in-law for the summer, one time. And my mother was a schoolteacher and sometimes she'd get the newspapers after they was done with them. She'd cut the quilt patterns out of them then. The name of the quilts would be already on the pattern. That's why I knew how to name them. And now, some patterns I get is from the newspaper, too—I cut them out and fix them right on pasteboard. Anything I see on a piece of paper, I can sit down and look at it and piece it right up. I could always see a lady with a dress on and just imagine the pattern of it. I'd go home and get me a piece of paper and sit down and cut me out a pattern for a dress just like she had on. I wouldn't need no pattern to go by, no book or nothing. I'd just see somebody with something on and I'd go and make it up for myself.

But lots of them are made-up quilts. See, there's no pattern for those. I just sit down and start to sewing them up. I call them make-ups. See, that's your own mind. You make it up by looking at something and imitating it. You draw it off in your mind, see. Then, when you get it cut out you put it together and see if it's in the right shape. Practically all my quilts are make-ups. Of course some are out of that book, but after I'd pieced them up once out of the book, I just kept them patterns in my mind. I didn't need the book to look at no more. My Pineapple quilt, that's pieced up like a star, see, but it's really a Pineapple. I saw one in the grocery store—it wasn't peeled—and I just looked at it to see how it was made. I didn't have no pattern for it. I just looked at the shape of that pineapple in the store there, and tried to make me a quilt like that. See, it's easy, if you count your blocks—it's four. You get you one solid piece straight and then cut the three corner pieces.

And like that wheel [tape recorder reel] going around there—I can look at that wheel and imagine me a quilt from it. I can take me some paper and cut out a pattern and piece me up a quilt just like that. Just by looking at it I could do that. I guess I'd call it a Tape Recorder quilt. That would be my name of it, since that's it's name, ain't it? Many of my quilts I've pieced up just by looking at things that way. Now I did one of the initial of my name, Pecolia. I was just sitting around one time and didn't have nothing else to do. So I said, "I just believe I'll make me a piece that will be the start of my name." I call it a P quilt. I just took me a piece of paper and drew that P with a pencil. You make it like if it was printed somewhere. Then you take your scissors and cut that P out. You got you a pattern then, see. Then you get your material and cut it on out by the pattern. You piece your straight piece that away, and you put them two ends on it then. That gives you a P. I want to make more letters, just like I made that P. I bet I could even do the whole alphabet.

One time I said to my stepdaughter, "Theresa, I'm going to piece me up a pattern of the Star." I love the Star. It's my favorite pattern because it's so beautiful. Just about the prettiest quilt you can piece is a Star. It just seems like it always shows up more better. And I think the biggest quilt I got is that Star. I can travel so fast with it—I can sew it up fast, I mean. See, it's an eight-point star. You get the middle of that first. When you get that right, see, then you can go on. Getting that middle first, that's the main thing. If you get that one straight, then you can get the rest right. But no piece is going to fit, unless it fits directly in those points there. You've got to have all your pieces cut just alike so it'll fit. If you ain't got it cut right, it ain't going to fit. You can't *make* it fit to save your life. If you don't get them cut correct, you just have a messed-up quilt. You have to just bag it up and do it again better. Then when you get them eight pieces just alike you sew those together. Then you fit them solid blocks into each one of them corners. See, with the Star, you can make it as large as you want, and you can make it as small as you want. You can make the pieces larger, just so you have them to fit right.

I been wanting to piece quilts ever since I saw my mother doing it. I wanted that to grow up in me—how to make quilts. I thought it was fun, you know, seeing her do it. I didn't know it was as hard work as it is. But that's hard work: piecing, putting them pieces together, and quilting them. It's hard work, but I love it. That's my talent; making quilts is my calling. Of course I been doing it since I was a child, so it don't go hard with me now, anyway. I do love to do it. Two things I love to do: to cook and to piece quilts. And since I learned when I was a kid, I haven't forgotten it. I still makes them; I guess I ain't going to never stop quilting. I always say, "Well, I think I'll stop piecing for awhile." But I guess as long as I can see, I'll still be trying to thread a needle. I wouldn't want nothing to happen to my quilts after I pass on. I want people to keep them to remember me. They'll say, "Well, I knew one old lady, that's all she did was to piece quilts." I'd like them to remember me quilting.

From the Logbooks

WALTER ANDERSON

Walter Anderson was born in New Orleans in 1903. Encouraged by his mother, who studied pottery at Newcomb College School of Art, he attended Parsons Institute of Design in New York and the Pennsylvania Academy of the Fine Arts. In 1928, he became business manager for his brother's ceramics shop, Shearwater Pottery, which is still in operation in Ocean Springs, Mississippi. Soon after, he married Agnes Grinstead, who wrote a book called Approaching the Magic Hour *about their life together. Residing in Ocean Springs until his death in 1965, Anderson spent much of his time on Horn Island, recording minute happenings of the flora and fauna that would inspire his watercolors, block prints, and line images. The following entry, from a handwritten manuscript at the Mississippi Department of Archives and History, is taken from his unpublished logbooks of the late 1940s. In this meditation on the pelican, Anderson expresses one of the great themes of his work—the interrelatedness of all things.*

AFTER YOU HAVE lived on the island for awhile there comes a time when you realize that the pelican holds everything for you. It has the song of the thrush, the form and understanding of man, the tenderness and gentleness of the dove, the mystery and dynamic quality of the nightjar and the potential qualities of all life.

In a word you lose your heart to it. It becomes your child and the hope and future of the world depend upon it.

You share in all of its reactions and conditions of life, you awake with it, you feel the change from the cave of sleep to the beginning of consciousness and desire. You hear its cries of hunger with the need to cry to the first mover, the primum mobile, the sun and light of the world for whatever it is that you need yourself—food, light, warmth, change.

The cloud which comes between you and the rising sun is the mother, the voice of the wind in the rushing squall is the sound of her flapping wings and the deluge of rain and ecstatic satisfaction of desire is the rush of warm food from her throat and the cloud past, and the burst of light which comes is the realization of day and light and life and the joy of living which has come and gone with the cloud of the mother and the satisfaction of desire.

The individual is created, but as the ecstasy passes, order comes and with it consciousness of number and the splitting of the single ego into thousands of young living beings, all alike in their condition, heads all turned with backs to the sun vibrating pouches, open beaks and the day has begun. The pelican strata on the island in the gulf life has begun.

Below them, supporting them, are the tough and twisted mangroves also a survival over seemingly impossible conditions of life collecting and holding their own earth in the face of year after year of attacking ocean, they by an incomprehensible contradiction manage to give off an atmosphere of pervading sweetness so that literally each small yellow white blossom holds a drop of pure nectar so that a cluster taken into the mouth will have an unmistakeable taste of honey. Tenacious of life they propagate themselves in at least three ways, by division from branches, layering, by seed, and by tubers rising from their roots. Above the twisted and knotted stems, which suggest Burnham beeches, in their contorted position and development, anyone walking through them is astonished and pained by their toughness and unwillingness to give place. They have a singularly agreeable and conventional arrangement of foliage, the leaves growing as an obvious development of the branches and not fastened like Christmas tree ornaments at the ends of twigs.

They grow from three to fifteen feet in light on the island although I have heard that they grew even taller in the tropics. Those of four or five feet with flattened tops are the ones most frequently chosen by pelicans for nesting places.

Below them another strata of life lives and moves among the mangrove stems; these are the turtles, with delicately decorated garments ingeniously spotted and painted, reminding one of a Dulac illustration and are constant with the other flora and fauna of the island.

They live horizontally, move horizontally. Their world, the world of the birds, is above them. They live in the twilight beneath the mangroves. They take their time from the tide which changes and from the sun which to them is constant. Above them is the city of the birds which comes between them and the sun. The rush and flap of wings means another messenger from the sun. They are condemned to their horizontal way of life, rejoice in their limitations and watch their world grow smaller with each new discovery instead of larger as with the great like Michelangelo and Alexander whose world grew just beyond the reach of their outstretched hands. . . .

Marie Hull: 1890–1980

M A R Y D . G A R R A R D

*Marie Atkinson was born in Summit, Mississippi, in 1890, and moved
with her family to Jackson in 1906. Having graduated from Belhaven
College, she attended the Pennsylvania Academy of the Fine Arts in Philadelphia. After her marriage to the architect Emmett Johnston Hull, she
taught, painted, and exhibited her work in New York, San Francisco,
and Chicago, winning numerous prizes. She studied old masters in
Spain and France, and she and her husband traveled widely together,
often by train at night to maximize time spent in museums. She was
influenced by such well-known teachers as John F. Carlson, Robert Reid,
Frank Dumond, and Robert Vonnoh. In the following preface to the catalog for the Marie Hull exhibition at Delta State University in 1990,
Mary Garrard, art historian and professor of art history at American
University in Washington, D. C., commends Hull for her career as both
painter and teacher. Garrard points out that Hull's major strength as a
painter was in her ability to adjust her style to the subject in such diverse
images as white sharecroppers, black servants, dramatic landscapes, Romanesque churches, and stylized flamingoes.*

A L T H O U G H I A M an art historian with a special interest in women
artists, my chief reason for wanting to write this preface is that, like
Marie Hull, I am a native Mississippian. Unlike her, I have long lived
away from Mississippi, but there is a rough parallel between us which
draws me to her life. Just as her artistic imagination was fed by contact
with European and northern American cities, my own writing and
thought are continually nourished by my relationship with Mississippi.
And so there is something I understand about her and about being a
kind of cultural agent, on a very personal level.

In the early 20th-century, when few artists or art students crossed the
Mason-Dixon line unless to stay, Marie Hull's pattern of activity was
unusual. Here was a painter who studied anatomy, landscape, portrai-
ture at the Pennsylvania Academy, the Art Students' League and elsewhere, with some of the best teachers in America (John F. Carlson,
Robert Reid, Frank Dumond, and Robert Vonnoh); who spent eight
months in Spain and France, studying old masters and contemporary
art while producing a staggering number of paintings and watercol-

ors—yet who returned to work and teach in Jackson, Mississippi, for the next half-century, all the while travelling and exhibiting in other parts of the country.

Her cross-pollinating career was even more exceptional for a Southern woman. As Jessie Poesch's research suggests, female artists of Hull's generation typically practiced their art in the region where they were trained—Helen Turner and Selma Burke went East; Alice Ravanel Smith stayed in the South. Kate Freeman Clark studied, worked, and exhibited in New York City, but stopped painting when she returned to Holly Springs, Mississippi. Josephine Crawford and Angela Gregory studied and traveled abroad, but didn't teach art when they returned to New Orleans. By contrast, Marie Hull made an artistic reputation both in and outside the South (roughly half her solo and group exhibitions were in non-Southern sites), brought avant-garde ideas into her painting and her teaching, was a charter member and early president of the Mississippi Art Association, and became an active force in the growth and development of art in Mississippi.

What is there in such an artistic career that is distinctively female? On the surface, very little, unless one counts that, had she been a man, with her talent and energy she might have taught in a university or perhaps chaired an art department. Hull's work is not sex-stereotyped. Her artistic influences were largely from male artists or from masculine-associated styles: Cezanne in the early years; Cubism (and her own student Andrew Bucci) in the middle years; and in her late works, Abstract Expressionists, such as Kline or Baziotes. The very fact of her ability to change her style frequently is something we associate with the masculine avant-garde. Picasso comes to mind, and Hull's series of flower paintings, each in a single color key, reminds me of Picasso's experiments in his early "periods."

Yet we do not see here the usual sort of style development, that sort of logical progression that art historians readily discern, in which one idea leads to another to form a personal narrative and to reveal the artist's private journey to transcendence. Hull's style changes appear to be motivated instead by a wish to adapt to purpose and place. Somber, monumental realism is used to dignify images of white sharecroppers or the artist's black servants; intense colors and vibrant brushstrokes present a landscape as a felt experience; solid drawing anatomizes a bowl of flowers. Romanesque churches call forth abstract geometry, while flamingoes demand the stylized arabesques of art nouveau. In her late paintings, such as Mississippi River or Mississippi Spring, Hull's response to particular places conditions even the most contemporary of styles. She makes inspired use of Rothko's broad horizontal banding, giving it 'a local habitation and a name,' to convey the enormous weight of a Delta sky, its pressure upon the earth, the tense stability of the seasonal cycle.

We might see Marie Hull's adjustment of style to subject as a female trait since accommodation and flexibility are often attributed to "women's ways." Yet inasmuch as these are also civilized virtues, we might equally consider the kind of style change a rebuke to art-world bad manners—such as the assertion of personal artistic ego over every other concern. In her reflection of other values—attachment to community, to teacher-student relationships, to place, to the ideal of "quality"—Hull is surely as quintessentially Southern as she is female. Nevertheless, I think that her career as influential artist and teacher in the South is the more exemplary in gender terms. For, given the social constraints on women in her day, her influence was perhaps possible only in the context of a power traditionally handed over in America to women: the education of young minds in the civilizing and world-expanding realms of art and music.

Marie Hull's first teacher, Aileen Phillips, was in 1910 the only trained art teacher in Jackson. She had studied in Europe and at the Pennsylvania Academy. In about 1947, in Indianola, I took my first art lessons from Mrs. Ada Neill, our own "lady art teacher." I wish I knew where she had studied, but I don't. The only cue is my remarkable ability to produce a Corot-like landscape in pastel at the age of ten. The imprint of the teaching of Aileen Phillips and Marie Hull may have been less literal than that of Mrs. Neill, yet these women shared with each other and many more the capacity to create, to inspire creativity, and to bring new aesthetic ideas to communities across the country.

It is impossible to overestimate the importance of such a contribution. It may not have been uniquely female, but it was very likely predominantly so. When the role of women in American art education is fully studied, Marie Hull will undoubtedly find her place in that history, for her work as an art teacher is an achievement that not only complements but equals her considerable talent and success as a painter.

The Arrival of B. B. King

CHARLES SAWYER

In his authorized biography, journalist/photographer Charles Sawyer traces B. B. King's arduous journey from the Mississippi cotton fields to fame as a blues singer in Memphis and beyond. Born near Itta Bena, Mississippi, on September 16, 1925, Riley B. King lived for a time with his grandmother in Kilmichael, Mississippi, and sang at the Holiness Church where the preacher Archie Fair taught him chords on his electric guitar. When Riley's mother realized she was dying, she called her nine-year-old son to her bedside and admonished him to be kind to his fellow human beings. The following excerpt, from the chapter entitled "Mississippi Share-Croppers," picks up King's life when, at seventeen, he moved from Kilmichael, where he had worked for a man named Flake Cartledge, to Indianola for better pay—a dollar a day. He soon started up a band called the Famous John Gospel Singers with his cousin, Birkett Davis. He gained a foothold as a singer in 1947 when he went to work for a new black radio station, WDIA, where he was called the Pepticon Boy because of the health tonic he advertised. He later became known as the Beale Street Blues Boy, then simply B. B., so named for the Memphis street filled with nightclubs that nurtured many famous blues singers. With the popularity of his song "Three O'Clock Blues," King's career was launched. In the 1950s he and his band often gave three hundred performances a year on the "chitlin' circuit," a hardship made almost unendurable by Jim Crow laws that kept them out of "whites only" restrooms on the road. King performs annually at a concert in his honor in Indianola, Mississippi, where friends note that he has not forgotten his mother's instructions to be kind.

BIRKETT DAVIS, Riley's cousin and former singer with Riley's gospel group before Birkett left Kilmichael, told Riley about the better cotton farming down in the Delta and the day wages available there when he visited him at the Cartledge place in 1942. In the back of his mind, Riley was thinking about forming a new and better singing group with cousin Birkett. He had bought a guitar from a Kilmichael man, Denzil Tidwell, for $2.50 borrowed from Flake Cartledge, and continued singing spirituals with his chum Walter Doris, Jr., who often came to his cabin. In the winter of 1942–43, he wrote to Cousin Birkett asking him to help him move to the Delta. His cousin came to the rescue in a borrowed car, carrying sufficient cash to pay what Riley owed Flake Cartledge. In the spring of 1943, not quite eighteen years old, Riley moved to Indianola, Mississippi, in the heart of the Delta.

The Delta was just coming into its full power as one of the richest agricultural regions in the world. Most of the Delta was reclaimed from swampland, canebrakes, and pine forests. In the first third of the nineteenth century, it had been a wilderness; only a small portion was arable. Now, in the middle third of the twentieth century, the land was cleared, the swamps dried up, and the danger of flooding greatly reduced by work under the Flood Control Act of 1928, which diverted the Mississippi River in many places to eliminate the tortuous crooks and loops. The shortened river deepened its bed, lowering the water level by up to seven to fifteen feet. By 1943, when Riley came looking for work, a majority of Delta acres were in crops, and most of it was in cotton.

Riley got work with an Indianola planter, Johnson Barrett, who owned slightly less than 350 acres and rented more than he owned, for a total of around 1,000 acres under cultivation. This was a modest operation, hardly qualifying to fit the romantic image of the plantation as an empire of 2,000 acres or more spreading out for miles in every direction from the pillared manse. The Barrett plantation was a farm, larger than the average (56 per cent of all Delta farms of the time were less than 80 acres), but considerably smaller than the truly large plantations of 2,000 acres and more which controlled 21.5 per cent of the arable Delta land. Barrett was called a "planter" by custom, but that name calls up images quite different and less appropriate than does the term "farmer," which pictures him in bib overalls rather than wearing a white suit and holding a mint julep on the manor porch. The plantation in Indianola, comprised of four contiguous tracts bought from four different owners in 1936, was not the first attempt by Barrett to establish a substantial farm in Mississippi. In the years before, he had twice gone broke; and a third time, in 1935, he had been burned out of his house in Philip, Mississippi.

Working the Barrett plantation in Indianola were roughly fifty families, all but two of them farming on shares—the other two were cash tenants—plus six tractors and six mule teams. All these were under the direction of a black man, Booker Baggett, who had started working for Barrett in 1940 as a tractor driver. Baggett had worked his way up to a position of responsibility unprecedented for a black man in that area of the Delta. When Barrett fired his nephew for mismanaging the little general store he kept on the plantation to provide for the families farming his land, Barrett went out to the field and called his top hand, Baggett, off the tractor and told him to take over running the store. Inside two months, Baggett brought the store into the black, and Barrett was so impressed that he promoted him to plantation manager. Both the pay—$2.50 a day—plus housing, food, and an automobile, and the responsibility were unheard of for a black man at the time. His responsibility went far beyond what was ordinarily given to the black "straw boss," also known as the H.N.I.C. for "Head Nigger In Charge." He kept the plantation accounts and was authorized to do all hiring and firing, to make withdrawals from the bank, and to charge equipment and materials with local merchants. Often whites came on the plantation and refused to take Baggett's word that he was the boss—only to be sent back to him by Barrett who told them unequivocally, "Booker's in full charge." It took a cool hand on Baggett's part to handle such people when they came back with their feathers ruffled.

Like his benefactor in Kilmichael, Flake Cartledge, Riley's new employer, planter Johnson Barrett, was an ordinary man in most regards, with a few progressive ideas about race. Barrett was a plain-spoken, self-made man who was easily irritated by what he considered needless mistakes, and expected his employees to work with unflagging strength and no complaints. He took an abiding interest in the welfare of his employees, and was known to write off the debts of his sharecroppers in bad years. At the same time, some tenants believed that in good years Barrett gave them less than the true market price he received for their share. According to one employee, who saw Barrett's record books, their suspicions were well founded. Among blacks in the Indianola area, Johnson Barrett was reputed to be unusually liberal for the time, yet no saint either.

Fifteen and twenty years before Riley arrived in Indianola, two events took place that profoundly changed plantation management, and had a subtle but important effect on his life personally. These were the mass production and marketing of row tractors by International Harvester, begun in 1922, and the design of a moistened-spindle mechanical cotton picker. These two machines—the row tractor and the mechanical cotton picker—changed cotton farming from a labor-intensive to a capital-intensive business, and abolished small-plot sharecropping by hand. The change took thirty years to accomplish, and Riley arrived at the Barrett plantation just as the swing was gathering momentum.

Riley worked on the Barrett plantation as both a sharecropper and a tractor driver, for which he was paid day wages of $1. As a tractor driver, he had a skill—albeit a modest one—though less modest in those days than it is now. He no longer worked with his muscle alone. Moreover, he was especially good with his machine and became highly valued by both Barrett and Booker Baggett. Before many months had passed, Riley had a crop in the ground, a skilled job working for a tough, fair-minded farmer under a black man, a new singing group, and a sweetheart. The singing group was a five-man chorus including Riley and cousin Birkett, led by John Matthews. They called themselves "The Famous St. John Gospel Singers" and patterned themselves after well-known groups like The Famous Golden Gate Quartet, The Trumpeteers, and The Dixie Hummingbirds. Riley accompanied them on his guitar when they sang at dozens on dozens of local churches. Occasionally, they gave live performances broadcast on WGRM in Greenwood, Mississippi. Meanwhile, Riley was moonlighting on his spiritual music by playing blues on street corners Saturday nights. (Blues was not a new musical interest for him; he had listened to blues records back in Kilmichael and had heard bluesman Bukka White, his mother's cousin, when Bukka came on rare occasions to visit his kin in Kilmichael.) He discovered that by using his weekly wage as traveling money to go to other Delta towns and cities, he could double or triple his net profit working the streets, singing blues and playing his guitar. His profits singing blues, plus his exposure to many leading blues and jazz musicians who played in Indianola, turned his musical interest away from spirituals.

Indianola was a main stop on the network of roadhouses and juke joints that dotted the landscape of the Deep South. The local joint there was run by Johnny Jones and called simply "Jones' Night Spot." At Jones', he saw Sonny Boy Williamson, Robert "Junior" Lockwood, and Louis Jordan, to name a few of the leading black musicians that passed through on the "chitlin circuit," as it was called. He managed to strike up an acquaintance with some of them and became afflicted with the malaise that strikes every provincial youth who comes in contact with highly mobile outsiders: envy of their sophisticated ways, their style of dress and, in this case, their musical proficiency and versatility. Riley's feet began to itch, his ears to burn, his heart to pound. He began practicing blues in earnest, listening to recordings purchased from a local fix-it shop proprietor named Willie Dotson. From the very first his taste was eclectic, running a spectrum from old-style bluesman Blind Lemon Jefferson to the pioneering jazz guitarist, Charlie Christian.

In 1943, soon after coming to Indianola, Riley registered for the draft and in 1944 was called to Camp Shelby for his physical exam. He stayed several days before being pronounced physically fit for service and allowed to return home. Johnson Barrett was short of hands then and was concerned that he not lose a good tractor driver; he told Riley he would apply to the draft board for an occupational deferment on his behalf and advised him that getting married would improve his chances of being deferred. Riley promptly married his sweetheart, Martha Denton, on November 26, 1944. He was nineteen; she was slightly younger. Riley's deferment as an employee in an essential industry was granted, and Riley and his new bride moved in with cousin Birkett Davis. Like millions of other men of draft age, Riley faced the alternative of remaining at his job—like it or not—or facing the draft. It was an unpleasant predicament for many, but people accepted such unpleasant circumstances as normal for wartime and not an injustice made especially for them. Riley's case was no different from the cases of steelworkers in Pittsburgh or doctors, providing medical care over vast remote areas of the country, except in one respect: he was a sharecropper, now obliged by the conditions of his deferment to go on sharecropping for the duration of the war. At times he felt that his status was little different than that of the convict laborers employed in public works projects, though he realized his conditions were dramatically better than those poor souls. It might never occur to the deferred steelworker in Pittsburgh and the G.P. in Idaho that they were indentured servants; but to black sharecroppers in Mississippi, deferment from the draft sometimes looked like a degenerate form of slavery.

While he waited out the war, Riley's musical ambition grew steadily, fueled by the radio programs he heard broadcast from Memphis. At this time, there still was no major radio station in the country that tailored its programming to black audiences, but stations KFFA in Helena, Arkansas, KWEM in West Memphis, Arkansas, and WHBQ in Memphis, Tennessee, had occasional programs of black music, usually performed live in the radio studio or at talent night on the stage of one Memphis theater or another. When he was released from the hold of selective service, Riley tried vigorously to convince the St. John's Gospel Singers to leave Indianola in search of fortune. Soon it became clear that if he was to make the break, it would have to be alone; his singing partners had families and worried, with good reason, that their children might suffer from their ambitions if they joined Riley on the road. Martha King, Riley's wife, had suffered a miscarriage and they were still childless.

When Riley boasted of his musical ambitions to the other tractor drivers on the Barrett plantation, Booker Baggett baited him: "You'll never do any of those things, Riley, so long as the earth stands."

"Mr. Booker," Riley replied, "someday I'm going to drive up in a brand-new car and give you a dollar. Then you'll know I wasn't jivin' when I said I'd do these things."

Memphis stood as a beacon. It was a main center of black entertainment in America; more active, perhaps, even than New Orleans, and unlike New Orleans to the south, it was a stepping stone to the North. Memphis, only 120 miles north of Indianola, must have seemed as though it was off the edge of the earth to a young black man of twenty who had never set foot out of Mississippi. It stood there hounding him to come: the southernmost outpost of the elusive mysterious North, center for black nightlife, home of Beale Street, where the best bluesmen alive played in crowded dives.

In May 1946, around the time when his cousin Birkett and the other sharecroppers on the Barrett plantation drew their first furnish of the season, the final straw came Riley's way and sent him north. It happened on payday, when Riley put his tractor under the shed for the night. Impatient to get his pay, he bounded off the machine as it came to rest; but the hot engine gave a few extra churns, and the tractor lurched forward, knocking the tall exhaust stack against the edge of the roof and breaking it off. Realizing that planter Barrett would be furious, he dashed home, told Martha to move in with her relatives, that he was going straight to Memphis, slung his guitar over his back, and walked out to Highway 49 without collecting his pay. Along the way, he met a pal, Walter Kirkpatrick, and persuaded him to come along. Riley carried his guitar and had $2.50 in his pocket. Walter had half a sausage for the two of them. Riley had only the vaguest idea of what to do once in Memphis. His plan boiled down to one thing: find cousin Bukka. He had no address for bluesman Bukka White (who was actually his mother's cousin). In fact, he wasn't even positive Bukka was still living in Memphis. But that was where he'd last had word from him. Twenty years old, Riley King left the Barrett plantation, heading north up the Mississippi Delta, bound for Memphis.

A Feast Made for Laughter

CRAIG CLAIBORNE

Born in Sunflower, Mississippi, in 1920, Craig Claiborne has written dozens of cookbooks and was food editor for the New York Times *for over thirty years. A graduate of the Lausanne Professional School of the Swiss Hotel Keepers Association, he has been described as a maverick who elevated and widened America's culinary taste. In this cookbook/memoir Claiborne credits his mother, Kathleen, and his sister, Augusta, for his gift. Mrs. Claiborne opened a popular boardinghouse in Indianola during the twenties, a time of economic difficulties. It was said that "Miss Kathleen's" food was so delicious that bachelors shunned marriage to continue eating there. As recounted here, the scholar John Dollard lived at the boardinghouse while researching* Caste and Class in a Southern Town. *Claiborne vividly describes the ambiance of his mother's table and analyzes the three distinct categories of southern cooking: soul, Creole, and French. In the following excerpt from section one, called "A Feast Made for Laughter," he tells the stories of an untraditional Thanksgiving at the boardinghouse and of how Miss Kathleen came to be featured in the May 1948 issue of* Liberty *magazine.*

THERE IS ONE aroma that, more than any other, rekindles concrete thoughts of my mother in the kitchen. This is the smell of chopped onions, chopped celery, chopped green pepper, and a generous amount of finely minced garlic. This was the basis for, it seems to me in recollection, at least half of the hundreds of dishes that she prepared, and it is a distinctly southern smell. (A great southern chef, Paul Prudhomme of New Orleans, once told me that in Cajun and creole kitchens, chopped onions, celery, and green peppers are referred to as the Holy Trinity.)

And there is one dish, her own creation, and using this base, that I recall most vividly. This was chicken spaghetti, which she almost invariably made for special occasions—birthdays, holidays, Sundays. The boarders and her own family loved it and it has remained throughout my many years in the world of food a special favorite.

There were two holidays each year—Christmas and Thanksgiving—when my mother stipulated that meals would not be served to boarders, all of whom went to visit relatives or friends anyway.

I remember one nonturkey Thanksgiving that came about because the three children in the family announced that they were bored with a daily diet of poultry. A vote was taken. Almost in unison we asked for Mother's baked spaghetti. On that day we had it fresh from the oven for the midday Thanksgiving dinner; reheated for supper.

When the vegetables were cooked (they always remained al dente) a little ground beef was added and a tomato sauce containing cream, Worcestershire sauce, and Tabasco sauce. Worcestershire sauce and Tabasco sauce were primary ingredients in my mother's kitchen. Once the meat and tomato sauce were finished, the time came for the assembly of the dish. A layer of sauce was topped with a layer of cooked spaghetti or vermicelli, a layer of shredded chicken, and a layer of grated Cheddar cheese. The layers were repeated to the brim of an enormous roasting pan, ending with a layer of cheese. The pan was placed in the oven and baked until it was bubbling throughout and golden brown on top. The spaghetti was served in soup bowls with grated Parmesan cheese and two curious, but oddly complimentary side dishes—sliced garlic pickles and potato chips.

In my childhood, it would never have occurred to anyone to analyze or categorize the kind of food we dined on from my mother's kitchen. It was simply "southern cooking." In retrospect, it fell into three categories—soul food, which is a blend of African and American Indian; creole cookery, which is a marriage of innocent Spanish and bastardized French; and pure French, desserts mostly, from the first edition of *The Boston Cooking-School Cook Book.* To my mind that book was, in its original concept, the first great cookbook in America. For years it had no peer (Mrs. Rorer's works notwithstanding) and it was my mother's kitchen bible.

My mother had an incredible aptitude in her ability to "divine" the ingredients of one dish or another. She could dine in New Orleans and come back to reproduce on her own table the likes of oysters Rockefeller, oysters Bienville, the creole version (so different from the original French) of rémoulade sauce with shrimp.

There was another advantage to the old-fashioned southern kitchen: the talent and palate of the American Negro. I am convinced that, given the proper training in the kitchen of a great French restaurant, any American black with cooking in his or her soul would be outstanding.

With rare exceptions, all the servants in our kitchen arrived with a full knowledge of soul cooking, which is broad in scope. Essentially, it encompasses the use of all parts of the pig, more often than not boiled, plain, or with other ingredients. Pig's feet, pig's tails, hog jowl, and that most soul of all foods, chitterlings, the small intestines of pigs. It has always amused me, since I first encountered the regional cooking of France, to know that one of that nation's most prized and delectable of sausages—called andouille or andouillettes—is nothing more than chitterlings blended with various spices, onions or shallots, white wine, and so on, and stuffed into casings. For what it's worth, a New Year's party without grilled andouillettes in my house is as unthinkable as an absence of at least a couple of bottles of champagne. Once a year in my childhood home, Mother had a chitterling supper. Chitterlings, cooked and served with vinegar and hot pepper are, to some noses, a bit odoriferous. Therefore, the boarders were advised that they were invited to the chitterling supper, but if they found the aromas less than fastidious, they were cordially invited to find another place to dine.

The standard items of soul food that appeared almost daily at my mother's table were one form of greens or another, always cooked with pieces of pork, the feet, hocks, belly, and so on, sometimes salted, sometimes smoked. The greens were of a common garden variety, such as mustard greens, collard greens, and turnip greens. These would be put on to boil with a great quantity of water and salt and allowed to cook for hours. Once cooked, the liquid is much treasured by southern palates. It is called "pot likker" and you sip it like soup with corn bread. If you want to be fancy, you can always make corn meal dumplings to float on top of the greens. Black eye peas are also a regional treasure, some people think the finest of all staples. These, too, are cooked for a long while (preferably from a fresh state; if not, frozen; if not frozen, dried; and if none of these, canned).

One of the most distinguished roomers and boarders in my mother's house was a scholarly gentleman, well known in academic circles, the late Dr. John Dollard, a highly praised Yale psychologist and social scientist. Dr. Dollard had come to Indianola to do research on a book called *Caste and Class in a Southern Town* and with what might have been an uncanny sense of direction or perception, had chosen my house as his base of operation.

Dr. Dollard, a patient, kindly, amiable man was, of course, a Yankee and thus had a "funny accent." The other boarders did not take kindly to him for no other reason than that he was an "outsider." In the beginning he criticized the cooking of the greens, complaining that there was not a vitamin left in the lot. And as a result of his well-intentioned explanations and at the base encouragement of the other boarders, my mother willingly committed one of the most wicked acts of her life. Dr. Dollard was placed at a bridge table, covered, of course, with linen and set with sterling, and he was served a mess of raw greens that he ate with considerable and admirable composure and lack of resentment. Always the detached and critical observer, I found my mother's role in this little game almost intolerable, although I said nothing.

Odd coincidences have occurred often in my life. One day, a decade or so ago, I wandered into the photographic studio where portraits bearing the title *New York Times Studio* were taken. I glanced at an assignment sheet and saw the name John Dollard, Yale.

As I walked out, John walked in.

"John," I said, "I'm Craig Claiborne."

"How's your mother?" he asked. "She's a great woman."

With one possible exception, the dishes prepared by my mother that I liked best were the creole foods. As I have noted, to this day, like the madeleines of Proust's childhood, I can smell chopped onions, celery, and green peppers, cooking together in butter or oil. This, to my mind, is the creole base, and it is a combination that often perfumes my own kitchen.

My mother would purchase one of Mr. Colotta's (Mr. Colotta was the only fish dealer for miles around) finest red snappers from the Gulf Coast brought in that morning, encased in ice, and weighing almost twenty pounds. A fish that size would barely fit in the oven. It would be baked and basted with oil and the creole base and it was as succulent and tender as anything I've ever tasted here or abroad. Her shrimp creole with the same base was robust and glorious.

It would be easy to recite the entire roster of her creole and other southern specialties. A remarkable Brunswick stew, an incredibly good barbecue sauce with tomato ketchup, Worcestershire sauce, and vinegar as a base. She made a delectable assortment of gumbos—crab, oyster, and plain okra. (The word gumbo, I was to learn in later life, derived from the Bantu word for okra.) Her deviled crab was spicy, rich, and irresistible. . . .

Beaten biscuits are a blend of flour, lard, and butter that is worked together by hand. You then add enough milk to make a stiff dough, which is rolled out and literally beaten with any handy sturdy instrument. It might be a rolling pin, a shortened broom handle, even a hatchet or ax. You beat the dough, folding it over as you work, for the better part of an hour until it blisters. The dough is then rolled out, cut into small round biscuits, and pricked in the center with a fork. . . .

There are dozens of dishes that come to my mind when I think of my mother's kitchen—fantastic caramels, divinity fudge, a luscious coconut cake with meringue and fresh coconut topping, the best, richest pecan pie in the world, incredible fried chicken, great shrimp rémoulade, chicken turnovers in an awesomely rich pastry served with a cream sauce—but two of the dishes that she made for very "party" occasions had a curious appeal for my childhood palate. Sunday dinner, which was served at twelve-thirty in the afternoon, was always paramount among our weekly meals and if she wished to offer the boarders an uncommon treat she would serve them as a first course toast points topped with canned, drained white asparagus spears, over which was spooned a hot tangy Cheddar cheese sauce. This dish was generally garnished with strips of pimiento.

Another for which she was renowned was a three-layered salad composed of a bottom layer of lime gelatin chilled until set, a middle layer of well-seasoned cream cheese blended with gelatin and chilled until set, and a top layer of delicately firm tomato aspic. The salad was cut into cubes, garnished with greens, and topped with a dab of mayonnaise.

Years later, when I was working for the American Broadcasting Company in public relations, I knew a reporter for the old, once thriving monthly called *Liberty* magazine. Her name was Beulah Karney and she was food editor of that journal. She once asked me casually if I could name the best cook in the South and I specified my mother. Beulah traveled to Mississippi and interviewed "Miss Kathleen." In the May 1948 issue there appeared an article entitled "The Best Cook in Town" and it described my mother's boardinghouse. Pursuant to a good deal of recent research, I found that issue in the New York Public Library.

One sentence stated "the six paying guests, all bachelors, said there wasn't much point in getting married when Miss Kathleen's food was so good." Four recipes were printed, including one for Miss Kathleen's Party Salad, that three-layered affair.

After World War II when I had settled in Chicago, my mother wrote in a school child's composition book a collection of her favorite recipes. They are in her own handwriting. There are recipes for Karo Caramels (The Candy You All Liked and All the Others So Much), Galatoire's Trout Marguery, Oysters Rockefeller, Mrs. Robert Johnson's Rice Pudding (Do You Remember The Lovely Meal We Had With Them In Chicago), Great Grandmother Craig's Grated Potato Pudding, Italian Ravioli, Grand Hot Cakes, Sister's Sausage, Charlotte Russe, and a Craig Wedding Punch, the recipe for which was more than two hundred years old.

I Dream a World

LEONTYNE PRICE

Leontyne Price is one of Mississippi's international greats. She was born in 1927 to a black midwife in Laurel, Mississippi, and set out on her road to opera stardom when she was given a toy piano at age five, as she recalls here in the chapter entitled "Leontyne Price." With the aid of the Alexander F. Chisholm family, she was able to attend the Juilliard School of Music on a scholarship after graduating from Central State College in Ohio. In 1949, at age twenty-one, she sang to an overflow crowd in the Victory Room of the Heidelberg Hotel in Jackson, causing the sponsors to quickly arrange a second sitting. Highlights of her spectacular career include the female lead in Porgy and Bess, *Cio-Cio-San in* Madame Butterfly, *and the title role in Richard Strauss's* Ariadne and Naxos. *After her performance in* Aida *at La Scala in Milan in 1958, she received twenty-one curtain calls. On January 27, 1961, she made her Metropolitan Opera debut as Leonora in Verdi's* Il Trovatore, *the moment she describes as her proudest. In October of that year she became the first African-American to open the season at the Metropolitan in her role as Minnie in Puccini's* La Fanciulla del West.

MY MOTHER is responsible for having delivered more babies than any midwife in the history of Jones County, Mississippi. To this date, she is my greatest inspiration.

The way I was taught, being black was a plus, always. Being a human being, being in America, and being black, all three were the greatest things that could happen to you. The combination was unbeatable.

I received a toy piano for Christmas at the age of five or six. I had an awful lot of attention. I was center stage from the time I received that toy piano. I felt a musical sense of direction. I had the disease then, I could tell, because you really have to be a monster very early.

I think we performers are monsters. We are a totally different, far-out race of people. I totally and completely admit, with no qualms at all, my egomania, my selfishness, coupled with a really magnificent voice.

In some of my operatic roles—maybe the strength of my portrayal of Aida—I reveal the wonderful thing that it is to be a black princess.

My mother took me to see Marian Anderson. [Anderson was the first black soloist to sing with the Metropolitan Opera Company in New York in 1955.] When I saw this wonderful woman come from the wings in this white satin dress, I knew instantly: one of these days, I'm going to come out of the wings. I don't know what color the dress is going to be but I'm going to be center stage, right there, where I saw her. The light dawned. It was a magic moment.

My proudest moment, operatically speaking, was my debut at the Metropolitan. It was my first real victory, my first unqualified acceptance as an American, as a human being, as a black, as an artist, the whole thing.

I was the first black diva that was going to hang on. My being prepared is the reason I didn't go away. That is really the substance of my pioneering. Marian [Anderson] had opened the door. I kept it from closing again.

I sang seven roles my first season at the Metropolitan Opera, I was that prepared. My first invitation to the Metropolitan I refused, because I was not.

Art is the only thing you cannot punch a button for. You must do it the old-fashioned way. Stay up and really burn the midnight oil. There are no compromises.

Accomplishments have no color.

The Prices and the Chisolms have been friends all our lives. Those two families helped to bridge the gap in Laurel. My aunt was in the Chisolms' domestic service for fifty years. My parents were married on their estate. After I graduated with a teacher's degree from Central State College in Ohio, they were my sponsors for my New York studies at Juilliard.

Nobody ever thought of a career, nobody had that much money to gamble on it, which is the reason that some young people even now don't go into the classical field unless they have a sponsor. It's too difficult, too dangerous.

My father never understood it but he thought it was the most glorious thing he had ever heard in his life, that his baby girl would have this ability to understand all this stuff.

I don't love anything more than hearing my own voice. It's a personal adoration.

Listening to my recordings is like filing your pores with inspiration, and where better to get it from than yourself, because that substance is a combination of everyone who contributed something, your mama, your papa, the community, your teachers, everybody and everything. Applause is the fulfillment. From Mississippi to the Met. That's the pinnacle. That forty-two minute ovation [for *Aida*] was like having climbed the mountain. . . .

Once you get on stage, everything is right. I feel the most beautiful, complete, fulfilled. I think that's why, in the case of noncompromising career women, parts of our personal lives don't work out. One person can't give you the feeling that thousands of people give you.

I have never given all of myself, even vocally, to anyone. I was taught to sing on your interest, not your capital.

I do like being in competition with me.

I never thought any institution was more important than myself. I think that happens, for example, in Hollywood. You let the institution take you over and you are vulnerable, which means that when they get ready, they can discard you.

I wasn't uncomfortable singing at the inaugural ceremony for my friend William Winter, the governor of Mississippi, because I thought I belonged there. It was as much my capital as his.

We should not have a tin cup out for something as important as the arts in this country, the richest in the world. Creative artists are always begging, but always being used when it's time to show us at our best.

You should always know when you're shifting gears in life. You should leave your era, it should never leave you.

Now I'm doing recitals, orchestra things, master classes. If somebody thinks I can still sing, I've got a wheelchair in the wings. But I have not retired. From pressure I have retired, but I'm not ever going to retire from anything else.

The Soul of Southern Cooking

KATHY STARR

Before starting her own catering business in Hollandale, Mississippi, Kathy Starr was a nurse. In her cookbook, The Soul of Southern Cooking, *she provides us with tasty recipes and a glimpse into the life of her great-grandparents, who were sharecroppers. Of special interest is her grandmother, who was one of the first black postmistresses in Mississippi and later ran a cafe called the Fair Deal. As Vertamae Grosvenor says in her foreword to this cookbook, African-American soul food is uniquely southern; it is "a good-eating, creative, imaginative cookery, generous and earthy like the people who created it." The following selections from Starr's introduction and a section called "Spring" make abundantly clear why this cuisine is rightfully called* soul *food.*

M Y L O V E O F cooking started early. I was learning from my grand-mama by the time I was five years old, which was in the late fifties. She had a cafe known as the Fair Deal, and it was located over on Blue Front, across the railroad track in Hollandale. Blue Front was a string of little cafes where everybody gathered on the weekend. It was the only place blacks had to go, to get rid of the blues after a week's hard work in the cotton fields. Everybody lived for Saturday night to go to Blue Front and get a whole- or a half-order of buffalo fish or a bowl of chitterlings. People didn't like catfish then like they do now. As soon as the fishermen came by with the big buffaloes, Uncle Ira would get out in the back and start cleaning them.

The every-Saturday-night meal and the prices during my time were:

> Chitterlings and Hot Sauce (50 cents a bowl)
> Fried Buffalo Fish (60 cents; $^1/_2$ order, 35 cents)
> Flatdogs (15 cents)
> Hamburgers (25 cents)
> Regular dinners ($1.35)

My grandmama, who everybody called "Miz Bob," would always start a Saturday night with one hundred pounds of chitterlings and seventy-five pounds of buffalo. Once the people started drinking, the hunger would start, and before 11:00 p.m. all of the fish and chitterlings would be sold out. They would be eating those hamburgers and flatdogs (fried bologna sandwiches), too.

During that time beer was legal, but the hard stuff was not. But if you wanted a half-pint or a pint of whiskey or corn liquor, you could get it at Fair Deal because Grandmama and the chief of police had an "understanding," which was as good as a license to sell. Otherwise, it would have been a fine or jail. The chief had his way of coming by. He'd get his little tip and then we'd put the liquor on the table. This meant you could eat, drink and be merry.

The Seabirds (Seeburg juke boxes) would be jammin' all up and down Blue Front with Howlin' Wolf, Muddy Waters and B. B. King. Sometimes they would be there in person over at the Day and Night Cafe. The great blues singer Sam Chatmon came to Fair Deal often. People danced, ate, drank, and partied all night long till the break of day. Saturday night without a fight was not known. But the people always knew that, no matter how intoxicated you got, you couldn't fight in Miz Bob's cafe. If you wanted to fight, you would step outside and knuck it out.

My grandmama served dinner in the middle of the day. She considered it a disaster if dinner wasn't ready by twelve noon. A lot of her regular customers were farm and oil mill workers. The section workers on the Y & M V Railroad (Yazoo and Mississippi Valley, later Illinois Central) were her regular boarders. They paid her every two weeks when the railroad paid off. The girls at the pressing shop were also regulars.

Every morning about 5:00 a.m. my grandmother would get ready to put the dinners on. I remember crossing the railroad tracks on cold November mornings. The wind would be howling, and the pecans were rattling down on the tin roofs of the shotgun houses. Sometimes you could hear the towboat whistling out on the Mississippi River fourteen miles away. We'd pass the cottonseed oil mill. Whenever it was running, it always smelled like they were making ham sandwiches or cooking fried chicken. The compress was running too, day and night, pressing those bales of cotton. When I'd get over to Fair Deal, I'd crawl up on top of the drink box under the counter and go to sleep to the thumping and hissing of the compress. And I'd nap until the good smells and sounds woke me up—big pots of greens and vegetable soup simmering on the stove and Grandma stirring up the corn bread. . . .

Spring in the Delta is a beautiful time. In March farmers can get in the fields and start breaking up the land and plowing. They still use the old saying that when the pecan trees bud, you can plant corn, and when the pecan buds are as big as a squirrel's ear, you can plant cotton.

When I was a child, I used to love to go out in the fields and pastures, looking for wild greens and poke sallet, and sometimes wild onions and garlic. The onions and garlic were so strong, we didn't use them often. For Easter, we always had a nice ham, and we always had mustard greens.

Easter dinner

Baked Ham
Potato Salad
Mustard Greens
Candied Sweet Potatoes
Yeast Rolls
Cornbread
Coconut Cake
Pecan Pie
Iced Tea

Spring was fishing time too, and early in the morning or late in the afternoon, we'd go down to the creek bank, and throw in our lines. If it was still too chilly to sit on the ground, we'd turn our bait buckets upside down and sit on them. It was nice to come home with a string of white perch and breams to change the winter diet, and sometimes a big turtle for soup.

Gardens were planted early so the vegetables would come in as soon as possible. Blackberries and dewberries would begin to ripen all along the railroad track. (When I was a kid, we always called them wild berries, just like we called all birds, like quail and doves, wild birds.) My grand-mama says if you were riding the Bigleben train from Hollandale to Leland, sometimes the conductor would let you off to pick a hat full of berries, while the train was stopped at some little station. Back in the old days at my great-grandfather Fleming's, when spring came they'd still have hams in the smokehouse, sweet potatoes in the "sweet potato pump," corn in the corn crib (the little shed to store corn for the horses, cows and chickens), and fresh ground meal. But everyone was waiting for the little chickens to become broilers and the English peas and butter beans to be ready for the table.

Jellies, Pickles, and the Ladies Who Made Them

CHARLES EAST

Born in 1924, Charles East grew up in Shelby and in Cleveland, Missis-sippi. He served as director for the Louisiana State University Press from 1970 to 1975 and has worked as a freelance writer for numerous maga-zines and newspapers. His fiction has appeared in such journals as the Virginia Quarterly Review, *the* Southern Review, *and the* Yale Re-view *and was collected in a book called* Where the Music Was, *pub-lished in 1965 and reprinted by the University of Georgia in 1995. As this reminiscence from* Southern Living *shows, East is a careful ob-server of a world where even a jar of preserves has a notable social history.*

I KNEW THE people of our Mississippi Delta town for the jellies they made, the peaches and figs they preserved, the cucumber or green-tomato pickles they "put up." Mrs. Ernest Bullock, for instance, I still remember for her voice, her smile, but most of all for her pear relish. My Cousin Addie Bland achieved a kind of local fame, especially among the Methodist ladies, for her chow-chow and mustard pickles.

In the Depression years of the 1930s canning and preserving were an inevitable part of small-town Southern life, but I suspect they were, as much as anything, part of a system by which neighbors and relatives communicated their caring for each other. Whenever my grandmother got up to leave Cousin Addie's house after a visit, my cousin would send her on her way with a jar of something special.

Each lady had her secret, so that none of the jars of pickles or pre-serves of one tasted—or for that matter looked—exactly the same as another's. These jars often bore homemade labels—occasionally giving the name of the lady who made them, but more commonly the year, and sometimes the precise date. A practical consideration in view of the fact that jars could accumulate on pantry shelves and that one should never open the pear preserves from, say, 1939 before those from 1937.

Now, this was not a custom restricted to our town. In the summers my grandmother and I would make our annual trek to Fairhope or Mobile and return laden with jars of watermelon-rind preserves that her sister, my Aunt Alice, had given her.

From our visits with Cousin Maggie Smith in Wilson, Louisiana, we would bring home bread-and-butter pickles—a recipe, by the way, that has never been duplicated, even by Claussen or Vlasic. I can see her now, checking the tops of the jars with her strong hands before she presented them to my grandmother. It amazed me that this exceptional woman, once the mayor of her town—indeed the first woman to be elected mayor in the state, and this in the 1920s—could make wonderful quilts and put up bread-and-butter pickles.

My own grandmother, so often the recipient of all this bounty, favored plums and blackberries. When blackberry season came, we were off, my father at the wheel, headed for the wild bushes that grew along country roads and back of the levee. Or she would buy gallon buckets of berries from the vendors who came knocking at our door in the berry season. "How much you want?" she'd ask, and the seller of berries would announce "Two bits" or "Four bits," depending on how large the bucket was and how well the day had gone, and whether the berries that year were plentiful.

On the other hand, the plums that she turned into jelly always came from our own backyard, from the large tree that stood outside my window. I remember the sweet smell of the kitchen when the plums or the berries were cooking, the juice boiling up in heavy brass pans that had found their way to Mississippi from the kitchen of a Louisiana plantation. Or the smell of cloves if it was pickles.

But it was not all pears or plums or blackberries. One family friend made quince jelly; another mayhaw. Once, on an outing at the Sunflower River, we came upon a thicket of ripe scuppernongs and harvested enough for a batch of jelly that lasted through the next winter.

There they sat on our pantry shelves—the jars of scuppernong jelly next to Cousin Maggie's bread-and-butter pickles next to Cousin Addie's chow-chow, on the shelf above Aunt Mattie Steadman's fig preserves and Mrs. Bullock's pear relish. And on the shelf above that, a row of empty jars, washed and rinsed and ready to be returned, for that was the understanding between them.

What they left was a legacy of Southern largesse, but more than that—the memory of allspice and cloves, of the deliciously tart taste of plums and the sweet taste of figs, each jar with a name and a face to go with it.

F R O M

Bodies & Soul

AL YOUNG

*Born in 1930 in Ocean Springs, Mississippi, Al Young has written
poetry, novels, essays, and screenplays, but he always comes back to music
in one form or another. In addition to being a writer and teaching at
Stanford and the University of California, among other places, he is also
a professional musician. In 1988 when Young spoke to students at Delta
State University in Cleveland, Mississippi, he said, "You have a rich life
here. You have a life rich in history, rich in culture, rich in people." In
this essay, called "If I Had Wings Like Noah's Dove," written in 1964,
he recalls his desire, at the age of seven, to be a cowboy, until his grandmother pointed out the scarcity of black cowboys. This "musical memoir"
describes his quest to find a substitute. In the following passage, Young
celebrates his discovery of music—gospel, folk, blues, and classical—and
pays tribute to the great musicians, many of them Mississippians, who
so deeply affected him.*

I T W A S M Y grandmother—Mrs. Lillian Campbell of Pachuta, Mississippi—who passed down to me the first folk songs I ever learned, and
they were mostly old Negro spirituals along the order of "Steal Away,"
"Meetin' at the Buildin'," "Didn't My Lord Deliver Daniel," and "Pha-
roah's Army." There seemed to be hundreds of them that she would
half-sing and half-hum in the classic fashion that musicologists have
learned to call "moaning." Morning, noon and nighttime, from dawn
to dark, one song would turn into another or back into itself as Mama
drew water from the well, washed, milked, cooked, swept, scrubbed,
gardened, quilted, sewed, doctored, scolded, and wrung the necks of
chickens. Often I would study her at the kitchen woodstove, getting up
a big iron pot of something for early-afternoon dinner and moaning to
herself while she smiled out the window at fig trees or at a particular
red bird. Music was merely one of her ways of getting through days.

We didn't have electricity, running water, gas or a car; nor did we
have any idea that what we sang or listened to was American folk music.

At the age of seven, I made up my own folk song in the manner of
Hank Williams who was knocking everybody down out there by then

with his "Hey, Goodlookin'," and "Move It Over." Mama would crack up when I sat out in the porch swing with my little cigar box guitar and whined:

> *O Hopalong Cass'dy*
> *You treated me nasty*
> *when I was in Texas, Tennessee. . . .*

I wanted to grow up and be a cowboy. Like all the other boys my age, I wanted to go galloping across plains giving crooks the uppercut, the same as Tex Ritter, Gene Autry, Roy Rogers and all the others; hammering out a tune by the campfire nights, and just generally being It. It was Mama who put the facts to me one rainy afternoon when Cousin Jesse and I were lollygagging around the woodpile by the fireplace, polishing up our cap pistols, tickled that it was too wet to be out in the field picking cotton.

"Boys, y'all ever heard tell of a colored cowboy? You ever seen one at the picture show or in a funnybook?"

Of course, we hadn't. There was nothing out on the Negro cowboys at that time, although I was later to learn how many of them there had actually been. That was one dream I had to gradually let go.

But I hung onto the music as it went charging through my blood in the form of gospel, folk song, blues, country & western, rhythm & blues, pop, bebop, cool, modern, classical, international—and then came the first fun chord I learned to strum on a real guitar. Suddenly I was back into folk.

By then, I'd become a freshman at the University of Michigan, Ann Arbor, and the Cold War was massacring hearts and minds. A few days after I moved into South Quad, the resident House Mother had me to lunch, along with the roommate they'd placed me with. His name was Bill McAdoo and he was older; a workingclass political firebrand from Detroit. Bill's mother was Jewish and his father Black. At one point during our simple repast of mash potatoes, shiny gravy, tinned peas and something called City Chicken, our blue-haired Dorm Mother squinted across the table. "I'll have you boys know," she glowered and announced, "that we believe in taking regular showers and baths around here."

At the end of that first semester, I flew the coop. I moved out of all dormitories into the world at large where the living was never easy, but where at least there was room to breathe. Not having been raised white, Republican or middle class, I had no recourse but to go my own way, and I've been going my own way ever since. If you were different in

those days, you were automatically slap-sticker-labeled Communist, or
Red or Pinko at worst, and Beatnik at best. I was never even either. I'd
done a lot and read a lot—or so I thought—but, leery of schools, I was
starving for lasting knowledge, spiritual growth and stimulating friendship. Classes weren't enough somehow. Fraternities seemed both fatu-
ous and stifling. And all the beautiful girls of the colored aristocracy
were busy planning their coming-out parties or sensibly stalking their
own kind—boys from good backgrounds with good hair and lucrative
futures. Not much had changed since earlier days at Hutchins Interme-
diate in Detroit when I sat backstage with Mary Jean Tomlin, later to
become Lily, at some school show in which we were both performing,
speculating about what became of talented kids who didn't come from
privileged families.

In college I gravitated toward activities germane to my natural interests, and toward people who, like myself, remained open to experience.
So it wasn't surprising to find myself taking up with budding writers,
poets, playwrights, dreamers, journalists, intellectual mavericks, politi-
cos, painters, sculptors, photographers, actors, hipsters, renegades,
math visionaries, townies, composers; all manner of self-invented mis-
fits, including, of course, musicians.

Music soothed. Music helped. Music helped soothe the loneliness
and my sense of uncertainty, just as it eased the sting and nagging strain
of color prejudice, social awkwardness, McCarthy Era paranoia and the
all-around savagery of blooming adolescence itself; a beastly climbing
rosebush with thorns no more imaginary than the wounds they open.
Red with passion and hopelessly romantic, it eventually took a witty
professor of Spanish to thoughtfully point out that the writers who were
románticos by and large lived very short lives (1803–1836) whereas the
classicists tended to have gravestones that read 1795–1889. As it had
done for my grandmother, music still got me through days.

Occasionally I would sit up all night by myself, grave, determined not
to turn in before I had mastered some difficult Leadbelly lick or
learned the changes to something Sonny Terry and Brownie McGhee
had recorded. I was learning stuff from everybody: Blind Willie Johnson, Snooks Eaglin, Reverend Gary Davis, chain-gang prisoners taped
by Alan Lomax at Mississippi State Penitentiary (Parchman Farm), Ode-
tta, Blind Blake, Woody Guthrie, Mississippi John Hurt, Lonnie Johnson, Elizabeth Cotton, John Lee Hooker, Robert Johnson, Bascom
Lunsford, Jean Ritchie, Pete Seeger, The Weavers, Josh White, Big Bill
Broonzy, Muddy Waters, Howlin' Wolf, Bo Diddley, Harry Belafonte,
Len Chandler, Cynthia Gooding, Jesse Fuller, Theodore Bikel, Sister

Rosetta Tharpe, The Staple Singers, Lightnin' Hopkins, Charles Mingus, Ray Charles, and from sources all around me.

All of it was "ethnic" as far as I was concerned. I mean, I took the late Bill Broonzy's word for it when he made that remark of his that went: "Anything a man can play is folk music; you don't hear no dogs or cats or horses singing it, do you?" At the time I wasn't aware that Louis Armstrong had said something similar long before that. I was hung up for a spell on quite a few backwoodsmen and citybillies, to say nothing of all those meditative foreigners with their thumb pianos, bouzoukis, balalaikas and sitars.

As I came upon other amateurs given to similar habits, we would work out songs, tunes and pieces and get together regularly to swap material and techniques as well as show off our fragile accomplishments. These get-togethers, when they weren't strictly for fun, were called hoots, and hoots were serious and very big at college.

If a hootenanny was jubilant enough, you were apt to hear English majors doing field hollers; pre-meds having a go at lumberjack songs; students of library science singing about robbing banks and hopping freight trains; business administration people getting all wrapped up in "Hallelujah, I'm a Bum"; eighth-generation Yanks armed with banjos, fiddles and mandolins, sounding more like Confederates than Flatt & Scruggs and the Foggy Mountain Boys; future ballistics missile experts working up a sweat on "Ain't Gonna Study War No More"; kids reared in traffic jams reminiscing about "The Old Cotton Fields Back Home."

There were doctrinaire folkniks who took themselves and their image quite seriously. I can see now how, in many ways, they helped usher in the great costume phenomenon that would overtake the Western World by the time the Sixties ended. Personally, I had grown weary of workshirts, neckerchiefs, buckskin coats, clunky boots, railroad caps, peasant dresses and blouses, cowboy hats, Levi suits, leather vests, Paul Bunyan shirts and thrift shop resurrections long before that overly studied mode of dress gave way to Jesus gowns, capes, plumage, Shakespearian garb, Salvation Army bandleader coats, paratrooper gear, dashikis, Cossack uniforms, Mao jackets, coolie togs, aviator helmetry, sharecropper bibs and sundry Me-Tarzan-You-Jane getups.

At length, I came to perform; sometimes around town as a single and other times with well-rehearsed string combos such as those formed variously with the likes of Marc Silber, Perry Lederman, Bernie Krause, Joe Dassin and Felix Pappalardi. Marc became a guitar maker and opened—first in New York and then in Berkeley—a shop called Fretted Instruments. Perry hooked up with Indian sarodist Ali Akhbar Khan and became immersed in ragas and a personal mysticism. Bernie went on to replace Eric Darling in the Weavers and later teamed with fellow synthesist Fred Beaver to form Beaver and Krause, a pioneering fusion repertory unit. Joe Dassin, son of film director Jules Dassin, returned to France where he became a pop music idol before suffering a fatal heart attack in Tahiti in 1980. As for Felix Pappalardi, the only bona fide conservatory trainee among us—who was equally at home on guitar, bass, fiddle and trumpet—he launched the rock band Cream, became an international success and remained highly visible and respected as a player, arranger and producer on the New York music scene.

Show business was something I could never hack, not on any sustained basis. It got to the point where it felt too much like jail. It also didn't seem to matter where I worked—the Midwest, the East, the West Coast. I took care of business on the gig; I always delivered. The money, especially at college, paid for rent, food, clothing, free time, and also kept my digs overrun with staples such as books, records, tapes and beer. But then I would catch glimpses of myself, a captive on the stand or on stage all those professional nights when I would've been happier writing or reading or—rather than merely singing about it—actually be out walking with my baby down by the San Francisco Bay.

Perhaps I did become, after all, that singing cowboy my grandmother lovingly discouraged. Then again, for all I know, I might very well still be in show biz. But I've changed my axe and I've changed my act, and the changes never seem to stop coming.

Roadfood

JANE AND MICHAEL STERN

*The Sterns are a husband-and-wife team who have traveled the byways
all over America and sampled food from lesser-known, out-of-the-way
places. In* Roadfood, *published in 1992, they find many good things
to say about local eateries in Mississippi—from Smitty's in Oxford to
Weidman's in Meridian. Possibly the most unusual of such places is
described in the following piece, "Mendenhall Hotel Revolving Tables,"
where diners choose from twelve different kinds of vegetables and four
different kinds of meat every day. This hotel dining room, like a coquettish southern belle, is hidden away in the little town of Mendenhall, south
of Jackson.*

A MEAL AT THE Mendenhall hotel is an inspiring reminder of
how the word "restaurant" originated: as a place to restore strength
and good spirits when far away from home.

The main thing that inscribes the Mendenhall in the *Roadfood* Hall
of Fame is the amount of food it tenders. If you have not personally
luxuriated in any of Dixie's classic communal dining rooms, such as
Mrs. Wilkes's in Savannah, or the Hopkins Boarding House in Pensacola, you can hardly imagine how much there is to eat. A vista of vittles
is spread before you: baskets of steaming hot biscuits, cracklin' cornbread, yeast rolls, and sweet muffins; a dozen or more vegetables and
ultra-customized vegetable casseroles, fried chicken (*de rigueur* at any
good boarding house meal), ham and pork chops and barbecued beef
and Brunswick stew, and peach cobbler and icy pitchers of pour-it-your-
self pre-sweetened iced tea.

Pay one price (under ten dollars) and eat all you want; and when
you are done, find a rocking chair on the front porch and snooze a
spell. It is not exactly power lunch, and gourmets won't find the latest
trendy food on the table; but for those in search of authentic American
cooking, there is no restaurant experience that can compare to this
grand old hotel in the small town that was once a stop on the rail line
between Jackson and Hattiesburg.

It was back in 1915 that Mrs. Annie Heil, owner of what was then
called the Heil Hotel, started serving meals to trainmen and travelers
who stopped for a quick half-hour lunch on their way north or south.

Because they had no time to dally over a menu or a course-by-course meal, Mrs. Heil came up with a system to serve them fast: round-table dining, for which she sat everyone at a big round table with a lazy Susan in the center where the whole meal was unfurled and ready for fast eating action. The wheels of good food have been spinning ever since, at the Mendenhall Hotel and at a few other citadels of Dixie cooking in this part of Mississippi.

What fun it is to eat this way! It's practical, too. Cuts down on the reaching, stretching, and pass-it-to-me's that obstruct ordinary boardinghouse meals. All the platters, bowls, casseroles, bread baskets, pitchers, and condiment jars are within easy reach. When you want something, spin it and grab. Whenever a serving tray on the lazy Susan starts looking empty, a member of the staff snatches it back to the kitchen and returns with a full one.

What most visitors remember best about a visit to the Mendenhall Hotel are the arrays of vegetables—perhaps a dozen different kinds at every meal, ranging from locally grown, garden-fresh tomatoes (yes, we know; technically, tomatoes are a fruit) to legendary southern-style whipped yams, streaked with marshmallows and scented with vanilla; creamed corn; mighty bowls of butter-rich squash and luscious creamed spinach.

As for *how much* it is polite and proper to eat at such a meal, take a hint from the house motto displayed in a pretty needlepoint sampler on the wall of the Mendenhall Hotel dining room: "EAT 'TIL IT OUCHES."

FROM

Along the RFD

ROSE BUDD STEVENS

*Rose Budd Stevens was a pen name for Mamie Davis Willoughby. Begin-
ning in the 1940s, this remarkable woman wrote newspaper columns
from her home at Shady Rest Farm near Liberty, Mississippi, in Amite
County. Her topics included making lye hominy, hog killing, and local
characters like Dillon Sandford, who refused to get out of bed for over
forty years. In columns such as "Farm Names Never Change," she con-
vinces the reader of the stability of rural Mississippi culture, while in
"The Strange Visions of Aunt Lue," she tells about the long-held supersti-
tions of an aging black woman. In the following entry, "Mama's Christmas Baking," Stevens informs us of a lost delicacy.*

BACK IN DAYS of yore when Christmas baking time came around
Mama always had plenty of help. We delighted in getting coconut
grated for at least two cakes. Nuts (pecans, hickory, a few bought Brazil
nuts and of course one small bag of French walnuts—without these two
last mentioned nuts it simply wouldn't have been real Christmas) were
picked out and stored in fruit jars. Mama let us help with cutting and
slicing the candied peel and fruits, most of which had been prepared
by her hands weeks before.

If cash was a stranger to Shady Rest we would be sent to the field to
find a pie melon to be used to candy down; this was used as citron in
fruit cakes.

Every double yolk egg would have been saved for several weeks past;
larger than the general run of eggs would also be put aside for Mama's
baking spree.

A secret store of sugar would be brought out. Salted down butter
would be put to soak and then washed until it was as pure and sweet as
could be. Spices would be ground or pounded for fruit cakes.

Molasses was always on hand, and flour for the dipping out of a barrel bought when the last bale of cotton was sold.

Perhaps it took a bit of managing for Mama to turn out her sweet
cooking; we never realized this, and only knew we were in for a few days
of good times and fun in the old kitchen, heated by a fireplace and
wood stove.

The best thing I remember about Christmas baking was the delicious little "try" Mama would cook for each child, whenever a batch of batter was mixed. Lives there a soul over thirty-five who doesn't remember the dab of cake batter baked in a small tin plate, a syrup can lid, or the lid of a baking powder can . . . *"to see"* if enough baking powder had been added, perhaps too much sugar, therefore calling for a mite more flour and a drop or so of milk.

Often too generous a hand had been dipped in the butter crock . . . or Mama had been called away from the mixing bowl as she opened the flavoring bottle, to kiss a crying child or to help Daddy look for something . . . then the question . . . "did I flavor or not?" All of these questions were answered by the simple method of baking a "try."

The try belonged to the children! No if about it!

I remember Mama always tasting the batter to see if it was to her liking. Always our hearts yearned toward her taste buds not being up to par, for then we knew she would open the kitchen table drawer, take out as many small "try pans" as there were children around the table.

We had our choice of baking powder lids, with K.C. or Calumet imprinted thereon. We were allowed to grease and dust with flour our selected lid. Mama would dip a level full tablespoon of batter for each lid.

Bourbon

WALKER PERCY

Known for his award-winning novels, including The Moviegoer *and* The Last Gentleman, *and his serious philosophical essays collected in such works as* The Message in the Bottle *and* Lost in the Cosmos, *Percy also had a remarkable sense of humor. In the following essay he delivers a delightful meditation on bourbon, the quintessential southern drink. With allusions to Proust and Faulkner, he presents his closest associations with the drink, including an escapade with a Bellevue nurse that might well have been the inspiration for the misadventures of Will Barrett in* The Last Gentleman.

THIS IS NOT written by a connoisseur of bourbon. Ninety-nine percent of bourbon drinkers know more about bourbon than I do. It is about the aesthetic of bourbon drinking in general and in particular of knocking it back neat.

I can hardly tell one bourbon from another, unless the other is very bad. Some bad bourbons are even more memorable than good ones. For example, I can recall being broke with some friends in Tennessee and deciding to have a party and being able to afford only two fifths of a $1.75 bourbon called Two Natural, whose label showed dice coming up five and two. Its taste was memorable. The psychological effect was also notable. After knocking back two or three shots over a period of half an hour, the three male drinkers looked at each other and said in a single voice: "Where are the women?"

I have not been able to locate this remarkable bourbon since.

Not only should connoisseurs of bourbon not read this article. Neither should persons preoccupied with the perils of alcoholism, cirrhosis, esophageal hemorrhage, cancer of the palate, and so forth—all real enough dangers. I, too, deplore these afflictions. But, as between these evils and the aesthetic of bourbon drinking, that is, the use of bourbon to warm the heart, to reduce the anomie of the late twentieth century, to cut the cold phlegm of Wednesday afternoons, I choose the aesthetic. What, after all, is the use of not having cancer, cirrhosis, and such, if a man comes home from work every day at five-thirty to the exurbs of Montclair or Memphis and there is the grass growing and the little family looking not quite at him but just past the side of his head, and there's Cronkite on the tube and the smell of pot roast in the living room, and inside the house and outside in the pretty exurb has settled the noxious particles and the sadness of the old dying Western World, and him thinking: Jesus, is this it? Listening to Cronkite and the grass growing?

If I should appear to be suggesting that such a man proceed as quickly as possible to anesthetize his cerebral cortex by ingesting ethyl alcohol, the point is being missed. Or part of the point. The joy of bourbon drinking is not the pharmacological effect of C_2H_5OH on the cortex but rather the instant of the whiskey being knocked back and the little explosion of Kentucky U.S.A. sunshine in the cavity of the nasopharynx and the hot bosky bite of Tennessee summertime— aesthetic considerations to which the effect of the alcohol is, if not dispensable, at least secondary.

By contrast, Scotch: for me (not, I presume, for a Scot), drinking Scotch is like looking at a picture of Noel Coward. The whiskey assaults the nasopharynx with all the excitement of paregoric. Scotch drinkers (not all, of course) I think of as upward-mobile Americans, Houston and New Orleans businessmen who graduate from bourbon about the same time they shed seersuckers for Lilly slacks. Of course, by now these same folk may have gone back to bourbon and seersucker for the same reason, because too many Houston oilmen drink Scotch.

Nothing, therefore, will be said about the fine points of sour mash, straights, blends, bonded, except a general preference for the lower proofs. It is a matter of the arithmetic of aesthetics. If one derives the same pleasure from knocking back 80-proof bourbon as 100-proof, the formula is both as simple as $2 + 2 = 4$ and as incredible as non-Euclidean geometry. Consider. One knocks back five one-ounce shots of 80-proof Early Times or four shots of 100-proof Old Fitzgerald. The alcohol ingestion is the same:

$$5 \times 40\% = 2$$
$$4 \times 50\% = 2$$

Yet in the case of the Early Times, one has obtained an extra quantum of joy without cost to liver, brain, or gastric mucosa. A bonus, pure and simple, an aesthetic gain as incredible as two parallel lines meeting at infinity.

An apology to the reader is in order, nevertheless, for it has just occurred to me that this is the most unedifying and even maleficent piece I ever wrote—if it should encourage potential alcoholics to start knocking back bourbon neat. It is also the unfairest. Because I am, happily and unhappily, endowed with a bad GI tract, diverticulosis, neurotic colon, and a mild recurring nausea, which make it less likely for me to become an alcoholic than my healthier fellow Americans. I can hear the reader now: Who is he kidding? If this joker has to knock back five shots of bourbon every afternoon just to stand the twentieth century, he's already an alcoholic. Very well. I submit to this or any semantic. All I am saying is that if I drink much more than this I will get sick as a dog for two days and the very sight and smell of whiskey will bring on the heaves. Readers beware, therefore, save only those who have stronger wills or as bad a gut as I.

The pleasure of knocking back bourbon lies in the plane of the aesthetic but at an opposite pole from connoisseurship. My preference for the former is or is not deplorable depending on one's value system—that is to say, how one balances out the Epicurean virtues of cultivating one's sensory end organs with the greatest discrimination and at least cost to one's health, against the virtue of evocation of time and memory and of the recovery of self and the past from the fogged-in disoriented Western World. In Kierkegaardian terms, the use of bourbon to such an end is a kind of aestheticized religious mode of existence, whereas connoisseurship, the discriminating but single-minded stimulation of sensory end organs, is the aesthetic of damnation.

Two exemplars of the two aesthetics come to mind:

Imagine Clifton Webb, scarf at throat, sitting at Cap d'Antibes on a perfect day, the little wavelets of the Mediterranean sparkling in the sunlight, and he is savoring a 1959 Mouton Rothschild.

Then imagine William Faulkner, having finished *Absalom, Absalam!,* drained, written out, pissed-off, feeling himself over the edge and out of it, nowhere, but he goes somewhere, his favorite hunting place in the Delta wilderness of the Big Sunflower River and, still feeling bad with his hunting cronies and maybe even a little phony, which he was, what with him trying to pretend that he was one of them, a farmer, hunkered down in the cold and rain after the hunt, after honorably passing up the does and seeing no bucks, shivering and snot-nosed, takes out a flat pint of any bourbon at all and flatfoots about a third of it. He shivers again but not from the cold.

Bourbon does for me what the piece of cake did for Proust.

1926: as a child watching my father in Birmingham, in the exurbs, living next to number-six fairway of the New Country Club, him disdaining both the bathtub gin and white lightning of the time, aging his own bourbon in the charcoal keg, on his hands and knees in the basement sucking on a siphon, a matter of gravity requiring cheek pressed against cement floor, the siphon getting going, the decanter ready, the first hot spurt into his mouth not spat out.

1933: my uncle's sun parlor in the Mississippi Delta and toddies on a Sunday afternoon, the prolonged and meditative tinkle of silver spoon against crystal to dissolve the sugar; talk, tinkle, talk; the talk mostly political: Roosevelt is doing a good job; no, the son of a bitch is betraying his class.

1934: drinking at a Delta dance, the boys in bi-swing jackets and tab collars, tough-talking and profane and also scared of the girls and therefore safe in the men's room. Somebody passes around bootleg bourbon in a Coke bottle. It's awful. Tears start from eyes, faces turn red. "Hot damn, that's good!"

1935: drinking at a football game in college. U.N.C. vs. Duke. One has a blind date. One is lucky. She is beautiful. Her clothes are the color of the fall leaves and her face turns up like a flower. But what to *say* to her, let alone what to do, and whether she is"nice" or "hot"—a distinction made in those days. But what to *say?* Take a drink, by now from a proper concave hip flask (a long way from the Delta Coke bottle) with a hinged top. Will she have a drink? No. But it's all right. The taste of the bourbon (Cream of Kentucky) and the smell of her fuse with the brilliant Carolina fall and the sounds of the crowd and the hit of the linemen in a single synesthesia.

1941: drinking mint juleps, famed Southern bourbon drink, though in the Deep South not really drunk much. In fact they are drunk so seldom that when, say, on Derby Day somebody gives a julep party, people drink them like cocktails, forgetting that a good julep holds at least five ounces of bourbon. Men fall face-down unconscious, women wander in the woods disconsolate and amnesiac, full of thoughts of Kahlil Gibran and the limberlost.

Would you believe the first mint julep I had I was sitting not on a columned porch but in the Boo Snooker bar of the New Yorker Hotel with a Bellevue nurse in 1941? The nurse, a nice Upstate girl, head floor nurse, brisk, swift, good-looking; Bellevue nurses, the best in the world and this one the best of Bellevue, at least the best looking. The julep, an atrocity, a heavy syrupy bourbon and water in a small glass clotted with ice. But good!

How could two women be more different than the beautiful languid Carolina girl and this swift handsome girl from Utica, best Dutch stock? One thing was sure. Each was to be courted, loved, drunk with, with bourbon. I should have stuck with bourbon. We changed to gin fizzes because the bartender said he came from New Orleans and could make good ones. He could and did. They were delicious. What I didn't know was that they were made with raw egg albumen and I was allergic to it. Driving her home to Brooklyn and being in love! What a lovely fine strapping smart girl! And thinking of being invited into her apartment where she lived alone and of her offering to cook a little supper and of the many kisses and the sweet love that already existed between us and was bound to grow apace, when on the Brooklyn Bridge itself my upper lip began to swell and little sparks of light flew past the corner of my eye like St. Elmo's fire. In the space of thirty seconds my lip stuck out a full three-quarter inch, like a shelf, like Mortimer Snerd. Not only was kissing out of the question but my eyes swelled shut. I made it across the bridge, pulled over to the curb and fainted. Whereupon this noble nurse drove me back to Bellevue, gave me a shot and put me to bed.

Anybody who monkeys around with gin and egg white deserves what he gets. I should have stuck with bourbon and have from that day to this.

F R O M

Last Train to Memphis

P E T E R   G U R A L N I C K

*Guralnick's biography of Elvis Presley, published in 1994, traces the life
of the singer from his earliest years in Tupelo, Mississippi. Presley's first
public singing came about through a talent contest for children sponsored
by the local radio station WELO, where Mississippi Slim was a star. In
1945 when he was ten, Presley sang "Old Shep" and won fifth place.
The following excerpt, from the chapter "Tupelo: Above the Highway,"
describes the contest and a little of what Tupelo was like in the years
when the popular musicians of the day might pass through this northeast
Mississippi town and feed the secret passion of a small, unobtrusive boy
who would become the king of rock and roll. Presley's immense fame resulted from his ability to create a synthesis of diverse sources as gospel,
blues, and country music. His style was the embodiment of paradox,
since, as many scholars contend, it depended on a white man singing
like a black man. In the conservative 1950s, his performances stirred
controversy. With his wild hip gyrations, Presley became an icon for teen-
agers and a threat to many parents. He is probably the most famous
Mississippian of the twentieth century.*

W E L O   H A D   B E G U N broadcasting on South Spring Street, above
the Black and White dry goods store, on May 15, 1941. There were a
number of local talents involved in starting up the station, including
Charlie Boren, its colorful announcer, and Archie Mackey, a local
bandleader and radio technician who had been instrumental in establishing Tupelo's first radio station, WDIX, some years earlier, but the
hillbilly star of the station in 1946 was a twenty-three-year-old native of
Smithville, some twenty miles to the southeast, Carvel Lee Ausborn,
who went by the name of Mississippi Slim. Ausborn, who had taken up
guitar at the age of thirteen to pursue a career in music, was inspired
by Jimmie Rodgers, though Hank Williams and Ernest Tubb became
almost equal influences in the forties. Probably his greatest influence,
however, was his cousin Rod Brasfield, a prominent country comedian,
also from Smithville, who joined the Opry in 1944 and toured with
Hank Williams, while his brother, Uncle Cyp Brasfield, became a regular on the Ozark Jubilee and wrote material for Rod and his comedy
partner, Minnie Pearl. Though Mississippi Slim never attained such

heights, he traveled all over the country with Goober and His Kentucki-
ans and the Bisbee's Comedians tent show and even played the Opry
once or twice, largely on the strength of his cousin's connections. Just
about every prominent musician who passed through Tupelo played
with Slim at one time or another, from Merle "Red" Taylor (who furnished the fiddle melody for Bill Monroe's "Uncle Pen") to college-
bound youths like Bill Mitchell (who in later life, after a career in politics, would win many national old-time fiddle contests), to weekend
pickers like Slim's uncle Clinton. "He was a good entertainer," recalled
Bill Mitchell, "put on a pretty good show, love songs with comedy (he
came from a family of comedians)—it was a pretty lively show. The people really enjoyed it." In addition to a regular early-morning program
on weekdays, Slim had a noontime show every Saturday called *Singin'*
and Pickin' Hillbilly that served as a lead-in to the Jamboree, on which
he also appeared. This was where Elvis first encountered the world of
entertainment.

Archie Mackey's memory was of a young boy accompanied by his
father. "Vernon said that his boy didn't know but two songs," said
Mackey, another Jamboree regular, who claimed that he had Elvis sing
both, with Slim accompanying him on guitar. Some have suggested that
Slim was reluctant to play behind an "amateur" and that announcer
Charlie Boren practically had to force him to do so, while others have
sought credit for first carrying Elvis to the station. It's all somewhat
academic. Like everyone else, he was drawn by the music and by the
show. He was not the only child to perform, though according to Bill
Mitchell most of the others were girls. And, it seemed, none of the
others felt it like he did.

"He was crazy about music," said James Ausborn, Slim's kid brother
and Elvis' schoolmate at East Tupelo Consolidated. "That's all he
talked about. A lot of people didn't like my brother, they thought he
was sort of corny, but, you know, they had to get a mail truck to bring
all his cards and letters. Elvis would always say, 'let's go to your brother's
program today. Can you go up there with me? I want him to show me
some more chords on the guitar.' We'd walk into town on Saturday, go
down to the station on Spring Street [this was the broadcast before the
Jamboree], a lot of times the studio would be full but my brother would
always show him some chords. Sometimes he would say, 'I ain't got time
to fool with you today,' but he'd always sit down and show him. Then
maybe he'd sing him a couple of songs, and Elvis would try to sing them
himself. I think gospel sort of inspired him to be in music, but then
my brother helped carry it on."

Music had become his consuming passion. With the exception of a couple of playmates who shared his interest, like James, or who might have looked up to him for it, no one really noticed. His uncle Vester, who said that his mother's people, the Hoods, were "musicians out of this world," never noticed the transformation. Frank Smith saw him as one of the crowd, not really "eager" for music—"he just liked it." Even his parents might have missed this development in their closely watched son: "He always knew," said Vernon, as if he and Gladys had even doubted, "he was going to do something. When we didn't have a dime, he used to sit on the doorstep and say, 'One of these days it'll be different.'"

If you picture him, picture someone you might have missed: a wide-eyed, silent child scuffling his feet, wearing overalls. He stands in line in the courtroom, waiting his turn to tiptoe up to the mike. His small child's voice carries a quavering note of yearning—other children get up and do letter-perfect recitals, big burly men frail on their beat-up guitars, but Elvis cradles his like a bird. After the broadcast is over, as the crowd slowly dissipates, the little boy hangs around on the outskirts of the group, watching Mississippi Slim and the other musicians pack up. He walks out behind them onto the courthouse square, with the statue of the Confederate soldier facing the Lyric Theater, the movie house that he and his friends never go to because it costs fifteen cents, a nickel more than the Strand. He hangs around on the edge of the crowd, nervously shifting from one foot to the other, desperately side-stepping every offer of a ride back to East Tupelo. He is waiting for an invitation, and in his determination to wait he shows the kind of watchful perseverance that is the hallmark of his solitary style. Maybe his friend James will say something to his brother, will suggest that they go off and have a Nehi together. Meanwhile he hangs on every word that is spoken, every glance exchanged: talk of the music, talk of the Opry, what cousin Rod Brasfield had to say that last time he was in town.

He soaks it all in. While others allow themselves to be distracted, his nervous attention never wanders; his fingers are constantly drumming against his pants leg, but his gaze bores in on the singer and the scene. Does he hang around with Slim? It's hard to imagine where. He dreams of *being* Slim. He dreams of wearing a western shirt with fancy pockets and sparkles and a scarf around his neck. Slim knows all the Opry stars. He knows Tex Ritter—the boy has heard the story a dozen times, but he doesn't mind if he hears it one more time from James: how Tex Ritter was making a personal appearance over in Nettleton with one of his movies, and Slim said to his little brother, "You want to go? You talking all the time about Tex Ritter, I'll show you that me and him is friends." So they went over to Nettleton, where Tex played a few songs before they showed his film, and then he signed some autographs. He had his six-guns on. Then all of a sudden he looked out and said, "I'll be damned, there's old Mississippi Slim sitting out there in the front row," and he stopped everything he was doing and went out and shook his hand. Then he said, "You come on right up here, and why don't you do a song for us." When he shook James' hand, James thought his hand was going to break, that was the kind of grip old Tex Ritter had. That was exactly the way it happened.

"I took the guitar, and I watched people," Elvis recalled, "and I learned to play a little bit. But I would never sing in public. I was very shy about it, you know." Every Saturday night he would listen to the Opry. He and Gladys and Vernon, his cousin Harold (whose mother, Rhetha, has died and who lives with them part of the time), maybe Grandma Minnie, too, now that Grandpa has lit out and she is living with them mostly—you had just better not run down the battery before the Saturday-night broadcast. The adults laugh and exchange glances at some of the jokes and tell half-remembered stories about the performers: Roy Acuff and Ernest Tubb, the Willis Brothers and Bill Monroe, here's that Red Foley to do "Old Shep" that Elvis sung at the fair. The music can carry you off to faraway places. But no one really knows. Daddy loves him. Mama will take care of him. There is nothing in his life that they do not know except for this. It is his secret passion.

FROM

Stand By Your Man

TAMMY WYNETTE

Wynette Pugh, who would later become the famous country singer Tammy Wynette, was born in Itawamba County in 1942. Her father died a year later with a brain tumor. She was reared primarily by her maternal grandparents, whom she called Mama and Daddy. As she describes in the following passage from her autobiography, published in 1979, the woman who would later be asked to join the Grand Ole Opry grew up picking cotton. In this excerpt from chapter one, she ponders the many ironies of her life: that the woman whose theme song is "Stand by Your Man" has been married five times, that the woman who had no indoor plumbing when she first married now has nine bathrooms, that the woman whose girlhood dream was to meet the great country singer George Jones not only met but married him. Although Jones and Wynette divorced in 1975, they began singing on tour together again in 1995.

MAMA DID MOST of the disciplining, but Daddy had his stern side too. He whipped me only three times in my life, but I remember every one of them. I got the worst one when I was about ten. It was on a Saturday and there was a county fair in Tupelo that I couldn't wait to get to. But it was harvest time so we all had to pick cotton that day. Daddy said if I picked a certain amount by noon—I think it was fifty pounds—I could quit and go on to the fair. I got up before dawn and started off the day cheating by picking before sunup. Cotton still damp from the dew weighs more, and I wanted to pick my allotted pounds as fast as possible. But when time came to quit I knew my sack didn't weigh enough, so I committed the ultimate sin of a cotton picker—I weighted my sack down with rocks. Cheating on the weight is bad enough, but rocks in a cotton sack are a real danger and one that I had been warned against for as long as I could remember.

If a rock strikes the metal pipe that sucks the cotton from the back of the truck up into the gin, it can cause sparks and set the whole place on fire. But I was determined to make it to the fair. So I drug my sack to the scales and after it was weighed I took it off to the side and very carefully took out every rock I'd put in—or so I thought. Then I climbed on the back of Daddy's old Case tractor so I could reach the wagon hooked to it, and I dumped the cotton out myself to make sure

I hadn't missed any rocks. After that was done, I headed for the house to clean up. Daddy got on the tractor and started for the gin, which was no more than fifty yards away. By the time I reached our front porch he was in line waiting for his turn at the pipe, so I stopped to watch. I saw him pull the wagon under the suction pipe and then, not two minutes later, I saw smoke. I knew instantly what had happened and I thought, "Oh my God, I've set the gin on fire. I'm dead now." It was a community gin, and I could just see all the cotton picked by us and the neighboring farmers going up in smoke. I saw Daddy unhook the wagon and start for the house on the tractor. I couldn't see the men inside the gin, but I knew they'd be working frantically to put out the fire, and the only reason Daddy would be leaving at a time like that was to get *me.*

I jumped off the porch and ran for the fields, looking back over my shoulder at him coming on that tractor. When he reached the house, he got down and started after me on foot. I was way out in the cotton fields by then, running and looking back, crying and begging him not to whip me. He didn't run after me. He didn't even speed up his walk. He just kept coming. He called to me, "The faster you run, the harder I'll whip you when I catch you," but I kept on going. Then suddenly I tripped and fell down, hitting my knee on a sharp rock. It hurt really bad and blood was running down my leg. I thought, "Oh, this is great because now he won't whip me." When he got to me I was bawling and holding my knee. I showed it to him expecting sympathy, but he just looked at it and said, "I'll take care of that after I've taken care of this." He pulled up a cotton stalk and whipped me good with it. Every time the stalk hit my legs, it stuck in my flesh because he hadn't pulled off the dry pods. But as much as it hurt I knew I deserved it.

The fire burned three or four hundred pounds of cotton before they got it put out, and Daddy had to make that up. So I had to pick the amount that had burned without pay. But he let me go to the fair that afternoon anyway. Many farmers didn't pay their families to work in the fields, but Daddy always did. I got about $2 for every hundred pounds I picked. I don't remember how much I could pick a day at that age, but I know as I grew older I got up to $4 per hundred pounds, and I could pick 170 or 180 pounds a day. The most I ever picked in one day was 204 pounds, which was really a lot for a girl.

Just as our social life revolved around the church, our home and school life revolved around the crops. I was just three weeks old when I was first taken into the cotton fields. Since my father was too sick to work by the time I was born, my mother had to pick cotton to earn money for us. She'd take me with her and lay me on a quilt on the ground. Then she'd spread another quilt on the branches of a tree above me and sprinkle that with insect powder to keep the ants off me. She'd work in the fields all day long, stopping just when she had to nurse me. But my first memory of the cotton fields is riding on Mother's pick sack when I was three or four years old. A pick sack is made of heavy cotton canvas, and it's about six feet long, according to how tall the picker is. An adult sack would be five to seven feet long. It has a strap that goes across the shoulder, padded with cotton so it won't hurt so much when the sack gets full. I would sit on top of Mother's sack, and she'd pull me along between the rows as she picked. I was sent out to pick, myself, when I was six or seven years old, and I continued to work in the fields until I left home to get married at seventeen.

The men planted the cotton in early spring, and if it came up skimpy we'd have to go back in and plant more to make a good solid row. When the cotton stalks grew to eight or ten inches high, we'd go in with a hoe and chop a space around each one so they would have room to branch out. Two or three weeks later we'd go back in with hoes and clear out the grass, because it would grow up as tall as the cotton in no time. Sometimes we'd do as many as three hoeings before harvest time. Then came the picking, which we all dreaded. On the first picking you had to be careful to get everything that was open. If you could look back down your rows and see any white spots, that meant you "goose picked" the cotton, or did not pick it all from the boll. Then you'd have to go back and clean up your rows. It was a matter of pride not to leave them messy. You walked between the rows, picking two at a time, and there would be two or three pickings each harvest, according to when the bolls ripened and opened. Picking cotton tears your hands up because the dry bolls have stickers that prick the skin and make it fester up and bleed. Your back aches from bending over all day, your hands are sore and itchy, and your knees throb from crawling on the ground to reach the lowest cotton bolls. I can remember being so exhausted after a day in the fields that I'd literally cry if company showed up at the house at night. You couldn't go to bed as long as company was there, and all I ever wanted to do after picking cotton was to go straight to bed.

School terms were arranged around planting and harvesting, so we were on a different schedule from city children. We started school in October after the harvest, but if all the crops weren't in by then, due to bad weather, they gave us the time off we needed to get everything picked before winter. School let out in May; then we had June off before we started the first picking in July. We picked in July, August, and September from dawn till dark with the Mississippi sun beating down full strength all day. If we were working anywhere near the road where people could see us, Daddy made us wear pants and long-sleeved shirts. But if we were picking way back in the fields, we could wear bathing suits and get a suntan. My skin tans easily, so by the end of every summer I was black. I still like to keep a suntan, but I'm thankful that I now get mine on the beach in front of my house in Florida or by my pool in Nashville, and not in a cotton field.

The only thing that got me through those long, hot days during harvest was daydreaming. I don't remember what I fantasized about when I was real small, but during my adolescence I daydreamed a lot about singing professionally. One of my favorite fantasies as a teenager was to imagine myself standing on a stage singing with my country music idol, George Jones. There I'd be, down on my hands and knees, fingers all cut and scratched, knees sore as boils, dusty and dirty, picking that dang cotton as fast as I could, with a vision going around in my head of George Jones asking me to sing with him in front of thousands of people. Even my best girlfriend would have laughed if I'd shared that fantasy. It was so farfetched it was ridiculous. Yet a few years later, I would not only be singing on the same stage with George Jones—I would be his wife.

PART SIX

Lives and Legends

Prince Among Slaves

T E R R Y   A L F O R D

*The following excerpt from a book by historian Terry Alford can only hint
at the remarkable story of Abd al Rahman Ibrahima, a slave owned by
Thomas Foster of Natchez. Ibrahima (Abraham) was a most unusual
slave, for in his native land before capture, he was a prince in Timbo of
Futa Jalon in the Republic of Guinea. As the following description shows,
Ibrahima's adjustment to slavery was piercingly painful. Although he
had a wife in Timbo, Foster arranged for him to marry a slave named
Isabella. When the marriage unexpectedly worked out, Ibrahima gained
a measure of stability in a foreign land. He lived long enough to have
his royal status verified by a distinguished white man named Dr. Cox,
who had known Ibrahima's father in West Africa. This excerpt from
Chapter 3, "A Common Slave," reveals the backbreaking labor in the
cotton and tobacco fields the former prince performed to make his master
a rich man. Ironically, Ibrahima and Foster were both born in 1762 and
died in 1829.*

T H O M A S   F O S T E R ' S dream of affluence surged ahead. In 1795
he began to accumulate real estate. First he bought five-hundred acres
of land on St. Catherine's Creek from Dr. Flower and the Calvit family
for $1,250. Two years later, when his mother reached the age of seventy,
he bought her plantation for a pittance. Mary gave as a gift to Thomas's
first-born son, Levi, then still a minor, 170 additional acres. To this
Thomas added eighty-five acres from his brother William, whose land
adjoined his own to the north. In addition, a grant of some 650 acres
on distant Buffalo Creek was made to him by the Spanish. In 1799
Thomas purchased four lots in the town of Natchez, which was being
developed on the bluff above the river. For these quarter blocks, two of
them on the main street (and one of those with a house on it), Thomas
paid $1,800. In no case was it necessary for Thomas to sign a note for
the balance of his purchases. Every cent was paid immediately.

Cotton explains his ample purse. The establishment of Whitney gins
after 1795 meant a new age for Natchez, since that gin could clean
tenfold as much cotton as the roller method could. The crop quickly
eclipsed all others, as planters produced one thousand, two thousand,
even twenty-five hundred pounds per acre. Though the boom was remi-

niscent of tobacco days, this prosperity was firmly based. The cotton was of good quality and, after the government burned one planter's harvest because he had wet it to increase its weight, it improved even more. In 1800 cotton sold for a quarter dollar a pound cleaned. Single bales at New Orleans fetched twenty to thirty dollars.

Since women worked in the cotton fields along with men, Thomas mustered about ten hands by 1798. Each produced five to eight hundred pounds of clean cotton apiece. They faced a crop less challenging than tobacco. The routine was basically plowing, planting, hoeing, harvesting, and clearing the fields of old stalks. Exact jobs varied with the season of the year, and time had to be made for raising corn, tending livestock, fencing, and so forth. As the Fosters made the clothes that were worn on the plantation, some cotton would be kept. Most of it, however, was put in bags and sent to nearby gins, where it would be cleaned, the ginners keeping one fifth to one eighth for their trouble. In time it would find its way to an English textile mill. *Hottohoh,* as cotton was called in Futa, was well known to Ibrahima. It grew wild, but was also cultivated near the houses of the Jalunke in land enriched by the wastes of the village. At Timbo the cotton would be carded and spun by the free and slave women and sent to a caste of weavers who transformed it into cloth. Of course, this cotton was not grown for export, but there was a more important difference to Ibrahima. Cotton cultivation at home was the labor of women.

Other tasks on the plantation were more to his liking, such as working with the cattle, a natural employment for any Pullo who happened into slavery. According to the Spanish census of 1792, Thomas Foster owned twenty-five head of cattle. Over the years, as the plantation grew, this number did, too, until by the 1820s he owned 140 head. Thomas is credited with twenty hogs in the Spanish census, a number that also swelled in time. Ibrahima would have been loath to touch one at home, but this is a point his biographers pass over in silence. Did he escape the common pork diet of the District? Precedents are at hand, such as "Nero," a Muslim slave in South Carolina who drew his meat ration in beef, not pork, according to entries of the farmbook of his owner. Natchez diets could also be supplemented with venison and other game. Still, there is no information on Ibrahima's diet. Obviously, though, his enslavement put an end to regular meals of mutton, the dish most popular with the aristocracy of Futa.

Horses provided another link between the old and new that did not seem as bizarre as the upside-down world of farming. Thomas owned both work and riding horses. The number was about ten to fifteen, rather constant over the years. Every now and then a stray was taken up on the plantation. When that happened, it would have to be brought to the barn, where appraisals of the animal were made. Thomas brought oxen to the plantation in later years, and he also kept a number of mules. All livestock received a brand of *T* over *F*, with an underbit in the left ear as an extra precaution of ownership.

Horse racing was a serious business in the District. Its purpose, ostensibly, was to improve the blood of Natchez stock, but "like the fabled Upas tree of Java," a minister wrote, "it poisoned the moral atmosphere in all the region round about." A track operated during the 1790s on the creek several miles below the plantation. Thomas, fond of this sport, was often on hand for the races. One story makes Ibrahima his groom at the turf, a claim that is credible since he was extremely familiar with horses and racing. On a particular day, the account continues, Thomas raced and won against the lanky and uncouth Andrew Jackson of Tennessee. But Jackson was more interested in Thomas's groom than in his horse, and he even offered to buy Ibrahima. The planter refused. This tale, like that of Ibrahima's brandy-laced wedding feast, is probably just a piece of local pride by which the "heiristocracy" has distinguished itself over the years. Andrew Jackson did run a trading post in a long cabin north of Natchez during the winter of 1789–90. In 1791 he was married in Natchez, and in late 1811 he was back in the region slave trading. But this story, completely unsubstantiated as it is, must be viewed skeptically. If it has any value at all, it does not concern racing, or Jackson, but Thomas Foster, who knew how wisely the money for Ibrahima had been spent.

Thomas allowed Ibrahima and Isabella the small privileges, such as working a garden for themselves. With a pass in his pocket, Ibrahima would take any surplus produce into town to sell. He also sold Spanish moss, which was dried and fashioned into a cool "moss mattress" much preferred for summer sleeping. These activities brought Ibrahima humbly onto the fringe of Natchez's cash economy, an economy not widespread in Futa. More important, perhaps, it allowed him to mingle with the slave population in Natchez on Saturdays and Sundays, a time equivalent for religious and social activity to Fridays in Futa. Hardly any language other than Ibrahima's own could have given him conversational ability with Africans on such a wide scale. A herder of Baguirmi, or a Tokolor warrior, despite differences in the manner of speaking, could understand him without great difficulty. These occasions were his only chance to pick up news from Africa. Tidbits were provided by newly arriving Africans from Futa or neighboring states. Little is known of this international slave-trade grapevine, but it did exist, as Ibrahima discovered. Some years after he had been at Natchez, he met a person from home.

"Abduhl Rahahman [Ibrahima]!" the man cried at seeing him, dropping his face to the earth.

It was a tribute of respect to Ibrahima, done out of habit, though then wildly out of place. The person is identified only as "a Negro from [Ibrahima's] father's dominions." Possibly he was a Jalunke who had been sold or stolen from the country.

People such as this could bring Ibrahima news from home. It was sketchy and distorted reporting, but it was news of his family and country, the only news he was likely to get. Ibrahima learned, for example, that his father had died shortly after his capture. The event occurred in northern Futa while Sori was preparing for a *jihaad* in N'Gaaba. Ibrahima's brother Saadu took their father's turban and had himself crowned the fourth *almaami*. He was a "pious, learned, and ascetic" king, according to traditional history, who "never imparted a false oath, never took a person's goods, never touched the wife of his neighbor." If morality had been the sole requisite for holding power, the brother would have grown gray at the job. But a son of Karamoko Alfa wished power himself. With the help of elders, the son arranged a coup about 1795 in which the *almaami* was knifed to death. Many of Saadu's followers died, too, and one suspects even Ibrahima might have perished as well, had he been present.

How much the prince knew of the details of these events is not clear, but he did find out the succession of monarch and something of their fates. He lived at Natchez under the impression that his father had died in a civil war. Actually, and rather ironically, the old warrior had gone peacefully in his bed. Ibrahima thought Saadu had ruled briefly, just a matter of days. In fact, his brother ruled about seven years, those terrible first years of Ibrahima's own life in Natchez. He was correct to believe, however, that Saadu had been murdered. Though his informants rearranged some details and compressed the span of years in their reporting, it is apparent that Ibrahima received at least the headlines, as it were, of the news from home.

Timbo was not the only place where the government was changing hands. Natchez and the remainder of the east bank of the Mississippi River above the thirty-first parallel were ceded to the United States by Spain in 1795. When the Spanish delayed evacuation, Thomas and his brothers, part of what has been termed "the religious element on Pine Ridge," proved restless, disaffected subjects. Tense days passed, but at length the Spanish gave up, departing in March, 1798. The Natchez District became the Mississippi Territory.

Natchez above the bluff took shape in this decade. . . . The great planters were already beginning to build their ostentatious mansions in and near Natchez. Fine furniture, billiard tables, and four-wheeled carriages appeared. A consignment of goods arriving from Bordeaux at the time included almonds, linens, white silk stockings, kid gloves, and playing cards. In August, 1798, the Territory received its first American governor, the Massachusetts Federalist Winthrop Sargent. . . .

"Slavery, though disagreeable to us northern people," [surveyor Andrew] Ellicott wrote in the fall of 1797, "it would certainly be expedient to let continue in this district." It made the whites licentious and idle, "as is generally the case where slavery is tolerated," but it was in the fabric of society. The Natchez Permanent Committee, in a petition to Congress signed by [Daniel] Clark, begged leave "to represent that a great part of the labor in this country is performed by slaves . . . without which, in their present situation, the farms in this district would be but of little more value to the present occupiers than equal quantity of waste land." Expediency had its day, for the law organizing the Territory allowed the system to continue. Still, some of the planters were aware of the iniquity of their property in people. "That we deprive the [slaves] of the sacred boon of liberty is a crime they can never forgive," Sargent told a gathering of militia officers in 1801. "Mild and humane treatment may for a time continue them quiet, but can never fully reconcile them to their situation."

In Natchez the Fosters were part of a group constantly wanting to tighten the policing of the slaves. John, an *alguacil* (constable) during Spanish rule, damned Governor Sargent for tolerating the blacks' drinking, profanation of Sundays, and weekend games of dice and chuck-penny. Fresh from an encounter with two of his own runaways, Thomas condemned the territorial slave law in 1805 "because it does not provide for taking such runaway slaves as go armed and make resistance when pursued." The brothers' worst fears were never realized, however. Though the District simmered at times, it never boiled over. No insurrection occurred to equal that at Pointe Coupée, Louisiana, in 1795, or even that at Timbo during Saadu's reign, when thirty revolutionaries were executed. There were proportionately more blacks at Pointe Coupée, it is true, and the Anglo-American was severer in his police than the Spaniard or the Frenchman. But more subtle considerations must be added.

Ibrahima was a professional soldier, an officer and an strategist. Who better to lead a vengeful slaughter across Pine Ridge? The fact is that he inclined strongly the other way. There were never enough Muslims as Natchez to develop New World Islamic communities comparable to those in South America or to organize revolts like those in Bahia, Brazil, in the 1820s and 1830s, which were really cisatlantic holy wars, directed not only against whites but against pagan and Christian blacks as well. Lacking the fellowship of numbers, beset with language and identity problems, Ibrahima felt a strong temptation to do his own time, what a frontier preacher termed "the Negro's eleventh commandment—every man mind his own business." Important, too, were his own beliefs and prejudices. Torn from the nexus of his social and personal relationships, he fell back on what was transcendent, his faith and a pride in his culture.

It took him years to recover from the shock of what had happened to him, to escape the despondency and self-neglect that engulfed each new arrival. Later still, his language, customs, and incomplete entry into American life made him seem bizarre, not only to whites but to American-born blacks, too. With a hauteur befitting a Pullo prince, Ibrahima, in turn, did not feel the non-Muslim Africans and Americans were his equals, despite the way whites lumped all of them together. The plantation was his reality now, as much as it was Thomas's, and the tug was powerful to identify his interests with those of his owner, not against them. Sarah's "smile and touch," Thomas's "uncommon benevolence" aside, the seeds of his accommodation had been sewn at Timbo.

Ibrahima's tall form became a familiar sight over the years at the market in Natchez, but his bearing became less than noble. From the day his hair had been cut, he had neglected it entirely. It became coarse and mazy, and he left it short, an ornament that no longer concerned him. His skin, much battered by the sun, grew weathered and dry. He lost interest in how he looked and had little time for cleanliness. Even the great Fulbe regard for one's hands was impossible to maintain when they became the calloused companions of froes and weeding hoes and oxcarts. "The privations incident to the lower order of community," as a friend termed it, ate into his health, spirit, and self-respect.

He remained a model of probity, hard-working and dependable at whatever he gave his attention. He never drank, he never cursed, he was never caught in a falsehood or dishonest act. He meant to survive, and he did, but the personal price was staggering. A man who knew him intimately for two decades said that—despite the passage of the years, despite the love of his wife, the cheer of his family, despite the respect of his owner—in all the time he had known Ibrahima, he had never seen him smile.

FROM

The Legend of the
Free State of Jones

RUDY H. LEVERETT

When Jones County constituents chose J. D. Powell as delegate to the state
convention in 1861, they did so because they expected him to vote against
secession, to which the inhabitants of this sparsely populated county were
opposed since they had very few slaves or cotton to fight for and little
sympathy for what they considered to be a rich man's war. But when
Powell saw that the outcome had already been determined in favor of
secession, he changed his vote. These were the conditions that supposedly
led a man named Newton Knight to secede from the Confederacy. Whether
he actually did so cannot finally be determined because of the many con-
flicting stories in both the northern and the southern press. Consequently,
this account by historian Rudy Leverett of Newt Knight and his followers
is simply called "The Legend".

ON 12 JULY 1864, the *Courier* newspaper in Natchez, a town
then long since occupied by the Union army, announced to the world
that Jones County in southeastern Mississippi had seceded from the
state and formed its own government with its own army. This new nation, readers were told, called itself the Republic of Jones. It had its
own commander-in-chief, a Major R. Robinson; a secretary of war, the
Honorable A. C. Williams; foreign ministers; and a congress. The *Cou-*
rier writer explained that since the state and Confederate governments
did not acknowledge the right of a county to secede, notwithstanding
their own involvement with secession from the Union, those governments had declared war against the Republic of Jones, and a desperate
battle had been fought. By this account, the armies of the Republic,
under the command of Major Robinson, had routed the Confederate
forces sent from Mobile under the command of Colonel Mowry. Following this battle, an armistice was declared, during which the belligerents
tried to resolve their differences, but failed even to arrange a cartel for
the exchange of prisoners of war. When negotiations collapsed, according to the story, the Republic recalled its ministers and prepared to
resume the conflict. The congress of the Republic debated the prospect

of forming an alliance with the United States but abandoned that idea on the grounds that the United States had already made clear its position on the question of secession by its war with the Confederacy. Finally, the newspaper declared that the Republic paroled the Confederate prisoners captured in its battle with Colonel Mowry's army and that the Republic expelled from its borders all persons who refused to declare loyalty to the Republic of Jones.

As proof of the veracity of its story, the *Courier* printed a copy of what it called a dispatch, sent from the battlefield by Major Robinson to his secretary of war announcing the victory over Colonel Mowry. Also printed was a copy of another document alleged to be a parole issued to a Confederate soldier named Ben Johnson. An editorial appearing elsewhere in the same issue of the *Courier* provided two additional details pertaining to the new nation: not only did the Republic of Jones have its own army, but it had its own navy as well; and, due to a shortage of paper in Jones County, paroles issued to POWs had been written on the bark of birch trees.

As far as is known, the legend of the Republic of Jones began with the publication of the 12 July *Courier* article. Within a few days of its initial appearance, the article was reprinted in Yankee newspapers from New Orleans to New York. The story, in anything resembling the form given it by the *Courier,* was not carried in Southern papers for a great many years. However, as much as three months before the publication of the *Courier* story, Southern papers had carried news articles on certain events in Jones County that formed the basis for a different, but related, legend. In mid-April of 1864 Southern-oriented papers had published accounts of the expedition of Confederate Colonel Robert Lowry into the northern parts of Jones County for the purpose of suppressing and punishing the criminal activities of a band of deserters led by Newton Knight. The Southern news articles were mildly concerned with showing that the Jones County deserters were criminals rather than pro-Union partisans but contain nothing that even remotely suggests an attempt by the deserters to establish an independent, sovereign nation. Nevertheless, in the course of time, the legend that grew in southeastern Mississippi around Newt Knight's deserters and their skirmishes with Colonel Lowry became assimilated into the legend of the Republic of Jones as developed in the Northern-oriented press. Newt Knight replaced Major R. Robinson as the leader of the Republic, and Colonel Lowry replaced Colonel Mowry or Maury as the leader of the Confederate forces, thus producing the main outline of the modern legend of the Republic of Jones.

The full details of just how the two strands of the legend came together may never be known. But in 1886, a generation after the end of the Civil War, an article titled "A Confederacy Within a Confederacy" was published in the *Magazine of American History*. This article, attributed to G. Norton Galloway, "Historian of the 6th Army Corps," contributed additional details to the story of the Republic. According to Galloway, about whom nothing else is known, the name of the new nation was the "Jones County Confederacy." Its president was Nathan or "Nate" Knight, "a man of intense force of character, bold, defiant, and without fear, but one of the most illiterate citizens of Jones County." In addition to its chief executive and his cabinet, the Jones County Confederacy is said to have had a bicameral legislature, which publicized its statutes by nailing copies of them to the trunks of trees. Galloway further informs us that this little "Confederacy" had a population of some twenty thousand people, most of whom were "refugees from the Davis government." Galloway estimated the size of Knight's army at ten thousand, and he named General Lowry as the Confederate officer sent to crush the rebellion in Jones County.

The credibility of the Galloway article received an impressive boost in 1891, five years after its publication, from Harvard University history professor Albert Bushnell Hart. Writing in the *New England Magazine*, Hart indirectly endorsed the historicity of the Galloway story by citing its details as an example of what he believed to be the few instances of conflict during the Civil War between the Confederate government and its constituent state and local governments. Hart added no new substance to the legend but lent it the authority of his name and institution. The article which appeared in two successive issues of the *Nation* magazine in 1892, sparked a heated debate about the truth of Galloway's claims, thereby further publicizing the story to a nationwide audience. This debate involved correspondence between Hart's adversary, Dr. Samuel Willard, and Mississippi governor, J. M. Stone, as well as an exchange of letters between Stone and former Mississippi governor Robert Lowry. The debate over the truth of Galloway's story was pursued in the *Publications of the Mississippi Historical Society,* where, over the following twelve years, two important papers were published on the subject, in 1898 and 1904.

None of the writers mentioned so far claimed firsthand knowledge of the events they described. The first witness to claim such personal knowledge from a national forum was Union Major Eli Lilly of the Ninth Indiana Cavalry Regiment. Lilly, the founder of the pharmaceutical company that bears his name, was captured in late summer or early fall of 1864 and imprisoned at Enterprise in Clarke County, Mississippi. Speaking at the National Encampment of the Grand Army of the Republic at Indianapolis, Indiana, on 6 September 1893, the year following the debate in the *Nation,* Major Lilly told his audience what had happened to him and his fellow prisoners in November 1864 while they were awaiting exchange at Enterprise:

> One night an old darkey came to our quarters and announced that "de Republic ob Jones is a-comin up here and dey'l rob and kill ebery one ob you." After investigation we found that there existed in Jones County, about thirty miles southwest of us, an organization called the "Republic of Jones" which held supreme control over Jones County and the surrounding country. They had their President, Vice-president, Cabinet and an army of several hundred men, banded together for mutual protection, general plunder, and to keep out of the Confederate army. If a small force was sent to conscript them they would pitch in and wipe them out. If a large force was sent they would take to the swamps and pine barrens and could not be found. So they maintained themselves throughout the war.
>
> It seems the location so near them of a lot of unguarded prisoners supposed to have plenty of money, watches, and good clothing was a temptation they could not withstand.

Major Lilly's basic claim that the Union POWs at Enterprise were threatened by the Republic of Jones was corroborated twenty-one years later by another of the Union prisoners who had been held at Enterprise. In 1914, former Lieutenant W. A. Duckworth of the 110th Colored Infantry Regiment published an article in the *Annals of Iowa* that confirmed Lilly's story but echoed some of the claims now familiar to us from earlier sources. Duckworth's principal contribution was the introduction of the name of Newton Knight in its correct form into the Northern strand of the legend of the Republic of Jones.

In 1919, the material from the Natchez *Courier* article and that from the Galloway story were brought together in the *Literary Digest,* in part via certain New York newspapers, in a story titled "The American 'Republic of Jones' of 1864." This article influenced other writers such as Mary L. Looram, whose story published in *The Outlook* in 1920 was heavily indebted to it. That same year the *Literary Digest* piece was reprinted in Jones County by the Laurel *Daily Leader* newspaper. This seems to be the first publication of what was essentially the Northern version of the legend in the place where the legendary events were supposed to have taken place. The following year the New Orleans *Item* newspaper printed an interview of Meigs O. Frost with Newton Knight, then a very old man, which allowed Knight to go on record with his version of many events associated with the legend. Knight died less than a year after this interview, but the publication of Frost's article seems to mark a shift in the development of the legend toward greater reliance upon Southern sources, especially upon the Jones County folklore associated with Newt Knight; the legend retained, however, many of the elements of the Northern strand. The work of Craddock Goins, which appeared in 1941 in *The American Mercury*, and that of Jack D. L. Holmes published in *The Civil War Times Illustrated* in 1965 are examples of this trend.

The Jones County folklore dealing with the activities of Newt Knight during the Civil War exists basically in oral form. The principal written versions of this material are the privately published works of Knight's son, Thomas Jefferson Knight, and another member of that family, Ethel Knight. The work of the former includes a "muster roll" of Newt Knight's "company" of deserters and a list of that company's "battles" with Confederate forces, both of which are attributed to Newt Knight himself. In these local materials "Captain Knight," as he is often called, is portrayed variously as a sort of rustic Robin Hood character dedicated to protecting helpless women and children from Confederate tax-collectors; as a Confederate army deserter-tuned-traitor dedicated mainly to saving his own hide; and as a Union loyalist committed to fighting a guerrilla war behind Confederate lines. Standard episodes of the Knight legend include his being drafted and consenting to serve only as a hospital orderly; his deserting the Confederate army when the Congress passed its "Twenty Nigger Law," thereby proving that it was "a rich man's war and a poor man's fight"; his killing of a senior Confederate officer and subsequent organization of his own para-military company; his capture of a Confederate supply train; his killing of two Confederate tax-collectors; his raid on a Confederate supply depot; and various of his "battles" with the "cavalry" forces of Colonel Lowry.

Important for our understanding of the development of the legend is the fact that, in Jones County folklore, it is always Colonel Lowry who is the principal adversary of Newt Knight. Colonel Henry Maury and his earlier expedition against the deserters in Jones County play no explicit role in the Knight stories. [The *Courier* article, which gave Colonel Maury's expedition such a pivotal role in the creation of the Republic of Jones did not mention Newt Knight or Colonel Lowry at all but named Major R. Robinson as the leader of the Republic and its armed forces. Moreover, to the extent that politics enters as a theme into the Knight legend, it focuses on the question of Knight's dubious loyalty to the Union, not on the dream of establishing a new state that would be independent of both the Union and the Confederacy.]

With the convergence of the Northern and Southern strands of the legend, the story of the secession of Jones County became well-known locally. Even so, it does not constitute a significant theme in the local lore about Newt Knight. Local tradition does not hold, for example, that Captain Knight killed Major Amos McLemore, the senior Confederate officer in the area, as an act of revolutionary political purpose. Nor does local tradition hold that Knight organized his company of deserters as a revolutionary army. Rather, these episodes are recounted, as often as not, for their inherent literary value. The story of McLemore's murder, for example, is a famous Southern ghost story, which has been collected by Kathryn Tucker Windham in her *13 Mississippi Ghosts and Jeffrey* under the title "Out of Devil's Den." The secession story is sometimes cited by natives as well as by professional writers as the explanation of the county's ancient cognomen, the Free State of Jones, a name that has come to have more or less vague associations with the Knight legend. In 1936, for example, James H. Street published "The Story of Ellisville" in his book, *Look Away! A Dixie Notebook,* in which Street credits Knight as the author of the county's nickname but stops short of claiming that the Free State of Jones was a sovereign nation with Knight as its president. There are other local traditions concerning the origins of the county's nickname. Street later developed the material in his story into a best-selling novel titled *Tap Roots,* which, in 1948, was released by Universal-International as a motion picture under the same title. The film starred Van Heflin, Susan Hayward, and Boris Karloff, with Julie London and Ward Bond acting in supporting roles.

In the years since 1864, the legends of Newt Knight and the Republic of Jones have been treated in dozens of newspapers and magazine articles, books, personal memoirs, public addresses, scholarly essays, and a variety of literary media. It has become an established part of the folk literature of the Southern people. Like many folk legends, these tales are historically ambiguous, structurally fluid, thematically complex, and richly textured with the life and culture of a particular people. They deal poignantly with such universal themes as loyalty, honor, belonging, love, sacrifice, betrayal, defeat, reconciliation, and redemption. Accordingly, they owe no special debt of fidelity to the historical facts about Jones County, Mississippi, or to the biographical facts concerning any of that county's residents, past or present. The simple fact would seem to be that the legend of the Republic of Jones and the history of Jones County, Mississippi, are as logically independent of each other as are, say, the accounts of the city of Troy given respectively by Homer and Schliemann. That, of course, is not to say that the legend bears no relationship whatever to historical facts but only that such relationships as do exist may turn out to be quite indirect and surprising.

Library of Southern Literature

C H A M P   C L A R K

*John Franklin Allen of Baldwin and Tupelo, Mississippi, began a long
and colorful career in Congress in 1884. In one mock-serious oration
before the house, he successfully argued for amending an appropriations
bill to include twenty thousand dollars for a fish hatchery in Tupelo,
soon referred to by locals as John Allen's hatchery. A portion of this speech
gives an idea of the contagious power of his humor: "[T]hose of you who
know anything of the history of your country will remember the conten-
tions and contest that lasted for many years between the French, English,
and Spanish governments for the ownership of the Mississippi territory.
I am informed by those familiar with the real designs of those great nations at that time that the real motive of all of them was the ownership of
Tupelo." The following anecdote " 'Private' John Allen" which gives an
account of how Allen was sent to Congress, was provided by Champ
Clark, a congressman from Missouri, who wrote the preface to* Jefferson's Complete Works *and was editor for* Modern Eloquence.

THE DRY-AS-DUSTS solemnly asseverate that humor never did
any good. They are cocksure of that. Now, let's see. How did Private
John Allen of Mississippi get to Congress? He joked himself in. One
"fetching" bit of humor sent him to Washington as a national law-
maker. The first time John ran for the congressional nomination his
opponent was the Confederate General Tucker, who had fought gal-
lantly during the Civil War and served with distinction two or three
terms in Congress. They met on the stump. General Tucker closed one
of his speeches as follows: "Seventeen years ago last night, my fellow
citizens, after a hard-fought battle on yonder hill, I bivouacked under
yonder clump of trees. Those of you who remember as I do the times
that tried men's souls will not, I hope, forget their humble servant when
the primaries shall be held."

That was a strong appeal in those days, but John raised the general
at his own game in the following amazing manner: "My fellow citizens,
what General Tucker says to you about the engagement seventeen years
ago on yonder hill is true. What General Tucker says to you about having bivouacked in yon clump of trees on that night is true. It is also
true, my fellow citizens, that I was vedette picket and stood guard over

him while he slept. Now then, fellow citizens, all of you who were generals and had privates to stand guard over you while you slept, vote for General Tucker; and all of you who were privates and stood guard over the generals while they slept, vote for Private John Allen!" The people caught on, took John at his word, and sent him to Congress, where he stayed till the world was filled with his renown.

Lanterns on the Levee

WILLIAM ALEXANDER PERCY

*Born in 1885, William Alexander Percy was a true Renaissance man.
In addition to being a planter and businessman, he was a poet and
philosopher who transformed the rugged river town of Greenville into an
oasis for writers such as David Cohn, Shelby Foote, Ellen Douglas, and
Hodding Carter. In 1931, this confirmed bachelor adopted three teenage
boys on the death of their mother, his deceased cousin's wife. One of these
boys, Walker Percy, would one day become an award-winning writer himself. In* Lanterns on the Levee, *Will Percy described and defended an
aristocratic South that would soon pass. In this first chapter, "The
Delta," Percy reveals his knowledge of the place's history as well as his
love for the people.*

M Y C O U N T R Y is the Mississippi Delta, the river country. It lies flat,
like a badly drawn half oval, with Memphis at its northern and Vicksburg at its southern tip. Its western boundary is the Mississippi River,
which coils and returns on itself in great loops and crescents, though
from the map you would think it ran in a straight line north and south.
Every few years it rises like a monster from its bed and pushes over its
banks to vex and sweeten the land it has made. For our soil, very dark
brown, creamy and sweet-smelling, without substrata of rock or shale,
was built up slowly, century after century, by the sediment gathered by
the river in its solemn task of cleansing the continent and deposited in
annual layers of silt on what must once have been the vast depression
between itself and the hills. This ancient depression, now filled in and
level, is what we call the Delta. Some say it was the floor of the sea itself.
Now it seems still to be a floor, being smooth from one end to the other,
without rise or dip or hill, unless the mysterious scattered monuments
of the mound-builders may be called hills. The land does not drain into
the river as most riparian lands do, but tilts back from it towards the
hills of the south and east. Across this wide flat alluvial stretch—north
and south it measures one hundred and ninety-six miles, east and west
at the widest point fifty miles—run slowly and circuitously other rivers
and creeks, also high-banked, with names pleasant to remember—
Rattlesnake Bayou, Quiver River, the Bogue Phalia, the Tallahatchie,
the Sunflower—pouring their tawny waters finally into the Yazoo, which

in turn loses itself just above Vicksburg in the river. With us when you speak of "the river," though there are many, you mean always the same one, the great river, the shifting unappeasable god of the country, feared and loved, the Mississippi.

In the old days this was a land of unbroken forests. All trees grew there except the pine and its kindred, and, strangely enough, the magnolia. The water-oak, the pecan, the cypress, and the sweet-gum were perhaps the most beautiful and home-loving, but there were ash and elm, walnut and maple, and many others besides. They grew to enormous heights, with vast trunks and limbs, and between them spread a chaos of vines and cane and brush, so that the deer and bear took it for their own and only by the Indians was it penetrable, and by them only on wraiths of trails. Wild flowers were few, the soil being too rich and warm and deep, and those, like the yellow-top of early spring, apt to be rank and weed-like. A still country it must have been then, ankle-deep in water, mostly in shadow, with mere flickers of sunshine, and they motey and yellow and thick like syrup. The wild swans loved it; tides of green parakeets from the south and of gray pigeons from the north melted into its tree-tops and gave them sound; ducks—mallard, canvasback, teal, and wood-duck—and Canadian geese, their wedges high in the soft air of autumn like winter's first arrows, have still not deserted it.

Such was my country hardly more than a hundred years ago. It was about then that slavery became unprofitable in the older Southern states and slave-holders began to look for cheap fertile lands farther west that could feed the many black mouths dependent on them. So younger sons from Virginia, South Carolina, and Kentucky with their gear, live-stock, and chattels, human and otherwise, started a leisurely migration into the Delta. Forests were cleared, roads constructed (such dusty or muddy roads!), soil shaped into fields, homes built. They settled first on the banks and bends of the river, later on the banks and bends of the smaller streams, for those were high ground over which the then yearly inundations of the river, as yet uncurbed by levees, never quite reached. There is still a great curve of the shoreline called Kentucky Bend, and another, mostly sandbar now, called Carolina.

The roads they built were local affairs, connecting plantation with plantation or with hamlets which grew slowly and without booms into our present small towns. In wet weather, of which we have much, they were bottomless, and old-timers believed they could never be anything else.

The real highway was the river. All life, social and economic, centered there. The river steamers furnished transportation, relaxation, and information to the whole river people. In our town the *Pargo* landed regularly on Sunday, usually between eleven o'clock and noon. Everybody would be at church, but when she blew, the male members of the congregation to a man would rise and, in spite of indignant glares from their wives and giggles from the choir, make their exits, with a severe air of business just remembered. With the *Pargo* came the week's mail and gossip of the river-front from St. Louis to New Orleans and rumors from the very distant outside world. If the occasion was propitious a little round of poker might be started and a few toddies drunk. They were a fine fleet, those old sidewheelers which plied between St. Louis and New Orleans and stopped on signal at the various plantations and river settlements—the *White,* the *Pargo,* the *Natchez,* the *Robert E. Lee.* The last and least of them was the *Belle of the Bends,* which as a small boy I could never see steaming majestically through the sunset to the landing without a fine choky feeling. They had pleasant outside cabins opening on an enormous white dining-saloon, decorated in the most abandoned gingerbread style, which after supper became a ballroom. Almost as comfortable as our ocean liners of today, they were far easier and more sociable; anybody who was anybody knew everybody else, and each trip was rather like a grand house-party, with dancing and gambling and an abundance of Kentucky whisky and French champagne. The ladies (who never partook of these beverages—maybe a sip of champagne) were always going to New Orleans for Mardi Gras or to shop or to hear the opera (well established there before it was begun in New York) or to visit cousins and aunts in the Louisiana and Natchez territory; and as those were days of enormous families, cousins and aunts were plentiful. There never was a Southern family that was a Southern Family some member of which, incredibly beautiful and sparkling, had not opened the ball with Lafayette. For years apparently his sole occupation was opening balls in New Orleans, Charleston, Natchez, and St. Louis. After looking at a hundred or more badly painted portraits of these belles I am a firm believer in this tradition.

If the ladies loved going to New Orleans, the men-folks were never at a loss for reasons to take the same trip. Memphis was hardly more than country town. The commission merchants (forerunners of the modern bank, co-operative association, Federal Land Bank, insurance company with funds to invest) had their offices in New Orleans and it was they who supplied the planters with the cash for their extensive and costly operations. Here was an ever ready reason to board the boat going south, and one that made unnecessary any reference to the lottery, the races, the masked balls, the fantastic poker games, the hundred and one amiable vices of that most European and sloe-eyed of American cities.

Our Delta culture stemmed from an older one and returned to it for sustenance and renewal, but it lacked much that made the older culture charming and stable. We had few of those roomy old residences, full of fine woodwork and furniture and drapery, which excellent French or English architects built in the Natchez and Charleston neighborhoods and in the Louisiana sugarcane territory. The few we had have caved into the river or burned. But a library was as portable as a slave, and excellent ones abounded—leather-bound sets of the *Spectator,* the *Edinburgh Review,* the works of Mr. Goldsmith and Mr. Pope, *Tom Jones* and *A Sentimental Journey,* translations of Plutarch and Homer, amazing poems about plants and flowers by the grandfather of Darwin, *The Faerie Queene* and Bobbie Burns. (I never came across a copy of Shelley or Keats or Wordsworth in these old collections.) On the bottom shelf would be a fat Bible, the front pages inscribed with long lists of deaths and births in a beautiful flourishing hand. On the top shelf, presumably beyond the reach of the young and impressionable, would be the novels of George Sand and, later, of Ouida. *Paul and Virginia* too was a favorite, but who can now recall that title, though no book ever had more warm and innocuous tears shed over it?

I recall one survivor of that generation, or rather of the one immediately following it. Aunt Fannie, my great-aunt by marriage, was in looks all that the Surry of Eagle's Nest and Marse Chan school of writers would have you believe elderly Southern gentlewomen invariably were. She had exquisite slender white hands, usually folded in idleness on her lap; upon her neat curly white hair, parted in the middle, reposed a tiny white thing of frills and lace which may have been a cap but which looked more like a doily; her face was small and white, with truly a faded-flower look; her dress was black and fitted well and with a sort of chic her still slender figure; she smelled faintly of orris-root, a bit of which she usually chewed with no observable cud-motion. (I don't know why old ladies abandoned orris-root—it's the right smell for them. But, after all, there are no old ladies now.) It was not these things, however, but certain little personal eccentricities of Aunt Fannie's that endeared her to me as a child. She would suddenly drop into a little nap, sitting bolt upright in her chair and with the animated company around her pretending not to notice it. Or, equally inexplicably and with equal disregard of surroundings, she would sob gently and delicately and wipe quite real tears from her eyes with her diminutive orris-scented handkerchief. I attributed this phenomenon to some old and overwhelming sorrow which she carried in her heart and was too proud and ladylike to reveal. Only years and years later I learned that these engaging little habits of hers arose from another little habit: Aunt Fannie took her grain of morphine every day. Being the only wicked thing she ever did, it must have been doubly consoling.

Nevertheless it was this same Aunt Fannie who, a newly arrived bride from Nashville, by raising a moral issue threw the countryside into violent commotion, almost caused a duel, and established a social distinction in our country which has survived more or less to this good day. She gave a house-warming, a large affair, with dancing and champagne and a nougat from New Orleans. In selecting her guests she flatly refused to invite a prominent planter because he openly and notoriously lived with a Negro woman. For some reason the logical duel did not take place; the planter found it easier to move from the community than to live down the stigma or to acquire a paler bolster-companion. Aunt Fannie's husband died, she saw the war and poverty and reconstruction, she raised a daughter and saw her die, she lived on into a new order unsure of itself and without graciousness—if a bit of morphine would blur the present and brighten the past for her, who could have had the heart to deprive her of it?

But, after all, I suppose my paternal grandmother, Mur, was more typical than Aunt Fannie, more illustrative of the class to which she belonged. Left on the plantation during the war, alone with her three babies, while my grandfather, an opponent of secession and a lukewarm slave-owner, was away fighting to destroy the Union and preserve the institution of slavery, she not only raised her little brood single-handed and under the handicap of increasing poverty, but managed the thousand-acre home place. When the effect of the Emancipation Proclamation was realized by the slaves, they became restless, unruly, even dangerous. Her position was one of great difficulty, if not of peril. One evening in the spring of 1864 she learned that the remaining slaves (for many had run away) had met and decided not to plant or work the crop. She immediately called them together and ordered them to meet her in the field the next morning at sun-up. They were there and so was she, sitting in a rocking-chair at the end of the turn-row. (Rocking-chairs have disappeared, a great and symbolic loss.) They met in this manner every morning till July, when the crop was laid by. When the war ended and my grandfather returned penniless, his family managed to live for a year or more on the proceeds from the sale of that cotton crop. At that time my grandmother was twenty-nine, very pretty, with a keen sense of the absurd, and how she could play Strauss waltzes!

Indeed, indeed, the lily-of-the-field life of the Southern gentlewoman existed only in the imagination of Northern critics and Southern sentimentalists, one about as untrustworthy as the other. They had too many duties even in slavery days to be idle. It is true, charm was considered the first and most necessary course in female education, as it is among French women today, and this seems to me sound, because it was a gregarious, sociable, and high-spirited world into which they were born, much addicted to dances and parties of all sorts and visitings and love affairs, and whether that world was delightful or vulgar depended on whether or not the women were ladies. To manage a single household competently is a sizable job. These women on country estates so isolated as to be of necessity self-sustaining and self-governing had the direction of the feeding, clothing, education, health, and morals, not only of their own families, but of the dark feudal community they owned and were responsible for. When there were no bakeries or corner grocery stores of Kress's and Woolworth's, they had to know how to make cloth, bake bread, smoke meat, design quilts, pickle and preserve, nurse and concoct medicines, and supervise the cooking of all and sundry. They held Sunday school for their own and the darkies' children and generally taught white and black alike reading, writing, arithmetic, and the Bible. From them we inherit those golden recipes which give the lie to foreign critics when they say Americans know nothing of gustatory joys, eat to live, and are unaware that good cooking is one of the few things that make life bearable. What of Virginia hams, Maryland terrapin, Charleston roe and hominy, New Orleans gumbo-filé, griades, fourchettes, sea-food—oysters, crabs, shrimp, pompano, red snapper, crawfish, sheepshead—and the hundred exquisite ways of preparing them known to the Creoles, not to the Parisian? What of coffee, dish-water in the North, chicory abroad, but strong and hot and clear and delectable on any Southern table? And the hundred varieties of hot breads? Oh, the poor little boys who never put a lump of butter into steaming batter-bread (spoon-bread is the same thing) or lolled their tongues over pain-perdu! There should be a monument to Southern womanhood, creator of the only American cuisine that makes the world a better place to live in.

Instead, you will find in any Southern town a statue in memory of the Confederate dead, erected by the Daughters of something or other, and made, the townsfolk will respectfully tell you, in Italy. It is always the same: a sort of shaft or truncated obelisk, after the manner of the

Washington Monument, on top of which stands a little man with a big hat holding a gun. If you are a Southerner you will not feel inclined to laugh at these efforts, so lacking in either beauty or character, to preserve the memory of their gallant and ill-advised forebears. I think the dash, endurance, and devotion of the Confederate soldier have not been greatly exaggerated in song and story: they do not deserve these chromos in stone. Sentiment driveling into sentimentality, poverty, and, I fear, lack of taste are responsible for them, but they are the only monuments which are dreadful from the point of view of aesthetics, craftsmanship, and conception that escape being ridiculous. They are too pathetic for that. Perhaps a thousand years from now the spade of some archaeologist will find only these as relics of and clues to the vanished civilization we call ours. How tragically and comically erroneous his deductions will be!

My memorial to Southern cookery would be more informative. Or one to Southern hospitality, concerning which so many kindly things have been said. And that tradition too must have begun in those earlier times. In such a purely agrarian and thinly populated country there were no hotels or lodging-houses of any kind. The traveler could buy neither bed nor food, but had to hope some resident would give them to him as an act not so much of hospitality as of sheer humanity. A stranger in the Navajo country of Arizona or in Arabia experiences the same difficulty today and has it solved for him in the same way—the natives receive him as their guest. Frequently this must have been trying to the ladies of the household. I have always heard, though I will not vouch for the story, that a stranger dropped in for the night on one of my Louisiana kinsmen and remained a year. The stranger was Audubon, the ornithologist. My French grandmother, whom I called Mère, was not quite so cordial. Neither her plantation home nor her English vocabulary was large. When my grandfather, whom I called Père, unexpectedly appeared one nightfall with a number of friends who had been bear-hunting with him, she first said to him: "Mais, Ernest"—and he quailed, for it was one of her favorite phrases and it could mean all manner of things, but it always *meant*—then she observed to the guests: "Welcome, messieurs, I can eat you but I cannot sleep you." She was a remarkable woman, and very firm.

Well, she has joined the lovely ladies who opened the ball with Lafayette, and the forest country, only half conquered in her day, has become an open expanse of cotton plantations, though woods, unkempt remnants, still cling to their edges and rim the creeks and bayous. Railroads have come, and almost gone, thanks to the shoving and obese trucks and busses. The roads are now of concrete or gravel and there are thousands of miles of ugly wires crossing the landscape bearing messages or light. The river town has a White Way, picture shows, many radios, a Chamber of Commerce, and numerous service clubs. We have gone forward, our progress is ever so evident.

And the river? It is changed and eternally the same. The early settlers soon began to rebuff its yearly caress, that impregnated and vitalized the soil, by building small dikes around their own individual plantations. This was a poor makeshift and in time, not without ruction and bitter debate, was abandoned in favor of levee districts which undertook to levee the river itself at the cost of the benefited landowners within the districts. After reconstruction no more vital problem perplexed Delta statesmen than how to convince the Federal government of the propriety of contributing to the cost of building levees. At first they failed, but later niggardly aid was doled out—a bit some years, others none. Only within the last fifteen years has the government accepted the view urged for half a century by our people that the river's waters are the nation's waters and fighting them is the nation's fight. The United States Engineers under the War Department are now in full charge of levee revetment work from one end of the river to the other.

But this work has not changed the savage nature and austere beauty of the river itself. Man draws near to it, fights it, uses it, curses it, loves it, but it remains remote, unaffected. Between the fairy willows of the banks or the green slopes of the levees it moves unhurried and unpausing; building islands one year to eat them the next; gnawing the bank on one shore till the levee caves in and another must be built farther back, then veering wantonly and attacking with equal savagery the opposite bank; in spring, high and loud against the tops of the quaking levees; in summer, deep and silent in its own tawny bed; bearing eternally the waste and sewage of the continent to the cleansing wide-glittering Gulf. A gaunt and terrible stream, but more beautiful and dear to its children than Thames or Tiber, than mountain brook or limpid estuary. The gods on their thrones are shaken and changed, but it abides, aloof and unappeasable, with no heart except for its own task, under the unbroken and immense arch of the lighted sky where the sun, too, goes a lonely journey.

As a thing used by men it has changed: the change is not in itself, but in them. No longer the great white boats and their gallant companies ply to and fro on its waters. A certain glamour is gone forever. But the freighters and barge lines of today keep one reminder of the vanished elder packets—their deep-throated, long-drawn-out, giant voices.

And still there is no sound in the world so filled with mystery and long-ing and unease as the sound at night of a river-boat blowing for the landing—one long, two shorts, one long, two shorts. Over the somber levels of the water pours that great voice, so long prolonged it is joined by echoes from the willowed shore, a chorus of ghosts, and, roused from sleep, wide-eyed and still, you are oppressed by vanished glories, the last trump, the calling of the ends of the earth, the current, cease-lessly moving out into the dark, of the eternal dying. Trains rushing at night under the widening pallor of their own smoke, bearing in wild haste their single freightage of wild light, over a receding curve of thun-der, have their own glory. But they are gone too quickly, like a meteor, to become part of your deep own self. The sound of the river-boats hangs inside your heart like a star.

Fabulous Provinces: A Memoir

T . D . Y O U N G

Thomas Daniel Young was born in Louisville, Mississippi, in 1919. Emeritus Professor of English at Vanderbilt, he has written extensively about southern literary figures such as Andrew Lytle. In this account, Young describes how his father, Will Young, set up his medical practice in 1902 at Boone in Neshoba County, where he would deliver over four thousand babies during his fifty-six-year practice. This vignette offers a clear example of why Young often argued that, although the plane of life in Mississippi is low, the quality of life is high (from chapter 1, "Son, Are You a Doctor?").

W I L L   W A S   A L M O S T asleep when the conductor suddenly opened the door of the day coach and yelled, "Artesia, next stop! Artesia in five minutes." He sat up, stretched, and stepped into the aisle and began collecting his luggage. He pulled down an old cardboard valise that contained almost all of his worldly belongings, then, more carefully, laid beside it a paper bag in which were packed scissors, forceps, bandages, stethoscope, and assorted salves and pills. He had been given these items the evening before, following his graduation from the University of Nashville School of Medicine. At the reception honoring the graduates, each brand-new M.D. had been given the same packet. Will had just written his name on the package and was going to leave it in the library when he encountered Dr. Larkin Smith. Smith, his favorite teacher, examined the contents of the parcel. "They've given you everything you will need to practice medicine," Dr. Smith remarked (sarcastically, Will thought), since it had been Smith who had consistently—and alone among Will's teachers—emphasized that disease is caused by bacteria. It was true that others had *mentioned* the possibility as an interesting theory, but these men remained committed to the notion that some maladies were caused "by breathing the unwholesome damps" while others were caused by an excess of the "humors" and could be treated successfully by removing the contaminated blood. In exasperation Dr. Smith had once remarked to his class: "The only

Will, after letting the horse drink from a trough beside the store, de-cided he had better get some food for himself and the horse. He had no idea when he would find another store. He tied the horse to a hitch-ing post and walked through the front door. As his eyes gradually ad-justed to the gloomy interior, he was struck by the aroma of leather, cheese, apples, and aging wood—altogether, a pleasant aroma. Then a voice asked from the back of the store, "Can I do something for you?" The voice came from a wiry little man standing in the enclosure at the back of the store marked POST OFFICE, BOONE, MISSISSIPPI.

"Yes. I need some dinner, and so does my horse."

The man closed the latticed wooden gate to the post office and came to the front of the store. "I'm Melvin Barnhill. Don't believe I've seen you before."

"No, I guess you haven't. I'm a stranger in these parts. Just passing through on my way to the Cleveland community, down in Neshoba."

They shook hands and began talking about the weather and the crops; but Melvin Barnhill did not offer to wait on Will. Instead, he said: "I was about to close up here and go to the house for dinner. Why don't you put your horse in the barn and come with me?" Will thanked him, admitting that, since it had been almost two days since he had had one, he would indeed like a hot meal. Barnhill went back to the post office and put up the few remaining pieces of mail, then came back to the front of the store, and they walked over to Barnhill's house to-gether. As they neared the house, about twenty-five yards from the store, Barnhill yelled, "Edgar! Come here!" He told the fourteen-year-old boy who appeared to take Will's horse to the barn, unsaddle it, and give it some corn. Then they went up the steps to the front porch of an enclosed dog-run house and entered a long hall, which served as a din-ing room-sitting room. Soon joined by Edgar, they sat down at the table. Mrs. Barnhill, a large woman with a noticeable limp, entered and sat at the end of the table nearer the kitchen, where she could more easily replenish the dishes of food on the over-burdened table. Opposite her was her husband and on his right were Will and Edgar. Opposite them were two other boys—Grady, about two years younger than Edgar—and Roy, two years Grady's junior. Before them stood a veritable feast of summer vegetables: new peas and potatoes in a rich butter-cream sauce, fried squash, turnip greens, radishes, spring onions, crusty biscuits, cornbread muffins, coconut cake, and freshly baked egg custard. Beside each plate was a half-pint goblet of milk, which, since it was taken from the cows earlier that day, had cooled in a tightly closed molasses pail at the bottom of the well.

Almost an hour later, Will, filled to capacity, joined the family on the front porch. Melvin Barnhill sat in a cane-backed chair tilted against the wall, fighting food-induced drowsiness. In the kitchen, his wife was clearing the table. The boys were sprawled on the porch. Eventually Grady restlessly got up and went to the front steps. Noticing that he had a decided limp, Will said to him: "Come over here a minute, son. Why are you limping so? What's wrong with that foot?"

"I don't know. Had it a long time. People say I got a bone felon." He sat down at Will's feet, and Will took the foot in both hands. Looking at it carefully, he could see that constant walking in dew-covered grass, farmlots, fields, and woods had not only bruised the foot more or less permanently but had also dangerously infected it.

Will asked Edgar to go to the barn and fetch his saddle bags. When the boy returned, Will removed a scalpel and a bottle each of alcohol and iodine. He had Roy and Edgar hold Grady while he washed the affected part of the foot with alcohol, then lanced it and allowed it to drain. Finally, he applied iodine and dressed the foot with a bandage.

Melvin Barnhill, who had been watching this procedure with great interest, waited until Will had finished, then asked: "Son, are you a doctor?"

"I guess so. At least, that's what they told me in Nashville." Will looked back at Grady. "But let's wait and see if this fellow lives. Then we'll know for sure."

The boy's father considered this bit of wit for a moment. "We sure do need a doctor around here," he said at last, as much to himself as to Will. At the same time, the statement sounded like a question. Melvin was obviously getting at something. "The nearest one is ten miles away, and he's overworked as it is," Melvin continued. "If you'd settle here, you could use the side room where I store feed, and I wouldn't charge you a penny rent."

Will inspected the room and decided that it would do. By early afternoon the next day, they had cleared out the room, and Will hung a sign outside the front door that read: w.a. young, m.d. Around five o'clock, Will received his first patient, an elderly black man with the "spring mizries." Will gave him a "bedtime capsule" with instructions to take two tablespoons of castor oil before breakfast. The man gave Doctor Young two dollars. Thus began a practice that would last nearly sixty years.

FROM

Black Boy

RICHARD WRIGHT

*Born near Natchez in 1908 to a sharecropper father and a sickly mother
who taught school when she could, the child Richard Wright was moved
around from relative to relative. In chapter 7 of his autobiography, published in 1945, Wright describes how his first story, called "The Voodoo
of Hell's Half Acre," came to be printed when he was only fifteen. In his
dreams to be a writer he got little support from his grandmother, with
whom he lived in Jackson, Mississippi, from his mother, who was paralyzed, or from his older relatives. Yet writing would one day free him from
the poverty and Jim Crow laws that bound him. Wright, who exiled himself from Mississippi by moving to Memphis, Chicago, New York, and
finally Paris, would one day be considered one of Mississippi's foremost
writers. His best-known work,* Native Son, *was published in 1940.*

SUMMER. Bright hot days. Hunger still a vital part of my consciousness. Passing relatives in the hallways of the crowded home and not
speaking. Eating in silence at a table where prayers are said. My mother
recovering slowly, but now definitely crippled for life. Will I be able to
enter school in September? Loneliness. Reading. Job hunting. Vague
hopes of going north. But what would become of my mother if I left
her in this queer house? And how would I fare in a strange city? Doubt.
Fear. My friends are buying long-pants suits that cost from seventeen to
twenty dollars, a sum as huge to me as the Alps! This was my reality in
1924.

Word came that a near-by brickyard was hiring and I went to investi-
gate. I was frail, not weighing a hundred pounds. At noon I sneaked
into the yard and walked among the aisles of damp, clean-smelling clay
and came to a barrow full of wet bricks just taken from the machine
that shaped them. I caught hold of the handles of the barrow and was
barely able to lift it; it weighed perhaps four times as much as I did. If I
were only stronger and heavier!

Later I asked questions and found that the water boy was missing; I
ran to the office and was hired. I walked in the hot sun lugging a big
zinc pail from one laboring gang of black men to another for a dollar
a day; a man would lift the tin dipper to his lips, take a swallow, rinse

out his mouth, spit, and then drink in long, slow gulps as sweat dripped into the dipper. And off again I would go, chanting:

"Water!"

And somebody would yell:

"Here, boy!"

Deep into wet pits of clay, into sticky ditches, up slippery slopes I would struggle with the pail. I stuck it out, reeling at times from the hunger, pausing to get my breath before clambering up a hill. At the end of the week the money sank into the endless expenses at home. Later I got a job in the yard that paid a dollar and a half a day, that of bat boy. I went between the walls of clay and picked up bricks that had cracked open; when my barrow was full, I would wheel it out onto a wooden scaffold and dump it into a pond.

I had but one fear here: a dog. He was owned by the boss of the brickyard and he haunted the clay aisles, snapping, growling. The dog had been wounded many times, for the black workers were always hurling bricks at it. Whenever I saw the animal, I would take a brick from my load and toss it at him; he would slink away, only to appear again, showing his teeth. Several of the Negroes had been bitten and had been ill; the boss had been asked to leash the dog, but he had refused. One afternoon I was wheeling my barrow toward the pond when something sharp sank into my thigh. I whirled; the dog crouched a few feet away, snarling. I had been bitten. I drove the dog away and opened my trousers; teeth marks showed deep and red.

I did not mind the stinging hurt, but I was afraid of an infection. When I went to the office to report that the boss's dog had bitten me, I was met by a tall blonde white girl.

"What do you want?" she asked.

"I want to see the boss, ma'am."

"For what?"

"His dog bit me, ma'am, and I'm afraid I might get an infection."

"Where did he bite you?"

"On my leg," I lied, shying from telling her where the bit was.

"Let's see," she said.

"No, ma'am. Can't I see the boss?"

"He isn't here now," she said, and went back to her typing.

I returned to work, stopping occasionally to examine the teeth marks; they were swelling. Later in the afternoon a tall white man wearing a cool white suit, a Panama hat, and white shoes came toward me.

"Is this the nigger?" he asked a black boy as he pointed at me.

"Yes, sir," the black boy answered.

"Come here, nigger," he called me.

I went to him.

"They tell me my dog bit you," he said.

"Yes, sir."

I pulled down my trousers and he looked.

"Humnnn," he grunted, then laughed. "A dog bite can't hurt a nigger."

"It's swelling and it hurts," I said.

"If it bothers you, let me know," he said. "But I never saw a dog yet that could really hurt a nigger."

He turned and walked away and the black boys gathered to watch his tall form disappear down the aisles of wet bricks.

"Sonofabitch!"

"He'll get his someday!"

"Boy, their hearts are hard!"

"Lawd, a white man'll do anything!"

"Break up that prayer meeting!" the white straw boss yelled.

The wheelbarrows rolled again. A boy came close to me.

"You better see a doctor," he whispered.

"I ain't got no money," I said.

Two days passed and luckily the redness and swelling went away.

Summer wore on and the brickyard closed; again I was out of work. I heard that caddies were wanted and I tramped five miles to the golf links. I was hired by a florid-faced white man at the rate of fifty cents for nine holes. I did not know the game and I lost three balls in as many minutes; it seemed that my eyes could not trace the flight of the balls. The man dismissed me. I watched the other boys do their jobs and within half an hour I had another golf bag and was following a ball. I made a dollar. I returned home, disgusted, tired, hungry, hating the sight of a golf course.

School opened and, though I had not prepared myself, I enrolled. The school was far across town and the walking distance alone con-sumed my breakfast of mush and lard gravy. I attended classes without books for a month, then got a job working mornings and evenings for three dollars a week.

I grew silent and reserved as the nature of the world in which I lived became plain and undeniable; the bleakness of the future affected my will to study. Granny had already thrown out hints that it was time for me to be on my own. But what had I learned so far that would help me to make a living? Nothing. I could be a porter like my father before me, but what else? And the problem of living as a Negro was cold and hard.

What was it that made the hate of whites for blacks so steady, seemingly so woven into the texture of things? What kind of life was possible under that hate? How had this hate come to be? Nothing about the problems of Negroes was ever taught in the classrooms at school; and whenever I would raise these questions with the boys, they would either remain silent or turn the subject into a joke. They were vocal about the petty individual wrongs they suffered, but they possessed no desire for a knowledge of the picture as a whole. Then why was I worried about it?

Was I really as bad as my uncles and aunts and Granny repeatedly said? Why was it considered wrong to ask questions? Was I right when I resisted punishment? It was inconceivable to me that one should surrender to what seemed wrong, and most of the people I had met seemed wrong. Ought one to surrender to authority even if one believed that that authority was wrong? If the answer was yes, then I knew that I would always be wrong, because I could never do it. Then how could one live in a world in which one's mind and perceptions meant nothing and authority and tradition meant everything? There were no answers.

The eighth grade days flowed in their hungry path and I grew more conscious of myself; I sat in classes, bored, wondering, dreaming. One long dry afternoon I took out my composition book and told myself that I would write a story; it was sheer idleness that led me to it. What would the story be about? It resolved itself into a plot about a villain who wanted a widow's home and I called it *The Voodoo of Hell's Half-Acre.* It was crudely atmospheric, emotional, intuitively psychological, and stemmed from pure feeling. I finished it in three days and then wondered what to do with it.

The local Negro newspaper! That's it . . . I sailed into the office and shoved my ragged composition book under the nose of the man who called himself the editor.

"What is that?" he asked.

"A story," I said.

"A news story?"

"No, fiction."

"All right. I'll read it," he said.

He pushed my composition book back on his desk and looked at me curiously, sucking at his pipe.

"But I want you to read it *now.*" I said.

He blinked. I had no idea how newspapers were run. I thought that one took a story to an editor and he sat down then and there and read it and said yes or no.

"I'll read this and let you know about it tomorrow," he said.

I was disappointed; I had taken time to write it and he seemed distant and uninterested.

"Give me the story," I said, reaching for it.

He turned from me, took up the book and read ten pages or more.

"Won't you come in tomorrow?" he asked. "I'll have it finished then."

I honestly relented.

"All right," I said. "I'll stop in tomorrow."

I left with the conviction that he would not read it. Now, where else could I take it after he had turned it down? The next afternoon, en route to my job, I stepped into the newspaper office.

"Where's my story?" I asked.

"It's in galleys," he said.

"What's that?" I asked; I did not know what galleys were.

"It's set up in type," he said. "We're publishing it."

"How much money will I get?" I asked, excited.

"We can't pay for manuscript," he said.

"But you sell your papers for money," I said with logic.

"Yes, but we're young in business," he explained.

"But you're asking me to *give* you my story, but you don't *give* your papers away," I said.

He laughed.

"Look, you're just starting. This story will put your name before our readers. Now, that's something," he said.

"But if the story is good enough to sell to your readers, then you ought to give me some of the money you get from it," I insisted.

He laughed again and I sensed that I was amusing him.

"I'm going to offer you something more valuable than money," he said. "I'll give you a chance to learn to write."

I was pleased, but I still thought he was taking advantage of me.

"When will you publish my story?"

"I'm dividing it into three installments," he said. "The first installment appears this week. But the main thing is this: Will you get news for me on a space rate basis?"

"I work mornings and evening for three dollars a week," I said.

"Oh," he said. "Then you better keep that. But what are you doing this summer?"

"Nothing."

"Then come to see me before you take another job," he said. "And write some more stories."

A few days later my classmates came to me with baffled eyes, holding copies of the *Southern Register* in their hands.

"Did you really write that story?" they asked me.

"Yes."

"Why?"

"Because I wanted to."

"Where did you get it from?"

"I made it up."

"You didn't. You copied it out of a book."

"If I had, no one would publish it."

"But what are they publishing it for?"

"So people can read it."

"Who told you to do that?"

"Nobody."

"Then why did you do it?"

"Because I wanted to," I said again.

They were convinced that I had not told them the truth. We had never had any instruction in literary matters at school; the literature of the nation or the Negro had never been mentioned. My schoolmates could not understand why anyone would want to write a story; and, above all, they could not understand why I had called it *The Voodoo of Hell's Half-Acre*. The mood out of which a story was written was the most alien thing conceivable to them. They looked at me with new eyes, and a distance, a suspiciousness came between us. If I had thought anything in writing the story, I had thought that perhaps it would make me more acceptable to them, and now it was cutting me off from them more completely than ever.

At home the effects were no less disturbing. Granny came into my room early one morning and sat on the edge of my bed.

"Richard, what is this you're putting in the papers?" she asked.

"A story," I said.

"About what?"

"It's just a story, granny."

"But they tell me it's been in three times."

"It's the same story. It's in three parts."

"But what is it about?" she insisted.

I hedged, fearful of getting into a religious argument.

"It's just a story I made up," I said.

"Then it's a lie," she said.

"Oh, Christ," I said.

"You must get out of this house if you take the name of the Lord in vain," she said.

"Granny, please . . . I'm sorry," I pleaded. "But it's hard to tell you about the story. You see, granny, everybody knows that the story isn't true, but . . ."

"Then why write it?" she asked.

"Because people might want to read it."

"That's the Devil's work," she said and left.

My mother also was worried.

"Son, you ought to be more serious," she said. "You're growing up now and you won't be able to get jobs if you let people think that you're weak-minded. Suppose the superintendent of schools would ask you to teach here in Jackson, and he found out that you had been writing stories?"

I could not answer her.

"I'll be all right, mama," I said.

Uncle Tom, though surprised, was highly critical and contemptuous. The story had no point, he said. And whoever heard of a story by the title of *The Voodoo of Hell's Half-Acre?* Aunt Addie said that it was a sin for anyone to use the world "hell" and that what was wrong with me was that I had nobody to guide me. She blamed the whole thing upon my upbringing.

In the end I was so angry that I refused to talk about the story. From no quarter, with the exception of the Negro newspaper editor, had there come a single encouraging word. It was rumored that the principal wanted to know why I had used the word "hell." I felt that I had committed a crime. Had I been conscious of the full extent to which I was pushing against the current of my environment, I would have been frightened altogether out of my attempts at writing. But my reactions were limited to the attitude of the people about me, and I did not speculate or generalize.

I dreamed of going north and writing books, novels. The North symbolized to me all that I had not felt and seen; it had no relation whatever to what actually existed. Yet, by imagining a place where everything was possible, I kept hope alive in me. But where had I got this notion of doing something in the future, of going away from home and accomplishing something that would be recognized by others? I had, of course, read my Horatio Alger stories, my pulp stories, and I knew my Get-Rich-Quick Wallingford series from cover to cover, though I had sense enough not to hope to get rich; even to my naïve imagination that possibility was too remote. I knew that I lived in a country in which the aspirations of black people were limited, marked-off. Yet I felt that I had to go somewhere and do something to redeem my being alive.

I was building up in me a dream which the entire educational system of the South had been rigged to stifle. I was feeling the very thing that the state of Mississippi had spent millions of dollars to make sure that I would never feel; I was becoming aware of the thing that the Jim Crow laws had been drafted and passed to keep out of my consciousness; I was acting on impulses that southern senators in the nation's capital had striven to keep out of Negro life; I was beginning to dream the dreams that the state had said were wrong, that the schools had said were taboo.

Had I been articulate about my ultimate aspirations, no doubt someone would have told me what I was bargaining for; but nobody seemed to know, and least of all did I. My classmates felt that I was doing something that was vaguely wrong, but they did not know how to express it. As the outside world grew more meaningful, I became more concerned, tense; and my classmates and my teachers would say: "Why do you ask so many questions?" Or: "Keep quiet."

I was in my fifteenth year; in terms of schooling I was far behind the average youth of the nation, but I did not know that. In me was shaping a yearning for a kind of consciousness, a mode of being that the way of life about me had said could not be, must not be, and upon which the penalty of death had been placed. Somewhere in the dead of the southern night my life had switched onto the wrong track and, without my knowing it, the locomotive of my heart was rushing down a dangerously steep slope, heading for a collision, heedless of the warning red lights that blinked all about me, the sirens and the bells and the screams that filled the air.

One Writer's Beginnings

EUDORA WELTY

Although Eudora Welty's accomplishments are well known all over the world, she was born in Jackson, Mississippi, in 1909, and she has been "underfoot" there, as she once put it, most of her life. She graduated from Mississippi University for Women, attended Columbia University School of Business, and then went to work for the Works Progress Administration (WPA), taking notable photographs of people whose lives were marked by the depression. She has received the Pulitzer Prize, the American Book Award for fiction, France's Legion of Honor, and many, many other prizes for her short stories, including those collected in A Curtain of Green *and* The Golden Apples, *and novels, such as* The Ponder Heart, Losing Battles, *and* The Optimist's Daughter. *Her "sense of place" anchors the reader in the particulars of a place through the five senses and is considered to be one of her major contributions to fiction. In this excerpt from a section of her memoirs, called "Listening," she explores mysteries heard and overheard when she was a child. Praised for her careful rendering of characters' expressions, idioms, and dialects, Welty began to develop this ability during those early years of listening.*

IN THAT VANISHED time in small-town Jackson, most of the ladies I was familiar with, the mothers of my friends in the neighborhood, were busiest when they were sociable. In the afternoons there was regular visiting up and down the little grid of residential streets. Everybody had calling cards, even certain children; and newborn babies themselves were properly announced by sending out their tiny engraved calling cards attached with a pink or blue bow to those of their parents. Graduation presents to high-school pupils were often "card cases." On the hall table in every house the first thing you saw was a silver tray waiting to receive more calling cards on top of the stack already piled up like jackstraws; they were never thrown away.

My mother let none of this idling, as she saw it, pertain to her; she went her own way with or without her calling cards, and though she was fond of her friends and they were fond of her, she had little time for small talk. At first, I hadn't known what I'd missed.

When we at length bought our first automobile, one of our neighbors was often invited to go with us on the family Sunday afternoon ride. In Jackson it was counted an affront to the neighbors to start out for anywhere with an empty seat in the car. My mother sat in the back with her friend, and I'm told that as a small child I would ask to sit in the middle, and say as we started off, "Now *talk*."

There was dialogue throughout the lady's accounts to my mother. "I said" . . . "He said" . . . "And I'm told she very plainly said" . . . "It was midnight before they finally heard, and what do you think it *was?*"

What I loved about her stories was that everything happened in *scenes*. I might not catch on to what the root of the trouble was in all that happened, but my ear told me it was dramatic. Often she said, "The crisis had come!"

This same lady was one of Mother's callers on the telephone who always talked a long time. I knew who it was when my mother would only reply, now and then, "Well, I declare," or "You don't say so," or "Surely not." She'd be standing at the wall telephone, listening against her will, and I'd sit on the stairs close by her. Our telephone had a little bar set into the handle which had to be pressed and held down to keep the connection open, and when her friend had said goodbye, my mother needed me to prize her fingers loose from the little bar; her grip had become paralyzed. "What did she say?" I asked.

"She wasn't *saying* a thing in this world," sighed my mother. "She was just ready to talk, that's all."

My mother was right. Years later, beginning with my story "Why I Live at the P.O.," I wrote reasonably often in the form of a monologue that takes possession of the speaker. How much more gets told besides!

This lady told everything in her sweet, marveling voice, and meant every word of it kindly. She enjoyed my company perhaps even more than my mother's. She invited me to catch her doodlebugs; under the trees in her backyard were dozens of their holes. When you stuck a broom straw down one and called, "Doodlebug, doodlebug, your house is on fire and all your children are burning up," she believed this is why the doodlebug came running out of the hole. This was why I loved to call up her doodlebugs instead of ours.

My mother could never have told me her stories, and I think I knew why even then: my mother didn't believe them. But I could listen to this murmuring lady all day. She believed everything she heard, like the doodlebug. And so did I.

This was a day when ladies' and children's clothes were very often made at home. My mother cut out all the dresses and her little boys' rompers, and a sewing woman would come and spend the day upstairs in the sewing room fitting and stitching them all. This was Fannie. This old black sewing woman, along with her speed and dexterity, brought along a great provision of up-to-the-minute news. She spent her life going from family to family in town and worked right in its bosom, and nothing could stop her. My mother would try, while I stood being pinned up. "Fannie, I'd rather Eudora didn't hear that." "That" would be just what I was longing to hear, whatever it was. "I don't want her exposed to gossip"—as if gossip were measles and I could catch it. I did catch some of it but not enough. "Mrs. O'Neil's oldest daughter she had her wedding dress *tried on,* and all her fine underclothes feather-stitched and ribbon run in and then—" "I think that will do, Fannie," said my mother. It was tantalizing never to be exposed long enough to hear the end.

Fannie was the worldliest old woman to be imagined. She could do whatever her hands were doing without having to stop talking; and she could speak in a wonderfully derogatory way with any number of pins stuck in her mouth. Her hands steadied me like claws as she stumped on her knees around me, tacking me together. The gist of her tale would be lost on me, but Fannie didn't bother about the ear she was telling it to; she just liked telling. She was like an author. In fact, for a good deal of what she said, I daresay she *was* the author.

Long before I wrote stories, I listened for stories. Listening *for* them is something more acute than listening *to* them. I suppose it's an early form of participation in what goes on. Listening children know stories are *there*. When their elders sit and begin, children are just waiting and hoping for one to come out, like a mouse from its hole.

It was taken entirely for granted that there wasn't any lying in our family, and I was advanced in adolescence before I realized that in plenty of homes where I played with schoolmates and went to their parties, children lied to their parents and parents lied to their children and to each other. It took me a long time to realize that these very same everyday lies, and the strategems and jokes and tricks and dares that went with them, were in fact the basis of the *scenes* I so well loved to hear about and hoped for and treasured in the conversation of adults.

My instinct—the dramatic instinct—was to lead me, eventually, on the right track for a storyteller: the *scene* was full of hints, pointers, suggestions, and promises of things to find out and know about human beings. I had to grow up and learn to listen for the unspoken as well as the spoken—and to know a truth, I also had to recognize a lie.

It was when my mother came out onto the sleeping porch to tell me goodnight that her trial came. The sudden silence in the double bed meant my younger brothers had both keeled over in sleep, and I in the single bed at my end of the porch would be lying electrified, waiting for this to be the night when she'd tell me what she'd promised for so long. Just as she bent to kiss me I grabbed her and asked: "Where do babies come from?"

My poor mother! But something saved her every time. Almost any night I put the baby question to her, suddenly, as if the whole outdoors exploded, Professor Holt would start to sing. The Holts lived next door; he taught penmanship (the Palmer Method), typing, bookkeeping and shorthand at the high school. His excitable voice traveled out of their diningroom windows across the two driveways between our houses, and up to our upstairs sleeping porch. His wife, usually so quiet and gentle, was his uncannily spirited accompanist at the piano. "High-ho! Come to the Fair!" he'd sing, unless he sang "Oho ye oho ye, who's bound for the ferry, the briar's in bud and the sun's doing down!"

"Dear, this isn't a very good time for you to hear Mother, is it?"

She couldn't get started. As soon as she'd whisper something, Professor Holt galloped into the chorus, "And 'tis but a penny to Twickenham town!" "Isn't that enough?" she'd ask me. She'd told me that the mother and the father had to both *want* the baby. This couldn't be enough. I knew she was not trying to fib to me, for she never did fib, but also I could not help but know she was not really *telling* me. And more than that, I was afraid of what I was going to hear next. This was partly because she wanted to tell me in the dark. I thought *she* might be afraid. In something like childish hopelessness I thought she probably *couldn't* tell, just as she *couldn't* lie.

On the night we came the closest to having it over with, she started to tell me without being asked, and I ruined it by yelling, "Mother, look at the lightning bugs!"

In those days, the dark was dark. And all the dark out there was filled with the soft, near lights of lightning bugs. They were everywhere, flashing on the slow, horizontal move, on the upswings, rising and subsiding in the soundless dark. Lightning bugs signaled and answered back without a stop, from down below all the way to the top of our sycamore tree. My mother just gave me a businesslike kiss and went on back to Daddy in their room at the front of the house. Distracted by lightning bugs, I had missed my chance. The fact is she never did tell me.

I doubt that any child I knew ever was told by her mother any more than I was about babies. In fact, I doubt that her own mother ever told her any more than she told me, though there were five brothers who were born after Mother, one after the other, and she was taking care of babies all her childhood.

Not being able to bring herself to open that door to reveal its secret, one of those days, she opened another door.

In my mother's bottom bureau drawer in her bedroom she kept treasures of hers in boxes, and had given me permission to play with one of them—a switch of her own chestnut-colored hair, kept in a heavy bright braid that coiled around like a snake inside the cardboard box. I hung it from her doorknob and unplaited it; it fell in ripples nearly to the floor, and it satisfied the Rapunzel in me to comb it out. But one day I noticed in the same drawer a small white cardboard box such as her engraved calling cards came in from the printing house. It was tightly closed, but I opened it, to find to my puzzlement and covetousness two polished buffalo nickels, embedded in white cotton. I rushed with this opened box to my mother and asked if I could run out and spend the nickels.

"No!" she exclaimed in a most passionate way. She seized the box into her own hands. I begged her; somehow I had started to cry. Then she sat down, drew me to her, and told me that I had had a little brother who had come before I did, and who had died as a baby before I was born. And these two nickels that I'd wanted to claim as my find were his. They had lain on his eyelids, for a purpose untold and unimaginable. "He was a fine little baby, my first baby, and he shouldn't have died. But he did. It was because your mother almost died at the same time," she told me. "In looking after me, they too nearly forgot about the little baby."

She'd told me the wrong secret—not how babies could come but how they could die, how they could be forgotten about.

I wondered in after years: how could my mother have kept those two coins? Yet how could someone like herself have disposed of them in any way at all? She suffered from a morbid streak which in all the life of the family reached out on occasions—the worst occasions—and touched us, clung around us, making it worse for her; her unbearable moments could find nowhere to go.

The future story writer in the child I was must have taken unconscious note and stored it away then: one secret is liable to be revealed in the place of another that is harder to tell, and the substitute secret when nakedly exposed is often the more appalling.

Perhaps telling me what she did was made easier for my mother by the two secrets, told and still not told, being connected to her deepest feeling, more intimately than anyone ever knew, perhaps even herself.

So far as I remember now, this is the only time this baby was ever mentioned in my presence. So far as I can remember, and I've tried, he was never mentioned in the presence of my father, for whom he had been named. I am only certain that my father, who could never bear pain very well, would not have been able to bear it.

It was my father (my mother told me at some later date) who saved her own life, after that baby was born. She had in fact been given up by the doctor, as she had long been unable to take any nourishment. (That was the illness when they'd cut her hair, which formed the switch in the same bureau drawer.) What had struck her was septicemia, in those days nearly always fatal. What my father did was to try champagne.

I once wondered where he, who'd come not very long before from an Ohio farm, had ever heard of such a remedy, such a measure. Or perhaps as far as he was concerned he invented it, out of the strength of desperation. It would have been desperation augmented because champagne couldn't be bought in Jackson. But somehow he knew what to do about that too. He telephoned to Canton, forty miles north, to an Italian orchard grower, Mr. Trolio, told him the necessity, and asked, begged, that he put a bottle of his wine on Number 3, which was due in a few minutes to stop in Canton to "take on water" (my father knew everything about train schedules). My father would be waiting to meet the train in Jackson. Mr. Trolio did—he sent the bottle in a bucket of ice and my father snatched it off the baggage car. He offered my mother a glass of chilled champagne and she drank and kept it down. She was to live, after all.

Now, her hair was long again, it would reach in a braid down her back, and now I was her child. She hadn't died. And when I came, I hadn't died either. Would she ever? Would I ever? I couldn't face *ever*. I must have rushed into her lap, demanding her like a baby. And she had to put her first-born aside again, for me.

Of course it's easy to see why they both overprotected me, why my father, before I could wear a new pair of shoes for the first time, made me wait while he took out his thin silver pocket knife and with the point of the blade scored the polished soles all over, carefully, in a diamond pattern, to prevent me from sliding on the polished floor when I ran.

As I was to learn over and over again, my mother's mind was a mass of associations. Whatever happened would be forever paired for her with something that had happened before it, to one of us or to her. It became a private anniversary. Every time any possible harm came near me, she thought of how she lost her first child. When a Roman candle at Christmas backfired up my sleeve, she rushed to smother the blaze with the first thing she could grab, which was a dish towel hanging in the kitchen, and the burn on my arm became infected. I was nothing but proud of my sling, for I could wear it to school, and her repeated blaming of herself—for even my sling—puzzled and troubled me.

When my mother would tell me that she wanted me to have something because she as a child had never had it, I wanted, or I partly wanted, to give it back. All my life I continued to feel that bliss for me would have to imply my mother's deprivation or sacrifice. I don't think it would have occurred to her what a double emotion I felt, and indeed I know that it was being unfair to her, for what she said was simply the truth.

"I'm going to let you go to the Century Theatre with your father tonight on my ticket. I'd rather you saw *Blossom Time* than go myself."

In the Century first-row balcony, where their seats always were, I'd be sitting beside my father at this hour beyond my bedtime carried totally away by the performance, and then suddenly the thought of my mother staying home with my sleeping younger brothers, missing the spectacle at this moment before my eyes, and doing without all the excitement and wonder that filled my being, would arrest me and I could hardly bear my pleasure for my guilt.

There is no wonder that a passion for independence sprang up in me at the earliest age. It took me a long time to manage the independence, for I loved those who protected me—and I wanted inevitably to protect them back. I have never managed to handle the guilt. In the act and the course of writing stories, these are two of the springs, one bright, one dark, that feed the stream.

FROM

Memoirs

TENNESSEE WILLIAMS

Born in 1911, Pulitzer Prize-winning playwright Thomas Lanier Williams recalls in his memoirs his early years in Columbus, Mississippi, before his family moved to St. Louis. In the following excerpt from chapter 2, he gives one answer, from among several he would give, as to why he named himself after the neighboring state of Tennessee instead of Mississippi. At another time he said that Thomas Lanier "sounds like it might belong to the son of a writer who turns out sonnet sequences to Spring." Williams's early years in Mississippi manifested themselves in his well-known, much-produced plays such as The Glass Menagerie, A Streetcar Named Desire, *and* Cat on a Hot Tin Roof. *Stage great Jessica Tandy welcomed the chance to play Blanche DuBois, because, as she said, Williams knew how to create powerful women characters. His innovations in lighting, music, and narration are considered major contributions to the theatre. In the* Encyclopedia of Southern Culture, *the scholar Jacob Adler states, "The most important dramatist to come out of the South, Williams provided innumerable insights into southern life and character, conveying authenticity to southerner and non-southerner alike."*

I GUESS IT hardly needs stating that I had been the victim of a particularly troubled adolescence. The troubles had started before adolescence: I think they were clearly rooted in childhood.

My first eight years of childhood in Mississippi were the most joyously innocent of my life, due to the beneficent homelife provided by my beloved Dakin grandparents, with whom we lived. And to the wild and sweet half-imaginary world in which my sister and our beautiful black nurse Ozzie existed, separate, almost invisible to anyone but our little cabalistic circle of three.

That world, that charmed time, ended with the abrupt transference of the family to St. Louis. This move was preceded, for me, by an illness diagnosed by a small Mississippi town doctor as diphtheria with complications. It lasted a year, was nearly fatal, and changed my nature as drastically as it did my physical health. Prior to it, I had been a little boy with a robust, aggressive, almost bullying nature. During the illness, I learned to play, alone, games of my own invention.

Of these games I recall vividly one that I played with cards. It was not solitaire. I had already read *The Iliad* and I turned the black and red cards into two opposite armies battling for Troy. The royalty, the face cards of both Greeks and Trojans, were the kings, princes and heroes; the cards merely numbered were the common soldiers. They would battle in this fashion: I would slap a red and black card together and the one that fell upon the bedspread face up was the victor. By ignoring history, the fate of Troy was decided solely by these little tournaments of the cards.

During this period of illness and solitary games, my mother's overly solicitous attention planted in me the makings of a sissy, much to my father's discontent. I was becoming a decided hybrid, different from the family line of frontiersmen-heroes of east Tennessee.

My father's lineage had been an illustrious one, now gone a bit to seed, at least in prominence. He was directly descended from Tennessee's first senator, John Williams, hero of King's Mountain; from the brother Valentine of Tennessee's first Governor John (Nollichucky Jack) Sevier; and from Thomas Lanier Williams I, the first Chancellor of the Western Territory (as Tennessee was called before it became a state). According to published genealogies, the Seviers could be traced back to the little kingdom of Navarre, where one of them had been a ward of the Bourbon monarch. The family then became divided along religious lines: between Roman Catholics and Huguenots. The Catholics remained Xaviers; the Huguenots changed their name to Sevier when they fled to England at the time of St. Bartholomew's Massacre. St. Francis Xavier, credited with the conversion of many Chinese—a valiant but Quixotic undertaking, in my opinion—is the family's nearest claim to world reknown.

My paternal grandfather, Thomas Lanier Williams, II, proceeded to squander both his own and his wife's fortunes on luckless campaigns for the governorship of Tennessee.

Now the imposing old Williams residence in Knoxville has been turned into a black orphanage—a good ending for it.

The question I'm asked with most tedious frequency by interviewers and talk-show hosts is "How did you get the name Tennessee when you were born in Mississippi?" So that's the justification for my professional monicker—and I've also just indulged myself in the Southern weakness for climbing a family tree. . . .

Brother to a Dragonfly

WILL D. CAMPBELL

*No one embodies paradox like Will Campbell, a preacher without a
church. Born in 1924 and reared in Liberty, Mississippi, in Amite
County in the Piney Woods, Campbell came from an extremely poor family, yet he managed to become ordained as a Southern Baptist preacher
at seventeen, and went on to attend seminary at Louisiana College at
Pineville, then studied at Wake Forest, Tulane, and Yale. After reading
Howard Fast's book on social justice,* Freedom Road, *he parted ways
with traditional churches and other institutions and became head of the
southern office of the Department of Racial and Cultural Relations for
the National Council of Churches. He became involved in the civil rights
movement at the University of Mississippi and in Little Rock and Birmingham. He was the only white man to help organize the Southern
Christian Leadership Conference. His resignation from the National
Council of Churches in 1963 and his growing awareness of discrimination against southern poor whites marked another departure from traditional attitudes towards social reform. Singer, writer, and farmer as well
as preacher, Campbell lives with his family in Juliet, Tennessee. He is
author of such works as* The Glad River, Forty Acres and a Goat,
and Providence. *With his cane and black hat, the preacher Will B.
Dunn in the comic strip* Kudzu *is easily recognized as Campbell's double.
Although his autobiography is primarily an attempt to come to terms with
the death of his brother Joe, in the following passage from the section
called "Midday," Campbell explains how he became a preacher and how
the black hat became his trademark.*

M Y   P L U N G E into the preaching world came suddenly and without
much warning. . . . Our East Fork pastor, J. Price Brock, had taken an
interest in me and would sometimes take me on his preaching circuit.
The hour of preaching at each church was arranged to fit the convenience of the preacher. One at nine, another at eleven. Across the
county line, thirty miles of dirt road away, still another church would
meet at two in the afternoon. Then back to the last by seven that night.
He introduced me to his congregations and began to insist that I read
certain books. The first was a little handbook on personal timidity. He
had noticed that I never talked to anyone on his church fields unless

asked a question, would not go to the dinner table until specifically asked, did not shake hands unless the other's hand was offered first. He did not outright say that I had to overcome my shyness if I were going to be a successful preacher but I got the message. Such practical and social habits as that seemed more important than what I might believe about one theological point or another. Interesting that I should find the same thing true throughout years of theological training. The training was for success, not faithfulness to Christian orthodoxy.

Since Brother Brock went to school at what was then called "Baptist Bible Institute," now the New Orleans Baptist Theological Seminary, and must ride the train each weekend the hundred or so miles, his wife and two babies were left alone in the new East Fork parsonage. So I was asked to stay with them during the week and go to school from their house. That was, of course, considered an honor and each morning I would stand, yawning, on the front porch as all the school buses rolled by going to school. Then at the last minute Mrs. Brock, actually not many years older than my own sixteen, would drive me the quarter of a mile to the school house. I tried hard to time it so as to arrive just as the bell was ringing, for that meant that everyone would be in the front of the building as I was saying good-bye to the preacher's wife.

But my debut as a real preacher man had nothing to do with my relationship to the pastor. It started as a joke. In April the eleven members of our graduating class had gone the hundred yards from the schoolhouse to the churchhouse to practice for our forthcoming baccalaureate exercises which, as always, would be held in the East Fork Baptist Church. Mr. Ray Turner was in charge of the rehearsal. His wife, the meanest woman I had ever encountered, and the best English teacher, was assisting.

Someone had played the Washington and Lee March on the piano as we filed down the aisle, and we had remained standing to sing "Follow the Gleam." Something had gone wrong and it must be repeated. Somehow I had made my way to the dais and sat on the double chair reserved for the preacher. It was a holy position and I felt presumptuous and insecure sitting there. I had borrowed from Holland Anderson, one of our classmates, his big, black hat, looking like those worn by Italian priests and it, two sizes too large, covered my head and ears. When the class finished the singing of "Follow the Gleam," they were supposed to sit down. At the precise moment they sat, like a jack-in-the-box, I stood up, placing my hands firmly on the pulpit and looking down at them in judgmental fashion. I had intended to be cute, but not funny. At least not as funny as it apparently was. As they roared with laughter my ears burned with embarrassment. And yet I was more than pleased that I had made them laugh. I glanced quickly in the direction of the principal and his wife. I feared I had committed an act of sacrilege. But they were bursting with uncontrollable guffaws. I was a hit! There was no stopping me then. I went into contortions and gyrations, flailing away at the pulpit, making the veins stand out on my neck. It was a pantomime which would have been a credit to Bill Sunday at his best.

Walking back to the school someone, Gladys Anderson I think, suggested that we should ask Brother Brock to let us have a youth day service at church. Based on that performance, everyone thought it would be a good idea. So in five minutes it was all planned. I would be pastor, Evie Lee would play the piano, Delton as song leader, and so on through the list of church functions including collecting the offering, a job reserved for the deacons.

The youth day was set for late June and until the day came I spent more time practicing my sermon than doing anything else. I continued to work in the field, but if plowing, the sermon outline was tacked on the rung between the two plow handles where I could preach to the rear end of the horse. And I did it with varying enthusiasm. At times I wished that I had never appeared behind that pulpit. But most of the time I felt that I could not wait until the day arrived. Daddy asked on more than one occasion if I would be ready, stating that he had rather I not plow another day than to fail in my first preaching endeavor. He also pointed out one night when we were having our daily Bible readings that my voice was not very strong. I told him of a preacher secret I had heard from Norma Jane, Brother Brock's wife. She had told me that when they were first married she had him drink a glass of pineapple juice before he went into the pulpit on Sunday morning. I had already planned to have a can of pineapple juice on hand that Sunday morning as part of my last minute preparations.

Joe would, of course, come home from the CCC Camp for the occasion. Grandpa Will Parker would be there for sure, Aunt Dolly and other kin from "across the river."

The sermon was called "In the Beginning." The Scripture reading was, appropriately, the first chapter of Genesis, or at least major portions of it. The sermon told of how this was a beginning for us, of how our class could be compared to the creation story. The majority of it dealt with the fact that the Biblical account said, "In the beginning God created the heavens and the earth . . ." and that the rest of the Bible had to do with earth and what happened there and not with heaven. I was a sixteen-year-old fundamentalist, but for some reason which I have never understood I had never taken much to preachments about other worlds—above or below. It was, in many ways, heretical and modernistic for East Fork. But on that occasion I could have denounced Christianity as a capitalistic myth cunningly designed to keep the masses under control, and our youth choir could have sung Ukrainian folk songs, and our Sunday School superintendent could have lectured on "The Origin of Species," and all the people would have said "Amen." Never had they been so proud of us. I chided the oldsters and chastised them lightly for being irregular at Sunday night services and this was the most appreciated part of all. It meant that Dave was not to be a preacher who would tolerate sin, and would denounce it no matter how unpopular it made him. (Somehow the pride of some of those in attendance that day went sour when the little preacher years later turned to denouncing social sins.)

Everyone in the graduating class had some part in the service. And we were all roundly hugged and congratulated and commended for having done so splendidly. Uncle Hilary, or "Uncle Fork" as we called him, Grandpa Campbell's half-brother, father of my buddy Thaxton, or "Snooky," and the one who was considered a drunk though he was in fact a moderate drinker, allowed to all standing around after the service that they should remember that day for they would be hearing much from the little preacher. Ray Turner, a great teacher in any age, simply whispered, "Plow deep," the R.F.D. version of "Right on." Aunt Ida, not really Aunt but sister to Aunt Donnie, wife of Uncle Fork, who lived with them and was considered rich because she lived on some kind of mysterious disability insurance policy, kissed me and cried. Joe made no comment but gave me the kind of look that told me he had been extremely proud of what I had done. For I had stood up, laid my dollar Ingram watch on the pulpit—an act which had nothing to do with when I began or stopped for it was all written down, a fact which brought the only criticism from one aunt, which Mamma dismissed as jealousy because one of her boys was not making a preacher—and said my piece.

Somehow I did not feel as awed in the presence of Joe after that. His success as a company clerk, his being the one providing the bulk of the money, both in the family needs and when the two of us were out on social occasions, his uniform and his poise in the presence of girlfriends, had been enough to keep me in a state of wonderment.

Now I could claim a success of my own.

For I was a full-fledged preacher, entitled to buy Coca-Colas at clergy discount.

(The Original) Humorous Whiskey Speech

N. S. SWEAT, JR.

"Soggy" Sweat, law professor, judge, and district attorney, gave his fa-
mous "Whiskey Speech" during his first term in the legislature (1948–
52). As early as 1880 Lawrence County, in the southern part of the
state, banned alcoholic beverages. In 1908, the legislature enacted a
statewide prohibition law. In 1918, Mississippi became the first state to
approve the Eighteenth Amendment prohibiting liquor. Even after the
Twenty-first Amendment repealed prohibition, the "drys" in Mississippi
outnumbered the "wets" until 1966, making it the next to last state in
the union with a prohibition law. As Sweat's 1952 speech illustrates, a
politician's stand on the issue could make or break him. In 1957 at a
Young Democrats' banquet honoring Sen. Jack Kennedy, Sweat chastised
Kennedy for not including the speech in Profiles in Courage. *Sweat*
said, "I assume that either you have not heard my stand on whiskey or
have heard it and just can't believe it to be true. Therefore, I feel I should
enlighten you on my stand on whiskey." After he had delivered the speech,
Kennedy replied, "I want to say to the master of ceremonies that one of
the requirements for a statesman to be listed in my book is that he must
be dead, but I want him to know that he certainly does qualify in every
other way." With that he inscribed a copy of Profiles in Courage. *It*
said, "Be sure to keep a lookout for the next edition." Sweat died in
1996.

My Friends:

I had not intended to discuss this controversial subject at this particular
time. However, I want you to know that I do not shun controversy. On
the contrary, I will take a stand on any issue at any time, regardless of
how fraught with controversy it might be. You have asked me how I feel
about whiskey. All right, here is how I feel about whiskey . . .

If when you say whiskey you mean the devil's brew, the poison
scourge, the bloody monster, that defiles innocence, dethrones reason,
destroys the home, creates misery and poverty, yea, literally takes the
bread from the mouths of little children; if you mean the evil drink that

topples the christian man and woman from the pinnacle of righteous, gracious living into the bottomless pit of degradation, and despair, and shame, and helplessness, and hopelessness, then certainly I am against it.

But,

If, when you say whiskey you mean the oil of conversation, the philosophic wine, the ale that is consumed when good fellows get together, that puts a song in their hearts and laughter on their lips, and the warm glow of contentment in their eyes; if you mean Christmas cheer; if you mean the stimulating drink that puts the spring into the old gentleman's step on a frosty, crispy morning; if you mean the drink which enables a man to magnify his joy, and his happiness, and to forget, if only for a little while, life's great tragedies, and heartaches, and sorrows; if you mean that drink, the sale of which pours into our treasuries untold millions of dollars, which are used to provide tender care for our little crippled children, our blind, our deaf, our dumb, our pitiful aged and infirm; to build highways and hospitals and schools, then certainly I am for it.

This is my stand. I will not retreat from it. I will not compromise.

FROM

Coming on Back

WILLIE MORRIS

Born in Jackson, Mississippi, in 1934, writer Willie Morris grew up in
Yazoo City, a childhood he vividly recalls in his memoir North Toward
Home, *published in 1967. After graduating from the University of*
Texas, where he was editor of the Daily Texan, *he continued his educa-*
tion as a Rhodes Scholar at New College of Oxford University receiving
B. A. and M. A. degrees there. In 1963, having edited the Texas Ob-
server, *he became an editor for* Harper's *magazine. After Morris became*
editor-in-chief in 1967, he attracted such writers as Walker Percy, Nor-
man Mailer, and David Halberstam to the magazine's pages. As one
critic wrote, "He made Harper's *probably the most significant magazine*
in America." Morris accepted a writer-in-residence position at the Univer-
sity of Mississippi in 1980 and now resides in Jackson with his wife,
JoAnne Prichard, executive editor of the University Press of Mississippi.
Among his writings are Good Old Boy, James Jones: A Friendship,
The Courting of Marcus Dupree, *and* My Dog Skip. *The following*
excerpt from "Coming on Back" was first published in Life *magazine in*
May 1981, on the occasion of Morris's return to Mississippi.

I OFTEN DWELL on the homecomings I have made—the acutely
physical sensations of returning from somewhere else to all those dispa-
rate places I have lived. To the town of my childhood—Yazoo—it was
the precarious hills looming like a mountain range at the apex of that
triangle known as the Mississippi Delta, the lights of the town twinkling
down at night in a diaphanous fog. To the city of my college days—
Austin—it was the twin eminences of the University Tower and the
grand old State Capitol awash in light from very far away. To the citadel
of my young adulthood—Oxford University—it was the pallid sunlight
catching all in filigree the spires and cupolas of that medieval fortress
on its estuary of the Thames. To the metropolis of my ambition—New
York—it was the Manhattan skyline which seemed so forbidding, yet
was at once so compact and close-at-hand. To the village of my gentlest
seclusion—Bridgehampton—it was the Shinnecock Canal opening
onto that other world of shingled houses, flat fields and dunes, and the
blue Atlantic breakers.

It was in the East that I grew to middle-age. I cared for it, but it was not mine. I had lived nearly twenty years there, watching all the while my home ground from afar in its agonies, perceiving it across the distance, returning constantly on visits or assignments. The funerals kept apace, *Abide With Me* reverberating from the pipe-organs of the churches all too much, until one day I awoke to the comprehension that all my people were gone. As if in a dream where every gesture is attenuated, it grew upon me that a man had best be coming back to where his strongest feelings lay. For there, then, after all of it, was the heart.

Foremost, the remarkable literary tradition of Mississippi derives from the complexity of a society which still, well into the late Twentieth Century, had retained much of its communal origins, and along with that a sense of continuity, of the enduring past and the flow of the generations—an awareness, if you will, of human history. If modern industrialism and the national urge to homogeneity came to Mississippi later and with greater destructiveness than to other areas of the United States, if the traditional federal authority had to reach more than halfway to meet what finally became the better instincts of the place, then this had to do with the direness of its immemorial past.

William Faulkner, the poet and chronicler of Mississippi, understood how deeply we care for it despite what it was and is—the gulf between its manners and morals, the extraordinary apposition of its violence and kindliness. There is something that matters in a state which elicits in its sons and daughters of both races, wherever they live, such emotions of fidelity and rage and passion. I myself have often felt an ineluctible similarity with Ireland—in the spoken and written language, the telling of tales, the mischief and eccentricity of the imagination, the guilts and blunderings and angers, the religiosity at the base of things, the admiration of the hoax and of strong drink, the relish of company and of idiosyncracy for its own sake, the radiance and fire in the midst of impoverishment. These are qualities, I would discover, which still bounteously exist.

"Time is very important to us because it has dealt with us," Eudora Welty of Mississippi says. "We have suffered and learned and progressed through it." For instance, many of the people I know here of my age had great-grandfathers and great-uncles who fought in the Civil War. Some survived it, some did not, having fallen at Brice's Crossroads or Shiloh or Chancellorsville or Gettysburg, in that near obliteration of the young officer class which rivaled England, France, and Germany of the World War I generation. The experiences of these men have been

brought to their great-grandsons and daughters through diaries found
in attics, through the words handed down, and through the ancestral
relics: a pistol, a sword, old buttons, a shred of grey cloth.

Many Americans, to express it boldly, have remained afraid of Mississippi. I witnessed this fear time and again in the East, and I see it to this
day, into the 1980s. It was, after all, not too many years before that
D. W. Brogan, who was a British historian but might just as well have
been speaking for much of Northern sentiment, could describe Mississippi as the most savage and backward of the forty-eight American com-
monwealths. The Freedom Summer of 1964, when hundreds of
Northerners confronted here the intransigence of the police, the poverty and the cruelty, and went home with stories to tell, was only seventeen years ago. I remember as if it were yesterday sitting in a coffee
shop across from my editorial offices in New York City hearing the legendary Bob Moses, the civil rights leader, describing in his gentle way
what he had lived through in Mississippi. At this writing—March
1981—only nineteen years have passed since President Kennedy sent
30,000 federal troops to Ole Miss to assure the admission of its first
black student, James Meredith, when Governor Ross Barnett declared:
"I refuse to allow this nigra to enter our state university, but I say so
politely." These would still be severe realities to Americans who dwell
on those embarrassing times and find it almost impossible to compre-
hend the swift and emphatic transformations in the life of the state, as
the Deep South, in the late 1960s and through the 1970s.

Mississippi's most horrific specters have always been racism and poverty. My friend Ed Perry, chairman of the appropriations committee of
the state House of Representatives, complains over beer in the Gin Saloon in Oxford of the lack of funds for many essential services. "There's
no money!" he shouts. "We have to juggle. There just ain't no money."
He recalls what his grandfather, who was a farmer down in the hard
land of Choctaw County, once told him: "Mississippi was the last state
the Depression hit. Hell, we had a Depression long before the Depression. People were so poor they didn't even know they were in one."
The 1980 statistics revealed Mississippi to be so entrenched in fiftieth
place in per capita income that it will likely never reach Arkansas in
forty-ninth. The state consistently has had the highest proportion of its
people on medicaid and food stamps—it was first per capita in getting
federal funds—and much of the new industry brought down after
World War II tapped the reservoir of unemployment and easy labor by
strictly adhering to the minimum wage.

The Governor in 1981 warned that Mississippi was like "an emerging colonial nation" and must begin to be selective about the quality of industry brought into the state: high-skilled industry was desperately needed in an undercapitalized society. In passionate words he warned too against the rampant economic growth which had already ruined large areas of the Deep South, and he deplored the pollution and indiscriminate dumping of hazardous wastes which had made many of the lakes and streams of my boyhood lifeless.

An acquaintance in Yazoo county writes me of the Big Black Swamp, where he had just been deer-hunting. "I felt a sacred spot," he says, "—a kinship not only with my forebears, but with the land." His father and his uncle hunted in these same woods. So did his grandfather and great-grandfather and great-great-grandfather, the latter having come down here in the 1830s after the Choctaws had ceded their claim to the settlers. Now the Big Black woods are owned by big paper companies which lease out hunting rights. "Big Black Swamp has always been there," he laments, "a fixture, like the moon in the sky. When the paper companies feel they must 'harvest' their 'wood crop' there, will it become Big Black Parking Lot?" This economic colonialism has always been hand-maiden to the poverty.

The returning son, who grew up with these things, needs no statistics to remind him. The dilapidated shacks and the unpainted facades still abound, and although the paved streets and public housing in the older black sections of the towns seem prolific in contrast to the 1940s, a random drive through the rural terrain or the larger cities reveals much of that same abject impoverishment, mainly black but white as well. Out in the Delta, where time often seems not to have moved, the extremes haunt one as they always did (the homes of many of the rich white planters, it must be said, would be cottages in East Hampton, Long Island), but the very land itself seems bereaved with the countless half-collapsed, abandoned tenant shacks set against the copious Delta horizon. These are testimonials to the largest mass exodus of a people in history—the Southern black migration northward since World War II. The triumph of Allis-Chalmers is everywhere, and the farm machinery companies pervade the landscape in such numbers as to astound one who remembers the numberless black silhouettes in these fields a generation ago, picking or chopping, pausing ever so often to wave at the occasional car speeding by. Brother Will Campbell, the pastor to everyone in the Deep South, claims he was driving down a Delta road not too long ago and sighted a tractor moving up the furrows all by itself, without a driver. The variety and complexity of these prodigious machines overwhelm the eye, tempting one to believe that if they had existed in such prodigality in the 1850s, the North would have seceded from the South. They reaffirm one's intuition, too, that the sheer expense of them must make the Mississippi Delta planter more than he was a gambler against the crops and the elements—living high and on mortgage and sending his wives and daughters to the Memphis stores to shop bountifully on credit.

The truth, of course, is that Mississippi has changed phantasmagorically in some ways, and in others it has changed hardly at all. It is a blend of the relentless and the abiding. There are things here now which my grandfather, who was born shortly after the Civil War and who died in 1953, would find unfathomable. If he stepped out of his grave in the old section of the Raymond cemetery and came back to Jackson, I suspect the scene along Interstate 55 with its mile upon mile of franchise establishments would astonish and frighten him. Modern-day Capitol Street and the Metrocenter Mall would leave him mystified, as would the traffic snarls and giant apartment complexes and insurance chains along the quiet streets where we rode the Number Four bus. All around him he would discover a brisk new world, all growth and deracination and touched with the Yankee dollar.

Yet if my grandfather had been with me on a spring morning of 1980, driving from Jackson northeast to Oxford on the country roads, he would have been witness to the sights of his memory. Off the interstates and removed from the resounding nostrums of the New South, lies our remembered world, the world of my childhood: old men in khakis whittling in the shade of a crossroads grocery, a domino game on the back stoop of a service station, an advertisement for a backwoods mortuary on an R.C. Cola sign, and abandoned frame church with piles of used tires in front and a scrawled poster on top of them proclaiming "Fried Chicken, Two Miles," a conversation between an ancient black man and woman in a store which serves also as the Trailways stop:

"How you doin' today, Annie?"

"Not too pretty good, but givin' thanks for bein' here."

. . . It is the proximity of Oxford and the Ole Miss campus, each populated by about 10,000 souls, which has given my homecoming its poignance, for both have tender resonances of an older past. Youth and age are in healthy proportion, and the loyalty of the town to the university is both exuberant and touching. The courthouse in the middle of the Square and the Lyceum at the crest of the wooded grove are little more than a mile apart, which is appropriate, for it is impossible to imagine Ole Miss in a big city, and Oxford without the campus would be another struggling northeast Mississippi town. One can drive around the campus and absorb the palpable sophistication of a small Southern state university, and then proceed two or three miles into a countryside which is authentic boondocks terrain upon which the Twentieth Century has only obliquely intruded.*

Shortly after I came here I was sitting on a sofa with Miss Louise, William Faulkner's sister-in-law. We were discussing the histories of some of the people buried in the cemetery. "It's an interesting town," she said. I told Miss Louise that I agreed. "It's so interesting," I suggested, "I think somebody ought to write about it."

Faulkner's presence pervades our place, and living here has helped me know him better. His courage was of the Mississippi kind, and as with all great artists, he was a prophet on his own soil—about whites and blacks and the destruction of the land and the American Century and the human heart. W. H. Auden wrote on the death of William Butler Yeats, "Mad Ireland drove him to poetry," and Mississippi worked this way on Mr. Bill, for something moved in him when he finally decided to come back and write about the people and things he knew best, creating his mythical land out of the real fibers of everything around him. Yet in the time he was laboring in solitude on much of the finest work an American ever wrote, he was deeply in debt, Ole Miss had little or nothing to do with him, and the town was baffled and perplexed by him. To many he was a failed and drunken eccentric. When he may have wanted the approbation of the town and the university, in his most solitary and fruitful days, it was not there for him. When the town and the university at last considered it appropriate to sanction him, he had already long before, through his brave commitment to his words and his loneliness there at Rowan Oak, surrendered the expectation of any community benediction. Only after his death is he owned here. To this day an articulate gentleman from out in the county will tell anyone who wishes to listen that he knows for a fact Faulkner did not write those books. He did not have the gumption. They were written by a certain farmer who had a way with words, loved tall tales, and did not want publicity. This is reminiscent of Mark Twain's judgment that Shakespeare himself did not write his plays. It was some fellow with the same name.

"What if he had not had Hollywood to go to and make money?" a friend asked. He would have found *something* to make his stories possible, I suggested.

---

* In the year 1981, people without running water would still bring wooden buckets into town to the ice-house, which had a perpetual flow of water.

But he would become an industry in the town, ranking close to soy-beans, timber, merchandising, and Southeastern Conference football. Little clusters of Yankee and foreign tourists, including an unusual pro-portion of Japanese with their ubiquitous cameras, wander out to the grounds at Rowan Oak, or to St. Peter's Cemetery seeking his grave and those of his flamboyant kin, or search the unpaved roads of Beat Two for modern-day Snopeses, or stroll around the Square and the Confed-erate statue a little wide-eyed, wondering perhaps what might happen to them in Mississippi. A French scholar, asked what had most im-pressed him in his tour of the county, said: "I was fascinated by your peasants." Ole Miss conducts a sizeable Faulkner seminar every sum-mer and owns his wonderful old house set behind its magnolias and cedars, having won out over the University of Texas which wished to dismantle the house and move it to a site near Austin, trees and all.

This reverence would no doubt bemuse Mr. Bill, but never mind. I find his spirit imperishable in the country people I see here, and in the old black men who sit on their haunches around the Square and banter with the white merchants, and in the proudly individualistic story-tellers of the town, and in the landmarks of his prose—the dank Yocona swamps and the slow-flowing rivers and the piney woods on a dreary winter's day. He died two months before James Meredith came to Ole Miss. I never met him; too many years separated us. I would like to know what he would make of our native state after nearly twenty years. I have a vision of running into him in his tweed jacket and khakis, in front of Shine Morgan's Furniture Store perhaps, or Smitty's Cafe. "Come on, Morris," he will say. "Let's go sit on the porch and drink some whiskey and talk about what's been happenin' in Mississippi since I last left."

Soul to Soul

YELENA KHANGA

When Russian-born Yelena Khanga came to America in 1991 on a Rockefeller Foundation Fellowship, her quest was to find a record of her black American great-grandfather, Hilliard Golden, who had lived in Mississippi. A former slave, Golden had acquired and eventually lost 640 acres of land in Yazoo County. As Khanga writes in this excerpt from chapter 1, "Distant Worlds," she discovered much more than records. She also found people, blacks and whites alike, who surprised her with their interest and hospitality. Khanga's Russian eyes offer an unusual perspective on Mississippi and Mississippians.

IN FEBRUARY OF 1991, I drove north from Yazoo City in search of my great-grandfather's land. My guides were the writer Willie Morris and his wife, JoAnne Prichard, who had prepared themselves for the search with copies of nineteenth-century as well as modern maps. Even when you know exactly what you are looking for, finding a piece of farmland is a more complicated enterprise than finding a city block; we found ourselves stopping and starting, squinting at old and new boundaries on the maps.

I reached this point only after a number of false starts. Neither my mother and I nor our Chicago relations knew exactly where the Goldens had lived in Mississippi. My mother mistakenly thought her father had grown up in Clarksdale (north of Yazoo), because the town was mentioned on his U.S. Army record book. In fact, Clarksdale was simply the place where he reported for basic training after being drafted in 1918.

The real trail emerged only when, through the Rockefeller Foundation, I was able to enlist the help of scholars in Mississippi. JoAnne, an editor with the University Press of Mississippi, found the first clue. It was a reference to my great-grandfather's votes when he served on the Yazoo board of supervisors during Reconstruction in a book she edited in 1976.[1]

At the B. S. Ricks Memorial Library in Yazoo City, librarians Linda Crawford and Darlene Johnson took up the search as soon as they knew Hilliard Golden had indeed lived in Yazoo. Sifting through mildewed census records and property deeds in basements and even in an airplane hanger, they located the Golden property on an 1874 map so fragile they were afraid to hold it up to the light. Gradually these researchers put together a remarkable picture of what my great-grand-father achieved in his first decade after slavery.[2]

Hilliard Golden's name appears for the first time in the 1870 census, which reports that he already owned land valued at seven hundred dollars, a considerable amount of money at the time. That plot of land—moist, reddish-brown earth near the Yazoo River in the northeast section of the county—is exactly what we found on our drive.

It was a bitter-sweet moment when I stepped onto the land and ran my fingers through the soil. Now owned by whites, the land was being tilled by black workers. When I told them my great-grandfather had once owned this farm, they didn't believe me. They simply couldn't imagine that it had been possible for a black in the last century to own anything. I began to understand that the history of black landowners like my great-grandfather is as obscure to many Americans, even blacks, as it was to me when I was growing up in Moscow. Furthermore, the men refused to believe me until Willie and JoAnne backed me up; they needed the word of whites to convince them I was telling the truth. Once they believed me, they insisted I must carry away a piece of "my" earth. The workers loosened small pieces of soil, carefully packed them in a jar, and solemnly placed the glass container in my hands.

The discovery of my great-grandfather's land held a special poignancy for me not only as a woman of African-American ancestry but as a black Russian. Family history and background are extremely important to Russians—more so, I believe, than to most white or black Americans (although the contemporary revival of interest in "roots" is certainly making inroads on the cheerful imperviousness to genealogy that strikes me as an American national trait).

Many of my Russian friends come from distinguished prerevolutionary families, and they treasure the pictures, books, and artifacts that their parents and grandparents managed to preserve through the upheavals of the Soviet twentieth century. I never envied my friends their *things,* but I did envy them their certain knowledge of who their ancestors were and what they accomplished.

When I was growing up, it seemed to me that history began with my grandmother (and, of course, with the grandfather I never knew). How could I have had any real sense of my family's existence before we found ourselves in the Soviet Union? Emigration and the Cold War had shattered the family's links with America; if the rules of Soviet society had not changed dramatically in recent years, my mother and I would have gone to our graves knowing almost nothing about our American family.

My pride upon finding my great-grandfather's land has nothing to do with the sort of nonsensical ancestor worship in which people puff themselves up like pouter pigeons at the discovery of "noble" blood in their lineage. (In my country, the craze to uncover a Romanov or, at the very least, a Tsar's mistress in one's family tree is a comic by-product of the collapse of communism.) The Golden land tells me nothing about my ancestors' blood and everything about their character and persistence as they rose from slavery. From that Mississippi earth, even though it was eventually mortgaged and lost (probably to bankers), came the money for the private education of eight black children. In a real sense, it is one of the reasons my mother is a historian and I am a journalist. It is why Hilliard Golden's third- and fourth-generation descendants in Chicago are dentists and teachers and government administrators. The land gave us our start as a family.

Because I knew so little of my family's past when I was growing up in the Soviet Union, I always felt at some level that I was nobody from nowhere. In Mississippi I understood—not merely in my brain, but in the deepest recesses of my soul—that I come from a long line of somebodies. And I began to care for and identify not only with my own grandfather and great-grandparents but with all of the black men and women of past generations. My trip to Mississippi seemed to unlock a secret chamber in my heart. A part of me—the black part—was being reborn.

At every turn, I have tried to verify family legends, to be what Americans call a "hard-nosed reporter." Before I began spending time in America, my knowledge of the South was not second-hand but third-hand. My grandmother never traveled to Mississippi with my grandfather before they left for the Soviet Union; that would have been an invitation to a lynching in the twenties. Everything she knew of the South, she learned from her husband. Her picture of the South and of Mississippi—of lynchings, of absolute segregation, of every extreme form of racial oppression—was to a great extent frozen in time. In Moscow we knew about the civil rights movement of the sixties, but the knowledge was abstract.

As I made arrangements to visit Yazoo, I was somewhat afraid, not of physical violence, but of the subtle condescension I expected to see in the eyes of white southerners. I anticipated a look, as painful and difficult for me to describe as it is for me to see, that clearly telegraphs this message: "We tolerate you because you are a black Russian, an exotic member of your species. If you were an ordinary black American, we wouldn't be interested in you." I had seen that look flicker across the faces of certain northern whites, whose indifferent demeanor changed to bemused respect when I explained that I was Russian. In the South, I expected even more frequent encounters with what I have simply come to think of as The Look.

I was wrong. What I found in certain white southerners was an attitude of deep respect for both the white and black history of their region. I do not mean to suggest that the South lacks its full quota of white racists or that the whites I met were typical. The point is that neither my Soviet preconceptions nor the parochial (I now understand) warnings of certain northern American acquaintances had prepared me for the kind of white southerners who have pondered, understood, and grieved over the long, often tragic interaction between the races. In many respects—not the least of them being a willingness to sit, eat, drink, and endlessly debate obscure historical questions—these liberal southern intellectuals bear a marked resemblance to the best specimens of the Russian *intelligentsia*. I must explain that there is no precise American equivalent for the Russian term *intelligent*, which is usually translated as "intellectual" but means more: someone with a deep attachment to humanistic values and history. Mississippi's great native son, William Faulkner, is one of two or three American writers whose sensibility appeals most strongly to the true *intelligentsia* of my country. I sensed this cultural affinity in certain conversations in Mississippi and realized at the same time that such encounters would have been impossible in the South my grandfather knew.

There was also something very familiar to me—very Russian, if you will—about the pride taken by both blacks and whites in their particular corner of the world. In Yazoo, people place a high value on hospitality, and they all do their best to make a stranger feel at home. In truth, it's difficult to feel like a stranger for long. People who know about my family refer to me as "our Yelena"; if you have an ancestor who once lived in Yazoo, Yazoo continues to claim you as its own.

One night, Darlene and I were driving along the back roads and lost our way in a blinding rain. Darlene was relieved when we crossed paths with a local sheriff, who happened to be black. (The sight of black policemen in the South was another surprise for me. My mental image had been formed by old pictures of white sheriffs beating up civil rights demonstrators in the sixties.) The sheriff knew Darlene, but he immediately spotted me as a stranger because I was wearing my conservative

New York work clothes. "You're not from around here, are you?" he commented, waiting for me to explain my presence. "I'm from Russia," I replied. His eyes widened. "Russia? I thought everyone there was white." I assured him once again that I really did come from Russia and explained that I had found my great-grandfather's land. After I pulled out the map and showed him where the land was located, he seemed happier. "So your folks were really from around here," he said in a tone evincing considerable satisfaction at having placed me in a known universe.

While Yazoo's hospitality and intense interest in history reminded me of Russia in a positive way, certain other aspects of life evoked a negative déjà vu. The rural poverty around Yazoo—the sight of dull-eyed people sitting outside shacks that seemed to promise little more in the way of material comfort than antebellum slave quarters—truly shocked me. I hadn't encountered anything like it in America.

I have seen impoverished, drug-ravaged neighborhoods in America's cities, but rural poverty still conveys a special quality of isolation and despair to me. Both Russian and American cities—in spite of their very different economic and political circumstances—are filled with energy. In my native Moscow and my adopted New York, hopeful people on the move rub shoulders on a daily basis with those lacking any realistic prospect of improving their lot.

But on the way to my great-grandfather's land in Yazoo, I was oppressed by the sight of exhausted-looking laborers, working land they didn't own or sitting outside shacks and giving off a palpable aura of having nowhere to go and nothing to do. This brand of rural apathy is familiar to me, because I encountered it repeatedly in the Russian villages where I began my training as a reporter. For many years under the Soviet regime, villagers and farm workers were bound to the land by law as well as by poverty. The old laws required elaborate job and residency permits before anyone could move from the countryside to a large city, or even from a small city to a bigger one. (When I was born in 1962, my mother had to struggle with bureaucrats for months to arrange an apartment exchange that enabled my grandmother to move from Tashkent to Moscow to help take care of me.) The old Soviet system trapped farm workers in a static universe; villagers' lives were as far removed from the life of an educated Muscovite as a Yazoo farm laborer's life is from that of a Rockefeller.

I met so many helpful, hospitable people in Yazoo that I began to daydream about how nice it would be to live in a place close to my family roots and far from the competitive pressures of New York. The sight of rural poverty made me rethink this sentimental fantasy and reminded me why my ancestors left. How fortunate for the Golden family that my great-grandfather managed to educate his children before he lost his land! On the back roads, I watched young mothers, some of them teenagers, sit outside their rickety houses and stare into space as their children played in the dirt. With a different twist of fate, with a different great-grandfather, I might have been born into poverty myself. I might have been one of those vacant-eyed girls, growing old too soon and looking forward to nothing.

NOTES

1. Harriet DeCell and JoAnne Prichard, *Yazoo: Its Legends and Legacies* (Yazoo, Mississippi: Yazoo Delta Press), 1976.

2. JoAnne and Linda are white and Darlene is black—a fact I mention only because I had been misled by Soviet stereotypes about America, especially about the South, into assuming that only black historians would be interested in pursuing the story of a black family. On my trip to Mississippi, it was a pleasurable reeducation to discover so much interest on the part of scholars of both races.

On Fire

LARRY BROWN

Larry Brown was born in Oxford, Mississippi, in 1951. Before gaining recognition as a writer, he worked for the Oxford Fire Department from 1973 to 1990. He published his first novel, Dirty Work, *in 1989. He has published numerous short stories, and his collection* Facing the Music *won an award from the Mississippi Institute of Arts and Letters in 1989. The following excerpt from his memoir,* On Fire, *gives the reader a glimpse into the life of a firefighter and describes a rural black funeral after the death of one of Brown's closest friends in the fire department.*

WE ROLL THROUGH the door of the truck bay, our warning lights already revolving, flashing on the sidewalk and the big oaks along the street and the iron picket fence around the house across the street. The traffic stops for us and we turn left and head south down North Lamar, and Dwight stands on the siren and we pick up speed and race toward the first stop light a quarter mile away as the cars pull off to one side or I take the middle of the street and go around them, watching everything, watching the road, my speed, watching for people with their windows rolled up and the air conditioner going, or rock and roll turned up loud on their tape players, people who may not be able to hear me coming up behind them, people who might slam on their brakes. I never run a red light. Nobody with any sense driving a fire truck would run the red light at North Lamar and Jefferson because you can't see anything coming either way down Jefferson until you are under the light. The siren hurts our ears but Dwight stands on it and we stop and look both ways at Jefferson and then go on through, up to the Square where the road splits and both sides of the street can get blocked on you if people slam on their brakes and then you have to make your own road, go around somebody. The sound of the siren bounces off the high buildings on the Square and amplifies itself and now that we have everybody's attention, we turn right and floor it down Jackson Avenue toward a boy who is strangling to death on his own blood this hot summer night.

We catch the next light on green and blow the air horn just in case and then we can see the blue lights of the city police cars and the red lights of the ambulance and we slow down and pull in and stop the pumper in the street, put the pump in gear, apply the parking brake. I pick up the radio mike and report that we're 10–7, engaged in an assignment, and then I report what we're looking at, which is a white Ford Pinto on the right-hand side of the street, pointed the wrong way and wrapped around a telephone pole at the edge of the sidewalk. Dwight is out and pulling on his coat and gloves. Harry arrives behind us in the rescue truck and parks. I hang up the mike and get out, pull on my gloves, get my helmet from the compartment, and walk over and look into the car. The passenger door is open and a nurse is in the front seat with a young man who is lying across the buckets, jammed tight against the shifter, covered with blood, his legs twisted behind him in the smashed remains of the driver's door. The nurse is jabbing a piece of surgical tubing down his throat, shouting, *Breathe,* baby, *breathe!*

Harry is getting the entry saw out of the rescue truck and I walk back to the pump panel and pull the lever that opens the booster line, a rubberized one-inch handline that's on a reel above the pump panel, and then I throttle the engine up and watch the pressure gauge until the needle sits steady on two hundred psi and then I walk off and leave it. Dwight pulls the line down with one hand and drags it over to the car and lays it down in the street. Harry is bringing the saw and I go back to where the nurse is working with the boy. She looks up at me and tells me that we've got to do something quick and I say, We'll do all we can, lady. . . .

Harry gets the saw cranked and noses the carbide blade into the door and a shower of orange sparks starts flying around in a circle. We keep the hose ready in case gasoline ignites and I already know this isn't going to work. The whole weight of the car is against the door and we won't get it off without cutting down the pole. It doesn't look possible to remove him. It doesn't look possible that the boy could have gotten himself into this kind of shape. It looked like he's going to die right here with all of us trying to prevent it.

I tell them to keep sawing and I go back around to the other side of the car where the nurse is screaming for the boy not to die, shouting things at me, I don't know what, I don't listen, I don't care what she's saying, I'm looking at this car and trying to figure out some way to get the boy out of it as fast as I can. I lean over her with my flashlight and look at his legs. They're in that door behind him and the saw is running on the other side of the window, lighting up Harry's face and the safety goggles he has on. The boy breathes a little and then his breath catches in his chest and he makes that strangling noise again and she jabs the thing down his throat again. It's clogged with bubbles of air and blood and she keeps saying that we've got to do something, do something right now. She's about to get on my nerves and I wish to hell I did know what to do. I'm inside the car, crawling around, looking.

I get back out and look at the position of his body. And then I see it. He's got to come straight up. He's got to rise vertically out of that car like somebody levitating. The nurse tells me that they've got to call the rescue unit and I tell her, This is it, lady, this *is* the rescue unit and it's the only one you're going to get. I don't show her my First Responder patch, I don't tell her that I've been to the State Fire Academy to learn this shit, I don't tell her that if the city would open up its billfold I'd carve this car up like a Christmas turkey. I just go around to the other side and tell the guys who work with me to cut off the saw and let's get the windshield out.

We cover the nurse and the patient up with a blanket and then we take two fire axes and start chopping through the windshield, going around the edges, trying not to get glass splinters in our eyes, trying to remember to keep our face shields down. We go all the way around the top of the windshield and down both sides and then push it out over the hood and tear it loose from the gasket and throw it into the street like a dirty carpet. Then I'm up on the hood and reaching down through the hole for the shifter he's lodged against, that has his body hung. I push on it with all I have and it won't give. Somebody takes the blanket off the nurse and her patient and she's still working with him but he doesn't sound any better. I push against the shifter and it won't move. I say, Dwight, come here, help me. He crawls up beside me and lies down. I tell him that the boy is hung against the shifter, that we've got to bend it out of the way, but I'm not strong enough alone. I tell him to put his hand on mine on top of the shifter and he does. Dwight is a lot stronger than me and it starts to give. We push and strain, as hard as we can, and Dwight is nearly crushing my hand with his, but the shifter gives and bends over in the floor until it's away from him and not holding him anymore. Somebody has pushed the wheeled stretcher up near the car and we all reach and lift while somebody pulls traction on the patient, just in case he has a broken neck, and we slide the half-backboard in behind him and strap him to it and out he comes, onto the stretcher, the nurse walking beside him still jabbing the thing in and out of his throat, the respirator inside the ambulance only a few seconds away now, and they strap him down and load him up and get in with him and the doors slam and the ambulance screams down the street, the lonely wail of it washing over us as we stand and watch it go and listen to it fade away toward the hospital south of town.

I turn to Dwight and look at him. I'm glad he's so strong. I'm glad the boy didn't die. I understand why the nurse had no patience with us.

We roll up our shit and we go home. No thanks is needed from anybody. The city thanks us twice a month.

Now we are gathered in a little church in the woods, the yard of the church filled with muddy cars and muddy firetrucks, and we have all driven up a muddy road and we are here to say our last goodbyes to Dwight, who lies in his coffin in front of the pulpit. He was strong, but he had high blood pressure, and he wasn't careful about taking his medicine, and two days ago, when he was rabbit hunting with his uncle and his cousin, he had either a stroke or a heart attack and died quickly in the woods, before they could get him some help. I have never been in a black church before, and of all the hundreds of people here, the faces of firefighters in their uniforms are the only white faces.

The church will not hold all the people who have come here. The church has no paint on the outside. I cannot believe that he is dead, but they open the coffin and there he lies, with his mustache, without the glasses he always wore, and a seventeen-year-old son bends over him with streaming eyes and kisses his cheek.

The preacher is standing at the pulpit, but the service is not going to begin until everybody is seated. All the pews are full and people are still coming in. The funeral procession looked miles long. Chairs are brought in and set down in the aisles and people sit in them, maybe forty or fifty more. We sit in silence, sweating in the heat, the women fanning themselves with little cardboard fans on wooden sticks, things I haven't seen or seen people use since I was a child in my own church and saw women do the same thing. The people stop coming in and somebody closes the door.

From a curtain behind the pulpit a line of old women come in wearing choir robes. There's maybe a dozen of them. They hold no hymnals in their hands and the organ sits dead and silent in the corner. The women sit down and put their hands in their laps and they begin singing. They begin singing like angels and they sing about Heaven and Jesus and the love of God, and the hair wants to go up on my neck because it is unearthly and beautiful and my ears love it like no singing I've ever heard, and the preacher stands tall in his black velvet robe with a face of stone and stares at the wall of the church. We sit enraptured and I look at the people in fine clothes, some still in work clothes, fresh from the job, all of us here for this wonderful music.

The singing ends. Then it begins again. I don't know how long it goes on. It stops again. It begins again. And finally it stops for good.

The preacher is a huge man. He looks like Alex Haley, only blacker. This man is as black as midnight. He begins his sermon in a gentle voice, talking of how we all must one day throw off this mortal coil, the way Dwight already has, that his suffering is over, that God's got a better world waiting. He talks of how he remembers Dwight in church as a child, how he saw him accept Jesus as his savior. He raises his voice a little and his words begin to assume a rhythm, and he starts to move, and we start to move a little with him. His voice gets louder and some-body says Amen. Somebody says, Yes, Lord. His voice rises to a higher pitch and I can see people swaying. It's going to be something. They start to shout and talk back to him and we keep quiet. There are two things going on here at one time. It's looking as if it's going to get out of hand. Pretty soon the preacher's moaning and his voice has gotten high and tight and he's caught up in it and the whole place is caught up in it and I'm caught up in it too and it's all I can do to keep from shouting something out at him myself because he's got me feeling something. The man's a great preacher and he's got all these people right in the palm of his hand and he's making them jump and move and yell, Yeah! Amen! Tell it, brother! Sweet Jesus! I close my eyes and feel it. It goes on and on and it's hot in the church and the little walls reverberate with sound until the preacher slows down like a clock un-winding and by then just about everybody's crying, me too, no more Dwight.

We carry the casket down a slippery hill, mud on the ladies' shoes, black and white people walking together to the muddy hole we're going to lower him into. We stand around while the preacher says his final words, while Dwight's wife cries and their children cry. We all have little boutonnieres in our lapels and we take them off and put them in a small pile on top of a wreath of flowers that is there. They lower the casket and it comes to rest six feet down. There is a large pile of streaked clay with five or six shovels stuck into it. Nobody tells us to, but the firefighters pick up the shovels and we start shoveling the clay over him. It's not even dirt. It will hardly fall off the shovel blade. Sometimes you have to shake it off. It lands in sticky clumps, sodden, wet, thump-ing loudly on his shiny casket. It takes a long time. We change positions, we pass the shovels around among us, we rest sometimes. It's not a pretty place to be buried. The land is of poor quality, with nothing but scrubby trees and weeds around. It's very hot. We keep shoveling. I'm off duty. And you can bet that I'm going to take my uniform shirt off and wear a clean T-shirt into Ireland's and sit down and have a very large drink when I get back to Oxford.

"My Mother, in Memory"

RICHARD FORD

*Born in Jackson, Mississippi, in 1944, Richard Ford received a B. A.
from Michigan State University and an M.F.A. from the University of
California. With his wife, Kristina, he has lived in many places, from
Mississippi to Montana to New Orleans, and has written widely in such
periodicals as* Esquire, The New Yorker, *and* Harper's *about his restlessness, at times concluding, "I still think of Mississippi as home. But
then I was never really married to the idea of home in the first place."
Among his novels are* A Piece of My Heart, The Ultimate Good
Luck, Wildlife, *and* The Sportswriter. *In 1996, Ford won the Pulitzer Prize for* Independence Day, *a novel that delves into the root of the
American character. The following excerpt from "My Mother, in Memory" first appeared in* Harper's.

ALL FIRST CHILDREN, and certainly all only children, date the
beginning of their lives as extraspecial events. For my parents my arrival
came as a surprise and coincident with the end of World War II—the
event that finished the thirties in this country. And it came when my
mother had been married to my father fifteen years; when, in essence,
their young life was over. He was thirty-nine. She was thirty-three. They,
by all accounts, were happy to have me. It may have been an event that
made their life together seem conventional for once, that settled them;
made them think about matters their friends had thought about years
ago. Staying put. The future.

They had never owned a house or a car, although my father's job
gave him a company car. They had never had to choose a "home," a
place to be in permanently. But now, they did. They moved from Little
Rock down to Mississippi, to Jackson, which was the geographic center
of my father's territory and a place he could return most weekends with
ease, since my mother wouldn't be going with him now. There was
going to be a baby.

They knew no one in Jackson except the jobbers my father had called
on and a salesman or two he knew off the road. I'm not sure, but I
think it was not an easy transition. They rented and then bought a brick
duplex next to a school. They joined a church. Found a grocery. A bus
stop—though you could walk to the main street in Jackson from 736

North Congress. Also to the library and the capitol building. They had neighbors—older citizens, established families hanging on to nicer, older, larger houses in a neighborhood that was itself in transition. This was life now, for them. My father went off to work Monday morning and came back Friday night. He had never exactly done that before, but he liked it, I think. One of my earliest memories is of him moving around the sunny house on Monday mornings, whistling a tune.

And so what my beginning life was was this. A life spent with my mother—a shadow in a picture of myself. Days. Afternoons. Nights. Walks. Meals. Dressing. Sidewalks. The movies. Home. Radio. And on the weekend, my father. A nice, large, sweet man who visited us. Happy to come home. Happy to leave.

Between them, I don't know what happened. But given their characters, my best belief is that nothing did. That their life changed radically, that I was there, that the future meant something different, that there was apparently no talk of other children, that they saw far less of each other now—all meant almost nothing to how they felt about each other, or how they registered how they felt. Neither of them was an inquirer. They did not take their pulse much. Psychology was not a science they practiced. They found, if they had not known it before, that they'd signed on for the full trip. They saw life going this way now and not that way. They loved each other. They loved me. Nothing much else mattered.

I don't think my mother longed for a fulfilling career or a more active public life. I don't think my father had other women on the road. I don't think the intrusion of me into their lives was anything they didn't think of as normal and all right. I know from practice that it is now my habit to seek the normal in life, to look for reasons to believe this or that is fine. In part, that is because my parents raised me that way and lived lives that portrayed a world, a private existence, that *could be* that way. I do not think even now, in the midst of my own life's concerns, that it is a bad way to see things.

So then, the part of my life that has to do with my mother.

The first eleven years—the Korean War years, Truman and Eisenhower, television, bicycles, one big snowstorm in 1949—we lived on North Congress Street, down a hill from the state capitol and across from the house where Eudora Welty had been a young girl thirty-five years before. Next door to Jefferson Davis School. I remember a neighbor stopping me on the sidewalk and asking me who I was; this was a thing that could happen to you. Maybe I was nine or seven then. But when I said my name—Richard Ford—she said, "Oh, yes. Your mother is the cute little black-haired woman up the street." And that affected me and still does. I think this was my first conception of my mother as someone else, as someone whom other people saw and considered: a cute woman, which she was not. Black-haired, which she was. She was, I know, five feet five inches tall. But I never have known if that is tall or short. I think I must have always believed it was normal. I remember this, though, as a signal moment in my life. Small but important. It alerted me to my mother's—what?—public side. To the side that other people saw and dealt with and that was there. I do not think I ever thought of her in any other way after that. As Edna Ford, a person who was my mother and also who was someone else. I do not think I ever addressed her after that except with such a knowledge—the way I would anyone I knew.

It is a good lesson to learn. And we risk never knowing our parents if we ignore it. Cute, black-haired, five-five. Some part of her was that, and it didn't harm me to know it. It may have helped, since one of the premier challenges for us all is to know our parents, assuming they survive long enough, are worth knowing, and it is physically possible. This is a part of normal life. And the more we see them fully, as the world sees them, the better all our chances are. About my mother I do not remember more than pieces up until the time I was sixteen: 1960, a galvanizing year for us both—the year my father woke up gasping on a Saturday morning and died before he could get out of bed; me up on the bed with him, busy trying to find something to help. Shake him. Yell in his sleeping face. Breathe in his soft mouth. Turn him over onto his belly, for some reason. Feeling terror and chill. All this which she stood in the doorway to his bedroom in our new house in the suburbs of Jackson, pushing her knuckles into her temples, becoming hysterical. Eventually she just lost her control for a while.

But before that. Those pieces. They must make a difference or I wouldn't remember them so clearly. A flat tire we all three had, halfway across the Mississippi bridge at Greenville. High, up there, over the river. We stayed in the car while my father fixed it, and my mother held me so tightly to her I could barely breathe. I was six. She always said, "I smothered you when you were little. You were all we had. I'm sorry." And then she'd tell me this story. But I wasn't sorry. It seemed fine then, since we were up there. "Smothering" meant "Here is danger," "Love protects you." They are still lessons I respect. I am not comfortable on bridges now, but my guess is I never would've been.

I remember my mother having a hysterectomy and my grandfather,

Ben Shelley, joking about it—to her—about what good "barbers" the nuns at St. Dominic's had been. That made her cry.

I remember once in the front yard on Congress Street something happened, something I said or did—I don't know what—but my mother began running out across the schoolyard next door. Just running away. I remember that scared me and I yelled at her, "No," and halfway across she stopped and came back. I've never known how serious she was about that, but I have understood from it that there might be reasons to run off. Alone, with a small child, knowing no one. That's enough. . . .

And then my father died, which changed everything—many things, it's odd to say, for the better where I was concerned. But not for my mother. Where she was concerned, nothing after that would ever be quite good again. A major part of life ended for her February 20, 1960. He had been everything to her, and all that was naturally implicit became suddenly explicit in her life, and she was neither good at that nor interested in it. And in a way I see now and saw almost as clearly then, she gave up.

Not that she gave up where I was concerned. I was sixteen and had lately been in some law scrapes, and she became, I'd say, very aware of the formal features of her life. She was a widow. She was fifty. She had a son who seemed all right, but who could veer off into trouble if she didn't pay attention. And so, in her way, she paid attention.

Not long after the funeral, when I was back in school and the neighbors had stopped calling and bringing over dishes of food—when both grief and real mourning had set in, in other words—she sat me down and told me we were now going to have to be more independent. She would not be able to look after me as she had done. We agreed that I had a future, but I would have to look after me. And as we could, we would do well to look after each other. We were partners now, is what I remember thinking. My father had really never been around that much, and so his actual absence was, for me (though not for her), not felt so strongly. And a partnership seemed like a good arrangement. I was to stay out of jail because she didn't want to get me out. *Wouldn't get me out.* I was to find friends I could rely on instead. I could have a car of my own. I could go away in the summers to find a job in Little Rock with my grandparents. This, it was understood but never exactly stated (we were trying not to state too much then; we didn't want *everything* to have to be explicit, since so much was now and so little ever had been), *this* would give her time to adjust. To think about things. To become whatever she would have to become to get along from there on out.

I don't exactly remember the time scheme to things. This was 1960, '61, '62. I was a tenth-grader and on. But I did not get put in jail. I did live summers with my grandparents, who by now ran a large hotel in Little Rock. I got a black '57 Ford, which got stolen. I got beaten up and then got new friends. I did what I was told, in other words. I started to grow up in a hurry. . . .

Does one ever have a "relationship" with one's mother? No. I think not. The typical only exists in the minds of unwise people. We—my mother and I—were never bound together by guilt or embarrassment, or even by duty. Love sheltered everything. We expected it to be reliable, and it was. We were always careful to say it—"I love you"—as if a time might come, unexpectedly, when she would want to hear that, or I would, or that each of us would want to hear ourselves say it to the other, only for some reason it wouldn't be possible, and our loss would be great—confusion. Not knowing. Life lessened.

My mother and I look alike. Full, high forehead. The same chin, nose. There are pictures to show that. In myself I see her, even hear her laugh. In her life there was no particular brilliance, no celebrity. No heroics. No one crowning achievement to swell the heart. There were bad ones enough: a childhood that did not bear strict remembering; a husband she loved forever and lost; a life to follow that did not require comment. But somehow she made possible for me my truest affections, as an act of great literature would bestow upon its devoted reader. And I have known that moment with her we would all like to know, the moment of saying, "Yes. This is what it is." An act of knowing that certifies love. I have known that. I have known any number of such moments with her, known them even at the instant they occurred. And now. And, I assume, I will know them forever.

Neighborhoods

ELLEN DOUGLAS

Josephine Ayres Haxton, whose pen name is Ellen Douglas, was born in Natchez, married and raised her children in Greenville, and now resides in Jackson, Mississippi. Douglas has written many novels and short stories set in Mississippi, for which she has won such prizes as the Houghton Mifflin-Esquire Fellowship Award and the O. Henry Prize; she was the first recipient of the Mississippi Institute of Arts and Letters Award in 1979. Among her works are Black Cloud, White Cloud, Where the Dreams Cross, Apostles of Light, *and* The Rock Cried Out. *Douglas had been writer-in-residence at Northeast Louisiana University, the University of Mississippi, the University of Virginia, and Hollins College. The following essay, written for the* Atlanta Journal/Constitution *on July 19, 1996, in honor of the Olympics in Atlanta, adds new meaning to the term "sense of place."*

SOUTHERN WRITERS of fiction and poetry and the critics and academics of the literary world have been talking for a couple of generations about "Place" and "the Sense of Place." Does the sense of place still influence Southern writers? Are we now indistinguishable from the rest of the country? Has Southern place become the refuge of cliche-wielding sentimentalists and writers of gothic horror stories? Is the South disappearing? Has it, in fact, disappeared?

All this sometimes seems to me blown out of proportion. Of course every artist is working in a place—the place his imagination makes of the world around him. And of course the South has been a compelling and idiosyncratic neighborhood—horrendously ugly in spots, breathtakingly beautiful, its people dogged, as human beings are, by the moral ambiguities and idiosyncracies of their place and time. And I think it's still O.K. for us to claim the South, largely because we don't move around as much as some folk do. To a degree we stay in our neighborhood instead of abandoning it and building a new one.

The South, it's true, has seemed solid to me, permanent—green black magnolia trees with leaves as thick as shoe leather, dark cedars weighed down with moss, oaks with their great boles and powerful stretched-out arms. I've been lucky to live in this place, to know that my great-grandmother would still recognize our house, would know the lilies blooming by the door (might have planted them herself), would know the shards of glass embedded in concrete along the top of the red brick garden wall—against intruders.

Other writers have other neighborhoods, but always these are the places their imaginations make of the world.

But my neighborhood and theirs, those other writers, wherever they are, have gotten dislocated in our time in a large and different way—a dislocation that we are all called on to bear witness to. It happened the day we first saw the pictures of Earth from space; saw that the Earth is our neighborhood—the only place we have. Nothing before had shown us how small it is, how suspended in darkness, how fragile and lit up by the sun like a soap bubble floating in the void.

Perhaps by now, seeing it on the weather channel every day, we should be used to this new take on our neighborhood. But I can't get used to it. Over and over again I see the trees, lilies, shard-encrusted wall of my home float away on the fragile globe that is home to us all. And I know that it may vanish as a soap bubble vanishes.

Such terrible knowledge opens chasms at the writer's feet. I can no longer trust my neighborhood not to pop, whirling us off with it into the cold and dark. Easy to see, looking at the bubble, how it could dissipate in the void: A melt down, the ozone pierced, the final choking dose of poison, the weight of too many billion people, the loss of too many billion trees.

In the face of such knowledge to write fiction? To keep on writing?

And it's not the changing South, nor is it our mortality. We've always had to face change and death or close our eyes. But to lose the place all lives have sprung from? What to do, what to say about that possibility?

May be, since I continue to write, I do so out of habit, voice sounding its puny locust song, keeping on talking, as Faulkner said.

But my impulse is to do what every fiction writer knows she must not do: To preach, to sound the tocsin, to call us all to arms against the destruction of the world.

And to celebrate, too, to rejoice at the sight of our bubble, all blue and green and swirling clouds, to proclaim the miracle of it—our neighborhood—hanging there, alive, in the black void.

Acknowledgments

I wish first to thank JoAnne Prichard, executive editor at University Press of Mississippi, for her thoughtful suggestions and encouragement in helping me through the maze. I am especially grateful to the research committee at Delta State University for generous aid in funding the project. I want to thank Thompson Wacaster and the Phil Hardin Foundation for their selection of this project for grant support. I am indebted to Anice Powell and the staff at Seymour Library in Indianola, and I also appreciate the help of the staff at the Mississippi Department of Archives and History. I am deeply grateful to my husband, Claiborne, for his enthusiasm and perceptiveness. Thanks also go to other family members, including my sister, Mary Garrard, for her inspiration and valuable suggestions, Craig and Ray Skates, who went out of their way to be helpful, and Mary Jayne and Bill Whittington, Mabelle White, and Fay Clark, who were there at the right time. I am blessed with friends and partners Dorothy Shawhan, Elizabeth Sarcone, Carolyn Elkins and Leila Wynn, who share my love of books and who can be counted on for support and encouragement. Thanks also to Willie Morris, LeRoy Percy, Guytie Runnels, and Mary Ann Wells. Grateful acknowledgment is made for permission to reprint from the works listed as "Credits" on pages 461–66.

Credits

Excerpt from "Rough Riding Down South" by J. F. H. Claiborne first appeared in *Harper's New Monthly Magazine,* June 1862.

Excerpt from *Travels on the Lower Mississippi, 1879–1880: A Memoir* by Ernst von Hesse-Wartegg, edited and translated by Frederic Trautmann. Copyright © 1990 by the Curators of the University of Missouri. Reprinted by permission of the publisher.

Excerpt from *Olden Times Revisited* by W. L. Clayton, edited by Minrose Gwin. Copyright © 1982 by University Press of Mississippi. Reprinted by permission of the publisher.

"Mississippi" by William Faulkner first appeared in *Holiday,* April 1954. Reprinted by permission of Shelden Abend.

"The Singing River" from "Legends of the Mississippi Gulf Coast" by Ruth Bass. WPA files. Mississippi Department of Archives and History, Jackson, MS.

Excerpt from *Deep'n as It Come:* The 1927 Mississippi River Flood by Pete Daniel. Copyright © 1977 by Oxford University Press, Inc. Reprinted by permission of the publisher.

Excerpt from *On the Gulf* by Elizabeth Spencer. Copyright © 1991 by University Press of Mississippi. Reprinted by permission of the publisher.

"Mosquito Blues" by Dorothy Shawhan first appeared in *Delta Scene,* summer 1983. Reprinted by permission of the author.

PART THREE: **Conflict**

Excerpt from *A Lost Heroine of the Confederacy: The Diaries and Letters of Belle Edmondson* by Belle Edmondson, edited by Loretta and William Galbraith. Copyright © 1990 by University Press of Mississippi. Reprinted by permission of the publisher.

Excerpt from *Civil War Diary: 1861–1863* by Cyrus F. Boyd. Copyright © 1953 by Iowa State Historical Society. Reprinted with permission.

Excerpt from *The Civil War: A Narrative* by Shelby Foote. Copyright © 1958 by Shelby Foote. Reprinted by permission of Random House, Inc.

Excerpt from "Capture of Jefferson Davis" by Jefferson Davis. Typescript from Jefferson Davis and family papers. MSS collection. MS Department of Archives and History, Jackson, MS.

Excerpt from *Crusade for Justice: The Autobiography of Ida B. Wells* by Ida B. Wells, edited by Alfreda M. Duster. Copyright © 1970 by the University of Chicago Press. Reprinted by permission of the publisher.

Excerpt from *The Facts of Reconstruction* by John R. Lynch. Copyright © 1913 by Bobbs-Merrill Co.

Excerpt from *A Slaveholder's Daughter* by Belle Kearney. Copyright © 1900 by The Abbey Press.

"Progress of Women: A Speech to the Hypatia Club, 1898" by Nellie Nugent Somerville. Unpublished manuscript. Reprinted by permission of the Schlesinger Library.

Excerpt from *After Freedom* by Hortense Powdermaker. Copyright © 1939 by Atheneum.

"(The Original) Humorous Whiskey Speech" by N.S. Sweat, Jr. Copyright © 1952. Reprinted by permission of the author.

Excerpt from *The Magnolia Jungle* by P. D. East. Copyright © 1960 by Simon and Schuster. Reprinted by permission of P.B. East.

Excerpt from *Witness in Philadelphia* by Florence Mars, with the assistance of Lynn Eden. Copyright © 1977 by Louisiana State University Press. Reprinted by permission.

Excerpt from *Terror in the Night* by Jack Nelson. Copyright © 1992 by Jack Nelson. Reprinted by permission of Simon & Schuster, Inc.

Excerpt from *Coming of Age in Mississippi* by Anne Moody. Copyright © 1968 by Anne Moody. Used by permission of Doubleday, a division of Bantam Doubleday Dell Publishing Group, Inc.

Excerpt from *So the Heffners Left McComb* by Hodding Carter. Copyright © 1965 by Hodding Carter, renewed © 1993. Reprinted by permission of Brandt & Brandt Literary Agents, Inc.

"Mississippi: The Fallen Paradise" by Walker Percy first appeared in *Harpers,* April 1965. Reprinted by permission of McIntosh and Otis, Inc.

Excerpt from *The Little Light of Mine* by Kay Mills. Copyright © 1993 by Kay Mills. Used by permission of Dutton Signet, a division of Penguin Books USA Inc.

P A R T F O U R : **Social Fabric**

Excerpt from *The Jesuit Relations and Allied Documents: Travels and Explorations of the Jesuit Missionaries in New France* by Father Le Petit, edited by Reuben Gold Thwaites. Copyright © 1900 by Burrows Bros. Co.

Excerpt from *Border Romances,* by W. Gilmore Simms. Copyright © 1885 by Belford, Clarke, & Co.

Excerpt from *Mississippi Mayhem* by W. G. Barner. Copyright © 1982 by Leisure Press.

"Logging Time" by Agnes G. Anderson. Unpublished manuscript. Reprinted by permission of Mary Pickard, representative for The Family of Walter Anderson.

Excerpt from *"You Live and Learn. Then You Die and Forget It All"* by Ray Lum as told to William Ferris. Copyright © 1992 by William Ferris. Used by permission of Bantam Doubleday Dell Publishing Group, Inc.

Excerpt from *Sacred Space* by Tom Rankin. Copyright © 1993 by University Press of Mississippi. Reprinted by permission of the publisher.

"Sacred Harp Sings" by W. B. Allison. Unpublished manuscript. From WPA files. Mississippi Department of Archives and History, Jackson, MS.

Excerpt from *Once Upon A Time When We Were Colored* by Clifton Taulbert. Copyright © 1989 by Council Oak Books. Reprinted by permission of the publisher.

Excerpt from *Drums of the Toli* by Robert Hardee. Copyright © 1971 by Payne Publishing, Inc. Reprinted by permission of Nelda Temple.

"A Creature in the Bay of St. Louis" by Barry Hannah first appeared in *Sports Afield,* September 1994. Copyright © 1994 by The Hearst Corporation. All rights reserved. Reprinted by permission of the author.

Excerpt from *Families* by Wyatt Cooper. Copyright © 1975 by Wyatt Cooper. Used by permission of Bantam Books, a division of Bantam Doubleday Dell Publishing Group, Inc.

"Interview with Mrs. Arwin Deweese Turner" by Charlotte Capers. Unpublished interview. From WPA files. Mississippi Department of Archives and History, Jackson, MS. Reprinted by permission of the Mississippi Department of Archives and History.

Excerpt from *Fridays with Red: A Radio Friendship* by Bob Edwards. Copyright © 1993 by Simon and Schuster. Reprinted by permission of the publisher.

Excerpt from *America's Dizzy Dean* by Curt Smith. Copyright © 1978 by Chalice Press of St. Louis, MO. Reprinted by permission of the publisher.

PART FIVE: **Body and Soul**

Excerpt from *George E. Ohr* by Garth Clark. Copyright © 1978 by the Mississippi Department of Archives and History. Reprinted by permission of the department and the author.

Excerpt from *Father of the Blues* by W. C. Handy. Copyright © 1941 by Macmillan.

Excerpt from *Biedenharn Heritage: 1852–1952* by Emy-Lou Biedenharn (1962). Reprinted 1994 by Emy-Lou Biedenharn Foundation, Monroe, LA. Reprinted by permission of George T. Walker.

Excerpt from *In One Lifetime* by Verna Arvey. Copyright © 1984 by University of Arkansas Press. Reprinted by permission of the publisher.

Excerpt from *Dreams and Visions* by Theora Hamblett, in collaboration with Edwin E. Meek. Copyright © 1975 by Theora Hamblett. Reprinted by permission of Edwin E. Meek.

Excerpt from *My Husband, Jimmie Rodgers* by Carrie Cecil Williamson Rodgers. Copyright © 1935 by Southern Literary Institute. Reprinted by permission of Mrs. Ruth Rowe.

Excerpt from *Big Bill Blues* by William Broonzy, as told to Yannick Bruynoghe. Copyright © 1955 by Da Capo Press. Reprinted by permission of the publisher.

Excerpt from *Allison's Wells: The Last Mississippi Spa 1899–1963* by Hosford Latimer Fontaine. Copyright © 1981 by Muscadine Press. Reprinted by permission of John Fontaine.

Excerpt from *Mississippi Artist: A Self-Portrait* by Karl Wolfe. Copyright © 1979 by University Press of Mississippi. Reprinted by permission of the publisher.

Excerpt from *Local Color,* edited by William Ferris. Copyright © 1982 by William

Ferris. Reprinted by permission of Doubleday, a division of Bantam Double-day Dell Publishing Group, Inc.

Excerpt from the logbooks of Walter Anderson. Unpublished manuscript. From the uncollected works of Walter Anderson. Mississippi Department of Archives and History, Jackson, MS.

Preface to *Marie Hull: 1890–1980: Her Inquiring Vision* by Mary D. Garrard. Copyright © 1990 by Delta State University Art Department. Reprinted by permission of Collier Parker.

Excerpt from *The Arrival of B.B. King* by Charles Sawyer. Copyright © 1980 by Charles Sawyer. Used by permission of Doubleday, a division of Bantam Doubleday Dell Publishing Group, Inc.

Excerpt from *A Feast Made for Laughter* by Craig Claiborne. Copyright © 1982 by Craig Claiborne. Reprinted by permission of Doubleday, a division of Bantam Doubleday Dell Publishing Group, Inc.

Excerpt from *I Dream a World: Portraits of Black Women Who Changed America* by Leontyne Price, edited by Brian Lanker. Copyright © 1989 by Stewart, Tabori & Chang. Reprinted by permission of the publisher.

Excerpt from *The Soul of Southern Cooking* by Kathy Star. Copyright © 1989 by University Press of Mississippi. Reprinted by permission of the publisher.

"Jellies, Pickles, and the Ladies Who Made Them" by Charles East first appeared in *Southern Living*, May 1995. Copyright © 1995 by Southern Living, Inc. Reprinted with permission.

Excerpt from *Bodies & Soul* by Al Young. Copyright © 1981 by Al Young. Reprinted with permission of the author.

Excerpt from *Roadfood: The All New, Updated and Expanded Edition* by Jane and Michael Stern. Copyright © 1992 by Jane and Michael Stern. Reprinted by permission of HarperCollins Publishers, Inc.

Excerpt from *Along the RFD* by Rose Budd Stevens. Copyright © 1987 by University Press of Mississippi. Reprinted by permission of the publisher.

"Bourbon" by Walker Percy first appeared in *Esquire*, December 1975. Copyright © 1975 by Walker Percy. Reprinted by permission of McIntosh and Otis, Inc.

Excerpt from *Last Train to Memphis* by Peter Guralnick. Copyright © 1994 by Peter Guralnick. Reprinted by permission of Little, Brown and Company.

Excerpt from *Stand by Your Man* by Tammy Wynette with Joan Dew. Copyright © 1979 by Simon & Schuster.

PART SIX: **Lives and Legends**

Excerpt from *Prince Among Slaves* by Terry Alford. Copyright © 1977 by Harcourt Brace & Co.

Excerpt from *The Legend of the Free State of Jones* by Rudy H. Leverett. Copyright © 1984 by University Press of Mississippi. Reprinted by permission of the publisher.

" 'Private' John Allen" by Champ Clark from Edwin Anderson Alderman and

Index